TOWARD A SCIENCE OF TRANSLATING

TOWARD A SCIENCE OF TRANSLATING

WITH SPECIAL REFERENCE TO PRINCIPLES
AND PROCEDURES
INVOLVED IN BIBLE TRANSLATING

BY

EUGENE A. NIDA

LEIDEN
E. J. BRILL
1964

*To my colleagues in the Translations Department
of the American Bible Society*

TABLE OF CONTENTS

PREFACE

This volume, *Toward a Science of Translating*, has been largely prompted by the nature of field work in which I have been involved during recent years in Latin America, Africa, and Asia. An earlier book, *Bible Translating* (Nida, 1947a), though very useful to the Bible translator, is essentially only a practical handbook, with a kind of rule-of-thumb orientation. Increasingly it became obvious that in order to assist translators more satisfactorily it was necessary to provide something which would not only be solidly based on contemporary developments in the fields of linguistics, anthropology, and psychology, but would also relate the specific area of Bible translating to the wider activity of translating in general. The present volume is an attempt to fill this need.

As the title of this book implies, it makes no pretension to be a definitive volume, for in the present state of development in the field of semantics it is impossible to contemplate writing such a final work. However, there have been a number of important and fruitful developments in linguistics, both in the structural as well as the semantic areas, and these have contributed very significantly to the organization of this book.

Though the scope of translation theory in this volume is all-inclusive, the illustrative data are drawn primarily from Biblical materials, and especially so in the later chapters. This is not as great a disadvantage as it might appear at first glance, for no other type of translating has such a long history, involves so many different languages (at present more than 1,200), includes more diverse types of texts, and covers so many distinct cultural areas of the world. But though the examples are drawn primarily from Biblical data, this volume is not prepared with the average Bible translator in mind, for it is rather too technical in orientation. Nevertheless, it should serve as an important help to such translators as may have some background in present-day linguistic theory and it will be the basis of other more simply written books now in preparation, which will be aimed at teaching translation methods.

Very important help on this volume has been received from a number of colleagues and friends. I am especially indebted to the following: Robert G. Bratcher, Wesley Culshaw, H. A. Gleason, Joseph E. Grimes, R. W. Jumpelt, Jan Knappert, Terry Langendoen, Robert P. Markham, Fred C. C. Peng, Punya Sloka Ray, William Reyburn, William Samarin, William A. Smalley, G. Henry Waterman, and William L. Wonderly. Dorothy L. Tyler is to be thanked for her invaluable assistance in

editing; Anna-Lisa Madeira, Letha Markham, and Dorothy Ridgway for
their careful typing of the manuscript; Eleanor F. Newton and Cullen
Story for their work on the Bibliography; Richard Lesseraux for his
assistance in the preparation of diagrams; and Robert D. Morrow
for important help in proofreading.

Eugene A. Nida

New York
March, 1963

CHAPTER ONE

INTRODUCTION

The polyglot empire of ancient Babylon, with its hard-working core of multilingual scribes sending out official communications on cuneiform tablets to the far corners of the realm, is a far cry from the electronic equipment used today in simultaneous interpretation at the United Nations in New York. The basic problems of interlingual communication, however, remain the same, though in our day the terrifying potentialities of modern technology require us to increase our efforts to guarantee effective understanding between peoples. Whether one is dealing with translation in international gatherings, or with the highly publicized efforts to put machines to work translating masses of scientific abstracts, or with the pioneering efforts of missionaries translating the Scriptures for remote, primitive tribes, one thing is certain: at no time in the history of the world have there been so many persons as today who are dedicating so much time and effort to the task of translation.

OPPOSITION TO TRANSLATION

Though interlingual translation is accepted by all as a practical necessity, the task and its results have not been without detractors. Grant Showerman (1916, p. 100) has declared that "translation is meddling with inspiration," while Harry de Forest Smith (Brower, 1959, p. 173) has insisted that a translation of a literary work is as tasteless as "a stewed strawberry," and Max Eastman (1936) contends that "almost all translations are bad," for they are made by ordinary people who match the unusual foreign expression with the commonplace in their own tongue. Moreover, they add insult to injury by their desperate concern to be literary. [1]

There may well be reason to complain of translating when one examines closely what happens to a document in the process of being transferred from one language to another. As an experiment, the editors of *Politiken*, a newspaper in Denmark, sent a delightfully written essay of 700 words by J. V. Jansen to a succession of Swedish, German, English, and French translators. Finally, this successively retranslated article, which started out as a descriptive essay with "rhythmical sentences, simple phrases and well-chosen words, giving a vivid impression of forest smells, and colors, of abundant animal life and the dignity of nature and of labor," ended up as so prosaic a jumble that a Danish professor, who was asked to produce the final translation from French back into Danish, protested

[1] For a number of equally poignant criticisms of translations by well-known literary figures, see Mounin (1955).

that he could not see any point to his wasting time in translating material "that seemed to have been written by a school child." [1]

Some objections to translation have reflected theological considerations. The *Masseketh Sopherim* (Tractate of the Scribes), for example, reflects the medieval Jewish attitude toward the translation of the Old Testament into Greek by saying, "Five elders wrote the Law in Greek for King Tolmai (Ptolemy); and that day was a hard day for Israel, like the day on which Israel made the golden calf." The *Megillath Taanith* (The Roll of Fasting) describes thus the same translation: "On the eighth day of Tebeth the Law was written in Greek in the days of King Tolmai, and darkness came upon the world for three days," (Thackeray, 1917, pp. 89-93). Sir Thomas More was opposed to all Bible translations because the expressions used in them were contrary to the tradition of the Roman Church, a position emphasized by the strictures of the Council of Trent. [2]

Nevertheless, men have not always despaired of translation, for it has at least some advantages, even though, as some have said, "Nothing improves by translation except bishops." [3] Even so, Fitzgerald (1903, p. 100) would contend that "a live sparrow is better than a stuffed eagle." Though a translation may be like old wine in new bottles or a woman in man's clothing, the results can be both tasteful and alive, despite the judgment of early Renaissance Italian writers, who contended that translations are like women—homely when they are faithful and unfaithful when they are lovely.

Underlying all the complications of translation is the fundamental fact that languages differ radically one from the other. In fact, so different are they that some insist that one cannot communicate adequately in one language what has been said originally in another. Nevertheless, as linguists and anthropologists have discovered, that which unites mankind is much greater than that which divides, and hence there is, even in cases of very disparate languages and cultures, a basis for communication. This common core of human experience and the relatable modes of speaking about it do not, however, eliminate the striking and fundamental differences between languages. Moreover, the divergences seem to be not only far more numerous than the similarities, but also to provide many more obstacles to understanding than the similarities are able to clear away.

At the same time, the translator is under constant pressure from the conflict between form and meaning. If he attempts to approximate the stylistic qualities of the original, he is likely to sacrifice much of the meaning, while strict adherence to the literal content usually results in considerable loss of the stylistic flavor.

Similarly, the translator is caught in the dilemma of "the letter vs.

---

[1] This procedure has been described in an anonymous editorial, entitled "Transformation by Translation," *Living Age* 333.1117-1118 (1927).

[2] For a discussion of various theological aspects of translation, see Schwarz, 1955.

[3] Cited by Grand'combe, 1949.

the spirit," for in being faithful to the things talked about, he can destroy the spirit that pervades an original communication. At the same time, if he concentrates too much upon trying to reproduce the original "feeling" and "tone" of the message, he may be accused of playing loose with the substance of the document—the letter of the law.

To make matters even worse, translators must deal with a medium of communication which is constantly in process of change. To be a useful instrument for social intercourse, language must be able to admit new knowledge and new organization of knowledge. In a sense, it must fit reality or it is useless; but it cannot fit reality too closely, or it would be equally unserviceable, for language cannot uniquely specify all the infinitely different events. It must be able to classify and group experiences. Moreover, it must have sufficient generality of utility to be employed by the masses of the people, and not merely by some small coterie of initiates. It is therefore not a private code but a public system of symbols, constantly, if slowly, being remade to fit the exigencies of a changing world. Translators themselves, however, are responsible for a good deal of the change that does take place within languages, for as Julio Casares (1956) has so aptly said, "Translation is a customs house through which passes, if the custom officers are not alert, more smuggled goods of foreign idioms than through any other linguistic frontier."

Another problem facing the translator is the proper understanding of his own role. Is translating, for example, an art or a science? Is it a skill which can only be acquired by practice, or are there certain procedures which can be described and studied? The truth is that practice in translating has far outdistanced theory; and though no one will deny the artistic elements in good translating, linguists and philologists are becoming increasingly aware that the processes of translation are amenable to rigorous description. When we speak of "the science of translating," we are of course concerned with the descriptive aspect; for just as linguistics may be classified as a descriptive science, so the transference of a message from one language to another is likewise a valid subject for scientific description. Those who have insisted that translation is an art, and nothing more, have often failed to probe beneath the surface of the obvious principles and procedures that govern its functioning. Similarly, those who have espoused an entirely opposite view have rarely studied translating enough to appreciate the artistic sensitivity which is an indispensable ingredient in any first-rate translation of a literary work.

THE FIELD OF TRANSLATION

The general field of translation may be divided into three parts, following Jakobson (1959b, p. 233). The first type, or "intralingual" translation, consists essentially in rewording something within the same language. By this process we may interpret the verbal signs by means of other signs in the same language, a process much more frequently practiced than we generally imagine, and one basic to an adequate theory of meaning. [1] The second type, or "interlingual translation," may be called "translation proper," for it comprises the interpretation of the verbal signs of one language by means of the verbal signs of another. However, in interlingual translation we are concerned not merely with matching symbols (i.e. word-for-word comparisons) but also with the equivalence of both symbols and their arrangements. That is to say, we must know the meaning of the entire utterance.

A third type of translation may be called "intersemiotic," or transmutation, by which we mean the transference of a message from one kind of symbolic system to another. For example, in the U. S. Navy a verbal message may be transmuted into a flag message by hoisting up the proper flags in the right sequence. Similarly, a speech by a Kiowa chief may be transmuted into sign language without verbal accompaniment, to be understood not only by the speakers of other languages, but also by any other Kiowas who may be present.

In many instances, however, translating does involve certain rather severe restrictions imposed by the cultural contexts and linguistic literary styles, or media of communication. The translation of legal documents from English to Spanish, for example, involves some basic differences between English common law and Roman law. The translator of American comic strips is constantly beset by problems arising out of cultural specialties; for example, corned beef and cabbage—a dish that fits so well the character of Jiggs—just does not make sense in many cultures. Accordingly, Jiggs's favorite food becomes rice and fish in Southeast Asia, cabbage stuffed with hamburger in Turkey, and stewed codfish in Italy (McManus, 1952).

Stylistic restrictions are a particularly important element in the translation of poetry, for so much of the essence of poetry consists in a formal envelope for a meaningful content.

An even more trying set of formal restrictions resulting from the particular medium of communication is encountered in trying to dub in live sound for a foreign motion picture, for one must not only communicate the story but also—particularly in close-up scenes—match the timing, the syllabic structure, and even the corresponding facial movements. [2]

Of all the various types of translating, however, one can safely say that none surpasses Bible translating in: (1) the range of subject matter (e.g. poetry, law, proverbs, narration, exposition, conversation); (2) linguistic variety (directly or indirectly from Greek and Hebrew into more than 1,200 other languages and dialects); (3) historical depth (from the third century B. C. to the present); (4) cultural diversity (there is no cultural area in the world which is not represented by Bible translating); (5) volume of manuscript evidence; (6) number of translators involved; (7) conflicting viewpoints; and (8) accumulation of data on principles and procedures employed. It is thus with some justification that this volume

---

[1]   See the sections on the determination of meaning by substitution techniques and hierarchical structuring, in Chapter 5.
[2]   Caillé, 1960.

on the science of translating employs to a considerable extent the experience of Bible translators, as being useful in a wider study of the
theory and practice of translating. There is, however, no attempt to
restrict this treatment to Scriptural materials, for this volume is concerned with the entire range of translating. Nevertheless, even within
the scope of Biblical materials themselves there is an ample supply of
significant and representative data.

There are, of course, special problems involved in Bible translating
which do not affect other types of translating to quite the same degree:
(1) in comparison with purely contemporary materials, the Bible
represents a document coming from a relatively remote historical period;
(2) the cultural differences between Biblical times and our own are considerable; (3) the nature of the documentary evidence, though in some
ways very abundant (in contrast to other documents from classical
times), is crucially deficient in many matters of word division and punctuation; (4) arbitrary traditional divisions into chapters and verses have
tended to obscure meaningful connections; and (5) overriding theological
considerations have in some instances tended to distort the meaning of
the original message. Furthermore, not only does the Bible translator
have to confront the natural tendency to conservatism and mystery in
religious expression, but, as Campbell said so aptly in 1789, "There is an
additional evil resulting from this manner of treating holy writ, that the
solecisms, barbarisms and nonsensical expressions, which it gives rise to,
prove a fund of materials to the visionary, out of which his imagination
frames a thousand mysteries." [1]

THE PURPOSE OF THIS TREATMENT OF TRANSLATION

Isenberg (1953, p. 234) is quite right in stating, "The truth is that the
art of interpretation has by far outstripped the theory of interpretation."
The present work is an attempt to remedy this unfortunate state of
affairs by bringing to the subject of translation numerous insights which
have become increasingly significant in a number of related fields.

In Europe the earliest significant work in anthropological semantics
was that of Wilhelm von Humboldt (1836), who insisted upon profound
psychological and philosophical relationships between language on the
one hand and thought and culture on the other. [2] But undoubtedly the
most important influence in Europe on the development of a theory of

[1] George Campbell's introductory volume to his translation of *The Four
Gospels* (London: A. Strahan, 1789) is an outstanding scholarly treatment of
translation principles and procedures, especially as they are related to the problems
of the Bible translator.
[2] The distinctive viewpoints of Humboldt have given rise to a number of similar
studies by German scholars, including J. Trier (1931), G. Ipsen (1932), and L.
Weisgerber (1953-1954). These views on the relationship of language and culture
contributed considerably to the tendency for certain German theologians to develop
a theology out of language—a position against which James Barr (1961) has
effectively remonstrated.

meaning was exercised by Ferdinand de Saussure (1916), whose basic concepts of linguistic structures provided a basis for dealing constructively with semantic problems.

In the United States, where, in reaction against a "catch-all" kind of mentalism, semantic problems were for some time side-stepped by many linguists as being outside the realm of linguistics proper, Edward Sapir made initial and highly significant contributions (1930, 1944), while Benjamin Lee Whorf (1945, 1950) formulated additional and provocative concepts which sought to explain certain thought structures and many culture traits as being basically a reflection of the fundamental linguistic categories of the languages of the peoples in question. These studies were rapidly followed by important contributions by a number of anthropologically oriented linguists, such as Harry Hoijer (1948, 1953), Floyd Lounsbury (1955, 1956), and Zellig Harris (1952).

Anthropology has come a long way from its biological preoccupation in the last century to its present-day concern with symbolism and values, a process which was decisively influenced by Bronislaw Malinowski (1922, 1935) and which has been carried on by a number of anthropologists, including Ward H. Goodenough (1956), Anthony F. C. Wallace and John Atkins (1960), C. O. Frake (1961), and Harold C. Conklin (1962). This shift of emphasis has been of utmost importance to anyone studying the meaning of verbal symbols; for, from the careful analysis of kinship systems and the detailed descriptions of the ways in which people describe their own lives and environments, we have obtained unparalleled insight into the manner in which the meanings of words can be studied and classified.

General semanticists have been the active gadflies in contemporary discussions of communication. They have not been content with the explanations of the grammarians, who are concerned with the relationships of words to words, or of the logicians, who deal with the relationships of assertions to assertions. They have not even been satisfied with the traditional semanticist, who directs his attention to the relationship of words and assertions to the referents to which they supposedly correspond. Rather, they have become involved in the problems of the relationship of these words and statements to human behavior in general. These men are interested, not in the supposed categories underlying logical expression, but in the behavior of people during, and resulting from, the process of communication.

General semanticists, such as Rapoport and Hayakawa, have toned down some of the extravagant claims of the early pioneer Korzybski, but they have not overlooked the important contributions which the latter made. Especially in his "map analogies," Korzybski (1933) claimed that: (1) the map is not the territory (i.e. the word symbols are not reality, but only the surrogates for such); (2) the map does not include everything (i.e. words lump together various more or less similar things but do not precisely identify all the differences of experience); and (3) the map is self-reflexive. That is to say, the map must really include the map, or in other words, that language contains symbols by means of which one may speak about language—a language within a language, or as some linguists speak of it, a "metalanguage."

As the result of an intense concern for language as a symbolic system, symbolic logicians have also contributed some highly important insights into the problem of meaning, and thus to translation. It is almost inevitable that such men as Bertrand Russell (1940) and L. Wittgenstein (1953), who declared that "Alle Philosophie ist Sprachphilosophie," all philosophy is the philosophy of language, should have made important contributions to our understanding of symbols and their meanings. By means of certain new concepts in logic, including: (1) the propositional function, (2) the operational definition, (3) predictive evaluation as the criterion of truth, and (4) the theory of types, [1] the traditional logic of Aristotle was almost completely reversed. Instead of assuming that words have certain meanings, and that the task of the logician is merely to describe what is already an inherent property of such a symbol, the symbolic logicians set up entire systems of symbols, assigned meanings to them, and proceeded to manipulate them as means of testing their values and relationships. In a sense, words were dethroned from the exalted status assigned to them in the Platonic system of "ideas," and made to be tools for the manipulation of concepts. The practical result has been the recognition that words are essentially instruments and tools, and that communication is merely one type of behavioral event. In this area some of the most stimulating observations have come from Ernst Cassirer (1933, 1946, 1953) and Willard V. Quine (1959, 1960a and b).

Psychologists also have made important contributions to the study of meaning, not only in the area of Gestalt psychology, which is pre-eminently concerned with perception and conceptualization, and hence with symbolization, but also in behavioristic analyses. The earlier attempts to explain all meanings merely in terms of stimulus and response have proved quite inadequate, for the conditioning features of human behavior cannot be readily controlled as are those of animals in mazes. However, by setting up "behavioral predispositions" psychologists have been able to show the relationship between symbol and behavior in ways that provide important insights into the problems of response to meaning —features of the utmost importance to the translator attempting to reproduce in his audience something of the same effect which is understood to have existed in the response of the original hearers. In this connection one should refer to the research and theories of B. F. Skinner (1953, 1957) and Roger Brown (1954, 1956).

Some psychologists (cf. Miller, Galanter, and Pribram, 1960) have developed psychological theories which exhibit very marked parallelism to linguistic structures, for their fundamental concepts about the structure of human behavior correspond closely to the types of structures encountered in language. Moreover, these theories tie in with present-day developments in the field of cybernetics, and demonstrate rather clearly

---

[1] For a useful summary of these basic concepts see Anatol Rapoport, "What is Semantics?" in Hayakawa (1954), pp. 3-18.

that behavior involves much more than reflexes and re-enforcement. In fact, it can be adequately explained only by taking into consideration such factors as image, plan, testing, and feedback. If these theories prove correct (and they are rapidly gaining ground), they offer means of rather startling advances for correlating the findings of linguists and psychologists in the crucial area of communication.

Psychiatry also has contributed significantly to modern approaches to meaning, particularly through the insights of Jung and Erich Fromm, by highlighting the importance of symbols and the extent to which verbal symbols carry far more emotive significance than was earlier thought possible.

Philologists, for whom translation has been a familiar and long-studied field, have also materially assisted the present-day study of literature by focusing increasing attention on the total cultural context of literary production, rather than attempting, as so often in the past, to ferret out hidden motifs and wasting time on irrelevant reconstructions.

Persons directly concerned with basic problems of Biblical interpretation have also contributed to an understanding of fundamental semantic theory, as in the detailed studies of Joachim Wach (1926-1929), who analyzed the theories of interpretation in the nineteenth century, and in the penetrating insights of Karl Jaspers and Rudolf Bultmann in *Myth and Christianity* (1958).

On the basis of these many different types of contemporary studies which are related directly and indirectly to problems of semantic and linguistic correspondence, this volume attempts to provide an essentially descriptive approach to the translation process. If at times the principles and procedures appear to be prescriptive, it is only because, within the range of the type of translation being discussed, these elements have been generally accepted as being the most useful. The fundamental thrust is, of course, linguistic, as it must be in any descriptive analysis of the relationship between corresponding messages in different languages. But the points of view are by no means narrowly linguistic, for language is here viewed as but one part of total human behavior, which in turn is the object of study of a number of related disciplines.

In order to do justice to the wide range of problems involved in translation, and as a means of so treating such matters that there is least need for repetition or cross reference, this introduction is followed by a chapter on the history of translating. This chapter, directly or indirectly, touches upon most of the basic issues treated in more descriptive detail in later sections of the book.

Chapters 3-5 are concerned with the nature of meaning in its linguistic, referential, and emotive phases.

Chapter 6 deals with the dynamic dimension of language. The total amount of information received by a receptor may be quite different from what was intended by a source, and therefore the translator must be concerned with language not only as a code, but also as a communicative event.

Then, as a special element in the communicative process, the role of the translator is considered in Chapter 7; for the principles and procedures of translation cannot be fully understood or objectively evaluated without recognizing the important part played by the personal involvement of the translator.

The principles of correspondence in translation are treated in Chapters 8-9 in terms of types of translations, principles of translating, formal restrictions on translations, and types of correspondence. The actual techniques of adjustment are treated in Chapter 10. Translation procedures, as treated in Chapter 11, include such subjects as the analysis of the receptor language text, the selection of correspondences, and the basic differences in translation procedure for (1) work done by a committee and (2) that done by a single individual. A final chapter deals with the practical and theoretical developments and implications of machine translation.

In Chapters 8 through 10 the presentations may appear to be somewhat repetitive, for we are attempting in these chapters to look upon the same sets of data from various points of view. For example, in Chapter 9 we note the types of correspondences which exist between languages, but in Chapter 10 we deal with these same sets, but from the standpoint of the techniques of adjustment which need to be employed in reproducing these in languages having other basic structures. The essentially theoretical aspects of translation are treated in Chapters 3 through 6, while the practical implications and applications are handled in Chapters 7 through 12. Though it is true that the basic approach to translation is primarily "descriptive," nevertheless, it is based upon a concept of language which goes beyond the more narrow confines of a so-called "taxonomic grammar." In other words, following Noam Chomsky (1957), we are not content to look upon a language as some fixed corpus of sentences, but as a dynamic mechanism capable of generating an infinite series of different utterances. An adequate description of a language must in some way or other account for the capacity of the individual speaker of a language to generate such a stream of speech and to interpret what he hears, even though he has usually never heard the particular combinations before. This generative view of language seems to be particularly important for the translator, for in translating from one language into another he must go beyond mere comparisons of corresponding structures and attempt to describe the mechanisms by which the total message is decoded, transferred, and transformed into the structures of another language. To describe this process we must have more powerful tools than mere lists of correspondences, for in so far as possible we need to explain how one can take a unique message in the source language and "create" an equally unique message in the receptor (or target) language. This requires looking upon language in some generative manner. At the same time, this does not mean that other views of language have nothing to contribute or that they are irrelevant to the task. These other approaches are often quite helpful and entirely satisfactory if we are seeking primarily observational or descriptive adequacy, but if we are looking for a deeper level of comprehension, that is, for "explanatory adequacy"

(Chomsky, 1962), we must employ an approach to procedures which will help to explicate the generative capacities of language.

If the range of subject matter and the detail with which it is treated in the subsequent sections seem at times unduly difficult or surprisingly voluminous, it must be recognized that translation is essentially a very complicated procedure. In fact, in describing the communication process in translating, I. A. Richards (1953, p. 250) has said, "We have here indeed what may very probably be the most complex type of event yet produced in the evolution of the cosmos."

CHAPTER TWO

THE TRADITION OF TRANSLATION IN THE WESTERN WORLD [1]

Undoubtedly the most famous translation from the ancient world is the Rosetta stone, dating from the second century B.C., but found only in 1799; for it provided the key to unlock the secrets of ancient Egypt through the clue it gave to deciphering Egyptian hieroglyphics. The stone actually contains both a biscript, a text in two forms of writing—Egyptian hieroglyphic and later demotic characters—and a translation of them into Greek.

Evidence of formal translations does not, however, begin with the Rosetta stone, for in the third millennium B.C., Sargon of Assyria delighted in having his exploits proclaimed with elaborate embellishments in the many languages of his empire. The Babylon of Hammurabi's day (c. 2100 B.C.) was a polyglot city, and much of the official business of the empire was made possible by corps of scribes who translated edicts into various languages. Part of the work of these ancient translators evidently consisted in the compilation of lists of corresponding words in various languages, for some of these "dictionaries" have been preserved in cuneiform tablets from various locations and from differing periods. Some of the activity of ancient translators is also reflected in the much later account found in Esther 8:9, where it is said that the King's scribes were summoned to prepare an edict to be sent "to all the satraps and governors and princes of the provinces from India to Ethiopia, a hundred and twenty-seven provinces, to every province in its own script and to every people in its own language, and also to the Jews in their script and language."

A special form of translation developed in the Jewish community in the time of Nehemiah, around 397 B.C.[2] As the event is recorded in Nehemiah 7:73b—8:8, all the people gathered to hear the reading of the law in the square before the Water Gate, "And they read from the book, from the law of God, clearly (or with interpretation); and they gave the sense, so that the people understood the reading." The Jewish people who returned from captivity in Mesopotamia were no longer able to understand the form of Hebrew used in the Scriptures. Accordingly, if the people were to understand, translators (or interpreters) had to explain the contents in a form of Aramaic, the rapidly spreading Semitic trade language of the Eastern Mediterranean.

[1] Because of the peculiar nature of translation problems and traditions in the non-western world, we are here restricting ourselves to the tradition of which we are a part and which is exerting the dominant influence in the world today. For discussions of traditions in the non-western world, see several articles in *Babel*, volume IX, nos. 1 and 2 (1963).

[2] Some scholars date this as 445 B.C.

The only reliable account we have for the formal translation of some part of the Scriptures concerns the book of Ecclesiasticus, included in the Apocrypha. We learn, for example, that Sirach's book of Wisdom was translated into Greek in Egypt about 130 B.C. by his grandson. About this same time the Old Testament was translated into Greek by various scholars who were trying to meet the needs of the large Greek-speaking Jewish community in Alexandria, Egypt, where the Jews numbered some two-fifths of the population in this intellectual and commercial center of the ancient eastern Mediterranean.

The ancient Greco-Roman world, however, was well acquainted with translations and the techniques involved. As early as about 240 B.C., Livius Andronicus had translated Homer's Odyssey into Latin Verse, and Naevius and Ennius rendered a number of Greek plays into Latin. Quintilian, Cicero, Horace, Catullus, and the younger Pliny all gave serious study to translation problems. However, there was no systematic study of principles and procedures from the ancient world. They simply translated, and in many instances they rendered the Greek classics with great skill and insight.

Unfortunately, Bible translating did not in some respects fare as well as the classics, for there was a tendency to regard the "letter rather than the spirit," with results that were sometimes lamentable. Aquila, for example, in the second century A.D. made a painfully literal translation of the Hebrew Old Testament into Greek. Theodotian, also in the second century, tried to make some major improvements in this type of translating; and Symmachus, toward the end of the same century, went somewhat further in the direction of intelligibility, so that Jerome could say of his work, "He gave the sense of the scripture, not in literal language, as Aquila did" (Grant, 1961, p. 25).

Translations of the New Testament were made very early, and into a number of different languages. Beginning first with Syriac and Latin, the process of translation included Coptic (several different dialects), Ethiopic, Gothic, Georgian, and Armenian, to meet the needs of the rapidly expanding Christian community. With respect to the Latin translations, we know that many of these were quite literal, and some of them apparently rather haphazard. As a model in literalness the translators could, of course, point to certain sections of the Septuagint, which are often so literal as to be stylistically very awkward, and not infrequently downright bad Greek. [1] Certainly by the time Jerome was commissioned in 384 A.D. by Pope Damasus to produce a text of the New Testament, it was no easy task to choose between conflicting renderings and to deal with the vested interests of competing interpretations. In the preface to his work Jerome felt obliged to anticipate some of the criticisms by writing: "Who is there, whether learned or unlearned, who, when he takes up the volume in his hands and discovers that what he reads therein does not agree with what he is accustomed to, will not break out at once in a loud voice and call me a sacrilegious forger, for daring to add something

---

[1] Wikgren, 1947, p. 2.

to the ancient books, to make changes and corrections in them ?" (Grant, 1961, p. 36). Jerome was right, for his translation of the New Testament produced a storm of protest that followed him through the rest of his life— a life dedicated first and foremost to the translation of the Old Testament into Latin.

Jerome's approach to translation was probably one of the most systematic and disciplined of any of the ancient translators. He followed well-conceived principles, which he freely proclaimed and defended, and stated quite frankly that he rendered "sense for sense and not word for word." [1] Furthermore, he claimed the support of Cicero, who had translated Plato's Protagoras and other Greek documents into Latin. Cicero, for example, had declared: "What men like you ... call fidelity in translation, the learned term pestilent minuteness ... it is hard to preserve in a translation the charm of expressions which in another language are most felicitous .... If I render word for word, the result will sound uncouth, and if compelled by necessity I alter anything in the order or wording, I shall seem to have departed from the function of a translator."

Jerome also defended his principles of translation by citing the manner in which the Gospel writer Mark treated such expressions as the Aramaic *talitha cumi*, literally, "Damsel, arise," but which Mark rendered into Greek by the sense as "Damsel, I say to you, arise." Jerome further confirmed his principles by citing the manner in which the New Testament writers freely quoted or adapted the Hebrew original or the Septuagint translation. On the other hand, Jerome made some statements which seem to contradict this striving for the sense rather than the wording; but these statements are probably due to his theological controversies with Rufinus, who espoused even freer principles of translation than Jerome, at least in theory, was willing to adopt. Actually, the work of Rufinus and that of Jerome are not so different as has often been implied.

Any departure from past tradition not only brings criticism from those who retain their preference for the old ("And no one after drinking old wine desires new; for he says, 'The old is good'," Luke 5:39), but also inevitably raises questions for and from those who are justifiably confused by differences of translation. Thus the Goths inquired of Jerome which was the correct translation of the Psalter—Greek or Latin ? Which, they asked, was the more nearly correct translation of the Hebrew? With so many translations, some of which were very literal indeed, it is no wonder that the Gothic clergymen were confused, as many people still are today (Bratcher, 1961c).

During the Middle Ages in Western Europe, translating, with the exception of the Venerable Bede's translation of the Gospel of John in 735 A.D., was confined primarily to religious essays rendered into stiff, ecclesiastical Latin. In the 9th and 10th centuries, however, Baghdad became an important center for the translation of the Greek classics into

---

[1] Letter 57 to Pammachius on the Best Method of Translating, from *A Select Library of Nicene and Post-Nicene Fathers*, translated by Schaff and Wall, Volume 6, *Jerome: Letters and Select Works*.

Arabic. By the 12th century, Toledo, Spain, had become a center of learning and for the translating of Greek classics into Latin, but generally by way of intermediate languages such as Syriac and Arabic. Nevertheless, there were scholars who were not unaware of the basic requirements of translation. Maimonides, for example, toward the end of the 12th century, insisted that word for word renderings generally make for a doubtful and confused translation (Luzzatto, 1957, p. 63).

From the Renaissance to the Present

At the time of the Renaissance, Western Europe was, figuratively speaking, inundated with a flood of translations, largely from Greek, for it was the rediscovery of the ancient world which had produced the "rebirth" in Western Europe. Since at last translations were being produced for a much wider audience than the ecclesiastically trained scholastics, there was every incentive to put such translations into the language of the people, and accordingly many persons became engaged in such enterprises. Apparently, however, the general level of such translating of secular works was not high, for, as F. R. Amos (1920, p. 50) has noted, "In contrast to translators of secular works, Bible translators labored long and carefully." Moreover, most of the controversies about translation principles were focused on the efforts of Bible translators, who were engaged in activities strongly supported by some and as vigorously denounced by others.

Undoubtedly the dominant figure in the field of translation during the 16th century was Martin Luther. In order to understand the significance of Luther's contribution, it is important to know something of the pre-Luther period; for by the time Luther published his New Testament in 1522 (the entire Bible was completed only in 1534), there were already a number of translations in several major Western European languages, e.g. Dutch, German, Bohemian (Czech), English, and French. Moreover, the theory of translation was being influenced profoundly by such intellectual leaders as Erasmus. Furthermore, political and social factors contributed to the importance of the languages of the people, in contrast with courtly and ecclesiastical Latin—differences which even the Latin grammarians, in their attempt to teach good Latin, were compelled to emphasize. Hence, even these Latin rhetoricians encouraged people, at least indirectly, to regard their own language as having a distinct form and genius (Schwarz, 1945). Even though such a person as Nicolas von Wyle might argue for literal word-for-word translations, most translators insisted on following the spoken language of the people. In doing so they were, of course, rapidly undermining the traditional rhetorical principles inherited from the Middle Ages (Schwarz, 1944).

Nevertheless, despite earlier tendencies toward more meaningful translating, Luther deserves full credit for having sensed the importance of full intelligibility, especially in the heat of theological controversy. Luther not only defended his principles in general terms, namely, that only in this way could people understand the meaning of the Holy

Scriptures; he also carefully and systematically worked out the implications of his principles of translation in such matters as: (1) shifts of word order; (2) employment of modal auxiliaries; (3) introduction of connectives when these were required; (4) suppression of Greek or Hebrew terms which had no acceptable equivalent in German; (5) use of phrases where necessary to translate single words in the original; (6) shifts of metaphors to nonmetaphors and vice versa; and (7) careful attention to exegetical accuracy and textual variants. [1]

In view of Luther's theological leadership in the Reformation and his remarkable success in translating the New Testament into German, it is little wonder that William Tyndale, who first translated the New Testament into modern English, was ready to parallel quite closely what Luther had already done. Though Tyndale translated directly from Greek, and of course could not depend on German for lexical choices in English, nevertheless he has shown unmistakable dependence upon the principles of translation which Luther employed (Gruber, 1923). Undoubtedly these principles played a major role in the acceptance of Tyndale's work as a basis for later English translations of the New Testament.

Despite the great importance of Luther in the entire field of translation, not only through the example of his work, but also in his *Sendbrief vom Dolmetschen* (1530), discussed more fully below, the credit for the first formulation of a theory of translation must go to Etienne Dolet (1509-1546). Dolet published in 1540 a brief but unsurpassed statement of translation principles (Cary, 1955b).

Etienne Dolet was born in Orleans, France. After some preliminary study in Paris and later travel in Italy, he returned to France at the age of 21 and became deeply immersed in the humanistic movement, arguing with Erasmus, and becoming involved in numerous political and intellectual controversies. This involvement led inevitably to his being imprisoned at various times, with thirteen of his books condemned and burned by the authorities. Finally, after escaping from prison, he was arrested in Lyon and brought to trial on the charge of heresy for having "mistranslated" one of the dialogues of Plato in such a way as to imply a disbelief in immortality. Condemned as a confirmed atheist, Dolet, at the age of 37, was tortured and strangled, and his body was burned, with copies of his books.

Etienne Dolet, himself an excellent translator and a brilliant student of the classics, summarized the fundamental principles of translation under five headings:

1. The translator must understand perfectly the content and intention of the author whom he is translating.
2. The translator should have a perfect knowledge of the language from which he is translating and an equally excellent knowledge of the language into which he is translating.

---

[1] For a supplementary discussion of these matters, see Edward H. Lauer (1915) and Heinz Bluhm (1951).

3. The translator should avoid the tendency to translate word for word, for to do so is to destroy the meaning of the original and to ruin the beauty of the expression.
4. The translator should employ the forms of speech in common usage.
5. Through his choice and order of words the translator should produce a total overall effect with appropriate "tone." [1]

It is interesting to note that Dolet senses the prime necessity of the translator's being in full rapport with the spirit and intent of the original author, a sentiment emphasized and stated negatively by Luther when he said, "I contend that a false Christian or a person with a sectarian spirit cannot faithfully translate the [Scriptures]." Moreover, Dolet does not seek to distinguish between the relative degree of control the translator must have in the source and the receptor language. In theory, one should have perfect knowledge and control of both. Dolet's emphasis upon avoidance of literalism and upon the use of vernaculars is strikingly relevant for all types of translation aimed at a general audience, and his final word on the tone of the translation as reflected in its appropriate stylistic effectiveness is fundamental to all serious efforts in translation, regardless of medium or content.

Of course there was some disagreement with such principles as Etienne Dolet enunciated and Luther demonstrated in his translation. Men like Gregory Martin held to a basically obscurantist viewpoint, insisting that the authority of the Church Fathers came before the results of contemporary scholarship. But people like William Fulke (1583), who undoubtedly had considerable influence on the translators of the King James Version, insisted that ecclesiastical tradition must give way to common English usage. Fulke contended that "To translate precisely out of the Hebrew is not to observe the number of words, but the perfect sense and meaning, as the phrase of our tongue will serve to be understood" (Amos, 1920, p. 60).

An outstanding Bible translation from this early period is the Spanish work of Casiodoro de Reina, whose translation, published in 1568, was revised by his friend and colleague Cipriano de Valera in 1603. These men were in close touch with all the major intellectual developments in France, England, and Germany, and their knowledge, combined with unusual sensitivity to linguistic usage, resulted in the production of a remarkably fine translation. In various degrees of revision it has served the Spanish-speaking world as the principal Spanish Bible in circulation. Because of the declining importance of Spain as an intellectual center of European life, this translation had much less effect upon translation theory and practice than various English and German translations had. However, it should be recognized as an outstanding example of the flowering of literary achievement in Spain in the 16th century, combined with intellectual insights from the ferment of learning in the world of the Reformation.

---

[1] Dolet's principles are reproduced here in summary form with certain paraphrastic adaptations, based upon Cary's analysis (1955b).

The translators commissioned by King James I of England to produce a text of the Bible which could be authorized for reading in the churches did not develop new principles or theories of translation. Actually, they were not seeking to do something new, but rather to select the best of what had been included in previous translations, as the preface, *The Translators to the Reader*, clearly states. However, a text that could have been a series of tasteless compromises turned out to be a remarkably fine translation, owing to the unusually good sense the translators showed in matters of exegesis and their extraordinary sensitivity to the style of speech appropriate in public reading. They were refreshingly better than the Rheims-Douay translators, who floundered in a morass of awkward literalness and ecclesiastical verbiage. Even though at first the King James Version was roundly denounced, and such groups as the Pilgrims would have nothing to do with it—copies were not allowed in the May-flower Company—it finally won out. It served to cast a very long shadow over Bible translating in many languages for several centuries.

In contrast with the relative care exhibited by the translators of the Scriptures, those engaged in the translation of secular works in the 17th and 18th centuries showed an almost unrestrained freedom. This period has been quite appropriately called the age of *Les Belles Infidèles* (Mounin, 1955). As G. M. Young (1941) has commented, translators of this period were not always asking themselves, "Have I captured the exact shade or sentiment in that line?" Rather, they "brought their subject home in bulk." [1] During these centuries foreign models had considerable influence with literary people throughout Europe. Though many English translations were rather garbled abridgments and revisions, they were, for the most part, vigorous and meaningful (Hughes, 1919). Primarily, however, the freedom of this period implied, not so much a technique for giving the translator greater opportunity to display his own powers, as a means by which he could reproduce more truly the spirit of the original (Amos, 1920, p. 156).

Probably the dominant person who set the stage for a conscious freedom in translation was the poet Abraham Cowley (1656), who defended his translations of Pindar's Odes by saying, "If a man should undertake to translate Pindar word for word, it would be thought *one Mad-man* had translated another; as may appear, when a person who understands not the original, reads the verbal translation of him into Latin prose, than which nothing seems more raving . . . . I have in these two odes of Pindar taken, left out, and added what I please; nor made it so much my aim to let the reader know precisely what he spoke, as what was his way and manner of speaking."

Dryden (1680) did not approve of Cowley's rather radical approach to Pindar's Odes, and classified his translations as "imitation." Dryden felt that there were three basic types of translation: (1) metaphrase, a word-for-word and line-for-line type of rendering; (2) paraphrase, a translation in which the author's work is kept carefully in view, but in which

---

[1] See also John W. Draper (1921).

2

the sense rather than the words are followed; and (3) imitation, in which the translator assumes the liberty not only to vary the words and sense, but also to leave both if the spirit of the original seems to require. Dryden said quite frankly that, "It is impossible to translate verbally and well at [the same time. 'Tis much like dancing on ropes with fetter'd legs! A man may shun a fall by using caution, but the gracefulness of motion is not to be expected." Dryden proposed the golden mean of paraphrase, insisting that "Imitation and verbal version are in my opinion the two extremes, which ought to be avoided."

Alexander Pope (1715) followed very much the same position as Dryden, for he contended that "No literal translation can be just to an excellent original" . . . and yet "no rash paraphrase can make amends." Pope insisted that "The fire of the poem is what the translator should principally regard, as it is most likely to expire in his managing."

Batteux (1760) in France sounded a more cautious word during this same general period. His "rules" involved the preservation of word order wherever possible, the conservation of the order of ideas, the use of the same length of sentences, the duplication of conjunctions, and the avoidance of paraphrase. Batteux was not opposed to alterations if they were fully justified, but he was cautious and deeply concerned with the reproduction of form. In Germany a somewhat similar development had taken place, as reflected in Herder's translations and in A. W. Schlegel's verse rendering of Shakespeare's *A Midsummer-Night's Dream* (Purdie, 1949).

John Wesley's translation of the New Testament, published in 1755, had considerable influence on views of Scripture translating, for his work was strikingly ahead of his time. He reflected very well the secular concepts of translating, and in many of his decisions on technical theological problems and exegesis he anticipated much of what was later incorporated into standard translations.

In 1789 George Campbell of Aberdeen published an outstanding work on the history and theory of translation, especially as related to the Scriptures. In his two-volume work, of which the first is a 700-page introduction to his translation of the Gospels, Campbell treated Bible translation in a detailed and systematic way, with far greater breadth and insight than anyone before him had employed in dealing with the problems. He indicated by copious examples precisely where he differed in principle and practice from such translators as Jerome, Castalio, and Beza, and showed remarkable insight into problems of textual criticism. In his study of the key words of the New Testament he anticipated many later developments.

Campbell took considerable pains to point out the inadequacies of the King James Version; and, whether he was dealing with minor details or broad principles, he displayed an unusual combination of sound knowledge and common sense. Campbell (pp. 445-446) summarized the criteria of good translating under three principles:

    1. To give a just representation of the sense of the original.

2. To convey into his version, as much as possible, in a consistency with the genius of the language which he writes, the author's spirit and manner.

3. To take care that the version have, "at least so far the quality of an original performance, as to appear natural and easy."

Using these three fundamental principles, Campbell proceeded to point out their full implications, not only in the history of Bible translating, but also in the way in which the Greek text should be translated into contemporary English.

In the following year, 1790, Alexander Fraser Tytler (Lord Woodhouselee), an Edinburgh Scot, published a volume on *The Principles of Translation*, in which he likewise sets up three principles, as follows:

1. The translation should give a complete transcript of the idea of the original work.

2. The style and manner of writing should be of the same character with that of the original.

3. The translation should have all the ease of the original composition.

Quite justifiably, Campbell accused Tytler of plagiarism, but the latter insisted that his was purely a parallel development. However, Tytler's work has had far more influence than Campbell's, because he treated a wider range of subject matter, and concentrated on the secular field of translation, rather than dealing exclusively with the Scriptures, as Campbell had done.

Tytler's approach is rather startlingly modern at times, for he admits additions if they are fully legitimate; that is, if "they have the most necessary connection with the original thought, and actually increase its force"; likewise, he countenances omissions if the words are "confessedly redundant" and their omission "shall not impair or weaken the original thought" (p. 22). He gives sensible advice on problems of obscurities in the original text, saying that translators should exercise judgment and select the meaning which agrees best with the immediate context or with the author's usual mode of thinking. "To imitate the obscurity or ambiguity of the original is a fault and it is still a greater one to give more than one meaning" (p. 28).

Tytler explains the translator's function as a process in which "he uses not the same colors with the original, but is required to give his picture the same force and effect. He is not allowed to copy the touches of the original, yet is required, by touches of his own, to produce a perfect resemblance . . . . He must adopt the very soul of his author, which must speak through his own organs" (pp. 113-14). On the other hand, Tytler complains of Dryden's influence, for it was after Dryden that Tytler sees too great a freedom coming into vogue, a circumstance in which "fidelity was but a secondary object," and translation was considered "synonymous with paraphrase" (p. 45).

In a sense, Tytler's caution marked the close of one period of translation and the beginning of another, for with the opening of the 19th century a type of supersophistication arose which spread the idea that "nothing worth translating can be translated" (Young, 1941, p. 209). The classical revival of the 19th century and the emphasis upon technical accuracy, combined with a spirit of exclusivism among the intelligentsia, conspired to make that century as pedantic in its attitudes toward translation as it was toward many other aspects of learning. This tendency was strikingly illustrated in some translations of the *Arabian Nights' Entertainments*, which, though technically more accurate than their predecessors, nevertheless robbed the stories of their Eastern atmosphere. [1] The same tendency has been noted in various European translations (Thierfelder, 1955).

Undoubtedly the principal exponent—for English—of a more literal tendency in translating was Matthew Arnold, who tried to reproduce Homer in English hexameter, and insisted upon close adherence to the form of any original. Moreover, Arnold was quite unwilling to accept as a criterion of a translated work that it should have essentially the same effect upon the average reader today as it had for the original receptors. Arnold was not, however, translating for people in general, but for a select audience who knew the originals and could read the translation with their mind's eye on the Greek. His proposed test (1862) was that a translation should more or less reproduce the effect of the original for "the competent scholar." It is little wonder that such persons as Laurie Magnus (1931) have severely criticized Arnold for having rules which merely conveyed the text and slighted the spirit of the original work.

Perhaps the best illustration of the pernicious effects of a literalistic view of translation is to be found in the English Revised Version of the Bible (1881, 1885) and in the corresponding American Standard Version (1901). These versions are as literal as they can be and still make sense—the result of well-defined principles aimed at producing just such a translation. These translations have been very popular with theological students studying Greek and Hebrew, since they make excellent "ponies"; but they have never been popular with the Christian community of English-speaking people, for they simply do not communicate effectively, owing to their 16th century forms (in some cases more archaic than those of the King James Version) and the literal, awkward syntax. Note, for example, such passages as the following:

2 Corinthians 10:14-16

> For we stretch not ourselves overmuch, as though we reached not unto you: for we came even as far as unto you in the gospel of Christ: not glorying beyond our measure, *that is*, in other men's labors; but having hope that, as your faith groweth, we shall be magnified in you according to our province unto *further* abundance, so as to preach the gospel even unto the parts beyond you, *and* not to glory in another's province in regard of things ready to our hand.

[1]   See Anon. (1900).

2 Corinthians 3:10

> For verily that which hath been made glorious hath not been made glorious in this respect, by reason of the glory that surpasseth.

The words may be English, but the grammar is not; and the sense is quite lacking.

The 20th century has witnessed a radical change in translation principles. In the first place, new concepts of communication have developed in our shrinking world. Not only have semanticists and psychologists insisted that a message which does not communicate is useless, but advertisers and politicians, among others, have set a high premium upon intelligibility. Moreover, there has been a new sense of urgency in world affairs, and Victorian optimism among an intellectual élite has given ground to radical realism. Writers, editors, publishers, and translators have all been caught up in a new mode of communication, subject to a vast variety of pressures and responding to numerous needs.

During recent years five developments have had a significant effect on the theory of translation and its practice in various parts of the world. The first of these is the rapidly expanding field of structural linguistics. In Europe the influence of Ferdinand de Saussure has been unequaled, and more recently the work of Hjelmslev (1953) and of other members of the Linguistic Circle of Copenhagen has been very important. But the most creative work in relating linguistics to translation and literary criticism was carried out by the Linguistic Circle of Prague under the early stimulus of Trubetskoy (1939), and later followed up in the field of translation and stylistics by such men as Boh Havránek, Jan Mukařovský, Jiří Levý, and Vladimir Procházka. In the United States a number of linguists, e.g. Edward Sapir, Benjamin L. Whorf, Floyd Lounsbury, C. F. Voegelin, Harry Hoijer, Martin Joos, Joseph H. Greenberg, and Uriel Weinreich became increasingly concerned with problems of language and culture. With an orientation rather different from their European counterparts, they have likewise made important contributions to the field of semantics, and thus to translation. Perhaps one of the most significant contributions of modern linguistic science to the field of translation has been the liberation of translators from the philological presuppositions of the preceding generation. [1]

A second development is the application of present-day methods in structural linguistics to the special problems of Bible translation by members of the Summer Institute of Linguistics, also known as the Wycliffe Bible Translators. Beginning in 1935, this organization has worked in more than 200 languages in thirteen different countries, and has produced an impressive number of technical publications on languages and linguistic structures, as well as numerous translations of the Scriptures in so-called primitive languages. By means of summer training programs open to missionaries of various groups and going to many places throughout the world, it has had an extensive influence on the use

---

[1] See Vladimir Procházka (1942).

of modern linguistic approaches to the problems of translation and communication.

The third development is the program of the United Bible Societies, which began with an international conference of translators in Holland in 1947. The Societies have published since 1950 a quarterly journal called *The Bible Translator*. This program has been sponsored primarily through the efforts of the American Bible Society, the Netherlands Bible Society, and the British and Foreign Bible Society. At the same time, linguists associated with the American Bible Society have prepared extensive helps for translators that reflect not only general developments in linguistics, both in America and Europe, but also their own research and field work.

The fourth development has been the publication since 1955 of *Babel*, under the auspices of UNESCO. Published by the International Federation of Translators, this quarterly has informed translators not only of new lexical aids and changing conditions affecting professional translators in different parts of the world, but also of the new trends in theory and practice. The leaders of this program, Pierre-François Caillé, E. Cary, R. W. Jumpelt, and Erwin H. Bothien, have all made highly important contributions to a better understanding of contemporary theory, principles, and procedures in the field of translation.

The fifth development, machine translation, has unfortunately been publicized rather out of proportion to its present tangible results. Nevertheless, there has been some solid work in this area, particularly in such places as the Academy of Sciences of the USSR in Moscow, Birkbeck College (University of London), and in the United States at the Massachusetts Institute of Technology, Harvard University, IBM Research Center in Tarrytown, New York, Georgetown University, and the University of California at Berkeley. Even apart from any practical results which such research may ultimately produce, the thorough study of translation procedures required by machine translation programing has produced some important insights into semantic theory and elements of structural design. These factors are discussed more fully in Chapter 12.

BASIC CONFLICTS IN TRANSLATION THEORY

Despite major shifts of viewpoint on translation during different epochs and in different countries, two basic conflicts, expressing themselves in varying degrees of tension, have remained. These fundamental differences in translation theory may be stated in terms of two sets of conflicting "poles"; (1) literal vs. free translating, and (2) emphasis on form vs. concentration on content. These two sets of differences are closely related, but not identical, for the tension between literal and free can apply equally well to both form and content. However, in general the issues are not well defined. For the most part such expressions as literal vs. free, translation vs. paraphrase, and words vs. sense are essentially battle cries for those who wish to defend their own work or criticize the work of others. Rarely are these conflicting views analyzed in detail or the implications of such principles worked out carefully in actual practice.

The most literal type of translation, an interlinear one, can scarcely be called a translation in the usual sense of the term. However, some productions intended as fully accredited translations are almost as absurdly literal as an interlinear rendering. For example, Arias Montanus, in the Antwerp Polyglot (1551), in translating the Old Testament into Latin, employed some of the most literal renderings imaginable. He did not hesitate to make up new Latin words in order to translate the same Hebrew stem by a single corresponding Latin stem, and he flagrantly violated good canons of Latin usage. In Genesis 1:20, for example, his rendering *reptificent aquae reptile* is no better Latin than the English parallel would be, "Let the waters reptilify the reptile." [1] Simply because the Hebrew verb in question was a causative, Arias constructed a causative in Latin, but the formal parallelism completely distorted the meaningful relationship.

Such a tendency toward absurd literalism is by no means dead. During the past fifteen years a small group of earnest but misguided persons have been putting out a so-called Concordant Version in English, in which they have attempted always to translate the same Greek or Hebrew term by the same English word. Moreover, they have attempted to match grammatical forms and even to employ the same word order, if at all possible. The results are lamentable, for the attempt to be literal in the form of the message has resulted in grievous distortions of the message itself. [2]

A famous literal translation of the Old Testament was the work of Aquila (c. 125 A.D.), who composed barbarous Greek in an attempt to be faithful to the Hebrew original. Jerome's translation of the Hebrew Old Testament into Latin was radically different in principle, and accordingly in results, but in the New Testament Jerome was guilty of many awkward renderings which simply reproduced Greek sentences in Latin words. In his rapid work on the New Testament Jerome was more of an editor than a translator; in many instances he merely selected the least unsatisfactory rendering current in various existing Latin translations. So poor were certain aspects of Jerome's Latin that Cardinal Bembo, at the time of the Reformation, objected to reading the Latin Bible on the ground that it would corrupt his Latin style.

Sebastianus Castellio, who in 1551 published his Latin translation of the Scriptures with the avowed purpose of making them more attractive to cultured Latin-reading persons than were Jerome's rather awkward ecclesiastical renderings, went somewhat to the other extreme. His language was frequently too florid, and often quite exotic. However, at certain points he certainly improved on Jerome. For example, Jerome's

---

[1] This and numerous other literalisms are noted by George Campbell (1789), pp. 450 ff.

[2] Another very literal translation of the Old Testament has been prepared by Buber and Rosenzweig, who have displayed remarkable ingenuity in reproducing in German many of the formal and stylistic features of Biblical Hebrew. This translation is, however, more admired by scholars than read by common people desirous of understanding the sense of the message.

rendering of the statement, "For with God nothing shall be impossible" (Luke 1:37), as *non erit impossibile apud Deum omne verbum* is a strictly literal translation of the Greek, and certainly inferior Latin in comparison with Castellio's *nulla res est quam Deus facere non possit.* [1]

The differences between literal and free translating are, however, no mere positive-negative dichotomy, but rather a polar distinction with many grades between them. These grades may be well illustrated by the following renderings of Romans 8:1-4 in the American Standard Version, the Revised Standard Version, the New English Bible, and J. B. Phillips' New Testament in Modern English:

American Standard Version

There is therefore now no condemnation to them that are in Christ Jesus. For the law of the Spirit of life in Christ Jesus made me free from the law of sin and of death. For what the law could not do, in that it was weak through the flesh, God, sending his own Son in the likeness of sinful flesh and for sin, condemned sin in the flesh: that the ordinance of the law might be fulfilled in us, who walk not after the flesh, but after the Spirit.

Revised Standard Version

There is therefore now no condemnation for those who are in Christ Jesus. For the law of the Spirit of life in Christ Jesus has set me free from the law of sin and death. For God has done what the law, weakened by the flesh, could not do: sending his own Son in the likeness of sinful flesh and for sin, he condemned sin in the flesh, in order that the just requirement of the law might be fulfilled in us, who walk not according to the flesh but according to the Spirit.

New English Bible

The conclusion of the matter is this: there is no condemnation for those who are united with Christ Jesus, because in Christ Jesus the life-giving law of the Spirit has set you free from the law of sin and death. What the law could never do, because our lower nature robbed it of all potency, God has done: by sending his own Son in a form like that of our own sinful nature, and as a sacrifice for sin, he has passed judgement against sin within that very nature, so that the commandment of the law may find fulfilment in us, whose conduct, no longer under the control of our lower nature, is directed by the Spirit.

Phillips' Version

No condemnation now hangs over the head of those who are "in" Jesus Christ. For the new spiritual principle of life "in" Christ lifts me out of the old vicious circle of sin and death.

---

[1] This contrast and a number of others are cited by George Campbell (1789), pp. 480 ff.

The Law never succeeded in producing righteousness—the failure was always the weakness of human nature. But God has met this by sending his own Son Jesus Christ to live in that human nature which causes the trouble. And, *while Christ was actually taking upon himself the sins of men, God condemned that sinful nature.* So that we are able to meet the Law's requirements, so long as we are living no longer by the dictates of our sinful nature, but in obedience to the promptings of the Spirit.

The conflict between the dictates of form and content becomes especially important where the form of the message is highly specialized, as it is in poetry. The 17th century poet Sir John Denham fully recognized this problem and stated quite bluntly in his Preface to the Second Book of Virgil's Aeneid: "I conceive it a vulgar error in translating poets to affect being *fidus interpres.* Let that care be with them who deal in matters of fact or matters of faith; but whosoever aims at it in poetry, as he attempts what is not required, so shall he never perform what he attempts; for it is not his business alone to translate language into language, but poesie into poesie" (Tytler, 1790, p. 35).

Lyric poetry obviously cannot be adequately reduced to mere prose, for the original form of the "song" must in some way be reproduced as another "song." The meter may be different, but the overall effect must be equivalent if the translation is to be in any sense adequate. Thus, though in some instances the form may be neglected for the content (as in Rieu's prose translation of Homer's epic poetry), in the case of lyric poetry some approximation to the form must be retained, even with some loss or alteration of content.

The problems of literal vs. free and form vs. content have been discussed more recently in terms of other frames of reference. L. Forster (1958a), for example, has dealt with these difficulties in terms of "levels" of translation, as related to the size of the basic units which enter into the translation process. In the Middle Ages, he notes, the primary unit of translation was the word, while later it became the phrase and the sentence. A still further concept of translation takes in the entire work as the legitimate unit of translation. A somewhat similar characterization of translation procedures may likewise be described in three stages, on the basis of escape from the tyranny of (1) words, (2) grammar, and (3) stylistic form.

This same basic problem has been approached by T. F. Higham (1938, p. xxxvi) from quite a different point of view. In discussing the two major kinds of translation, Higham says: "The one sect aims at transporting us back to the poetry of Greece, and the other at bringing Greek poetry closer to our own. The former aim is deserving of respect . . . . On the other hand, it is evident that such translators are praised more often than read."

By close attention to literal wording and formal correspondence one can be transported back to an earlier culture or off to some contemporary, but foreign, one. However, literalness and formal agreement do not let us feel really at home in such a strange literary land, nor do they actually help us to appreciate as we should how this same message must have impressed those who first heard it. Without some adjustments in form and content, at times even rather radical, no literary translation can fully accomplish its real purpose.

SPECIAL THEOLOGICAL PROBLEMS

As the preceding discussion has demonstrated, the translating of the Bible raises certain special issues. This would be true of any document having a long history and involving the deep personal attachment of many people and the vast, vested interests of numerous institutions. But dealing with any religious document such as the Bible, one must bear in mind that its contemporary significance is not determined merely by what it meant to those who first received it, but by what it has come to mean to people throughout the intervening years.

The conflicts which have arisen over principles and procedures in Bible translating can be viewed from a number of different perspectives. Perhaps one of the most meaningful ways to study these problems is to note the differences of opinion which have arisen over issues of (1) inspiration vs. philology, (2) tradition vs. contemporary authority, and (3) theology vs. grammar. [1]

The inspirational vs. the philological points of view in Bible translation were well defined by the differences between Augustine and Jerome. Augustine, for example, fully accepted the tradition of Aristeas, together with later elaborations, concerning the alleged miraculous translation of the Septuagint by seventy-two men (six from each of the twelve tribes), who, in groups of two and in complete isolation from other translators, translated the entire Old Testament with such divine inspiration and control that the resulting thirty-six drafts were absolutely identical in all respects (Thackeray, 1917). St. Augustine recognized that the Greek text of the Septuagint does not always agree with the Hebrew. He explained the differences by saying that the Spirit "with divine authority could say through the translators something different from what he had said through the original prophets—just as, though these prophets had the two meanings in mind, both were inspired by the Spirit.... We will conclude, in the case of something in the Hebrew which is missing in the LXX that the Spirit elected to say this by the lips of the original prophets and not by the lips of their translators. Conversely, in the case of something present in the LXX and missing in the original, we will conclude that the Spirit chose to say this particular thing by . . . the seventy rather than . . . by the original prophets, thus . . . all of them were inspired." [2]

---

[1] Schwarz (1955) has dealt with the history of Bible translation in terms of the traditional, philological, and inspirational views. The situation, however, seems somewhat more complex than this analysis would imply, for in each aspect of translation there are opposing tendencies and counter currents. Accordingly, it would appear more satisfactory to highlight these tensions by presenting the issues in terms of contrasting positions.

[2] St. Augustine, *The City of God*, 18.43.

It would be difficult to state more clearly the case for the divine inspiration of translators. Moreover, this view has certainly not died out. For example, people not infrequently ask the Bible Societies whether they publish the King James Version in Japanese or the King James Version in Spanish, implying that they regard the King James Version as in a special sense divinely inspired. On the other hand, such implicit views of inspired translation, often arising out of ignorance of the full implications of the problem, can be matched by the "informed obscurantism" of those who insist that, in translating the Old Testament, one should correct the Hebrew Text at those points at which the Septuagint, as cited in the New Testament, differs from the Hebrew Old Testament.

In contrast to the views of St. Augustine and his present-day successors, Jerome was completely opposed to the idea of the divine inspiration of translators. In fact, he said that he did not know "who was the first lying author to construct the seventy cells at Alexandria." Jerome was fully on the side of a philological approach to translation, as his examination of and judgments on variant New Testament renderings and his long and arduous study of Hebrew for Old Testament translating amply testify. Jerome's attitudes, fully confirmed by similar approaches by Erasmus at the time of the Reformation, are shared by most present-day scholarship, which has not hesitated to point out instances of theological bias on the part of the Septuagint translators. [1]

One must recognize, however, that neo-orthodox theology has given a new perspective to the doctrine of divine inspiration. For the most part, it conceives of inspiration primarily in terms of the response of the receptor, and places less emphasis on what happened to the source at the time of writing. An oversimplified statement of this new view is reflected in the often quoted expression, "The Scriptures are inspired because they inspire me." Such a concept of inspiration means, however, that attention is inevitably shifted from the details of wording in the original to the means by which the same message can be effectively communicated to present-day readers. Those who espouse the traditional, orthodox view of inspiration quite naturally focus attention on the presumed readings of the "autographs." The result is that, directly or indirectly, they often tend to favor quite close, literal renderings as the best way of preserving the inspiration of the writer by the Holy Spirit. On the other hand, those who hold the neo-orthodox view, or who have been influenced by it, tend to be freer in their translating; as they see it, since the original document inspired its readers because it spoke meaningfully to them, only an equally meaningful translation can have this same power to inspire present-day receptors. It would be quite wrong, however, to assume that all those who emphasize fully meaningful translations necessarily hold to a neo-orthodox view of inspiration; for those who have combined orthodox theology with deep evangelistic or missionary convictions have been equally concerned with the need for making translations entirely meaningful.

[1] See Gehman (1949, 1950) and Gard (1955).

The problems of traditional vs. contemporary authority have affected translations more in the realm of exegesis and text than in style. But again Jerome was fundamentally on the right side, for he broke with entrenched tradition, both in respect to his edited New Testament (where he rejected many popular renderings in various older Latin versions) and in his Old Testament translation, which constantly ran counter to the sacrosanct Septuagint. The irony of Jerome's work was that through the centuries it came to be venerated by traditionalists, against whose counterparts at an earlier period Jerome had waged so valiant a fight. Ultimately the spirit of Jerome was sacrificed to the letter of his translation, and the Vulgate became the exegetical standard of the Roman Catholic Church, even supplanting the Greek text itself—not only officially, but emotionally. Cardinal Ximenes, for example, regarded the Latin Vulgate, which he printed in his Complutentian Polyglot between the Hebrew and the Septuagint, as being like the Lord between two thieves, with Hebrew the unrepentant thief.

The battle between traditional standards and contemporary learning was an important part of the Reformation. At that time it was Erasmus who campaigned for the Greek Text of the New Testament against the Roman Church's insistence on the Vulgate. Beza endeavored by means of his Latin translation to overcome many of the grievous errors of the Vulgate; but unfortunately Beza was too much motivated by theological interests to restrain himself when there was an opportunity to read into the text some choice Reformed Church doctrine. [1]

Luther understandably had to confront the problem of traditionalism vs. the new enlightenment. One key passage which became an issue for all Protestant Reformation translators is Luke 1:28, where the Vulgate rendering of *plena gratiae* "full of grace" (a key passage for those who claim that Mary is able to dispense grace), is obviously an inaccurate translation of the Greek participle *kekharitomenê*. Luther therefore rejected the earlier German rendering of *voll Gnaden* (based on the Vulgate) and used *holdselige*, a very close parallel to the Greek. This same problem was an issue for Tyndale in English and for Reina and Valera in Spanish.

The Roman Catholic Church has not, however, maintained the same intransigent attitude that characterized the Counter Reformation. Even a translation of the Bible into Spanish by Eloíno Nácar F. and Alberto Colunga in 1944 shows a number of significant departures from tradition, even though it retains certain Roman Catholic hallmarks, such as this *llena de gracia* "full of grace" in Luke 1:28 and several instances of "penance," when the Greek term is "repentance." In the excellent *Bible de Jérusalem* in French, the Jerusalem School has produced an outstanding piece of work, reflecting a degree of scholarship quite superior to anything produced by any other group of Roman Catholic scholars, though in Luke 1:28 this French text also adheres to the Vulgate tradition, while a footnote, as so often, serves to give the truer meaning.

[1] For a discussion of Beza's doctrinal bias, see George Campbell (1789), pp. 493 ff.

The issue of theology vs. grammar is a somewhat more subtle problem. Luther, for example, was certainly one who looked to grammar as a basis for exegesis. In fact, he makes it quite clear that the comments of the church fathers are no substitute for careful study of the original languages, "for in comparison with the glosses of the Fathers, the languages are as sunlight to darkness." [1] Nevertheless, in translating, Luther had two overriding concerns: (1) that the people might fully understand the language [2] and (2) that the theological implications of the Bible should be perfectly clear. Accordingly, (in Romans 3:28) Luther translated *dass der Mensch gerecht werde ohne des Gesetzes Werke, allein durch den Glauben.* This word *allein*, making the last phrase mean "through faith alone," quite understandably provoked the ire of Luther's enemies, who insisted that he was adding to the Scriptures. Luther, however, contended that this added word was fully justified by the theological significance of the passage as well as the grammatical structure, even if it were not to be found literally in the original. [3]

Modern translators have been somewhat more inclined to trust the text as it is, rather than to re-enforce its meaning. In other words, the Biblical writers are permitted to speak more for themselves, rather than to do special service to some theological cause which the translator himself may represent. Of course, as in any realm of human activity, complete objectivity in translation is impossible, for we ourselves are a part of the very cultural context in which and for which we are translating. However, present-day attention given to the serious study of the text of Scripture, rather than merely to its philosophical implications, is a healthy sign. It has had its impact not only on the average Bible student, but also upon most translators.

In one sense Luther was a strong adherent to the principle of grammar, especially the grammar of the receptor language—the one into which the translation was being made. In his day he probably did more to sweep away meaningless ecclesiastical verbiage than anyone else. His contribution is obscured by the fact that the innovations of the Reformation have become the traditions of our day.

Again today translators face the problem of meaningless vocabulary. Klaus von Bismarck (1957) states the issue quite bluntly: "The official language of the church and the 'pious' speech of most of its members make it plain that church communities as a whole are not really facing up to the problems of their time, but are simply passing many questions by with their eyes closed." Fortunately, in a number of Biblical translations now coming out in English and other world languages there seems to be a growing awareness of the necessity of vital communication. At last, some of the meaningless phrases are giving way to sometimes blunt, but intelligible, language.

[1] For an excellent summary of Luther's views on these issues, see Martin Luther, translated by Painter (1936).
[2] See Kretzmann (1934).
[3] For a translation of Luther's views on translating, see W. H. Carruth (1907).

CHAPTER THREE

AN INTRODUCTION TO THE NATURE OF MEANING

Basic to any discussion of principles and procedures in translation is a thorough acquaintance with the manner in which meaning is expressed through language as a communication code—first, in terms of the parts which constitute such a code; secondly, the manner in which the code operates; and thirdly, how such a code as language is related to other codes. These subjects are discussed in this chapter and the two succeeding chapters.

Fundamentally, a code consists of symbols organized into a system. Language, which is precisely such a code, consists of words (or other units) which are organized, according "to the rules of the grammar," into particular types of combinations. There are, of course, other codes, e.g. the gestures employed—certain movements organized into patterns of behavior. The traditional use of naval flags to signal battle formations and the succession of events is another type of communication code. Edward T. Hall (1959) has described the "silent languages" of time and space, those systems of communication which we employ to signal meanings by rather highly organized patterns of behavior involving time (e.g. when to call, how late one may be, and times for appointments) and space (e.g. how close we stand in speaking to a person, the arrangement of space in an office, and the location of certain types of events). Music and the pictorial arts can also be said to constitute a kind of language. However, in terms of the number of symbols and the complexity of organization there is, of course, no code comparable to language.

Some codes, such as Morse and semaphore, [1] are more strictly speaking "secondary" or "dependent" codes, for they are entirely subordinate to language, which is a primary code. Writing, similarly, is a kind of dependent code, for it depends primarily upon speech, though in some instances written codes may become, for historical reasons, far removed from any contemporary form of oral language.

Types of Symbols

The words of a language constitute what are generally called symbols, but symbols have often been treated by logicians and semanticists as only a special type of a much larger class of objects, namely, signs. Reichenbach (1947), for example, sets up three basic types of signs: indexical, iconic, and conventional.

The first (indexical) type of sign may be either (1) nonhuman, e.g. wet streets are a sign of rain and smoke a sign of fire, or (2) human, e.g.

[1] It is, of course, possible to regard such spelling-dependent codes as being tertiary, since writing is itself secondary to speech.

screams, cries, and laughter. Iconic signs have the special feature of participating in what they signal by means of their very form, e.g. a picture has the form of the object to which it "points," and an onomatopoeic expression, such as *putt-putt* or *choo-choo*, is presumably an imitation of the very sound made by the object in question.

Conventional signs are those we generally call symbols, for they are free from formal "contamination" with the objects to which they refer. Some of these conventional signs, or symbols, are not linguistic, e.g. the dollar sign and the mathematical symbols that mark addition, multiplication, or division. But most linguistic signs are completely conventional, for without such freedom of form from their referents they would not be adequately maneuverable or sufficiently applicable to the almost infinite variety of experience they symbolize. In other words, if we are to use language symbols efficiently to talk about a myriad of things, many of which we have never heard or seen, they must have a shape and a size which in no way tie them to their referents.

Some linguistic signs, however, do have an iconic quality, as noted above, for they suggest by their very forms the objects to which they refer. This quality does not apply solely to forms traditionally regarded as onomatopoeic, but also to certain types of "sound symbolism," often noted by linguists. Bloomfield (1933, p. 156), for example, pointed out the meaningful elements in *fl* in such a series as *flip, flap, flitter, flimmer, flicker, flutter, flash, flare,* and in the *gl* in *glare, glitter, glow, glimmer.* Jakobson, as well as a number of others, has dealt with the symbolic values of certain vowels. For example, the high front vowel [i] is seemingly more readily associated with sharp, bright, high, and light objects, in contrast with the lower back vowel [o], which is so often associated with dull, dark, low, and heavy objects (Jakobson, 1960, pp. 372-373, and Whorf, 1956, p. 267). Nevertheless, such iconic elements in the symbols of language are relatively rare, though not unimportant in the translation of poetry, where they are so difficult to reproduce with anything like their original values.

SYMBOLS IN CONTEXT

Not only are there different types of signs and symbols; there are also diverse kinds of contexts in which such elements may occur: (1) immediate, (2) displaced, and (3) transferred. In an immediate context a symbol is used to identify an object in the immediate environment. In such instances it is not difficult to determine the referent of the symbol, for one can point to it. On the other hand, this very proximity of the referent in the original utterance may result in obscurity in a later repetition of the communication, for without being able to reconstruct the original circumstances we simply cannot identify the original referent.

In a displaced context a particular object or person not present is the referent. This, of course, is the most common type of situation, for we use language primarily to speak of things or persons not in our immediate environment. In a transferred context, however, we use symbols in such a way as to transfer their applicability from one class of objects or situations to a related class. For example, we may say that *the land is poor* or *the soil is rich*. *Poor* and *rich* refer primarily to the quantity of certain types of possessions, but certain characteristics of *land* and *soil* may also be described by these same terms, for certain characteristics of these objects can be "associated" with richness and poverty. Sometimes this type of transfer involves only a slight shift from some central meaning to a peripheral usage, as in the case of *poor* and *rich* used of *land* and *soil*. Not infrequently, however, the transfer involves more than a single word and results in an expression which cannot be readily understood by any simple process of extension of meaning, e.g. *the apple of his eye, the horn of salvation, the children of the bridechamber,* and *gird up the loins of your mind,* to cite only a few Biblical idioms that are extremely difficult to translate.

THE TRADITIONAL APPROACH TO MEANING

Traditional views of meaning can be conveniently summarized in terms of (1) centripetal, (2) centrifugal, and (3) lineal concepts. The centripetal view concentrates on the "common denominator of meaning," for, when confronted with the task of defining the meaning of a word, people usually respond by looking for a common core of meaning which will pull together all usages into a single whole. Evidently, the fact that a word has a unity of form leads people to think that there must be a unity of meaning, and hence they try to find it. However, attempts to discover common denominators of meaning are usually ineffectual. For example, given the following series: *charge the bill, charge the line, charge the battery, they charged their lunch, he got a charge out of it,* and *charge of gunpowder,* the word *charge* can scarcely be defined in terms of a common denominator; the common core of meaning in these expressions is so small that any description of the meaning in such terms would be "thin and anemic."

In contrast to this view, one may take the opposite approach and look to the area of meaning involved. Thus one emphasizes the centrifugal aspect, for often the meaning of a word seems to be "riding off in all directions at once," so difficult is it to pin down the meaning to any one referent or closely related set of referents. On the other hand, we usually regard such series of meanings as possessing central as well as peripheral areas. Hence a purely centrifugal view of meaning appears inadequate.

One can also look upon meaning as lineal, as coming from a line of historical descent. Such an organization of a series of meanings is more often based upon our views of logic than upon actual history. However, the lineal view at least seems to go back to origins and to approach correctly what words *should* mean, for by *should* people usually refer to what the words formerly denoted. But even a lineal view, whether based upon history or logic, is not enough, for verbal symbols are living realities, with great plasticity, remarkably capable of being used in ever varying circumstances not easily restricted to logico-historical categories.

Accordingly, such traditional views of meaning as can be treated under such simple classifications as centripetal, centrifugal, and lineal are simply not adequate for a thorough investigation of meaning. They may help, but essentially they only point the way to more serious approaches to the problems.

VARIOUS SCIENTIFIC APPROACHES TO MEANING

A scientific approach to meaning widely used in the past is the traditional philosophical theory of "the mental image." This approach assumes that the real meaning of a word can be equated in some manner with the mental image associated with the symbol. [1] It has the advantage of seeming to simplify the study of meaning, for it is far easier to maneuver and classify the mental images than to sort and arrange the referents to which such word symbols might refer. In the long run, however, this "mental image" approach has proved relatively sterile, for it does not answer some of the basic questions about meaning. For example, to say that *triangle* means the mental image of an ideal triangle is not really satisfactory, for many shapes can be labeled triangles, and a mental image in the traditional sense cannot be an image of all these—certainly not all at the same time. The more abstract or generic the meaning of a term, the more difficult it is to produce a mental image that adequately reflects the function of this symbol. [2]

The behaviorist approach to meaning in terms of stimulus and response, using Pavlovian types of stimulus-response situations, corrected

---

[1] Certain of the principal philosophical approaches to meaning are: (1) the pre-Socratic, in which the word was regarded not only as a faithful reflection of reality, but in a sense as a kind of handle with which to control reality—for right words meant right thinking; (2) the Platonic position of nominalism, with the rejection of magical connections between words and referents and the assumption of purely human conventions as a basis for meaning, but with great importance attached to the relationship between the words and the ideas for which they stood; (3) the Aristotelian use of language as a system of correct classification of knowledge, since language not only expresses relationships, but also reveals them; (4) the Cartesian emphasis upon the separation of the phenomenal and the noumenal, thus producing a real tension between the symbol and the referent, a problem with which epistemologists since Descartes have continued to wrestle; (5) the position of the logical positivists (as well as the symbolic logicians), who have rejected the Cartesian formulation, based essentially upon Platonic concepts, and have not hesitated to use symbols to "define" reality (for they are only labels at best) and to construct whole symbolic systems; and (6) that of the existentialists, who relate object and name as an intuitive reality, for the name is an integral part of the existential experience—a position in some respects not too dissimilar from the pre-Socratic one.

[2] There is a sense, however, in which the use of the "image" of a symbol may be rehabilitated and made psychologically valid, if we use the framework suggested by Miller, Galanter, and Pribram (1960). Under these circumstances the *image* constitutes the conceptual point of departure for a *plan*. The image of a symbol, as a label for certain aspects of experience, actually serves both as a springboard for a plan to use the symbol and as a point of reference by which the use of the symbol may be evaluated—a kind of internalized system for truth testing. Under these circumstances the images become closely related to behavior, for they do not remain in some idealized realm apart from human behavior (as in Platonism), but are constantly affecting and being affected by experience.

some extravagant excesses in the traditional philosophical orientation. Psychologists insisted that no one could really test the meaning of mental images, since no one could get inside another's brain to see what went on there. One could always describe what went on in his own thinking, but such individual descriptions seemed too subjective to be valid for objective experimentation or measurement. Moreover, though the measuring of the responses of animals under closely controlled conditions was not too difficult, it was impossible to subject human beings to the same types of controls in order to get objective measurements of response to word stimuli. Furthermore, it proved hopeless to determine all the stimuli that might enter into any one person's use of a particular word as a response. As a result, behaviorists began to talk about "behavioral dispositions," a theory constructed on the basis of simpler types of animal reponses, which were presumed to underlie human responses. These projections, however, have proved to fall far short of an adequate explanation of linguistic phenomena. [1] Nevertheless, thorough psychological investigations of meaning have done much both to sweep aside previous mentalistic views and to focus attention on certain essential elements in communication, namely, the stimuli and the responses involved in both speaker and hearer.

A somewhat different approach to language and meaning characterizes the work of the symbolic logicians, also called logical analysts or linguistic analysts, who have been dissatisfied with traditional logic, on the ground that it merely prescribes how people ought to think. Furthermore, they did not see much future in following the psychologists in describing how people presumably do think. What seemed more fruitful from their standpoint was a thorough investigation of language, either as the tool by which people manipulate their thoughts or as the system which, as closely as any other, reflects their thinking. Accordingly, symbolic logicians scrutinized language carefully and exposed many problems passed over by others, or merely taken for granted as a part of logic itself.

Some symbolic logicians have divided their study of meaning into three main parts, usually called (1) semantics, (2) syntactics, and (3) pragmatics. [2] For the symbolic logicians, semantics deals with the relationship of signs (or symbols) to referents, corresponding roughly to what people usually think of as the meaning of words. However, this meaning is regarded in a distinct way, for the referential meaning of any symbol is defined in terms of classes of referents. The referents themselves are infinite in variety, but the symbols are "handles" for dealing with groupings of similar objects and events. This process of classification is of course essential, for "unless one categorizes, that is, classifies, there is no basis for forming any judgments as to expectancies, for objects and events are in themselves unique. To handle them, we must classify them" (Roger Brown, 1958, p. 224).

[1] See Noam Chomsky (1959).
[2] See Charles Morris (1946). A similar type of distinction was used by Charles Pierce (1934).

This classification takes place in two principal ways: (1) by segmentation and (2) by distinguishing shared qualities. In no two symbolic systems, that is, in no two languages, is this classification identical. For example, we segment the color spectrum in English into eleven basic color words, but in West Africa a number of languages make only three fundamental color distinctions: red, white, and black. [1] In the Parimiteri dialect of Waica, spoken in northern Brazil, the people seem to get along quite well with four basic color words, with the following groupings: (1) *waki*, 'red, reddish purple, yellow, and orange', (2) *ushi*, 'dark blue, dark purple, black, deep red, and brown', (3) *krokehe*, 'green', and (4) *au*, 'white, clean'. The Tarahumara in northern Mexico have five basic color words, including one term, *siyonomi*, which covers both green and blue.

The distinguishing of shared qualities may result in very complicated classifications. For example, the Hanunóo distinguish more than 1,800 different plants which grow in their region of Mindoro, in the Philippines. Such a classification differs appreciably from the way in which botanists classify these same plants; in fact, botanists classify these plants into somewhat less than 1,300 species (Conklin, 1962).

While semantics deals with the relationship of symbols to referents, syntactics is concerned with the relationship of symbol to symbol; for the meaning of expressions is not to be found merely in adding up symbols, but also in determining their arrangements, including order and hierarchical structuring. For example, the constituents *black* and *bird*, when occurring in juxtaposition, may have two quite different meanings. In one instance we say *blackbird*, with the primary stress on the first element, and in the second, *black bird*, with the primary stress on the second. But there are clear differences of meaning, for not all *black birds* are *blackbirds*. Similarly, a *greenhouse* is not a *green house*, and the *fat major's wife* may mean that either the major or the wife is fat. But symbolic logicians go far beyond such problems of obvious ambiguity in attempting to describe carefully all the basic relationships of words.

Pragmatics, in contrast to both semantics and syntactics, deals with the relation of symbols to behavior. This element of meaning is increasingly recognized as important, for in communication the effective meaning of any message is what gets through to the receptor. Hence, the reactions of people to symbols are fundamental to any analysis of meaning. Words such as *Americanism, Communism, propaganda, nigger, wop, dago, pantywaist, passion, playboy, sex,* and *death* carry with them certain associations, which are often determinants of behavior. The reactions with which we are concerned here are not, however, responses to the referents in question, but to the symbols, for the same referents can be symbolized by other words which do not carry the same behavioral overtones.

The pragmatic elements of meaning are especially important in the

---

[1] Basically such so-called color terms actually serve more to distinguish shades or density of color rather than actual hues. Furthermore, our translating of foreign terms by specific color words in English is almost always misleading, for the foreign expressions designate color areas or domains, something which we cannot accurately reflect by gloss translations.

study of religious vocabulary, for terms often carry a heavily charged pragmatic meaning quite out of proportion to any referential value. For example, among some Pentecostal sects the expression *Holy Spirit* becomes almost a fetish symbol, and the response of the Pentecostal audience to such a name is almost automatic, regardless of the content of the total message. In many religious systems, Christian and non-Christian, there is a steady tendency for many terms to shift within the pragmatic area from an ethical response to an esthetic one, a shift accomplished largely by the techniques of ritualistic embellishment. Thus many words deeply embedded in creeds have lost any immediate behavioral relevance to the people, but have become important emblems of emotional association.

The linguistic-anthropological approach to meaning has in many respects paralleled developments in symbolic logic, though the immediate area of study in the two fields is different and the approach seemingly quite divergent. This parallelism is attributable to the fact that both symbolic logicians and linguists are interested in the distribution of symbols, both in language, as the primary concern of linguistics, and in general behavior, as linguistics has touched the field of anthropology. Except for Edward Sapir there was a tendency before World War II for American linguists to shy away from semantic studies, since a concern for structural analysis dominated the scene. Moreover, following the lead of Leonard Bloomfield, they saw little merit in trying to define the content of meaning, since presumably such a definition could be produced only by all the descriptive sciences working together to describe man's total environment and behavior. However, Bloomfield has been somewhat misunderstood, for his seemingly negative approach to meaning was in a sense a definition by restriction, for he sought to define the semantic value of symbols in terms of lexico-behavioral distinctiveness, in contrast to other symbols and their corresponding areas of distribution. He was not one to repudiate meaning as irrelevant to language or linguistic study, for in describing the relation of form to meaning, he said: "In language, forms cannot be separated from their meanings. It would be uninteresting and perhaps not very profitable to study the mere sound of a language without any consideration of meaning [but] ... we must start from forms and not from meanings" (1943, p. 103).

During more recent years the stimulating work of Sapir and Whorf, together with increasing concern for symbolization in all fields of scientific inquiry, has resulted in a number of significant probes into the area of language and culture. Here the distribution of words is studied not merely in terms of where they occur within sentences, but also where they occur in all types of human behavior. Moreover, there is increasing evidence that these distributions are highly and intricately structured.

One reason for earlier tendencies to reject the relevance of the study of meaning to certain aspects of linguistics was the mistaken belief that one could not understand a word apart from some nonlinguistic acquaintance with it; and that such an acquaintance, moreover, involved evidence from one or more of the other sciences. Of course, such evidence is often quite impossible to adduce, as in the case of such words as *ambrosia*, *dragon*, *unicorn*, and *mermaid*, and in no instance is it necessary, for the meaning is of the symbol and not of the referent (Roman Jakobson, 1959b). In the study of meaning, attention has therefore shifted from concern with the referents to the distribution of the form within the total behavior, so that, as Bloomfield (1943, p. 102) states, "The features of situation and action which are common to all utterances of a speech form are the meaning of that speech form." Zellig Harris (1940, p. 227) makes this type of definition somewhat more explicit by stating: "The meaning of a linguistic form may best be defined as the range of situations in which that form occurs, or more exactly, it is the features common to all the situations in which the form occurs and excluded from all those in which it does not."

This type of functional definition of meaning not only provides a more useful tool with which to analyze meaning; but it also suggests the very process by which terms acquire meaning, namely, through contextual conditioning. For example, the Motilones in Colombia have borrowed the Spanish word *purísima* 'most pure' from the phrase *María purísima* 'Mary, most pure', but have given it the meaning of 'the devil', for they observed Spanish-speaking persons using this expression in identically the same types of contexts in which the Motilones called upon demonic powers.

This emphasis upon meaning in terms of behavior has come as a healthy antidote to traditional mentalism, for language as a mode of action is described as a system of symbols which signal behavior, and not merely as countersigns of or indices to thought. This campaign against unwarranted mentalism also had certain practical and even ethical overtones, strongly espoused by the general semanticists and cogently stated by Aldous Huxley (1940, pp. 16-17), who denounces "the apparently irresistible human tendency to objectify psychological states and project them, on the wings of their verbal vehicle, into the outer world." Words like *beauty*, *goodness*, *spirit*, and *personality* are classified by Huxley as "typical vehicles of objectification. They are the cause of endless intellectual confusion, endless emotional distress and endless misdirection of voluntary effort."

SEMANTIC FIELD VS. SEMANTIC CONTEXT

The principal differences between the diverse scientific orientations toward meaning seem to depend upon whether the focus of attention is upon the semantic field or the semantic context. Concern primarily for the semantic field is exemplified in the work of a number of scholars, e.g. Wilhelm von Humboldt, who was interested in language and "world view"; H. Osthoff (1899), who held that meanings cluster together in systems; R. M. Meyer (1910), whose essentially componential approach demonstrated that words could belong to different meaning systems; J. Trier (1931), who made a distinction between the lexical field and the conceptional field; G. Ipsen (1932), who developed a concept of meaning fields and analyzed several sets of Indo-European vocabulary; and Weisgerber (1953-54), who has sought to interpret certain aspects of culture from language structures. [1]

In the United States, the approaches to the problems of the semantic field have been of three major types: (1) taxonomic studies, dealing primarily with folk classifications of related terms, e.g. the diagnosis of disease among the Subanen of Mindanao (C. O. Frake, 1961), and botanical classifications in Hanunóo (H. C. Conklin, 1962); (2) the componential analysis of sets of vocabulary, beginning with A. L. Kroeber's work on the basic components of kinship systems (1909), and including Jakobson's important componential treatment of case systems (1936), F. Lounsbury's analysis of the Pawnee kinship system (1956), and Ward H. Goodenough's work on Trukese (1951, 1956); and (3) the analysis of semantic domains, as in the work of C. F. Voegelin and F. M. Voegelin (1957a), who described a number of important sets of semantic domains in the Hopi language.

In contrast with the analyses of the semantic field, treatments of the semantic context have focused attention on the situations in which lexical symbols occur, and how diverse contexts result in widely different meanings. Malinowski (1922, 1923, and 1935) gave particular prominence to the concept of the cultural context of linguistic utterances, while George Trager's work on the paralinguistic features of language (1961), e.g. hesitations, quality of voice, pitch, range, tempo, and rhythm, has introduced into a consideration of meaning a number of elements which are often only alluded to by other investigators of the linguistic context. In some ways, however, the most important work in defining the nature and types of semantic contexts has been done primarily by perceptive literary critics, such as I. A. Richards (1932, 1953, 1960).

An adequate theory of meaning cannot, however, remain tied either to the semantic field or to the semantic context, for both field and context are equally important, particularly if one views language as a dynamic structure, capable of producing an infinite number of meaningful combinations of symbols. In some way or other we must account for "the fluent speaker's ability to freely produce and readily understand all utterances of his language, including wholly novel ones" (Jerrold Katz and Jerry Fodor, 1962b). In a sense such a theory of language must be predictive, to determine that some strings of words will be acceptable to speakers of a language and that other strings of words will not be. Moreover, it should be able to predict that if certain utterances do occur, the speaker will interpret them in one way and not in another, that other utterances will be interpreted in more than one way (ambiguous expressions), while still further sets of utterances will be regarded as essentially equivalent in meaning (i.e. paraphrases of each other).

Katz and Fodor (1962, 1963), who have supplied a theory of semantics based essentially on Chomsky's theory of a generative grammar, have

[1] B. N. Colby in an unpublished paper, entitled "Eidos, Semantics and Ethnoscience," has dealt extensively with a number of these approaches to studies of semantic fields.

neatly and effectively incorporated the factors of semantic field and context as mutually interacting forces. In the first place, they depend upon a "dictionary" to provide descriptions of the semantic fields of the various symbols. These fields are defined on the basis of the hierarchically arranged sets of contrasting categories, which on any level can produce ambiguity or misunderstanding. Accordingly, they diagram the meaning of *bachelor*, in the following manner:

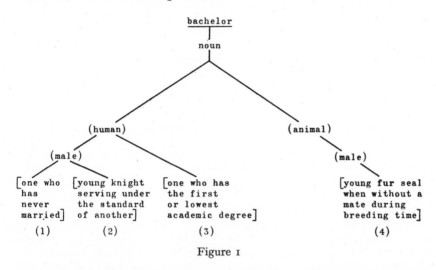

Figure I

The unenclosed elements are *grammatical markers*. The elements enclosed in parentheses are called *semantic markers* and the expressions enclosed in brackets are called *distinguishers*, which provide the terminal meanings. Such a schematic structuring can be said to define the semantic field, including the relationships between the various dictionary entries for a particular term.

In the actual use of language the speaker's ability to determine which of the four terminal meanings is intended depends upon the semantic context. For example the context *the ... who lives in the penthouse* will immediately rule out the meanings of "young fur seal" and "a young knight." It will also normally preclude the meaning of "one who has the lowest academic degree," unless by some highly idiosyncratic usage (depending upon special agreement or understanding between inter-locutors) this phrase *the bachelor who lives in the penthouse* is an abbreviation for *the bachelor of arts who lives in the penthouse.* The features of so-called "setting" which would provide the basis for this latter kind of idiosyncratic reading are, however, outside the normal scope of a se-mantic theory. When one encounters the expression *the bachelor who lives in the penthouse* it is not difficult to decide which of the four terminal meanings is the right one. In the first place, *who lives in the penthouse* indicates quite clearly that one is talking about a human and not an animal (for contrast, compare the context, *the ... which feeds along the rocky shores of the Pribilof Islands*). Secondly, in the absence of some further contextually defining element, e.g. *of arts* or terms specifying the accoutrements of knighthood, the reader will assume that the first meaning of *"male, one who has never married"* must be correct. He is able to decide this because the categories implicit in the phrase *who lives in the penthouse* coincide with the categories in the string terminating in the first meaning.

The semantic field of any lexical item is always much greater than the meaning which occurs within a specific context. In fact, it is precisely the function of the context to specify the particular "terminal meaning" intended by the speaker. [1] In some rare situations the context may be provided only by facts external to language, e.g. when a person points to the beak of a shoe-billed stork and says *That's a big bill*; but in general the linguistic context provides the basis for determining the specific terminal meaning, e.g. *a pelican's bill* and *a grocery bill*.

THE MEANING OF A SYMBOL AND THE COMMUNICATION EVENT

The tendency to think of the meaning of a word, e.g. *apple, boy, dog,* or *sun*, as apart from an actual communication event is fundamentally a mistake, for once we have isolated a word from its living context, we no longer possess the insight necessary to appreciate fully its real function. However, the value of a symbol in an actual communication event is sometimes difficult to define, since it has so many relationships. These relationships can be described, nevertheless, in terms of two principal functions. First, a symbol may be a kind of linguistic response to a situational stimulus. A child, for example, sees her doll and says, "Dolly, dolly." This event could be diagramed as follows:

$$S \text{ (situational)} \rightarrow R \text{ (linguistic)}$$

In this diagram S stands for the stimulus, which in this circumstance is the total situation in which the doll is present, and R stands for the response, in this instance a linguistic one, consisting of the utterance of the symbol *dolly*.

On the other hand, the parents may use the linguistic stimulus *dolly* in speaking to the child, "Go get your dolly." The response to this stimulus is presumably a behavioral reaction—the child goes to look for the doll. This communication event may be diagramed as follows:

$$S \text{ (linguistic)} \rightarrow R \text{ (situational)}$$

In this instance the stimulus is linguistic and the response is behavioral (or situational).

In most actual instances of communication, verbal symbols enter into a chain of stimulus-response situations, which can be diagramed:

$$S \text{ (sit.)} \rightarrow R \text{ (ling.)} = S \text{ (ling.)} \rightarrow R \text{ (sit.)}$$

Thus an original stimulus of a situational character may give rise to a

---

[1] See also Robert E. Longacre (1958), who has dealt with the problem of contextual conditioning of meaning as specifically related to translating.

linguistic response, which at the same time can act as a stimulus to a further situational, or behavioral, response.

It is precisely from just such sets of linguistic events that the learner of a language builds up a comprehension of the meaning of symbols. In fact, comprehension has been defined by I. A. Richards (1953, p. 251) as "an instance of a nexus established through past occurrences of partially similar utterances in partially similar situations—utterances and situations partially co-varying." This fundamental fact, that linguistic categories co-vary with nonlinguistic ones, is basic to any study of meaning (Roger Brown, 1958b, p. 307).

The human brain does not, however, simply record a finite series of utterances for possible future reproduction. This would mean that one could not say anything that he had not already heard nor interpret anything which had not already been understood. What does result is a complicated system of classification and structuring whereby the significant contrasts which are crucial to language usage are covertly, and sometimes overtly, recognized. The mind is able to isolate the lexical units which possess relatively free maneuverability, from the level of such morphemes [1] as *de-* (in *demobilize*) and *re-* (in *reassign*) to idiomatic expressions such as *jack-in-the-pulpit* and *go jump in the lake*. Moreover, the speaker of a language can respond in a systematic way to a number of different levels and types of contexts, e.g. overly sophisticated diction in contrast with slovenly pronunciation, pedantic word choices vs. colloquial usage, highly involved rhetorical patterns vs. simple conversational style, and urgency of the speaker's "tone of voice" vs. obvious indifference in speech. All of these factors, plus a number of others, play important roles in interpreting the intent of the message, for example, in terms of irony, humor, doubletalk, and sincerity. Effective communication is of course based upon mutually reciprocal re-enforcement between the lexical symbols and the context.

THREE DESCRIPTIVE DIMENSIONS OF MEANING

Because of the great diversities of both semantic fields and contexts it is very useful to distinguish three different dimensions of meaning, which in varying ways relate to both the semantic domains of individual words as well as to the conditioning contexts in which such words occur. They are most easily described in terms of a series of contrasts: (1) situational vs. behavioral meanings; (2) linguistic vs. extralinguistic meanings; and (3) intraorganismic vs. extraorganismic meanings (Lounsbury, 1955).

The contrast between situational and behavioral meanings involves a broad field of investigation, for this distinction includes both the stimulus-bearing parts of the context and the responses to it. For example, a particular blaze may constitute the stimulus for the verbal response *fire*. At the same time, the screaming of *fire* in a crowded building may be

---

[1] Certain submorphemic elements can also be recognized, e.g. the sound symbolism of *ush* in *gush*, *flush*, *blush*, *slush*, and *mush*.

the stimulus for panic. Thus in describing the meaning of *fire* we must include not only the stimulus situation involving rapid oxidation, but also the behavioral response to such a symbol. It might be argued that the reactions of the crowd are directed toward the referent of fire, not the symbol. On the other hand, announcing to a group that there is *a large, destructive conflagration in the building* will not produce the same types of reactions as the symbol *fire*, even though the former may be regarded as in some measure a valid lexical substitute for the latter.

The differences between the linguistic and extralinguistic aspects of meaning are often overlooked, since in general we tend to think only of the extralinguistic elements. That is to say, in speaking of such words as *boy, dog, tree*, and *hill*, we tend to consider these words only in relation to certain extralinguistic referents—the objects in question. When we do so, we are simply concentrating our attention on the extralinguistic distributions of these symbols. In other words, we are matching the occurrence of such symbols with the existence of certain types of extralinguistic objects in the environment. But these same words also have linguistic distributions. For example, in general they occur in a certain position in a sentence which we describe as occupied by a noun. Three of these words, *dog, tree*, and *hill*, may also occur in a position normally occupied by a verb, e.g. *they will dog his footsteps, the dogs can tree the coon*, and *he will hill up the corn*.

There are some linguistic symbols which have virtually no relevant extralinguistic distribution. That is to say, their occurrence must be treated almost exclusively in terms of linguistic distributions. For example, the English particle *to*, as it occurs before infinitives, e.g. *to go, to run, to kill*, can scarcely be "defined" in terms of some extralinguistic contexts. Rather, its distribution must be described in terms of other words. The same situation exists, of course, for many linguistic forms, e.g. *-ly* (*quickly, friendly*), *-th* (*width, depth*), and *de-* (*detach, deceive*). In many instances grammatical forms combine both linguistic and extralinguistic elements of meaning, as in such categories as number, mode, person, size, and shape, while grammatical case (e.g. nominative, accusative, dative, etc.) involves primarily the linguistic relationships between symbols.

Intraorganismic vs. extraorganismic factors play a very important part in any description of meaning, for such words as *revolution, blood*, and *love* not only refer to phenomena outside the body, but also tend to produce certain important reactions within the body. The intraorganismic meanings are of two basic types: (1) cortical, i.e. cognitive, referring to the cerebral processes, and (2) somatic, i.e. affective, referring to the physical reactions which occur when such symbols are either spoken or heard. Again, it is important to distinguish clearly between the referents of symbols and the symbols themselves. For example, in English there are a number of so-called four-letter words which refer to a number of body parts or functions. These words are regarded as vulgar, and the somatic reactions of most hearers to them are "unfavorable." However, the very same body parts and functions can be referred to by other symbols without any such somatic reaction. That is to say, the intraorganismic "meaning" is associated essentially with the symbol, and not with the body part or function.

These three dimensions of meaning are not in any sense separate sets of categories, for they continuously intersect one another. For example, situational meanings may be divided into intraorganismic and extra-organismic, for the situations which give rise to symbols may be either outside or inside a person. Similarly, the behavioral responses may be either intraorganismic or extraorganismic, either within the person or manifested outside the person, or both in as well as outside a person. Situational meanings may be similarly subdivided into linguistic and extralinguistic.

In general we regard referential meanings as situational, extraorga-nismic, and extralinguistic. Emotive meanings are primarily behavioral, somatic and intraorganismic. Linguistic meanings constitute a special class. To this extent, referential, linguistic, and emotive meanings parallel the distinction of semantic, syntactic, and pragmatic. However, the use of three sets of descriptive dimensions: situational vs. behavioral, linguistic vs. extralinguistic, and extraorganismic vs. intraorganismic, has the advantage of providing a much more detailed and precise manner of describing the relationship of the communicative event to the total cultural context in which it occurs. For practical purposes, we usually can get along quite well with the distinction of referential, linguistic, and emotive meanings, but where the problems become particularly acute this more refined descriptive tool is essential. This descriptive procedure, employing three dimensions, becomes especially helpful when we attempt to determine the differences in the manner in which the source and the receptors understand a particular communication. It is also very useful in analyzing more adequately the manner in which the different purposes of communication result in differences of meaning.

THE PURPOSES OF COMMUNICATION

A basic ingredient in any communication is the purpose of the human source producing the message. Symbols do not automatically flow out of such a human source, despite the saying about the person who "threw his mind into neutral and let his tongue idle on." The very processes of encoding a message imply certain purposes, even though they may be numerous, complex, and mixed. In general we take the intent of communication for granted, and it is only when we are confronted with problems of distrust, suspicion, and willful distortion that we recognize the full implications of intent.

If we are to understand fully the nature of the purposes or intent in communication we must describe these in terms of the communicative event, which consists essentially of three factors: source, message, and receptor. Since it is from this basic communication event that all meaning is ulti-mately derived, these factors are fundamental to any consideration of meaning, but they will be considered in detail only when we discuss the dynamics of communication in Chapter 6. At this point, however, by dealing with any communication event in terms of source, message, and receptor, we may describe the intent by analyzing the extent to which the focus of attention centers upon one or another of these elements or combinations of them.

It is, of course, impossible to assume that any one feature of the communication event occurs without reference to others; for at no time is communication really valid unless in one way or another all three factors of source, message, and receptor are involved. One may, however, describe the different intents of communication by indicating how one or another element or combination of elements may be brought into primary focus. For example, if the focus is essentially on the source, without any special concern for the message or receptor, then the intent is fundamentally a desire for self-expression, and may be termed expressive speech. If, however, the attention is shifted to the message, the intent may be either (a) designative, merely the listing of the referents in question, or (b) metalinguistic, in which the primary concern is the linguistic form of the message. If the attention is further shifted primarily to the receptor, the intent of the message may be described as suggestive, or seductive—an attempt to produce a response, but without special concern for the content of the message. If, however, one combines source and message as focal elements, the intention may be described as evaluative or appraisive, that is to say, the source not only designates some referent, but also provides his own evaluation of it. Similarly, if the focus of attention is the relationship between message and receptor, the intent is prescriptive or imperative—the receptor is told what he ought to do, in terms of the message. A form of communication in which the relationship of source to receptor is primary and in which the message is of minimal significance may be termed mystical. A communication in which all three elements seem to be equally relevant can be called identificational, for the source is not only vitally related to his message but exhibits a high degree of identification with the receptor, whose behavior he wants to influence.

The varieties of intent which messages exhibit are usually not of a "pure type," for generally the source has more than one intent. Even if his primary purpose is self-expression (as in some forms of lyric poetry), nevertheless, he is usually concerned with getting this message across to others. In many forms of speech, however, it is quite possible to detect an unmistakable "expressive" quality, more concerned with putting emotion into words than in communicating a message to others. At the same time, one seldom finds a purely designative message, one in which the source merely refers to phenomena. The source, as a part of the total context of communication, is usually so intrinsically bound up with the phenomena referred to in the message that he can scarcely designate without evaluating. Accordingly, he can rarely restrict himself to such an objective statement as, "The man said that someone had been murdered." Rather, he must declare that, "The man condoned the fact that...", "The man confessed that...", or "The man admitted that...."

When attention is focused almost exclusively on the message itself, it is possible to have two different "objects of concern": (1) the referents of the words, e.g. *John hit Bill*, in which one is concerned with the fact that one person hit another, or (2) the form of the message as a linguistic construction, e.g. in contrasting the active construction *John hit Bill* with the passive equivalent *Bill was hit by John*. In this second instance, we are not really concerned with a fight between two different individuals, but with the fact that we can manipulate the subject and the object of a sentence by altering the structure. A translator generally has little difficulty in dealing with the first type of intent, namely, the description of the referential interrelationships of a message. However, a translation of metalingual [1] material, in which the grammatical form of the message is focal, is extremely difficult. [2]

When the intent of a source is evidently a combined consideration of message and receptor, we may say that the purpose is imperative or prescriptive. In other words, the receptor is commanded to do so-and-so, or he is told that he should do so-and-so. On the other hand, the source may wish to produce some response in the receptor without any special attention to the message itself. For example, some marching songs have a great deal of military suggestiveness without any specific military content in the message. These suggestive communications are at the opposite pole from the expressive ones—where the attention is focused on the self-expression of the source. The suggestive power of certain poetry, combining sound symbolism, sensuous rhythms, and often relatively meaningless combinations of words, is in some respects the most difficult form of message to reproduce in another language. [3]

[1]   In this volume the words *metalanguage* and *metalingual* refer to that part of language which is used in speaking about language itself, namely, the terms designating all the various features of language and the way these are used in describing and talking about languages. This follows the widespread use of these terms by philosophers (Reichenbach, 1947) and agrees with a suggestion of Einar Haugen (1951). It is not, however, in line with the use of these terms by some linguists, who employ them to designate nonlinguistic symbolic systems.

[2]   Some detailed work on translating into French a commentary on the Greek text of the New Testament, written in English, but citing many translations from different parts of the world, has produced some highly involved problems, simply because the intent of many of the illustrations was not the referential meanings of the symbols, but the metalingual (or grammatical) values.

[3]   The purposes of communication have been variously classified. Reichenbach (1947, pp. 18-19) divides the uses of language into cognitive and instrumental, with the latter subdivided into informative, suggestive, and promotive (including imperative). For the purposes of the logician such a classification is quite useful, but it is too highly specialized to be widely applicable to language as used in everyday experience. I. A. Richards (1953, pp. 253-254) sets up seven basic purposes in communication—indicating, characterizing, realizing, valuing, influencing, controlling, and purposing, in which the last element is pivotal to the rest. Charles Morris (1946) has an even more complicated set of purposes, with intersecting types, and Roman Jakobson (1960b, pp. 352-354) sets up a system involving the following scheme:

	REFERENTIAL	
	POETIC	
EMOTIVE		CONATIVE
	PHATIC	
	METALINGUAL	*(Note 3 continued on p. 46)*

Religious communication has often had as a principal intent this suggestive response, accomplished by verbal symbols relatively devoid of semantic content. In fact, in some religious systems an unfamiliar language is used to create an effect of mystery, and in others some archaizing rituals virtually duplicate this situation by the use of little used or unfamiliar expressions. At various stages in the Judeo-Christian tradition there has been a conspicuous tendency to emphasize the mysterious and cabalistic elements in communication. However, with the awakening of the Renaissance, followed by the Reformation, and more recently by the twentieth-century scientific atmosphere of intellectual inquiry, this "suggestive" phase of religious language has been to some degree replaced by a greater emphasis upon the designative and evaluative aspects.

On the other hand, an anti-intellectual reaction has recently developed in certain segments of Christianity, with the result that language is being used more as a vehicle for establishing emotional security than for producing cognitive comprehension. Moreover, translators of the Scriptures sometimes find that peoples are perplexed, if not a little annoyed, with the seeming insistence of the translator that a religious text—whether indigenous or a translation of the Christian Scriptures—should make sense; for religious language and behavior have never been predicated upon the need for such intelligibility. In fact, at one time some Kekchis in Guatemala asked the missionary not to attempt to explain the "truths of their faith," for if such matters could be explained and understood, they would then "cease to be religion."

In addition to differences of intent in an original source, one must also face the fact that different peoples respond differently to the same message, for they interpret its intent differently. For example, some Pentecostals respond "pragmatically" to a passage of the Scriptures by engaging in shouting and dancing, while Episcopalians will respond "semantically" to the same passage. The first group interprets the intent as being primarily prescriptive and imperative, while the other presumes the intent to be more designative and evaluative.

Fundamental Features of Linguistic Symbols

This introductory analysis of the meanings of symbols has directly and indirectly touched upon a number of basic characteristics of linguistic symbols of particular importance for the translator's work. These include: (1) the essentially arbitrary character of verbal symbols; (2) the function of symbols to designate classes of referents; (3) the freedom of symbols; (4) the mapping of the totality of experience by means of lin-

---

[3] *Continued from page 45:*

This description of purpose follows the major elements in the communication model:

```
                      CONTEXT
                      MESSAGE
ADDRESSER                                    ADDRESSEE
                      CONTACT
                      CODE
```

guistic symbols; (5) language as a means of social interaction; and (6) the operation of linguistic symbols on two levels—(a) to describe the non-linguistic or practical world, and (b) to describe language itself.

1. *The Arbitrary Character of Linguistic Symbols*

Linguistic symbols reflect certain logical relationships between themselves and the extralinguistic (practical) world, e.g. in categories of number, distinctions in time, designations of participants in events (so-called person), and in the classifications of size, shape, and manner. Verbal symbols are, nevertheless, basically arbitrary, as evidenced in the following significant features:

   a. *The arbitrary relationship between the form of the symbol and the form of the referent.* There is no logical analogy, for example, between such symbols as *cat* and *dog* and the zoological referents for which they stand. This fact becomes self-evident if one compares corresponding words in other languages, e.g. Spanish *gato* and *perro*, French *chat* and *chien*, and German *Katze* and *Hund*. Even in onomatopoeic expressions the relationship between symbol and referent is basically arbitrary. Compare, for example, English *bowwow*, French *toutou*, Siriono (Bolivia) *hoho*, and Chacobo (Bolivia) *dashdash*, and Kipsigis (Kenya) *u'u'*.

   b. *The arbitrary relationship between classes of symbols and classes of referents.* Though series such as *cat, lion, feline* and *dog, wolf,* and *canine* reflect certain analogical similarities in the zoological world, they do not show in their linguistic forms any corresponding logical relationship. Similarly, segmentation of any semantic field, e.g. color, body parts, and kinship terms, is not based upon any strictly logical delimitation of "domains," for there are always striking anomalies.

   c. *The arbitrary relationship between classes of symbols and classes of symbols.* Even if languages do not "fit" the practical world, one might assume that they would be internally consistent, but grammatical classes are notoriously nonlogical. A close study of the grammatical referents of *he, she,* and *it* in English and of *der, die,* and *das* in German provides abundant evidence of essentially arbitrary relationships. So-called primitive languages are no less nonlogical. For example, in the Algonkian languages all persons and animals belong to a category of "animate gender," but so do the words meaning 'raspberry', 'kettle', and 'knee', in contrast with 'strawberry', 'bowl', and 'elbow', which "logically" belong to the "inanimate" class (Bloomfield, 1933, p. 272).

2. *The Description of Classes of Referents*

With the exception of proper names, which form a special class of symbols marking unique referents, linguistic symbols designate not single referents, but classes of referents. For example, the word *table* may be used for thousands of different objects. They include: diverse forms of furniture (provided there is a flat surface, which is usually horizontal, supported by legs or a pillar); food (*she sets a delicious table*); a plateau of land; an arrangement of words or figures (*table of weights and measures* or *table of statistics*); and a delaying motion (*he wanted to table the motion*).

Since most words symbolize classes of objects and not mere unitary items, we are faced with two problems: (1) the nature of the area (or domain) of a symbol, and (2) the boundaries between the domains of various related symbols. Theoretically, the area of meaning of a linguistic symbol should resemble the scatter of a typical old-fashioned shotgun blast, with a dense nuclear area and a tapering-off peripheral area. The relationship between such nuclear and peripheral meanings is often stated in terms of (a) frequency of usage (with the most frequent usages central and the less frequent ones peripheral) and/or (b) logical derivation, i.e. from what point one can go by the semantically "smallest steps" to all other areas of meaning. In terms of an internally consistent semology, however, we should determine nuclear and peripheral areas in terms of: (a) the number and relative significance of the componential features shared by the various meanings of a term, or (b) the patterns of co-occurrences, described in terms of either the context (following Joos) or the substitution possibilities.

Despite the theoretical validity of the shotgun blast pattern of nuclear and peripheral areas of meaning, such an ideal arrangement is rarely found, for the subareas of meanings of words are irregularly clustered in a multidimensional series of relationships. A more likely model of these relationships of meaning would be a diffuse nebula of somewhat irregular shape, having various concentrations and in some instances rather tenuous links.

If the problem of describing the area covered by a particular linguistic symbol is difficult, the assigning of boundaries is even more so. The basic reason is that no word ever has precisely the same meaning twice, for each speech event is in a sense unique, involving participants who are constantly changing and referents which are never fixed. Bloomfield (1933, p. 407) describes this problem by saying that "Every utterance of a speech form involves a minute semantic innovation." If this is so— and from both a theoretical and a practical point of view we must admit this to be a fact—it means that, in some measure at least, the boundaries of a term are being altered constantly. At the same time, of course, no two persons have exactly the same boundaries to words. That is to say, for precisely the same referent one person may use one linguistic symbol and another person a different symbol. The interminable arguments about terminology provide ample evidence that the boundaries of terms are not identical for all members of a speech community. Of course, there is a wide measure of agreement in the use of words; otherwise, human society could not function. Nevertheless, there are significant differences of word boundaries between semantic areas.

The fact that different members of the same speech community differ in their use of verbal symbols does not, however, constitute the only problem in assigning semantic boundaries between words. If we were to make a map of linguistic experience for any one person, by drawing lines in such a way as to enclose those features of the practical world symbolized by particular words, we should find that even for a single individual the same object in the practical world would be referred to by different words, depending upon such factors as linguistic context and emotive reactions. A map of semantic areas would thus be one, not in which all the territory is neatly divided off into well-defined regions, but rather one in which there are numerous instances of overlap and partial inclusion and exclusion. Moreover, even for one person a map of semantic boundaries would involve, not a single plotting, but hierarchical structuring, so that the same referent would be included within a number of different superimposed semantic areas.

If to this highly complex mapping of territory one then adds the maps of all other members of a speech community, it is easy to see how misunderstanding can arise. In fact, it is remarkable that people understand one another as well as they do. Understanding is possible only because people have the capacity of adjusting the grid of their own linguistic usage to that of someone else. Where there is sympathetic or empathetic motivation, understanding can be readily achieved, but where there is no such motivation, arguments can arise from the slightest linguistic provocation.

3. *The Freedom of Symbols*

Linguistic symbols are free because of two basic facts: (1) they are not tied to any one referent by virtue of some inherent formal identification (i.e. they are basically arbitrary and hence purely conventional); and (2) they are under constant pressure of change, since every speech event is essentially unique and therefore differs from all others. Linguistic symbols are semantically free to expand, to contract, to shift their centers, to die, and to be revived. This freedom is of inestimable value, for only through such freedom can persons employ symbols in new combinations or use them to describe objects which are new to the experience of the speech community. In fact, without such freedom no communication in the usual sense—much less translation from one language to another—would ever be possible. At the same time, such freedom is a liability, for the meanings of words can never remain fixed, but are forever shifting in one direction or another under pressure from one or another linguistic and cultural factor. Thus complete standardization of meaning is difficult to achieve for any living language, and even more so in branches of communication in which rapid advances and consequent numerous innovations are being made, e.g. nuclear physics, cultural anthropology, and structural linguistics.

This freedom of symbols means not only that a language can be used to describe new objects which come into the culture, e.g. a bicycle is an 'iron horse' (Loma of Liberia) and a 'fish-net horse' (Mano of Liberia), but also that a person can introduce new concepts into a speech community by using verbal symbols with certain contextual restrictions and amplifications. For example, Wulfila, who employed Gothic *Guþ* to

4

translate Greek *theos*, could do so—not because the Goths understood by *Guþ* what the Greek Christians meant by *theos*—but because this Germanic term could be adapted to make it roughly the equivalent of what *theos* had come to mean to Greek-speaking Jews and Christians; the Jews and Christians, in turn, had already radically altered the meaning of this word in using it as a symbol for their monotheistic God, symbolized in Hebrew as Elohim.

4. *The Mapping of All Experience by Linguistic Symbols*

In view of the infinite variety of referents in the practical world, it is remarkable that language can prove to be an adequate instrument for talking about any and all aspects of human experience. For example, there are between seven and one-half and ten million discernibly different shades of color, but in English even specialists use only about 3,000 color terms, and people in general use only some eleven basic color words (Conklin, 1962a). This mapping of experience by language must, of course, be limited to that portion of experience of which the people in question are aware, for people do not talk about things of which they are not conscious. However, when some part of their experience rises from a covert to an overt level, they are able to speak of it just as they can describe new objects that enter into their experience.

One of the principal reasons why some persons have supposed that certain languages (never their own, of course) could not be used to speak about certain aspects of experience is that they have not understood adequately the diverse ways in which different languages segment experience. One must recognize, for example, that for certain areas of experience, (1) some languages make more distinctions than others, and (2) no two languages agree completely in types of distinctions.

The fact that in certain areas of experience some languages make more distinctions than we do in English may come as a shock to some, but it is certainly true. For example, in Totonac, spoken in Mexico, there are six basically different words for "noise": (1) children yelling, (2) people talking loudly, (3) people arguing and turkeys gobbling, (4) people talking angrily, (5) a noise which increases constantly in volume, and (6) funeral noise. In Maya it is quite impossible to translate "search the Scriptures" without determining precisely what sort of 'searching' is involved, for there are three words meaning to 'search': (1) selecting the good from the bad or the bad from the good, (2) searching out something in a disorderly fashion, and (3) searching out in an orderly way, and with considerable attention to detail.

That some languages fail to make distinctions which are made in English is regarded by many English-speaking persons as evidence of a deficiency in these languages. However, an objective evaluation of these seeming "omissions" indicates that they can be fully justified, since the language in question merely follows another way of classifying experience. To illustrate, in Ifugao in the Philippines and in Moré, a language of the Haute Volta, 'hair' and 'feathers' are included under the same term, something which is certainly justified from a biological standpoint. In Kabba-Laka, a language of Chad, 'hear' and 'see' employ the same basic root, but a distinction may be made by adding 'eyes' and 'ears'. In Kekchi in Guatemala and Cuicatec in Mexico 'obey' and 'believe' are expressed by the same term, reflecting a classification quite parallel to the Biblical concept.

Different types of distinctions are, of course, numerous. They may involve, for instance, whole-and-part distinctions (e.g. Totonac distinguishes the top and the side of a mountain, but has no term for mountain as a whole), and types of collocations (e.g. in contrast with English *break a stick*, *break a string*, and *break an egg*, Shilluk uses 'break' only with objects such as wood, while strings are 'pulled in two', and glass or eggs are 'killed').

Different languages exhibit quite different concentrations of vocabulary, depending upon the cultural focus of the society in question. The Ponapeans of the North Pacific, as an example, have scores of words related to sweet potatoes; the Nuers of the Sudan have a very highly specialized vocabulary relating to cattle; the Arabs are famous for their hundreds of words applying to camels; and modern Western European languages employ thousands of technological terms.

Within any speech community there are always subgroups of specialists who have highly developed vocabularies for their areas of interest, e.g. medicine, witchcraft, and theology. Both in vocabulary and in the nature of the segmentation the language of specialists represents a highly specialized development.

5. *Communication within the Framework of the Society*

A communication is not intelligible if it is treated as an event abstracted from the social context of which it is a part. Rather, it must be analyzed in terms of its total setting, including the relationship of the participants to the code, their relationship to one another as members of a communicating society, and the manner in which the message acts as a link between source and receptor.

In any discussion of communication and meaning, one must recognize at the start, each source and each receptor differs from all others, not only in the way the formal aspects of the language are handled, but also in the manner in which symbols are used to designate certain referents. If, as is obviously true, each person employs language on the basis of his background and no two individuals ever have precisely the same background, then it is also obvious that no two persons ever mean exactly the same thing by the use of the same language symbols. At the same time, however, there is an amazing degree of similarity in the use of language among members of the same speech community. (In fact, speech becomes the principal means used by immigration officials to double check written documents.) Furthermore, this agreement is directly proportionate to the extent to which individuals participate in the same intercommunicating group or groups. In general, this means that they belong to the same socioeconomic group, for there is much greater intercommunication within such groups than among members of different groups.

A particular society, however, is not made up merely of geographically defined entities, whose members talk together merely because they are relatively contiguous. Moreover, within any society the roles of different persons are quite different with respect to communication. Actually, communication divides people into at least four principal groups, depending upon their roles in communication: (1) originators, e.g. medicine men, authors, philosophers, scientists, rulers; (2) purveyors of information, e.g. reporters, town-criers, gossipers, radio broadcasters, and teachers; (3) censors, e.g. elders, preachers, priests; and (4) receivers, e.g. children, common people, and those who are so old as to be no longer active in other communicative roles. Of course, the same person may perform one role and then another, depending upon his varied functions in the society. An individual may also change his role from time to time as he assumes different functions in the society. Nevertheless, whether the source of a particular message is basically an originator, purveyor, censor, or receiver has a great deal to do with the potential active response of the receptors, and also with the manner in which the receptors are likely to interpret the meaning of the message.

Among the various participants in any society there are two basic directions of communication: (1) horizontal, i.e. communication which takes place among those on approximately the same social level, e.g. mutual friends, men working at the same job, women in the same social club; and (2) vertical, whether (a) descending, e.g. policeman to thief, teacher to student, boss to employee, or (b) ascending, e.g. defendant to judge, and laborer to foreman. Most societies have the descending system of communication quite well organized, since it seems to follow readily from authority structures. However, the social feedback (ascending communication) which is so necessary if group activities are to be successful is usually only partially developed, even in a democratic society. The principal advantage of a democratic society over a totalitarian one is this fundamental feature of institutionalized communication feedback, whereby the governed can communicate effectively to the governing.

Within the total social context, the relationship of source and receptor of a specific message is by no means limited to narrowly linguistic factors. Other elements in the interpersonal exchange have an important bearing on the meaning and relevance of a message and the behavioral response to it. One must consider, for example: (1) the extent to which source and receptor possess a mutual sympathy or affection, and (2) the manner in which, in the specific situation, the source is able to convince the receptor that his best interests will be served by heeding the message. Such an interpersonal relationship may of course be developed by prior intercommunication. However, in such a situation behavioral symbols are generally far more important than linguistic ones. As the saying goes, "What you are speaks so loudly I cannot hear what you say."

If source and receptor are one and the same person, that is to say, if the source uses language to communicate to himself, he is employing language in a cognitive manner; for in this way he formulates propositions and then compares them with other propositions (as in deductive logic) or with his perceptions of reality (as in scientific observation). If he externalizes this inner speech, we say that he is "talking to himself."

Viewed as social interaction, intent may be described as representing several different levels:

1. What S (the source) wants R (the receptor) to understand by M (the message)—the theoretical norm.
2. What R understands by M—the practical norm.
3. What M means to the majority of persons in the S-R culture—the cultural norm.
4. What authorities on tradition (specialists: lawyers, professors, priests, *et al.*) in the S-R culture say S meant or should have meant by M—the legal norm.
5. What leaders of opinion say M ought to mean to R, irrespective o what S may have intended—the dynamic norm.

In the dynamic norm we are dealing with creative situations, as in the present-day interpretation of the Constitution of the United States in terms of new and different circumstances. Similar interpretations have been made of the Bible from time to time, viz. the successively revised exegeses of the first few chapters of Genesis.

6. *The Underlying Bases for Human Communication*

No adequate analysis of the nature of meaning can be made without a careful evaluation of certain underlying bases for human communication. Among these are certain elements in interpersonal relations which impose very great limitations on communication, while others make possible a high measure of mutual intelligibility.

The limiting factors in human communication consist of two basic facts: (1) no two people employ precisely the same symbols for the same types of experience (i.e. no two people have exactly the same background and hence all differ in their use of even the same language code); and (2) no two people employ the same symbols in exactly the same ways, i.e. in exactly the same types of arrangements. In other words, each person has his own distinctive style. This being the case, absolute communication between persons is impossible; in fact, it might seem that any effective degree of communication would be ruled out. Such, however, is not the case, for there are four basic factors which make possible a relatively high degree of mutual intelligibility, not only within a single language, but between members of different speech communities:

a. *The similarity of mental processes of all peoples.* Earlier concepts of a prelogical mentality of primitive peoples (espoused at one time by Lévy-Bruhl, but later rejected by him) simply do not reflect the facts, for there are no significant ways in which the mental processes of different peoples are appreciably distinct. Of course, the world views of peoples, as reflected in certain aspects of hierarchical structuring of vocabulary, do differ; but fundamentally thought processes are essentially the same, regardless of race or culture. Furthermore, even some tendencies to generalization appear to be very similar between peoples of widely different cultural background (Charles E. Osgood, 1960a).

b. *Similarity of somatic reactions.* Since somatic factors are so important in determining meaning (they constitute one of the important dimensions of meaning), it is significant that there is so relatively high a degree of agreement among peoples throughout the world. Certain automatic responses are universal, e.g. blushing and higher blood pressure in response to anger. Of course, the reasons for blushing and anger differ from culture to culture, but the form of the somatic response is remarkably similar. There are certain other semiautomatic somatic responses, e.g. laughing, smiling, and grimacing (in anger or pain), which are almost universal, but which may also undergo certain cultural conditioning; e.g. a smile in many parts of the Orient masks hostility, and among the Chols of southern Mexico laughter is a culturally accepted way of covering up sadness.

These somatic reactions, which involve the so-called sympathetic nervous system, are so commonly recognized that certain emotional and psychological states or reactions are often spoken of in terms of specific organs of the body. For example, the Mossis of Haute Volta in West Africa speak of most emotional states in terms of the heart (e.g. 'the heart is sweet' is joy, 'the heart is spoiled' is sorrow, 'the heart is shaded' is meekness, 'the heart is sterile' is jealousy). In Anuak, a Nilotic language of the Sudan, the liver is the center of emotions; e.g. 'shallow liver' is a tendency to become angry quickly, 'heavy liver' is sadness, 'sweet liver' is happiness, and 'white liver' is kindness. In Conob, a language of Guatemala, the viscera are regarded as the focus of emotional life. In Marshallese, a language of Micronesia, a number of psychological states are described in terms of the throat. In some of the Melanesian dialects of New Caledonian the skin is regarded as an important organ of emotional life. In still other languages one may find the gall, kidneys, and bowels used as focal elements in describing psychological states.

In some languages different organs fulfill different types of psychological functions. For example, in Achooli, a Nilotic language of East Africa, the liver serves as the seat of emotions and affections, the 'insides' as a center of feeling, the 'head' as a symbol of manner of activity, the 'eye' as the instrument of perception, conception, and intellectual grasp, the 'ear' as a means of understanding, and the 'mouth' as an expression of the will. When the word for each of these organs is combined with the adjective 'quick', there are a number of different interesting results; e.g. 'quick liver' means courageous, calloused; the expression 'quick insides' implies reluctance in yielding; 'quick head' denotes nimble activity; 'quick eye' indicates that the person is alert to grasp a situation; 'quick ear' implies ready understanding and good memory; and 'quick mouth' signifies that a person is stubborn.

What is important here is not that all languages have precisely the same types of idioms (they manifestly do not), nor that they all use such idioms (though most languages studied seem to have some expressions built along these lines); rather, it is important that, even though a people may not have exactly the same types of expressions as occur in other languages, they can nevertheless readily conceive of the underlying types of somatic experiences which make such expressions meaningful. Thus the similarity of somatic experience of all peoples provides at least a basis for intercommunication.

c. *Range of cultural experience.* Of the major elements of culture, namely, material, social, religious, linguistic, and esthetic, all societies participate in all phases and in rather analogous ways. Accordingly, even though specific behavior within any one area of life may differ, the range of common human experience is sufficiently similar to provide a basis for mutual understanding. Certainly the similarities that unite mankind as a cultural "species" are much greater than the differences that separate.

d. *Capacity for adjustment to the behavioral patterns of others.* Not only are children quite capable of adjusting completely to the pattern of any culture in which they are brought up (provided, of course, that they are not discriminated against); adults likewise are able to adjust their behavior, often almost automatically. (Consider our ability to adjust to the dialect of other persons.) We not only have the capacity of recognizing other "tokens" of behavior, but are also able to adjust to such tokens as an organized system. It would seem that we possess a kind of grid which we can employ to reinterpret experience in terms of some other conceptual framework, provided, of course, that there is a measure of willingness to do so and a degree of good will inherent in the activity.

Of course, individuals differ widely in their capacity to adjust. Moreover, such adjustment may be quite consciously undertaken and hence result from specific planned endeavor (as in most second-language learning by adults); or it may be developed almost entirely without such conscious planning, as with many born "mimics" and preadolescents who imitate their older models.

But despite the fact that absolute communication is impossible between persons, whether within the same speech community or in different communities, a high degree of effective communication is possible among all peoples because of the similarity of mental processes, somatic responses, range of cultural experience, and capacity for adjustment to the behavior patterns of others.

Language and Metalanguage

Language consists of a code which may be used not only to speak about the entire world of human experience, but also about the code itself. That is to say, we may use language not only to talk about a trip to Europe, but also to talk about the way in which we talk about the trip. When we use language to talk about language, we may conveniently call it "metalanguage." Such words as *word, sentence, clause, preposition, adverb, adjective, pronoun, noun,* and *verb* belong to metalanguage. Words such as *object, actor, action, goal, event, relation,* and *attribute* may be either language or metalanguage, depending upon whether they are used in speaking about ordinary aspects of experience or about the grammatical features of discourse. When we talk about the word *holy* as a verbal symbol, i.e. when we are trying to determine its meaning and use in the linguistic system, we are using it in a metalinguistic way; but when, in a discourse, we say *the paraphernalia of the medicine man is holy,* we are using language, not metalanguage.

This distinction between language and metalanguage is extremely important for the translator, since he must be constantly alert to the fact that the use of verbal symbols may readily shift from language to metalanguage. Moreover, the translation of metalanguage texts, e.g. grammar, is extremely difficult, for the linguistic "worlds" (i.e. the structures of diverse languages) which provide the linguistic referents differ from one another far more radically than do the cultural "worlds" which provide the nonlinguistic referents.

CHAPTER FOUR

LINGUISTIC MEANING

Before dealing with referential and emotive meanings (see Chapter 5), we must consider linguistic meaning; for, in the first place, this latter is much less understood, and hence more likely to cause confusion in our semantic analysis, and in the second place it structurally precedes referential and emotive meanings, which may be said to "begin where linguistic meaning leaves off." Certainly from the standpoint of an adequate theory of meaning, it is useful to begin with the meanings of grammatical constructions and to go on from these to a consideration of referential and emotive signification.

THE LINGUISTIC MEANING OF FORMS

In the phrase *old man* the total meaning of the phrase is not signaled by the referential or emotive values of the isolated words *old* and *man*, but a part of the meaning is derived from the construction itself. That is to say, the combination of attributive adjective and noun head also possesses a meaning, namely, that the first element qualifies the second. Similarly, in such phrases as *gray house, beautiful fur*, and *tall tree* it is the first component in each case which qualifies the second. Such a construction may actually be labeled a "qualifier-head phrase," as a means of designating this meaningful relationship between the constituent parts of the construction.

There are, of course, many different types of constructions and correspondingly diverse meaningful relationships between the constituent parts of grammatical constructions. For example, in the phrases *John left, Mary danced*, and *Bill played* the first constituent in each instance identifies the actor and the second the action, a kind of "actor-action" construction; while in the phrases *through the house, behind the store*, and *in the shed*, the relationship between the prepositions *through, behind*, and *in* and the following immediate constituents (consisting of the nouns with preposed determiner *the*) may be described as "relation-axis." Other basic grammatical constructions include "delimiter-head," e.g. *this man* and *one child*; "action-goal," e.g. *hit him* and *saw John*; and "equater-equated," e.g. *is fine, become sick*, and *appeared well*.

Linguistic meaning must be carefully distinguished from other types of meaning, for the linguistic signification of a form does not refer to anything outside of language itself, as does referential or emotive meaning, but rather to the meaningful relationships which exist within language. On the other hand, linguistic meaning is similar to referential and emotive meanings, for all types of meaning are derived essentially from the signaling of a relationship. In the case of referential meaning, these

57

relationships are the observed co-occurrences between the symbols and items in the cultural context (the things to which the words refer). In the case of emotive meanings, these are relationships between symbols and the psychological reactions of the participants in the communication. In the case of linguistic meaning we describe the recurring patterns of symbols which are linked to one another in significant ways. In every instance in which we are dealing with meaning we are essentially identifying a relationship and trying to describe the extent to which it may or may not be like some other relationship.

In attempting to determine the ways in which lexical symbols are relevantly related to one another, we discover that combinations of three or more words are usually structured into hierarchically arranged sets of binary constructions. For example, in the sentence, *The old man stared at us*, we do not relate *the* to *old*, *old* to *men*, *men* to *stared*, etc., but set up a structure which reveals the various layers of relevant combinations:

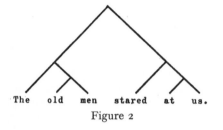

Figure 2

We can, of course, diagram this structure in various ways, e.g. with brackets:

$$\left\{\left[\text{The} \quad \left(\text{old} \quad \text{men}\right)\right] \left[\text{stared} \quad \left(\text{at us.}\right)\right]\right\}$$

Figure 3

by means of underlining:

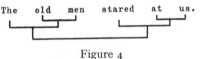

Figure 4

or by block diagram:

Subject-Predicate Sentence					
Noun Phrase			Verb phrase		
Article	Noun Phrase		Verb	Prepositional phrase	
	Adj.	Noun		Prep.	Pronoun
The	old	men	stared	at	us.

Figure 5

At every node in the tree diagram, and at every corresponding point in the other diagrams, there is a meaningful combination of symbols, which constitutes a construction. The meanings of these constructions do not, of course, depend upon the particular symbols, but upon the class of the symbols and their manner of association. For example, the following sentence has the same set of linguistic meanings in the corresponding constructions as the sentence cited in Figure 2, though the lexical symbols are entirely different:

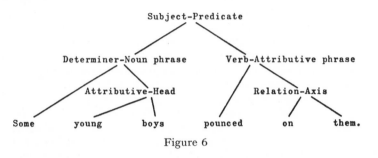

Figure 6

DIFFERENT MEANINGS IN APPARENTLY SIMILAR TYPES OF PHRASES

Though constructions made up of similar classes of words often have similar meanings, this is by no means always the case. For example, in the following phrases *his car*, *his failure*, *his arrest*, and *his goodness*, the relationship between *his* and the following nouns is in each instance quite different. In *his car* the expression is more or less equivalent to *he has a car*, but in *his failure* the corresponding expression would be *he failed*. For *his arrest* the corresponding form would be *he was arrested*, and *his goodness* is roughly equivalent to *he is good*. In other words, these four expressions *his car*, *his failure*, *his arrest*, and *his goodness* actually "go back to" different expressions.

We may describe *his car* (and other phrases of the same type, e.g. *his ball*, *his land*, *his house*, etc.) as meaning "A possesses B." *His failure* (and similar expressions such as *his mistake*, *his journey*, *his error*, *his attempt*, etc.) is equivalent to "A performs B"; while *his arrest* (and such other phrases as *his imprisonment*, *his embarrassment*, and *his involvement*) is equivalent to "A is the goal of the action B"; and *his goodness* (together with such expressions as *his kindness*, *his modesty*, and *his humility*) may be described as "B is the quality of A."

In accordance with traditional phrase-structure grammars, expressions such as *his car*, *his failure*, *his arrest*, and *his goodness* are treated as essentially the same, since they consist of a possessive pronoun, followed by a noun as the head word of the phrase. If, however, we relate these phrases to other elements in the grammar of the language, we soon discover that we have lumped together too many functionally diverse expressions.

The most effective means by which we may deal with these problems of diverse meaningful relationships between structurally similar types of expressions is to employ a generative type of grammar which makes full use of transformations (Chomsky, 1957, 1961b, 1962). A generative grammar is based upon certain fundamental kernel sentences, out of which the language builds up its elaborate structure by various techniques of permutation, replacement, addition, and deletion. For the translator especially, the view of language as a generative device [1] is important, since it provides him first with a technique for analyzing the process of decoding the source text, and secondly with a procedure for describing the generation of the appropriate corresponding expressions in the receptor language. Certain comparativists and descriptivists who are working with a limited corpus of written texts may find more traditional techniques somewhat easier to apply, but for the translator, who perhaps more than anyone else must take language in its dynamic aspect, a view of grammar as a generative device has many distinct advantages. [2]

In terms of a generative grammar, based on minimal kernel constructions and numerous transformations (worked out in terms of rewrite rules), such phrases as *his car, his failure, his arrest,* and *his goodness* are different because they obviously come from different kernels by way of different transformations. Their similarities consist in their sharing the common form *"his* plus noun phrase," but their structures are basically different. Accordingly, the meaningful relationships between *his* and the following nouns are different, for they depend on different meanings in the kernels from which they are transformationally derived.

Some of the most obvious transformations in English are passives from actives, e.g. *he was struck by the train* from *the train struck him*; questions from statements, e.g. *did he answer* from *he answered*; and negatives from positives, e.g. *he didn't leave* from *he left.* Certain other transformations may also involve embedding, e.g. *he went* in *I saw him go, I saw that he went,* and *I pled for him to go*; and *he was president* in *I knew that he was president, I wanted him to be president,* and *we elected him president.* A grammar based

---

[1] One must not think that a generative type of grammar is the only one which is valid. There are various types of grammars designed to explicate various levels of structure, but a generative grammar seems to be best designed to provide an adequate explanation of the overall functioning of a language, for it takes seriously the capacity of the speaker of a language to generate and to decode an infinite series of sentences. Moreover, it seems to explain most adequately the embedding of structures within structures and the relationship of parallel structures to each other.

[2] In addition, however, to the value of a generative grammar as an explanatory tool with greater adequacy than other methods, there are some psychological confirmations of transformational theory which seem to have special significance, particularly for the person interested in certain practical aspects of communication. Edward Coleman (1961) has produced some quite interesting experimental evidence to indicate that kernel elements are basic to a person's understanding of utterances. For example, it was noted that in one experiment the subjects tended to reproduce complex sentences in terms of their kernel sentence forms. In another experiment, it was found that subjects remembered more readily those expressions given in kernel form than those in nonkernel structures. Though his evidence is not conclusive, it is certainly indicative of significant correlations between linguistic structures and certain psychological processes.

entirely on immediate constituent analysis (i.e. consisting of a description of all the separate constructions which may occur in any complex structure—see Nida, 1960c) can of course describe all of these constructions, but it does not so efficiently relate the corresponding expressions in kernel and nonkernel constructions.

One of the distinct advantages of transformational techniques is the greater facility whereby ambiguous expressions can be analyzed and described. For example, the expression *fat major's wife* may mean that either the major is fat or the wife is fat. If the expression comes from the kernel *the fat major has a wife* the former meaning is intended; but if the expression is derived from *the major has a fat wife* then it is the second meaning. It so happens that the transforms of these two expressions are formally identical, and accordingly an ambiguity arises. Similarly, *he hit the man with a stick* may be derived from (1) *he hit the man* and *he hit with a stick* or (2) *he hit the man* and *the man had a stick*.

The diversity of transformational structures within a similarity of so-called formal structure may be very great. For example, *his fine car* and *their beloved ruler* may appear to be formally quite similar, but the meaningful differences are obviously very extensive; for while *his fine car* may be derived from the kernels *he has a car* and *the car is fine*, the phrase *their beloved ruler* comes from *they love him* and *he rules over them*. We can diagram the differences as in Figure 7:

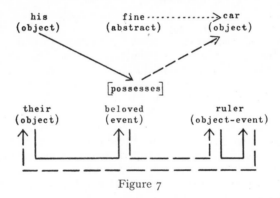

Figure 7

A similar problem may be seen in the phrase *his aged helper*, which though appearing to be quite similar to *their beloved ruler*, is actually very different, for it reflects quite different transforms, namely, *the man is aged*, and *he helps him*. The word *aged* may be interpreted as being both an event, i.e. *to age*, and an abstract, i.e. *to be old*. This phrase may therefore be diagramed as shown in Figure 8.

In Figures 7 and 8 a solid line combines the actor and the action (or event); a broken line relates the action to the goal, and a dotted line marks an attributive or "characterizing" relationship. Lexical items which must be added to fill out transforms are placed in brackets and markers of functional classes are placed in parentheses. It should be noted that a word such as *ruler*, though formally a noun, actually performs a double transformational role of identifying both an event and an object.

A careful examination of numerous transformations and the meaningful relationships between the parts reveals the fact that basically there are four principal functional classes of lexical symbols: object words, event words, abstracts, and relationals. These are similar to what Sapir (1944) noted, when he described the universal characteristic of the noun-verb dichotomy in languages and employed the basic classification of words into existents, occurrents, and qualities of existents and occurrents. Symbolic logicians also make certain important distinctions between words indicating objects, events, and attributes (Reichenbach, 1947), though they usually set up a special class of "logical words," some of

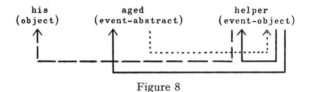

Figure 8

which we classify here as relationals, e.g. (in most contexts) *and* and *or*, and others as abstracts, e.g. *some, all,* and *not.* [1]

The classification here used for distinguishing object words, event words, abstracts, and relationals is not, however, based upon any system of logical categories, but merely upon the manner in which lexical items function in transformations, particularly as one transforms complex utterances into kernel expressions (i.e. back transformation). A particular lexical item may, of course, function in several different ways, depending upon the particular context in which it is used. For example, *stone* in *the stone is heavy, they will stone him,* and *he is stone deaf* is used first as an object word, then as an event word, and finally as an abstract.

We can make this analysis of the three functions of *stone* on the basis that in the context *the stone is heavy* the word *stone* occupies a position which "object words" may occupy and which gives rise to transformations distinctive of those involving object words. This is not the same as saying that *stone* is a noun, for one may also say *his touch is heavy,* where *touch* (as readily revealed in various transforms) identifies an event, not

---

[1] Wilbur M. Urban (1939, p. 118) also makes a point of distinguishing three basic classes — nouns, verbs, and adjectives — by which he really means objects, events, and attributes. Certain interesting parallel observations have been made by psychologists. Roger Brown (1958, pp. 247-248) notes that in children's speech most of the earliest words to be acquired are primarily object nouns. Moreover, in children's speech there seems to be much greater consistency between the formal classes of words and the semantic classes, i.e. nouns are mostly words for objects and verbs are words for events. As the form classes grow larger, however, they decline in this type of semantic consistency. One analysis showed that 83 per cent of children's nouns were essentially "object words," in contrast with 39 per cent of adult's speech. The convergence of several lines of investigation on these basic semantic entities would seem to add significant evidence as to their relevance.

an object, even though it is formally a noun in such a position. [1] In the context *they will stone him*, the word *stone* permits a passive transform, e.g. *he will be stoned by them*. Such a transform is quite impossible for *stone* in the context *the stone is heavy* but not at all impossible for *touch* in *it was touched by him heavily*, from an active *he touched it heavily*. Lastly, *he is stone deaf* illustrates a usage in which *stone* is restricted to relatively few transforms, e.g. *deaf as a stone*. Accordingly, from the total number of transformations in which the lexical unit *stone* may occur, we discover that there are three principal related classes of contexts. As a means of explaining these limitations we may say that *stone* has three principal functions: as an object word, as an event word, and as an abstract. We could, of course, reverse the procedure and say that there are three logical categories in the word *stone,* and that the distributions are dependent upon these. We prefer, however, to set up the classification on the basis of the linguistic functioning, but not merely in terms of the variety of distributions, but on the basis of the way in which such uses are transformationally related to one another, i.e. how one is derived from the other, whether by forward transformation (from kernel to terminal utterances) or by back transformation (from terminal types to kernels).

If we examine typical sets of transformational developments in various kinds of lexical units, we discover that the principal function classes consist of the following four principal types, with various subclasses: (1) "objects" e.g. *house, tree, leaf, sun, hill, man, rock, wall* (but not necessarily in all occurrences of these words); (2) "events" e.g. *run, walk, cut, talk, jump, go, sit, squirm*; (3) "abstracts": in such words as (a) *red, blue, small, many, one, two* (abstracts of objects); (b) *swift, slow, once, twice, often* (abstracts of events); (c) *hard* (e.g. *hard rock, worked hard*), *soft* (e.g. *soft coat, soft job*) (abstracts of either objects or events); or (d) *very* (e.g. *very many*), *too* (e.g. *too small*), *so* (e.g. *so swift*) (abstracts of abstracts); and (4) relationals, which serve to relate various objects, events, and abstracts: e.g. (a) object to object: *John and Bill, the men in the house, the book on the table*; (b) object to event: *the men in flight, the barking of the hounds*; (c) event to event: *run and jump, won in swimming*; (d) object to abstract: *an object of beauty, the color of a rose*; (e) abstract to event: *adept at winning, good for eating*; (f) abstract to abstract: *bad and lazy, beauty of holiness*.

In any particular language many words function in only one class. For example, in English *silly* and *tall* occur always as abstracts and *raccoon* and *moth* as objects, but some words may readily occur in more than one class, e.g. *tree, fox, dog, sail,* and *man*:

Objects	Events
The old tree fell.	The dogs will tree the coon.
The wily fox ran out.	He'll fox him.

[1] Note that though *the stone is heavy* and *his touch is heavy* may be transformed into *the heavy stone* and *his heavy touch* respectively, only the latter can be transformed into *he touches it heavily*.

Objects	Events
He saw the dog.	They will dog his steps.
The tattered sail drooped.	They will sail by steamer.
A stout man collapsed.	He tried to man the ship.

These contrasting distributions of *tree, fox, dog, sail,* and *man* might seem merely to emphasize the fact that nouns function as object words and verbs as events, but in many instances nouns may also signal events. For example, *forgiveness, redemption, pardon, failure, error, arrest,* and *mistake* are all essentially event words. Of course, what is important from the standpoint of transformations is that these nouns occur with the same kinds of associated words and in the same types of meaningful arrangements as do the corresponding verbs, e.g. *the forgiveness of sins (forgive sins), redemption of God (God redeems), his pardon (he is pardoned* or *he pardons), his failure (he failed), his error (he erred),* and *his arrest (he was arrested).* These nouns, which signal events rather than objects, reflect kernel expressions in which the corresponding event is expressed by a related verb. Similarly, nouns such as *goodness, kindness,* and *beauty* more often than not go back to kernels in which the corresponding abstracts are expressed by adjectives.

As we noted in the case of *ruler* in the construction *their beloved ruler,* the same word may function both as an event (with a goal) and as an object (the goal of the event *love*). This is true of many words. For example, *gift* in the phrase *his gift was joyfully received* identifies not only the object in question but signifies the fact that it was given (an event). Similarly, the word *heir* identifies not only an object (the individual in question) but states that something has happened or will happen, namely, that he inherits property, rights, title, etc. In a phrase such as *heirs of the promise* one level of back transformation may be stated as *those who inherit what has been promised.*

The value of transformational analysis and the accompanying clarification of meaningful structure can perhaps best be seen in the treatment of structurally diverse constructions with *of* in English. The following Biblical examples are typical:

1. will of God
2. sons of disobedience
3. forgiveness of sins
4. creation of the world
5. word of truth
6. glory of (his) grace

These phrases fall into the following classes, as determined by their back transforms:

1. B (object) performs A (event): *God wills.*
2. A (object) performs B (event): *sons* (in this context actually "people") *who disobey.*
3. B (event) is the goal of A (event): *sins are forgiven* or *forgives sins.*
4. B (object) is the goal of A (event): *creates the world.*

5. B (abstract) qualifies A (event): *the true word.*
6. A (abstract) qualifies B (event): *his glorious grace.*

There are three practical advantages to be derived from treating transformations in terms of four basic semantic elements: (1) we can often more readily see the equivalence of different formal structures possessing the same meaningful relationships, (2) we can more easily plot complex structures, without having to employ long series of related transformations from terminals back to kernels, and (3) we can more significantly highlight some of the contrasts between languages which tend to be otherwise obscured.

In the following four expressions the meaningful relationships between the event (*work, works*), the abstract (*excellent, excellence,* and *excellently*), and the object (*his, he*) are essentially similar:

1. his excellent work
2. the excellence of his work
3. he works excellently
4. his work is excellent

The kernel transform of these phrases is **he works excellently**, but if we diagram as in Figure 9 all four of these expressions we soon realize that the basic relationships are identical.

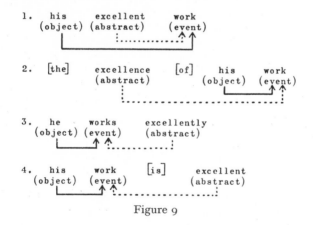

Figure 9

Though it is quite clear that the basic relationships in meaning are identical, nevertheless, the phrases are of course not exactly the same in value, for the first two are only nominal expressions, i.e. topics, while the last two are complete utterances, i.e. sentences. As a result we often need to distinguish two levels of linguistic meaning. First, that meaning which is derived from the kernel construction by way of the transformations, and secondly that meaning which is supplied by the particular terminal construction (the end result in the process of transformation from the kernel to the resulting expression).

When we are dealing with relatively complex expressions we can

5

employ one of two techniques to elucidate their transformational structures. First, we may draw up a long series of expressions, working up from kernels to terminal utterances or down from terminal utterances to kernels; or secondly, we may plot the relationship between the parts on the basis of identifying the four principal functional classes, which are basic to transformational analysis. In Mark 1:4 there is a relatively complex utterance in *John . . . preached the baptism of repentance unto the forgiveness of sins*. An expanded transform of this would be *John preached, you should repent and be baptized in order that God will forgive the sins which you have committed*. Such an utterance would have to be broken down into a series of other less complex transforms. We may, however, diagram this utterance as in Figure 10 by (1) setting up basic functional types of objects (O), events (E), abstracts (A), and relationals (R); (2) adding those which are implicit to the context and required by the transformational analysis; and (3) symbolizing the relationships between the constituent elements.

In an analysis of a Biblical text it is sometimes quite startling to find that a proper identification of the transformational function of certain lexical units turns out to be very different from what has been traditionally regarded to be the case. For example, words such as *grace* (as in *the grace of God*), *righteousness* (as used by Saint Paul in speaking of *the righteousness of God*) and *word* (in the expression *word of God*) refer primarily not to abstracts (as might be expected with *grace* and *righteousness*) or to objects (as in the case of *word*) but to events, i.e. *God manifests grace, God looks on for good, God is gracious toward; God declares righteous, God makes righteous; and God speaks, and God reveals (Himself)*.

KERNELS AND TRANSFORMS

The kernel constructions in any language are the minimal number of structures from which the rest can be most efficiently and relevantly derived. They are quite naturally not identical in all languages, but what seems to be very significant is that in so far as basic structures of different languages have been studied there appear to be many more parallelisms between kernel structures than between the more elaborated transforms. In fact, the remarkable similarities between the basic structures of different languages are increasingly becoming an object of study by linguists. For example, it has been found that all languages seem to have something equivalent to subject-predicate constructions. These may in some instances be more aptly termed topic-comment, but essentially they are very similar from one language to another. The speaker selects a subject and then makes a statement about it. In a high percentage of languages these subject-predicate kernel structures have an equational state type, e.g. *he is a man, the people become weary*, and an action type, *they fled* and *the man killed the lion*.

All languages appear to distinguish in some formal ways (but not of course with total consistency) between nouns and verbs, and in the most basic structures objects tend to be expressed primarily by nouns and events by verbs.

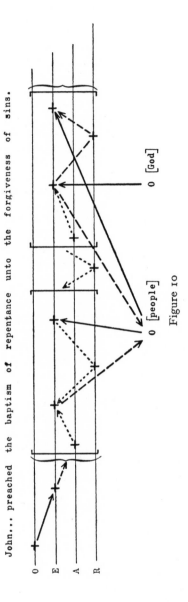

Figure 10

All languages also have ways of indicating the abstractions of objects and events. Sometimes this is done by formal classes of adjectives and adverbs, respectively, but in many instances abstracts of objects are treated as static verbs while abstracts of events are symbolized by particles, free or attached to verbs as affixes.

Relationships between words are indicated in a wide variety of ways; for example, morphological elements affixed to key words to indicate government (e.g. case) and agreement (e.g. number and gender), or particles, such as conjunctions, prepositions, and postpositions.

It may be said, therefore, that in comparison with the theoretical possibilities for diversities of structures languages show certain amazing similarities, including especially (1) remarkably similar kernel structures from which all other structures are developed by permutations, replacements, additions, and deletions, and (2) on their simplest structural levels a high degree of parallelism between formal classes of words (e.g. nouns, verbs, adjectives, etc.) and the basic function classes in transforms: objects, events, abstracts, and relationals.

Because of these two fundamental facts about language it is most efficient for us to develop an approach to translation which takes these facts fully into consideration. Instead of attempting to set up transfers from one language to another by working out long series of equivalent formal structures which are presumably adequate to "translate" from one language into another, it is both scientifically and practically more efficient (1) to reduce the source text to its structurally simplest and most semantically evident kernels, (2) to transfer the meaning from source language to receptor language on a structurally simple level, and (3) to generate the stylistically and semantically equivalent expression in the receptor language. In a sense this may seem to be a very roundabout way, for one would think that the simplest approach would be to match structure for structure in a long list of equivalences between languages. Of course, for languages such as English and German, French and Spanish, and Greek and Latin, where the formal structures are so similar, this can be done to an extent. On the other hand, such formal matching of structures often ends up in mechanically equivalent but stylistically unacceptable renderings. Moreover, the really competent translator, working even between closely related languages, usually tries to translate by "meaningful mouthfuls," not by structural units. What he actually does is to decode the meaning, transfer the content, and then generate another message in the receptor language.

The process of "decomposition and recomposition" may be described in the following steps, if for the time being we omit from consideration the referential and emotive meanings involved:

1. Analyze the source-language expression in terms of the basic kernel sentences and the transforms required to produce the utterance, while adding all implicit objects, events, abstracts, or relationships which are required by the processes of transformation. If we symbolize this process in terms of O (objects), E (events), A (abstracts) and R (relationals), ( ) for added elements, # for deleted elements, and underlining to show the

margins of morphological structures (i.e. grammatical words), we may obtain the following typical diagramatical representation of this first step in procedure in Figure 11.

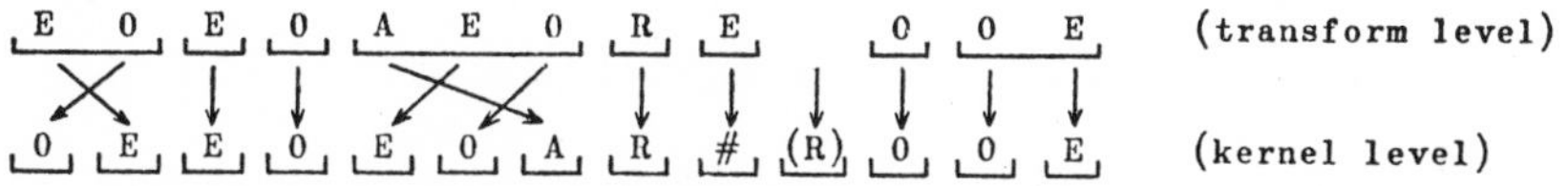

Figure 11

Note that in the original form a number of the basic functional elements are included in single words (this is very common in languages which have affixed subject and predicate markers). In the kernel transform of this, in so far as possible each functional element should be expressed by a separate lexical unit. In one instance in the above hypothetical diagram an event word is lost and a relational is added, while in several instances there are changes of order.

2. Transfer the kernel forms of the source language to the equivalent kernel forms of the receptor language. This is likely to produce some such shifts as the following:

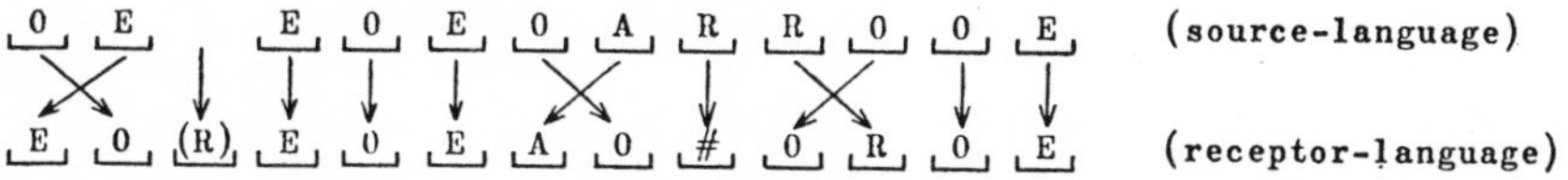

Figure 12

3. Transform the kernel utterances of the receptor language into the stylistically appropriate expressions. The following may symbolize this process:

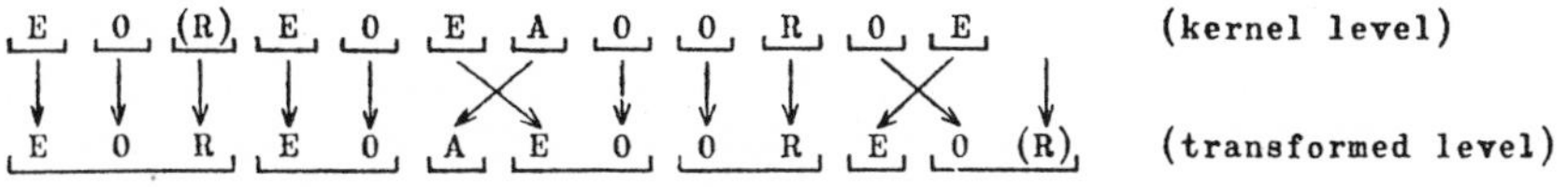

Figure 13

CHAPTER FIVE

REFERENTIAL AND EMOTIVE MEANINGS

While referential meanings are extralinguistic, extrasomatic, and situational (in terms of the contrasts noted in Chapter 3), emotive meanings are extralinguistic, somatic, and behavioral. Referential meanings refer primarily to the cultural context identified in the utterance, while emotive meanings relate to the responses of the participants in the communicative act.

Referential meanings are those generally thought of as "dictionary meanings," though any good dictionary always provides some evidence as to linguistic meanings by identifying the part of speech for each lexical unit. Moreover, for many words most dictionaries add important hints as to the emotive values, by listing forms as "vulgar," "obscene," "slang," pedantic," etc. Almost all native speakers of a language have a keen appreciation for these emotive meanings. That is to say, they have a "feeling" for the appropriateness of words in certain types of linguistic and cultural contexts, but these emotive meanings are very difficult to describe and define. For one thing, these "feelings" are almost impossible to objectify and classify, especially since they seem to differ appreciably from one speaker to another, and since the contrasts are problems of "more or less" rather than of "this or that."

Referential meanings are generally treated in terms of field and/or context, as noted in Chapter 3. In their simplest form, fields or domains may be described merely by listing the objects which may be referred to by a particular term, and the contexts may be identified by giving a list of typical utterances in which such a word may occur or has occurred. Usually the contexts are classified under the subdivisions of the domains, though in actual practice the subdivisions of the domains are made on the basis of the number and variety of contexts.

The domains of referential meaning are generally described in three ways: (1) by identifying the internal content of a domain, either by listing the referents in question or defining the necessary and sufficient features which will include the referents in question; (2) by contrasting the domain of one word with that of others (i.e. one does not describe the area covered by a particular lexical symbol, but simply defines the borders between this and other semantically contiguous symbols); and (3) by showing the extent to which the area of a particular word may be shared by other words, i.e. by listing synonyms. This last method is in fact a blend of the first two methods.

The description of domains may be done on what might be described as two levels. In the first place, one may deal with groups of related words, such as numerals, color words, and kinship terms; and since the referents in question are structured in relationship to one another, e.g. *grandfather* is to *grandmother* as *uncle* is to *aunt,* we can describe the referential structure of the lexical items which identify these referents. In the second place, one must also deal with individual words which appear to have little or no structured relationship to other terms, e.g. *sun, house, grass,* and *stick.*

What is needed for the analysis of semantic structure is a system which will combine a consideration of both domains and context, and which can relate single words in so far as possible to wider groupings. For the most part this need is satisfied by the approach of Katz and Fodor (1962b, 1963), described briefly in Chapter 3, but treated later in this chapter in greater detail.

The analysis of emotive meanings is by no means as easy as that of referential meanings, for the former seem to have no objective, describable domains. In fact, almost the only way in which we can analyze emotive meanings is by contexts, either cultural or linguistic. In describing emotive meanings on the basis of cultural contexts we either analyze the behavioral responses of others to the use of certain words (i.e. if we are studying a foreign language) or we try to diagnose our emotional attitudes toward words of our mother tongue. To objectify and to "measure" these psychological values, it is sometimes useful to get people to indicate their evaluations of words on a multiple-point scale, using such contrasts as good-to-bad, exalted-to-debased, enjoyable-to-painful, hot-to-cold, etc.

The second principal approach to emotive meanings is through the examination of linguistic contexts, that is to say, analyzing the co-occurring words which may prove diagnostic as to emotive values. For example, does a particular lexical unit normally appear in association with other units which may be described as occurring in settings which are vulgar, academic, conversational, etc.? And what are the "cue words" for such contexts?

In trying to construct any overall theory of semantic structure it is important that emotive meanings be related as closely as possible to referential ones, for not only are emotive meanings always present in varying degrees (even if the emotive value of a term is described as neutral), but they are part and parcel of the total system. Furthermore, within the referential domain of a particular word various areas may have radically different emotive values. Compare, for example, *passion* in the following three sets of contexts:

1. the passion of our Lord
   a passion play
2. a passion for music
   a passion for artistic expression
3. a passion killing
   a passion for sex thrills

TECHNIQUES FOR DESCRIBING THE REFERENTIAL MEANINGS OF SERIES OF RELATED WORDS

An analysis of the meanings of word symbols soon reveals that many words have structurally related domains. In a numerical series (i.e. *one, two, three, four,* etc.) the various units have meaning only in relation to preceding and succeeding units. Words such as *bear, mammal,* and *animal* are related in that they constitute a series with an increasingly larger range of inclusion. At the same time, one may find that words are parallel in certain types of contrasts. For example, in at least one respect—namely, sex—the meaning of *son* is to *daughter* as *nephew* is to *niece.* The semantic structures of such sets of words have been described primarily in the following ways: (1) chains (or strings), (2) hierarchies, and (3) componential plotting.

Chain Analysis

A typical chain or string of related meanings may be found in various sets of color terms which divide the spectrum into various units. As noted in Chapter 3, these related sets in various languages may be quite different, and in most instances they involve some degree of overlapping. That is to say, some colors may be referred to by either of two terms. This is, of course, as true of English terminology as of that of any other language.

Numerical systems would seem to be one instance in which there is no overlapping, for a series such as *one, two, three, four, five,* etc. appears by its very function to remove any possibility of ambiguity, as is generally true for English and a number of other languages in which considerable precision is attached to number series. [1] However, for some languages there is a good deal of overlapping. For example, in the Shiriana dialect of Shirianan, a language spoken on the Upper Uraricaa River of northern Brazil, [2] there are basically only five number words:

1. *pemi,* indicating that there is none. This contrasts with all other number terms, which are positive.
2. *moni,* one or a few, but not as many as *ŋami.*
3. *čarekep,* two, or more than one, but not as many as *čarami.*
4. *ŋami,* few, but in contrast with *čarami.*
5. *čarami,* many, usually five or more.

Even these very limited numbers are essentially relative in their meanings, and could only be diagramed as a series of overlapping areas, with certain indistinct and shifting boundaries, as in Figure 14.

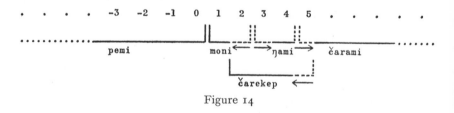

Figure 14

---

[1] Even in English numbers are sometimes not precise. For example, in the sentence *they had only two or three people there,* the phrase *two or three* may actually be a reference to several more than the precise numerical value of the terms in question.
[2] Data on the Shiriana dialect have been supplied by Ernest Migliazza.

Though a chain analysis may be quite useful in "plotting" the relationships existing in certain semantic structures, this procedure is actually not of great significance, since so few sets of words exhibit these relationships. Most semantic structures are far too complex to be treated by any lineal arrangement. It is for this reason that hierarchical and componential analyses are so much more useful and effective.

Hierarchical Analysis

In contrast with chains or strings of terms which describe merely linear relationships, the hierarchical structuring of symbols is a much more common and important type of relationship. Such hierarchical structuring of words is met with constantly, both in everyday colloquial usage and in formal writing. For example, it is not uncommon to hear a conversation including such a series as follows:

A. *The machine broke.*
B. *Where did you buy the old thing, anyway?*
A. *I bought it at the discount house.*
B. *Then toss the stuff out.*

In this series one referent is identified in four different ways: *machine, old thing, it,* and *stuff.* Obviously, the expressions *old thing, it,* and *stuff* can refer to many more objects than *machine.* In other words, the three substitute expressions may be called superordinate to *machine.* In formal writing, considerations of style demand that undue repetition be avoided by changing terminology often enough to obviate reference to the same phenomenon too often by the same words. Sometimes it takes a good deal of verbal juggling to do so, but it is part of the practical way in which, almost without realizing it, we deal with the problems of substitution and hierarchy. Of course, at times the substitutions may be more or less on the same hierarchical level. Such pairs of terms as *peace: tranquility* and *medicine man: witch doctor* are roughly on the same level, though one of the pair cannot always substitute for the other. However, they are more nearly equivalent in hierarchical level than are such pairs as *sin: adultery* and *good: generous,* for in such instances the second term of each pair is essentially subordinate to the first.

Some words are highly superordinate, e.g. *thing, object,* and *it.* That is to say, they may substitute for thousands of other words. On the other hand, such words as *flashlight, beaver,* and *goldfinch* have relatively limited ranges of substitution. The inclusive character of certain series of words may involve a number of gradations, e.g. a series of four terms: *kangaroo, marsupial, mammal, animal,* and a series of three: *mint, herb, plant.*

Certain important types of contrasts in hierarchical structures are diagramed in Figures 15-17, covering roughly similar areas of vocabulary in Miskito, a language of Honduras and Nicaragua, Khmu, a language of Laos, and English. In these diagrams the bottom line (given in English in the Miskito and Khmu diagrams) represents, not the lowest subordinate level, but one in which there is often the greatest degree of parallelism.

An even lower level in the case of Miskito would be personal names for men and women and various kinds of deer, rats, etc. The same would apply to the other diagrams as well. In ascending order, each level includes those terms on subordinate levels which are included within the brackets. Note that in the Miskito diagram (Figure 15) the expressions *diera rayakira*, literally 'things with life', and *diera siakwi*, 'green things', though seemingly only descriptive phrases, are actually exocentric lexical units, for they do not subdivide the class *diera* 'things', but rather refer to *witin*, which is in contrast to *diera*.

Several features of the Khmu diagram (Figure 16) should be noted.

1. The items occurring in the second hierarchical level (counting from the top) are classifiers used as substitutes for more specific terms. These classifiers are obligatory in the numerical system.

2. The distributions of the classifiers *tuut* and *sen* overlap. For *vine* one may substitute a term that identifies it as a member of the plant class, if it is alive; or, if it is used to tie objects, one must use a substitute which designates it as belonging to the rope class. This usage is not appreciably different from English practice, in which, depending upon the nature of the referent, *it* or *he* may be substituted for the word *spirit*.

3. Classifications may be exhaustive (even to the extent of overlapping), as in the second hierarchical order, or they may be "spotty" and incomplete, as in the third order.

The diagram of English hierarchical structuring (Figure 17) suggests several specific problems:

1. The same word may occur as a substitute on different levels. For example, *animal* contrasts with *person* on one level, but includes human beings on another. Similarly, *animal* as a substitute on the fifth level may stand in contrast to *insect*, *bird*, and *fish*, but on the fourth level, when it is in contrast to *plant*, it includes insects, birds, and fish.

2. There are differences of usage. Some persons insist that they would never call a tree a plant, regardless of the hierarchical level, but others do so freely.

3. Substitutes cannot be so neatly pyramided as the diagram implies, for one and the same term may fit more than one hierarchical structure. *She*, for example, belongs to more than one hierarchical structure, and even within a single structure may have differences of obligatory or optional usage. That is to say, *she* is an obligatory substitute for *woman*, but an optional substitute for such objects as large, sex-distinctive animals or birds, ships, and institutions.

4. There may be considerable overlapping of parts of classes, especially in limited contexts. For example, the word *thing* has a very wide substitution domain in the negative, where it may substitute for *animals* (*we didn't shoot a thing*), for *fish* (*we didn't catch a thing*), and for almost any object, including persons (*we didn't see a thing*).

Harold C. Conklin (1962) has employed a system of hierarchical structuring in dealing with a restricted set of botanical terms, representing a typical folk taxonomy. The basic eight levels of decreasing subordination are as follows:

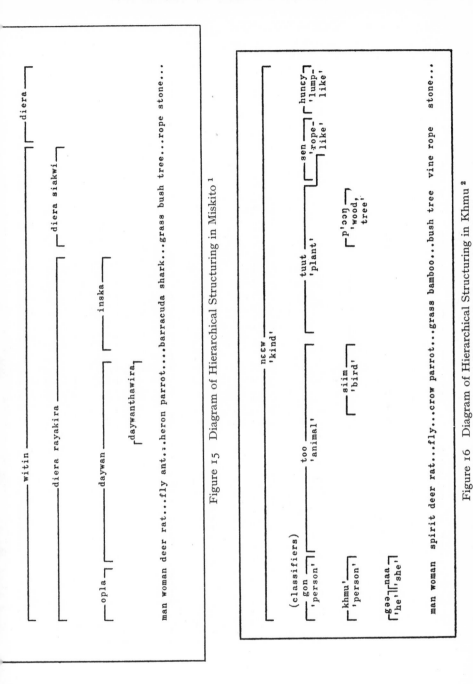

Figure 15 Diagram of Hierarchical Structuring in Miskito [1]

Figure 16 Diagram of Hierarchical Structuring in Khmu [2]

[1] Data for the Miskito diagram were furnished by Werner B. Marx.
[2] The Khmu data have been supplied by William A. Smalley.

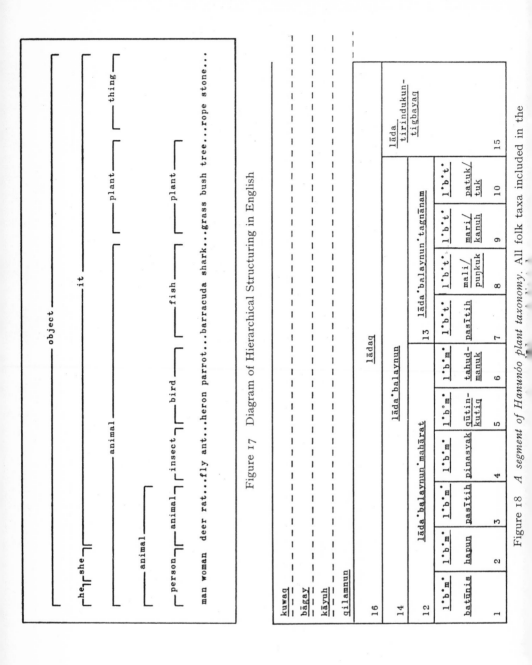

Figure 17   Diagram of Hierarchical Structuring in English

Figure 18   *A segment of Hanunóo plant taxonomy.* All folk taxa included in the

1. kuwaq	'entity' (i.e. something that can be named)
2. bāgay	'thing' (not a person, animal, etc.)
3. kāyuh	'plant' (not a rock, etc.)
4. qilamnun	'herbaceous plant' (not a woody plant, etc.)
5. lādaq	'pepper (plant)' (not a rice plant, etc.)
6. lāda·balaynun	'houseyard pepper (plant)' (not a wild pepper plant)
7. lāda·balaynun· mahārat	'houseyard chili pepper (plant)' (not a houseyard green pepper plant)
8. lāda·balaynun· mahārat· qūtin-kutiq	'"cat-penis" houseyard chili pepper (plant)', (not a member of any of the five other terminal houseyard chili pepper taxa such as lāda·balaynun· mahārat·tāhud-manuk, the "cook's spur" variety)

Conklin has diagramed the hierarchical structure involved in these terms as shown in Figure 18.

Conklin makes the important comment that, though the plants in folk taxa 16, 14, and 15 correspond rather closely to certain scientific classifications, the remaining twelve involve distinctions not recognized as significant botanical subspecies by taxonomic botanists who have classified the same flora. Moreover, certain aspects of the meaning of these lower level terms cannot be diagramed in this hierarchical type of structuring.

Certain general features of hierarchical structuring, outlined in the following paragraphs, are of considerable significance to anyone attempting to analyze the meanings of related sets of words.

1. As one ascends the hierarchical structure the terms generally become fewer and the domains larger. That is, the shift is from greater specificity to greater generic character. In certain instances, such as the Khmu data, a higher level may involve more terms, simply because it is more exhaustive. Note, however, that in each instance the second-level terms in the Khmu diagram completely include the domains of any lower-level terms.

2. The same word may occur on different levels. That is to say, it may have a more particular as well as a more general meaning. For example, in English *animal* may be a relatively low-level substitute if it includes only such terms as *wolf, sheep, dog, cat*, etc., but it may also substitute for the names of a much wider class of creatures, including *man, fish*, and *birds*, in the trichotomous folk classification of "animal, vegetable, and mineral." This situation poses a complex problem for the translator, for he must make certain that in finding a corresponding term in the receptor language he has represented not only a possible equivalent on some level, but the appropriate equivalent at the right level.

3. The identity of domains, both in terms of extent and level, determines to some extent the degree of synonymity between words. That is to say, certain aspects of synonymity depend upon the extent to which terms may substitute for each other at the same relative level. Of course, if terms are on widely differing levels, it is presumed that the domain of the subordinate term is completely included within the domain of the superordinate term. For example, *animal* may substitute for all the

occurrences of *wolf*, but these terms are on such disparate levels that they cannot be considered synonymous. On the other hand, *sorcery* and *witchcraft* may be regarded as roughly synonymous, because they are freely substitutable for each other in almost all contexts and exist on the same relative hierarchical order. *Magic*, on the other hand, may substitute for *sorcery* and *witchcraft* in many situations, but it may also substitute for *necromancy* and *legerdemain* as well as for such phrases as *mysterious enchantment, the use of occult powers*, and *the manipulation of supernatural influences*. This means that *magic* is on a higher level and not so synonymous with *sorcery* and *witchcraft* as these two are with each other.

4. Classifications tend to overlap at many points. That is to say, the same object may be identified by two different terms at the same level, depending upon the "perspective" or context. *Ship* in English, for example, may occur with either *it* or *she* as a substitute.

5. There are differences in classification between people within the same language-culture community. Specialists (e.g. scientists, medicine men, and priests) often differ in their usage from the common people. Moreover, there is always some degree of alternative usage at certain points in any system; otherwise it would never change.

6. Classifications tend to be rather spotty and unsystematic, especially in popular usage. So-called "scientific usage" is notably different in tending toward greater precision, systematization, and comprehensiveness.

7. All classes of words may be involved in such hierarchical structuring. Though common nouns are the easiest to classify and to understand, all classes of words have certain distributional patterns involving superordinate-subordinate relationships. For example, the English verbs *squirm, wriggle*, and *dance* are relatively low-level words in contrast to *go, come*, and *move*.

The hierarchical structure of lexical symbols also reveals certain important features about the language and culture of a people, as noted in the following paragraphs:

1. Every culture has its own distinctive manner of relating terms in a hierarchical structure. For example, in Kekchi, a Mayan language of Guatemala, there are three terms, *che', pim*, and *agwink*, which may be translated roughly as 'tree', 'bush', and 'plant' respectively, but the real distinctions are in no sense parallel to the corresponding terms in English. *Che'* means any large bush or tree of which the wood is useful. *Pim*, on the other hand, indicates bushes, grass, and weeds which have no such usefulness as wood and do not serve as food for human consumption. *Agwink*, however, identifies plants of which at least some portion is eaten by people.

2. The abundance of terms and the complexity of classification for any semantic area usually depend upon the focus of the culture as a whole, or upon the concentration of attention by persons forming a distinctive subculture (e.g. professional specialists, such as zoologists, witch doctors, or existential philosophers).

3. The hierarchical level of words may change. The level of the English words *sun* and *moon* has changed as the result of changes in astronomical knowledge. Formerly they referred to unique objects, and thus were on the lowest hierarchical level. Now, however, one may speak of stars as "suns," and the satellites of planets as "moons."

4. Languages differ most from one another as one ascends the hierarchical structure. On the very lowest levels, even below the level indicated in the Miskito, Khmu, and English diagrams (Figures 15-17), one often encounters considerable cultural specialization. However, by and large there are relatively fewer differences between languages in the lower levels than in the higher ones, since in the lower levels the terms tend to match more closely the perceptually distinguishable objects of the culture, but in the higher levels distinctions reflect conceptually based classifications of phenomena. In other words, when the distinctions are based primarily upon perception, there are fewer differences than when the differentiations result from conceptualization. For example, in Guaica, a language of southern Venezuela, there is little difficulty in finding equivalents for such English terms as *murder, stealing, lying, incest*, etc., but the terms for *bad, good, ugly*, and *beautiful* cover an area of meaning very different from that in English. To illustrate, Guaica recognizes, not a dichotomous classification of *good* and *bad*, but a trichotomous one, with the following distinctions:

a. 'Good' includes desirable food, killing enemies, chewing dope in moderation, putting fire on one's wife to teach her to obey, and stealing from any person not belonging to the same band.

b. 'Bad' includes rotten fruit, any object with a blemish, murdering a person of the same band, stealing from a member of the extended family, and lying (to anyone).

c. 'Violating taboo' includes incest, being too close to one's mother-in-law, a married woman's eating tapir before the birth of the first child, and a child's eating rodents. [1]

The tendency to think of so-called primitive languages as lacking highly generic vocabularies is ill founded. In Cuna, a language of Panama, for example, there are two very highly generic terms, *wilup* and *ikar*, which would be exceedingly useful if only we had them in English in speaking about communication and culture. *Wilup* means 'scar', 'weight', 'sign', 'symbol', 'proportion', 'measure', 'kind', 'type', 'primer', 'alphabet', 'picture', duty', and 'responsibility'. *Ikar*, on the other hand, means 'road', 'trail', 'way', 'plan of action', 'custom', 'manner', 'sanctions', 'pattern of behavior', 'ordinance', 'way of thinking', and 'culture'. When, in answer to objections that primitive languages lack generic vocabularies, such words with exceedingly wide areas of meaning are pointed out, the tendency is to criticize such languages as being "too loose" in their terminology. The truth of the matter is that certain languages spoken by so-called primitive peoples include some highly important generic and abstract terms, reflecting a remarkable level of

[1] These data on Guaica have been supplied by James Barker.

"sophisticatiòn." For example, the Toba dialect of the region of Saenz Peña in Argentina has five verbs with areas of meaning having important implications for philosophical inquiry:

1. eetec: 'to become, to eventuate, to happen (used particularly of a quality)'
2. huo'o: 'to exist, to have, to be in a relationship with'
3. saqca: 'not to exist, have, or be in a relationship with'
4. 'ot: 'to do, to make, to perform'
5. sit: 'to cause to be, to make possible'

One only wonders what Aristotle or Heidegger would have done had they worked out their philosophical insights in terms of these verbal contrasts. Moreover, this same language classifies all verbal forms by certain obligatory particles: (1) *ca* 'not present, either in time or space' (in expressions of time this may often refer to the future); (2) *na* 'present, coming'; (3) *da* 'present, standing'; (4) *ji* 'present, horizontal, or lying down'; (5) *ni* 'present, sitting or in a fixed position'; and (6) *so*: 'going away, not present, flying' (in terms of time, this refers to the past).

The fact that languages differ increasingly in the upper hierarchical levels means that the translation of abstract or generic materials is generally very complex, especially if the cultural contexts of the two languages are quite diverse. This means that such books as the Gospel of John, though seemingly simple in style and vocabulary, are actually very difficult to translate because of the numerous high-level generic and abstract terms. On the other hand, of all the books of the New Testament, the book of the Revelation—despite its extreme difficulty of interpretation—is perhaps the easiest to translate, because the vocabulary is so very specific.

5. There are two basic types of divisions in hierarchical structuring: (a) the horizontal, which marks the successive layers of specific to generic vocabulary, and (b) the vertical, which reveals some of the basic divisions. When such vertical divisions are multilevel, that is to say, when the cuts extend through several layers, they mark very important distinctions in the language, e.g. animate vs. inanimate, personal vs. nonpersonal, or natural vs. supernatural.

6. In that form of the language which is in common use by the average speaker the proportion of generic vocabulary to nongeneric vocabulary is apparently about the same in almost all languages. Of course, when certain specialists in a society set out to develop a generic or abstract vocabulary for some particular purpose (as when the philosophers of ancient Greece worked out so many terms for philosophical inquiry), the percentage of such terms naturally rises for that particular professional vocabulary. Though no extensive comparative analyses have been made of the vocabulary of languages, a systematic study of translation problems in several scores of languages seems to point to the fact that, in terms of the vocabulary in common use, languages do not exhibit striking differences in the relative percentages of lower vs. higher level vocabulary.

Since this observation seems to contradict what has frequently been said on the subject as the result of vocabulary sampling by linguistic and anthropological field workers, an explanation is needed. In the first place, concrete, low-level vocabulary is very easy to elicit and hence seems to be very abundant, while more highly generic or abstract vocabulary is difficult to obtain from an informant. Hence, one obtains at first a greater percentage of low-level terms. Moreover, many field investigators are inclined to conclude that practically all the terms which they have elicited are low-level vocabulary, while in actuality, if they explored the language more extensively, they would find that many of these words they obtained in specific contexts, apparently referring to a concrete object or particular event, actually have much wider domains. A third factor which influences the mistaken assumption about the absence of high-level vocabulary in some languages is that the high-level vocabulary of the language simply does not fit the investigator's language. Since he not infrequently has no linguistic tool other than his own language, either for eliciting such words or for describing their meanings, he tends to miss them, and hence denies their existence. Eskimo, for example, is often cited as a typical "concrete" language, with three words for different kinds of seals, but no word for seals as a class. It is true that Barrow Eskimo has three different words meaning 'gray seal', 'spotted seal', and 'bearded seal', respectively, but above this level this dialect of Eskimo goes to *nizuzutit*, meaning 'animal', and then to *niqsat*, referring to any kind of game. There is generic vocabulary, but not at the precise points in the hierarchical structure where English speakers would expect to find it. In Moré, a language of the Haute Volta in West Africa, there are actually six different verbs for 'carry', indicating (1) 'to carry in the hand', (2) 'to carry on the head', (3) 'to carry on the shoulder', (4) 'to carry on the back', (5) 'to carry on the hip', and (6) 'to carry along with one' (as on a bicycle). There is no term merely meaning 'carry', but there is another word, more generic than either *carry* or *take* in English, which includes all the events described by the six terms in question, plus many more.

7. The hierarchical structuring of related symbols is an extremely important index to a people's world view, for it is by language that people indicate their classifications of experience. Moreover, the classifications reflected in the hierarchical substitutions of words are even more revealing of a people's world view than are the categories embedded in the morphological structures. Categories such as mode, tense, person, aspect, number, and gender often reflect "ossified" structures which, though actively reflecting meaningful distinctions at an earlier stage in the language, are no longer responsive to change or indicative of living contrasts. Not that these underlying categorizations do not influence people's view of reality—usually quite unconsciously, of course; but there is no doubt that the hierarchical structure of superordinate and subordinate relationships is a far more active and precise picture of some of the contemporary ways in which people view their world.

Semantic analysis by hierarchical structuring is an important device for determining meaningful relationships of words to one another where

6

such words occur in patterns of substitution, that is to say, where super-ordinates may be substituted for subordinates, and vice versa. Moreover, some of the vertical divisions within large sets of hierarchically structured terms are usually very important for the semantic structuring of the language as a whole, and they often provide important hints as to certain basic distinctions in meaning within the semantic domains of single words. For example, if in the hierarchical structuring there is a clear-cut distinction between personal and nonpersonal, it is very likely that this dichotomy will be important in analyzing differences of meaning within the domains of many individual words. The English word *spirit*, for instance, has two rather widely differing areas of meaning, one for contexts in which spirit refers to a person-like "object," e.g. *he saw a spirit* and *the Spirit of God came upon him*, and another for contexts in which spirit designates an impersonal element, e.g. *he showed a lot of spirit* and *I like the spirit of the man*.

Hierarchical structuring does not, however, cover all types of vocabu-lary. For most relationals, a high percentage of abstracts, and a number of object words (e.g. kinship terms), hierarchical analysis is relatively useless.

Componential Analysis

In addition to linear plotting and hierarchical structuring, a third technique—componential analysis—may be employed to analyze the meaning of related series of words, provided that the relationships between terms are based on certain shared and contrastive features. [1] Effective componential analysis depends upon two major features: (1) a well-defined corpus of related terms, e.g. a kinship system, a set of case endings, and a pronominal series, and (2) the possibility of finding in nonlinguistic behavior (i.e. the distribution of these terms in the practical world) certain features which are determinate as to the basic contrasts between the symbols in question. For example, *father* and *mother* in English share the component of generation older than *ego* (the person central to the kinship structure in question), but they differ as to sex. The two components of generation and sex help us, therefore, to define the relationship of *ego* to *father* and *mother*. We can extend the number of kinship terms to include *grandmother, grandfather, grandson, granddaughter, son, daughter, uncle, aunt, nephew, niece, cousin*, etc. As we do so, it becomes evident that there are other important elements, e.g. descending generation in *son* and *daughter* (in contrast to ascending generation in *father* and *mother*), and lineality; for uncles and aunts are obviously not in the same relationship to ego as are his own parents. These components of meaning are of course testable in the nonlinguistic world, for we can confirm their validity in terms of biological relation-ships and marriage contracts.

[1] Some of the more important and illustrative treatment of componential analysis of meaning are given in: Jakobson (1936); Lotz (1947); Wonderly (1952b); Lounsbury (1956); McKaughan (1959); Austerlitz (1959); Wallace and Atkins (1960); Conklin (1962a). See bibliography.

In making a componential analysis of any group of related words there are five basic steps: [1]

1. Determining the limits of a "closed corpus" of data, i.e. limiting the study to a well-defined set of words which have multidimensional relationships consisting of certain shared and contrasting features.
2. Defining the terms as precisely as possible, on the basis of the objects involved. For example, for the English kinship term *uncle* we would specify father's brother, mother's brother, father's father's brother, and mother's father's brother, etc. [2]
3. Identifying the distinctive features which define the various contrasts in meaning, e.g. differences of generation, of sex, of lineality, etc.
4. Defining each term by means of the distinctive features. For example, father may be defined as first ascending generation, male, and lineal (i.e. direct line).
5. Making an overall statement of the relationship between the distinctive features and the total number of symbols classified. This is often done by means of some "plotting" or "mapping" of the semantic space.

By applying these five steps to a limited set of English kinship terms in which all the persons are in some measure biologically related (excluding those relationships defined only by marriage), we may illustrate clearly what is involved in a componential analysis, as follows:

1. The English terms chosen are *grandfather, grandmother, father, mother, brother, sister, son, daughter, grandson, granddaughter, uncle, aunt, cousin, nephew,* and *niece.*
2. These terms are then defined on the basis of the interrelationships involved (using in the following list the standard abbreviations of *Fa* for father, *Mo* for mother, *Br* for brother, *Si* for sister, *So* for son, *Da* for daughter):

grandfather:	FaFa, MoFa [3]	*uncle*:	FaBr, MoBr, FaFaBr, MoFaBr, etc.
grandmother:	FaMo, MoMo		
father:	Fa	*aunt*:	FaSi, MoSi, FaFaSi, MoFaSi, etc.
mother:	Mo		
brother:	Br	*cousin*:	FaBrSo, FaBrDa, MoBrSo,
sister:	Si		MoBrDa, FaSiSo, FaSiDa,
son:	So		MoSiSo, MoSiDa, FaFaBrSo,
daughter:	Da		FaMoBrSo, MoFaSiDa, etc.
grandson:	SoSo, DaSo	*nephew*:	BrSo, SiSo, BrSoSo, SiSoSo, etc.
granddaughter:	SoDa, DaDa	*niece*:	BrDa, SiDa, BrDaDa, SiDaDa, etc.

---

[1] In this section the methodology worked out by Wallace and Atkins (1960) is primarily followed.
[2] For the sake of simplicity uncles and aunts by marriage are excluded.
[3] Such abbreviations are to be read as "father's father" and "mother's father." All but the last element in such series is a so-called "genitive" or "possessive" form.

3. To determine the distinctive features of this set of words, we look for certain elements of meaning which are (a) shared by certain terms and (b) not shared by others. For example, we find that sex distinctions exist for all terms except *cousin*. A component of sex may then serve to divide all the other terms into two classes (male and female) and at the same time separate all these terms from *cousin*. On the other hand, a number of words differ primarily on the basis of generation. For example, *grandfather, father, son*, and *grandson* are all of the same sex, but differ essentially on the basis of being of different generations. On the other hand, *cousin* shows no such distinction. If we test all the possible interrelationships for a minimal number of distinctive features which will serve to define all these kinship terms, we end with the following three classes of components:

a. Sex (S): male (s_1) and female (s_2).
b. Generation (G): two generations above ego (g_1), one generation above ego (g_2), ego's own generation (g_3), one generation below ego (g_4), two generations below ego (g_5).
c. Lineality may be described in three degrees: (l_1), in which the persons involved are direct ancestors or descendants of ego, and (l_2) (colineals) and (l_3) (ablineals), representing two successive degrees of less direct lineality.

4. If we redefine the meanings of kinship terms on the basis of these componential features of sex, generation, and lineality, we obtain the following type of description:

grandfather:	$s_1g_1l_1$	*grandson*:	$s_1g_5l_1$
grandmother:	$s_2g_1l_1$	*granddaughter*:	$s_2g_5l_1$
father:	$s_1g_2l_1$	*uncle*:	$s_1g_{1-2}l_2$
mother:	$s_2g_2l_1$	*aunt*:	$s_2g_{1-2}l_2$
brother:	$s_1g_3l_2$	*cousin*:	$s\ g\ l_3$
sister:	$s_2g_3l_2$	*nephew*:	$s_1g_{4-5}l_2$
son:	$s_1g_4l_1$	*niece*:	$s_2g_{4-5}l_2$
daughter:	$s_2g_4l_1$		

It should be noted that in the above definition of terms by componential features it is necessary to list only three features for each "definition." At times, of course, a feature, e.g. *s* and *g* in the definition of *cousin*, has no accompanying numeral, for there is no subdivision of sexual or generational distinctiveness. In some instances, a feature includes two different grades, as for example, g_{1-2} in *uncle* and *aunt*.

5. The interrelationships of the various componential features may be conveniently described in two different ways: (1) by plotting the occurrences or nonoccurrences of such features, and (2) by mapping such differences in a kind of paradigmatic framework. The first type of description is illustrated in Figure 19.

Even a brief glance at Figure 19 indicates that there are certain systematic differences between the kinship terms. Both differences and similarities are more clearly shown by mapping semantic relationships, as in Figure 20.

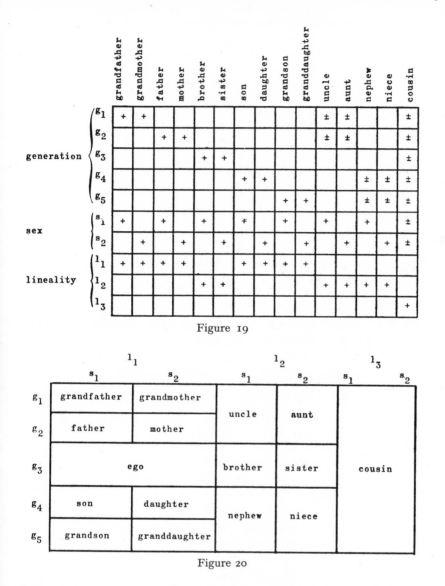

Figure 19

Figure 20

Important advantages of such a componential analysis of meanings are as follows:

1. Attention is drawn to the distinctive features which underlie the contrasts, without the distraction of many additional features which are not so basic to the functioning of the system.
2. Unsuspected features or distinctions in meaning are often discovered in the process of a thorough application of such a system.

3. By componential analysis the functioning of a system is revealed in its simplest terms.

Componential structuring and mapping may of course take on various forms, depending upon the types of defining features and their multidimensional relationships. For example, Conklin (1962a) has made a componential analysis of the pronominal structure of Hanunóo and mapped it on a three-dimensional model:

The pronouns of Hanunóo are as follows:

dah 'they'
kuh 'I'
mih 'we'
muh 'you'
tah 'we two'
tam 'we all'
yah 'he, she'
yuh 'you all'

The traditional dimensions of this structure are:

1. Person: first, second, and third
2. Number: singular, dual, plural
3. Exclusion: inclusive, exclusive

If, however, we set up a paradigm on this basis we have the following rather asymmetrical structure:

kuh	1s	*tah*	1d	*mih*	1pe (exclusive)
—		—		*tam*	1pi (inclusive)
muh	2s	—		*yuh*	2p
yah	3s	—		*dah*	3p

On the other hand, by determining the minimal obligatory features of distinctiveness, one can arrive at a more satisfactory, economical, and semantically verifiable solution. This means using three sets of componential features, involving three types of oppositions:

1. limited membership (L): unlimited membership (-L)
2. inclusion of speaker (S): exclusion of speaker (-S)
3. inclusion of hearer (H): exclusion of hearer (-H)

A description of meaning in terms of these componential features provides the following definitions:

dah	-L,	-S,	-H	'they'
yuh	-L,	-S,	H	'you all'
mih	-L,	S,	-H	'we' (excl.)
tam	-L,	S,	H	'we' (inc.)
yah	L,	-S,	-H	'he, she'
muh	L,	-S,	H	'you'
kuh	L,	S,	-H	'I'
tah	L,	S,	H	'we two'

These componential meanings lend themselves to a three-dimensional mapping, as shown in Figure 21.

It must be recognized, however, that semantic space may be orthogonal, i.e. regular and systematic, or it may be nonorthogonal, i.e. irregular and nonsystematic. For example, in the mapping of the meanings of the core of American English consanguineal kinship terms, we were able to use a symmetrical type of mapping, with regularity of shape and without holes in the pattern. However, if we had added the meaning of *uncle* and *aunt* to include persons not biologically related, i.e. uncles and aunts through marriage, the mapping of the space would have been irregular in shape,

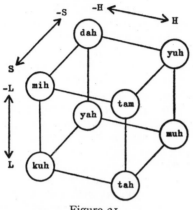

Figure 21

with a projection to take care of a feature of meaning not included in the restricted features whose relationships were so neatly plotted. [1]

Though componential analysis of meaning has many important advantages over a number of other techniques, one must recognize that such a procedure has a number of significant built-in limitations:

1. It is only applicable to restricted series of terms which have certain shared and contrastic features.
2. By analyzing only the minimal features of distinctiveness, many supplementary and connotative elements of meaning are disregarded, e.g. the emotive meaning in *mother* in contrast with *cousin*.
3. Componential analysis tends to define more what a term does not mean than what it does mean, for the distinctive features are really ways by which territories of meaning are "separated off" from one another, not means by which one "fills" such areas with meaning.
4. Though the componential features are fundamental to the functioning of a system, they are often not the focal elements in the consciousness of speakers. In other words, native speakers of a language will usually recognize the validity of componential features. However, they tend rather to think about areas of meaning and the classes of items which fit into such areas, rather than about the componential features which define the contrasts.

[1] For a treatment of orthogonal and nonorthogonal shapes of semantic territories, see Wallace and Atkins (1960).

TECHNIQUES FOR DESCRIBING THE REFERENTIAL
MEANINGS OF SINGLE WORDS

There are three fundamental ways in which we may describe the domain of referential meaning of individual lexical units. We may (1) name the class, usually by contrasting it with other classes, (2) identify the individual members of the class, generally by listing, or (3) describe the distinctive features of the class. The first meaning may be called a "type" (Morris' *designatum*)[1] or generalized meaning. The second "definition" is based upon the listing of tokens of the class (Morris' *denotatum*), and may also be called the particular meaning. The third type of meaning is based upon "sufficient and necessary features of the class" (Morris' *significatum*), or, in other words, the abstract meaning of the class. For example, we may define *chair*, first by contrasting the term *chair*, as the name of a class, from other possibly related classes, e.g. *bench, stool, position, post*. Secondly, we may define *chair* by listing the specific tokens of the class, e.g. *the chair in the living room, the chair of philosophy, the electric chair, he will chair the meeting*. In a sense, such tokens are almost unlimited, for such referents of *chair* are extensive. Thirdly, we may define *chair* by describing the sufficient and necessary features which distinguish it from all other objects. For example, *chair* in at least certain aspects of its meaning is described in The American College Dictionary (1947) as "a seat with a back and legs or other support, often with arms, usually for only one person." The American College Dictionary then goes on to list other meanings based upon tokens, not upon "sufficient and necessary features," for many symbols cover such a wide area of meaning that there is not a single cluster of defining features, but chains of such features.

If we apply the three-way distinction between class, token, and features of the class to the above analysis of certain core words in the English kinship system, we find that the tokens (or *denotata*) are the individual persons identified by such abbreviations as FaFa, MoFa, FaBoSo, MoFaDa, etc. The classes are the groups identified by such terms as *father, grandfather, uncle*, etc., including all the tokens which belong to any such classes (the *designata*). The distinguishing features of the classes (the *significata*) are the componential features of generation, sex, and lineality. The *significata* are, of course, the prerequisites of any class, but as has been noted the meanings of words are not limited to these prerequisites, for there are also other features, which may be called the probabilities or possibilities of the class. We may say that in certain usages the terms *father, dad, daddy, pop*, and *old man* all have the same *significata*, and that to this extent the *denotata* are identical. Thus the same referent may be identified by all these terms. But these words certainly have different emotive meanings, i.e. features which as possibilities and probabilities are far more "fluid" and difficult to describe than are the prerequisites involved in the *significata*.

In order to describe the domains of referential meaning of individual

[1]   See Charles Morris (1946).

lexical units, whether in terms of type, token, or features, there have traditionally been three kinds of techniques which have yielded the most helpful results: (1) derivational, (2) componential, and (3) distributional. Derivational analysis tends to concentrate on relating tokens to each other within the class. Componential procedures highlight the necessary and sufficient features of the class, and distributional techniques employ the elements of the linguistic context to provide clues to basic divisions of semantic domains.

DERIVATIONAL TECHNIQUES

By derivational techniques we mean those by which the meanings of terms are explained on the basis of assumed "chains" or "trees" of meanings showing how one meaning of a term is derived from another. This approach is most conspicuously involved in the average dictionary, in which the meanings are usually arranged in a logico-historical sequence. This sequence attempts to indicate not only the historical order in which meanings have arisen, but also something of the logical order of dependence of one meaning upon another. For example, the Liddell and Scott Abridged Greek-English Dictionary lists the principal meanings of *charis* as 'outward grace', 'loveliness', 'charm', 'kindness', 'goodwill', 'thanks', 'gratitude', 'influence', 'gratification', and 'delight', in an assumed derivational order by which one meaning appears to be derivable from or relatable to another. Many times such lists of meanings seem to be neatly classifiable, especially in such a dictionary as the Oxford English Dictionary. However, Allen Walker Read (1955, p. 41) points out that: "in the compilation of the Oxford English Dictionary the intermediate or transitional quotations were discarded as being 'ambiguous' or 'not clear', and the resulting neat patterns are false to actual usage."

Part of our problem in attempting to set up a series of meanings based on a presumed historical development is that often we do not know the history, even in languages with rather extensive documentation; for many uses may be quite extensive on a colloquial level before they ever appear in a document. Moreover, even when we know something of the history and can reconstruct a "line of descent" for various meanings, the patterns are generally not at all certain. For example, it is possible to diagram the various meanings of Hebrew *kbd, 'heavy', 'much', 'many', 'slow', 'abundant', 'burdensome', 'difficult', 'grievous', 'sluggish', 'dull', 'riches', 'respect', 'honor', and 'great', as in Figure 22 (Nida, 1958, p. 289).

This type of diagram has certain advantages, for it symbolizes, within a relatively limited space, a number of significant relationships of meaning. However, there are some serious drawbacks to this type of "derivational analysis," for: (1) the representation of relationships is oversimplified (several planes plus a dimension of time would be necessary if one were to diagram all the factors accurately); (2) the arrows imply a kind of etymological descent, which may or may not be correct; and (3) instead of two degrees of interrelationship (solid and dotted lines), there are actually several, with a considerable reciprocal

re-enforcement which can scarcely be shown on such a diagram. Hence
it must be recognized that any such plotting of meanings will inevitably
skew the basic relationships existing in the Biblical usage of this lexical
unit.

Analyses of meaning based on derivational procedures do, however
provide some very important insights, for any logico-historical grouping
of meanings tends to produce "tree structures" which show important

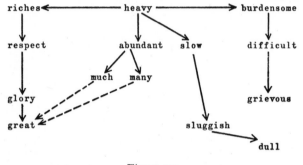

Figure 22

contrasts at certain nodes. In many instances, these points of branching
coincide with distinctions based on contrasting features, as noted in the
discussion of the meaning of *bachelor* in Chapter 3.

COMPONENTIAL TECHNIQUES

One striking defect in this diagram (Figure 22) of the meanings of the
Biblical Hebrew root *kbd* is the failure to reflect some of the obvious
features shared by different sets of meanings. For example, the meanings
of 'riches', 'respect', 'glory', and 'great' are culturally favored, while the
meanings of 'burdensome', 'difficult', 'grievous', and 'dull' are disfavored.
Certain of the meanings are related directly to physical weight and others
to derivable inertia. Still others express primarily an increased degree
of some quality. Since there are significant components of meaning
shared by some of the meanings and not by others, it is possible to apply
a kind of componential analysis to these meanings as a way of pointing
out more clearly certain of the interrelationships. These componential
features may be diagramed as in Figure 23.

This type of componential analysis, in contrast to the kind examined
in connection with sets of words, does not presume to identify all the
significant contrasts between various meanings of a term. It is merely a
method by which we may group certain sets of related meanings in a
significant way. In the above diagram, two of the components, namely,
"culturally desirable" and "culturally undesirable," are largely emotive,
rather than referential; and certainly these five components are not all
the "sufficient and necessary features" for defining the area of meaning
of the root *kbd*. On the other hand, such an analysis of meanings of a

single form has certain advantages, especially in the analysis of possible homonyms—terms identical in form, but unrelated in meaning, e.g. *pair, pare,* and *pear; read* and *reed;* and *light* (referring to brightness) and *light* (referring to weight). If there are no components or chains of components which unite any series of meanings, we may be quite certain that we are dealing with homonyms, not with highly divergent meanings of the same word.

Of course, these components must be carefully chosen for their cultural relevance and acceptability to native speakers of a language, for the native speakers are the ones who reshape the semantic structure of a language by recognizing the relationships which may not have existed previously. For example, historically the *by* of *by-law* is not the same as the *by* of *by-product,* or *by-path,* but for most American English speakers

	Heavy	Much	Many	Abundant	Great	Riches	Respect	Glory	Slow	Sluggish	Dull	Burdensome	Difficult	Grievous
Physical weight	+	±	±	±	±	+			±	±		+	±	±
Inertia	+	±	±	±		±			+	+	±	±	±	±
Culturally desirable		±	±	±	+	+	+	+						
Culturally undesirable	±	±	±	±					±	+	+	+	+	+
Increased degree					+			+		±	±			+

Figure 23

all these *by*s mean a subordinate or derivative sort of *law, product,* or *path.* Similarly, some persons identify *sex* in *sextette* and *rump* in *rumpus,* and for these persons the related forms have certain shared components of meaning (Read, 1949a).

At times a series of meanings of an apparently single term seem so disparate and unrelated that one questions the correctness of the presumed grouping of meaning. Particularly is this true when one deals with words occurring in cultural contexts entirely different from those familiar to one. For example, in Anuak, a Nilotic language of the Sudan, the word *jwok* occurs in at least ten rather widely different types of contexts (Nida, 1958, pp. 291-292):

1. "The one who made the world and everything in it is *jwok.*" In this type of context *jwok* is always referred to as a person, but any traits of personality are mentioned only in rather vague terms.
2. "The *juu piny* must be placated by offerings and sacrifices." The *juu piny* (*juu* is the plural form of *jwok*) are literally 'gods of the earth', most of whom seem to have been borrowed from the neighboring Nuers. For the most part they are malevolent and they differ in activity and power. The relationships (1) between the *juu*

piny themselves and (2) between the *juu piny* and the creator *jwok* are not defined.

3. "The family shrines are *jwok*." Small village and family shrines mark places where the *juu piny* are propitiated by offerings and sacrifices.

4. "That grove of trees is *jwok*." A few places are regarded as *jwok*. These are generally quite isolated from any village, are for the most part avoided, and seem never to be the site of any community ritual.

5. "The medicine man is *jwok*."

6. "The white man is *jwok*." Any person who has special abilities (something which is regarded as true of all white men) is spoken of as *jwok*.

7. "Radios, cars, airplanes, phonographs, and electricity are *jwok*." Any object whose functioning is inexplicable in terms of the Anuak frame of reference is *jwok*.

8. "Anything startling is *jwok*." The one exception to this is the appearance of a ghost (spirit of a deceased person), which is called *tipo*.

9. "The sick man has been taken by *jwok*." In this type of context the creator *jwok* may or may not be implied.

10. "What can we do now? It all depends on *jwok*." When people give up hope, as in the case of apparent fatal illness, they insist that the outcome is up to *jwok*, but there is no evidence that they always have in mind the creator *jwok*.

COMPONENTS	\multicolumn{10}{c}{CONTEXTS}									
	1	2	3	4	5	6	7	8	9	10
Extraordinary power	+	+	−	−	+	+	+	+	+	+
Personality: nonhuman	+	+			−	−			±	±
human	−	−			+	+			−	−
Fear	±	+	±	±	±	±	±	+	+	±
Respect	+	±	+	+	+	+	+		±	+
Unfamiliar cause-effect sequences							+	+	+	±
Objects (including persons)			+	+	+	+	+			
Processes							+	+	+	+

Figure 24

This series of ten meanings cannot be described in traditional ways, either by finding some common denominator of meaning or by setting up a derivational "tree." The interrelationships are highly complex. For this type of situation a description which takes into consideration certain componential features culturally relevant to Anuak life can be highly instructive and can provide a unity of perspective which would otherwise be lacking (Figure 24).

Once we have plotted the distribution of certain, but not necessarily all, of the relevant cultural features in a series of meanings of a term, we are in a much better position to recognize the manner in which various meanings are related, and the degree to which there is interdependence and re-enforcement. Moreover, in the selection of culturally relevant components of meaning we almost inevitably highlight the contrasts between words in various languages. For example, it might seem strange at first glance that in the above treatment of *jwok* in Anuak we have not indicated such traditional componential contrasts as ethical vs. non-ethical and secular vs. sacred. These distinctions were specifically not introduced precisely because they are not particularly valid or important in Anuak religious beliefs at this point. It is true that the creator *jwok* is usually benevolent and the *juu piny* are for the most part malevolent; and yet the benevolent or malevolent characteristics are not primary or absolute, and they are never related to ethical or nonethical standards. Even the distinction between secular and sacred (contexts 3 and 4) is poorly defined, and, in so far as it is employed, shows no one-to-one correspondence in the various meanings of *jwok*.

One feature of componential analysis which may not be fully evident at first, but which is structurally of great significance for any overall theory of semantics, is the fact that certain basic divisions take on a plus-minus (or binary) structure. The components themselves tend to reveal the underlying tree structure of hierarchically arranged sets of contrasting categories. These components are sometimes translated into "semantic markers" (see Chapter 3 and the concluding sections of this chapter).

FIGURATIVE EXTENSIONS OF MEANING

In attempting to deal with referential meanings we are constantly troubled by problems of figurative extensions of meaning, for many words possess domains with marginal protuberances which do not seem to fit into the regular patterns. For example, it is not too difficult for us to treat the central domain of *dog*, when we are dealing merely with the different species of *canis familiaris*, but we are often rather hopelessly lost when we branch out into figurative extensions, e.g. (1) a despicable fellow (*he's a dirty dog*), (2) constellations, *the Great Dog* and *the Little Dog*, situated near Orion, (3) mechanical devices for gripping or holding something, (4) an andiron, (5) pretension (*he put on the dog*), and (6) ruin (*he went to the dogs*). Nevertheless, these various extensions of meaning are part and parcel of the semantic structure of *dog*.

Figurative extensions of meaning arise primarily from the process of selecting one or more components of the meaning of a particular term (e.g. physical appearance, psychological disposition, spatial relationships as in part-to-the-whole, or functional similarity) and extending them to cover some object which has not been within the domain of such a word. If an object comes to be included permanently within the domain of a particular word, there is no longer an active figurative extension (i.e. a metaphor), but simply an increase in the area of meaning of the term in question.

The interpretation of figurative meanings must carefully consider these componential features, for whatever logical validity these figurative extensions may have is based entirely upon the shared componential features and not upon any total identity. For example, *a mighty fortress is our God* does not mean that God is literally a fortress, but that certain features regarded as characteristic of a fortress, e.g. strength, protection, safety, unassailableness, are also the qualities of God. In general such figures of speech are built upon some feature recognized by the people of a particular speech community as being dominant, e.g. wolf (prowling rapaciousness), fox (sneakiness, cleverness), pig (gluttony), skunk (foul repulsiveness). At times entirely different symbols may have roughly similar metaphorical value, for they share certain qualities which, when extended in figurative language, become approximately the same, e.g. *baloney, applesauce*, and *nuts*, all of which can be used to mean rejection of something as worthless.

Not all societies or speech communities make the same extensions. We, for example, do not employ *antelope* in metaphors, though this word is widely used in metaphors in Africa. Moreover, different languages may use the same term with quite different metaphorical significance. In American English the term *coon* (a shortened form of *raccoon*) is a contemptuous figurative name for Negroes, and on the basis of this association produces a number of further figurative extensions. The equivalent of *raccoon* in some American Indian languages of the Middle West is used with metaphorical extensions which involve culturally approved dexterity and intelligence. Languages also differ greatly in their styles of figurative expressions. For example, most animal metaphors in English, e.g. *fox, rat, bear, walrus, bull*, and *worm*, refer to presumed psychological characteristics. In Zuñi, however, the pre-Columbian metaphors employing animal words referred to physical characteristics, e.g. an individual's hands are "rough like the feet of a turkey"; someone is "as bald or downy-headed as an eaglet"; his eyes "protrude like a rat's"; he has "bony legs like a bird" (Stanley Newman, 1954).

Languages may also differ in the extent to which they employ metaphorical extensions, especially in certain areas of the vocabulary. In English, for example, we have a number of metaphors based on animals (e.g. *fox, rat, ass, goat, monkey*), insects (e.g. *louse, bug, fly*), flowers (e.g. *pansy, lily, rose*), vegetables (e.g. *tomato, beans, onions*), and fruits (e.g. *banana, apple*). However, English has nothing like the number of metaphors common in Brazilian Portuguese, in which almost all animals, fruits, and vegetables have certain metaphorical extensions of meaning, many with vulgar connotations.

Languages differ also in the readiness with which they admit new figures of speech. For example, Tarascan, a language of Mexico, which has a number of metaphors, does not readily admit new ones. In contrast, Cuna, a language of Panama, not only has many metaphors but admits new ones readily, apparently with considerable cultural approval, and even avidity.

An essential part of the communicative power of figures of speech is derived from the central meaning of the word, which still continues as an active force. Once the central meaning—which provides the basis for extension of some componential quality—is lost, the figure also loses its force; for the strength of the figure lies in the relationship established between the central, or core, meaning and the extension.

SEMANTICALLY ENDOCENTRIC AND EXOCENTRIC EXPRESSIONS

In the essentially arbitrary nature of language as a code, there is no way of knowing the meaning of a single symbol by merely examining its form. Thus there is nothing in the forms of such words as *boy, girl, dish, newt,* and *snow* which would tell us their referents. Similarly, there are many combinations of words to whose meaning the constituent parts offer little or no clue. For example, the Hebrew idiom *children of the bridechamber* refers to the wedding guests, and specifically to the friends of the bridegroom; but adding up the component parts of the phrase does not provide a clue to this meaning. The same situation applies to all kinds of so-called idioms, e.g. *heap coals of fire on his head, from the frying pan into the fire, keep your shirt on, twiddle your thumbs, a monkey wrench in the machinery,* and *bats in the belfry.*

Such expressions, for which the meaning cannot be determined on the basis of the constituent parts, constitute lexical units, whether they are single morphemes or combinations of morphemes, either so-called words (e.g. *pineapple* and *jack-in-the-pulpit*) or phrases (e.g. *bees in the bonnet* and *bats in the belfry*). These lexical units must be treated essentially as units, as the name implies, and a semantic analysis must also deal with them as with a single word; for the semantically relevant distribution of these units cannot be described in terms of its parts, but must be treated as a whole.

Most combinations of words are not lexical units, but rather what may be called semantically endocentric phrases, of which the meaning of the whole is deducible from the meanings of the parts; e.g. *he is in the house, I want something to eat,* and *between London and New York.* On the other hand, when combinations of words constitute single lexical units, they are semantically exocentric. In such a unit the meaning is not traceable to the signification of the parts or to their arrangement, but applies to the unit as a whole; e.g. *he is in the doghouse* and *between the devil and the deep blue sea.* Of course, the expression *he is in the doghouse* can be endocentric in meaning if it applies to Fido, but if the man of the house is the referent of *he,* the phrase is exocentric, for it means that the man is in trouble with his wife.

Fortunately, languages often supply clues as to whether expressions are endocentric or exocentric. If there is some very obvious doubt, for example, a language may introduce an element meaning 'like' or 'as'. Also, the stylistic form often provides clues to the exocentric character of certain expressions. Since poetic language tends to be more exocentric than prose, the fact that a phrase occurs in a metered context alerts the reader to the probability that it is exocentric, especially if there is a doubt as to its possible endocentric meaning. Moreover, in certain styles of writing, e.g. apocalyptic literature of Biblical times, the preponderance of exocentric phraseology provides a further contextual clue to interpretation.

DISTRIBUTIONAL TECHNIQUES

The third technique we may employ in dealing with a series of meanings of a single lexical unit consists of distributional analysis. It is based upon a frame-and-substitution method, fundamental to any description of distribution. We may concentrate our attention, however, either on (1) the frame, or context, as does Martin Joos (1958b) or (2) the types of substitutes, as treated by Nida (1963b).

In approaching the problem of meanings of single words, Joos selected a large number of uses, 500 in all, of the English word *code*, each, together with its context, on a separate slip of paper. He began his analysis by sorting the various meanings into separate piles. For example, a citation mentioning the Napoleonic Code went in the same pile with one mentioning the Soviet penal code. Other piles included "rigid moral code," "code of sexual morality," and still others included citations for plumbing and building codes and codes of ethics of physicians and lawyers. Ultimately there were fourteen different piles, representing a variety of related meanings. These are listed by Joos as follows (though given here with a somewhat different type of numeration):

1. Formalism: 'nuances can be codified' [pattern (of items) replacing continuous gradation]
2. Codification: 'official compilation of statutes is called a code'
3. Law: 'law is not a permanently fixed code determined by Time or J. Edgar Hoover'
4. Rule [public]: 'safety code'; Good Form [private]: 'code of good manners'
5. Custom [public]: 'the Dog Lovers' code'; Conduct [private]: 'code of honor'
6. Ethics: 'a meticulous perfectionist who strives to live by a rigid code' [the Golden Rule]
7. Morals: 'there is little left within the family or the moral code to hold marriage together'
8. Ritual: 'in the Communist code book, opposition is sabotage' [ritual expulsion of M, M, and K]
9. Crypto-secrecy: 'the aristocrat of the cipher family is code', 'indecipherable code dispatch'
10. Clique-language: '[teen-agers] "language"—or perhaps code would be a better word'
11. Condensation [public]: 'code of poetic diction'; Jargon [private]: 'operating room code'
12. Recoding [public]: 'plain international code'; Code-naming [private]: 'code name: "slang"'

13. Language: 'study of the message (and the code) lies in the province of linguistics'
14. Lexicon: 'taxonomic code of botany'

As the analysis continued, the relationship between the piles of meanings gradually became increasingly clear, not merely on the basis of obviously related sets of meanings, but by virtue of the fact that the contexts of certain meanings revealed significant groupings. For example, meanings 2-7 referred to regularity, and 8-14 had to do with symbolization. Likewise, features of public and private character of the codes showed some interesting distributions, for public could be applied to items 11-14 and 1-5, while private was applicable to item meanings 4-12. Thus there was some overlapping, and yet the areas of applicability were continuous. As was soon found to be the case, this series of meanings had to be treated as a circle, in which meaning 14 actually came next to meaning 1.

This grouping of meanings in a circle was discovered in two ways. First, wherever a use of *code* could be applied to more than one pile, it was applicable, with the exception of one instance out of the 500, to contiguous piles. Moreover, such an ambiguous meaning was, strangely enough, always applicable to an odd number of piles, in which case it was always assigned to the center pile. In the second place, collocations of attributive terms, e.g. *rigid, strict, ethical, religious,* and *military,* were almost always (only one exception in the many instances checked) applicable to contiguous piles. For example, *strict* could be used with meanings 3-7, *rigid* with meanings 4-7, *ethical* with meanings 5-7, and *religious* with meanings 6-8.

This classification of meanings of a term on the basis of its collocations is a kind of calculus, by which one may analyze not only the range of distribution, but also the significant classes grouped at various points. In each instance, however, attention is focused primarily on the types of co-occurring items. Such a technique of analysis is relatively objective and proves to be a very important tool for discriminating meanings and discovering semantic structure. It is, however, a decidedly involved technique, requiring a vast body of data and almost complete control of the lexical resources of the language.

The results of this treatment of *code* should, as Joos indicates, not be interpreted to imply that all sets of meanings will turn out to be circular. In fact, there may be a number of different "shapes" of such relationships. Furthermore, some sets of meanings will undoubtedly result in irregular and unsystematic shapes. However, it is important to note that underlying some of the apparently meaningless multiplicity of meanings can be found certain significant structural features.

Despite the complexity of this approach to semantic structure, it is possible to apply it in a limited way to the type of materials one finds listed in a concordance. A listing of words in contexts provides the very collocations needed for setting up some of the major divisions in meaning. Since, moreover, the corpus of Biblical materials is rather large, especially for the Old Testament, a concordance provides an excellent basis for the study of meaning, as scholars have realized for a long time. They have not, however, treated such meanings in terms of a comprehensive calculus, with varying degrees of overlapping positions. Usually they have attempted, rather, to define more or less rigidly the boundaries between various meanings, with results which seem neat, but are usually over-simplified and not reflective of the actual facts of language usage.

The distributional technique proposed by Nida (1963b) concentrates attention primarily on the substitutes, rather than on the frame. However, this substitution technique is much simpler to apply than Joos's analysis by context and in many ways is more useful, especially for the translator. In applying this technique one examines first a series of expressions containing the lexical unit in question, e.g. *chair* in the following phrases:

1. sat in a chair
2. the baby's high-chair
3. the chair of philosophy
4. has accepted a university chair
5. chairman of the meeting
6. will chair the meeting
7. the electric chair
8. condemned to the chair

The next step in the procedure is to find what substitutes for *chair* may be used in these phrases without introducing a different referent. The criterion for determining whether the referent is the same or different is the reaction of a native speaker of the language, i.e. whether he insists that in the substitution of another form one is "saying the same thing but in different words," or that one is saying something different. Another way of employing this type of restriction is to determine whether the altered expression could be used in substantially the same nonlinguistic (or practical world) context, i.e. in speaking about the same event or objects under the same total circumstances. For example, it is equally possible to say of a particular event *he sat in the chair* or *he sat in the piece of furniture*. Stylistically these two phrases are different, but they may be employed to refer to precisely the same event.

The substitutions employed in this type of semantic analysis are not, of course, the same as are required in formal analysis. For example, we could not use the substitute *baby's high piece of furniture*, just because in one instance *piece of furniture* was a substitute for *chair*. However, one can speak about the baby's *high-chair* as a *piece of furniture*. On the other hand, *chair* in phrases 3 and 4 is never substituted for by *piece of furniture*, but rather by *teaching position* or by *post*. In contexts 5 and 6 one may speak of *presiding over the meeting*, and in contexts 7 and 8 a typical substitute would be *death* or *execution*, e.g. *condemned to death*.

If we sort out the various types of substitutes which may be made within a frame, while still identifying (or speaking of) the same event or object in question, we arrive at four significantly different types of substitutions in the case of *chair*: (1) *piece of furniture*, (2) *position* or *post*, (3) *preside*, and (4) *death* or *execution*. These substitutions thus give us basic clues to four different areas of meaning of the word *chair*. These four different meanings, however, stand for whole clusters of contexts, and in proportion as they are widely separated from one another they are likely to give us clues to diverse ways of handling such meanings in other languages.

In instances in which a phrase appears ambiguous, e.g. *he took the chair*, we need only ask what type of substitute may be used in the practical situation to give us a clue to the specific areas of meaning involved. For example, this phrase may mean (1) *he took the piece of furniture* (and carried it away), (2) he accepted the *post* at the university, or (3) he began to *preside*.

The four meanings of *chair* as discovered by means of the possible substitutions (i.e. in speaking about the same events or objects, but with different words, and not necessarily in precisely the same formal frames as used in structural analysis) may be variously related, with a certain amount of overlapping. However, in proportion to the degree that such clusters of contexts and substitutions are separate from one another (i.e. have the fewest instances of overlapping), one can expect that other languages will have diverse ways of speaking about the corresponding phenomena.

This distributional technique may ultimately add up to essentially the same results as those found by Joos's approach. The advantages of concentrating upon the substitutions, rather than upon the frame, are: (1) the approach may be applied to a small number of instances; (2) relatively reliable data can be readily elicited from native speakers of a language; (3) the variety and range of substitutions lead readily into further explorations of related semantic areas; and (4) the extent of the semantic space between types of substitutions often provides important clues to lexical differences which are crucial for the translator.

This technique of setting up different classes of meaning on the basis of substitutions may also be regarded as a classification of meanings by the use of synonyms, a technique as old as dictionary making. The distinctive feature of this frame-and-substitution technique of semantic analysis is simply that it provides a formal basis for analyzing the classes and degrees of synonymity. After all, the extent to which certain words may substitute for others within certain linguistic and cultural contexts is precisely the most crucial element in semantic structure; for if, as linguists insist, the meaning of lexical units is essentially a matter of the potentiality of occurrence or distribution—whether within the language itself or within the total cultural framework—then the extent to which certain words share these distributions is a focal area for semantic analysis.

THE USE OF STRUCTURAL CONTRASTS FOR THE ANALYSIS OF MEANING

In the previous sections of this chapter we have examined a number of techniques for analyzing different aspects of referential and emotive meanings. All of these have varying degrees of usefulness as heuristic tools, and many are valuable for describing certain domains of meaning and some of the problems of contextual conditioning. None of these theories, however, provide a comprehensive system for semantic analysis, for in one or more ways they lack certain indispensable features. For one thing, these theories fail to show the relationship between those elements of meaning which are linguistically structured and those which are dependent upon nonlinguistic elements in the cultural setting. At the same time, in most instances referential meanings and emotive meanings are so isolated from each other that they seem structurally unrelated. Furthermore, it is extremely difficult in most cases to incorporate extensions of meaning into the structural analysis, and in fact peripheral meanings are in general carefully excluded, or "selectively forgotten." Another rather conspicuous failure is the lack of proper co-ordination between features of field and context.

What we require in an adequate theory of semantics is a system which will provide an explanation of the procedures whereby the native speaker of a language may interpret an infinite variety of messages, most of which are novel to him. We need to know how he is able to select the appropriate meaning of terms, how he recognizes ambiguity when it does exist, and how he senses that two quite different utterances are essentially paraphrases of each other. How does the hearer know, for example, that *green* in *green house* has quite a different meaning from what it has in *greenhouse*? How does he recognize that there is an obvious typographical error in the sentence *he will lead the book through*? And what tells him that the sentences *two cops dashed after him* and *a couple of policemen chased after him* are substantially equivalent in meaning? As indicated in Chapter 3, the most useful theory which has been developed to date is that of Katz and Fodor (1963), and in general the exposition which follows is based upon their highly important insights.

In attempting to explain how the speaker of a language can produce and understand any of an infinite series of utterances, including those wholly novel to him, a linguistic theory must, of course, carefully distinguish between grammar and semantics. In general we may say that the grammar is designed to explain that part of the language which depends upon the relationship of classes of words to one another, even though a class may have only a single member. Thus grammar deals entirely with the linguistic context of words. The semantic analysis of a language, however, attempts to explain primarily the relationship of individual words and combinations of words to the nonlinguistic contexts of utterances—whether on the level of referential or emotive meanings.

THE ROLE OF CONTEXT

The sentence *this coat is lighter* has two distinct meanings: (1) the coat does not weigh as much as another object (presumably another coat), and (2) the color of the coat is not as "dark" as another. This ambiguity is not based on any grammatical "duplicity" (overlapping of structures), but merely upon the fact that the word *lighter* has two "meanings," that is to say, is related to two different features of the nonlinguistic world. To make this sentence unambiguous all that we would have to do would be to add *in weight* (in which case the first meaning would be signaled) or *in shade* (in which case the hearer would understand the second meaning). It is not necessary, however, to employ such specific terms as *weight* and *shade*, for the proper meaning may be derived "indirectly" from expressions which point to the same areas of signification as a secondary rather than as a primary semantic specification. For example, *this coat is lighter, since it is made of vicuna cloth* is obviously a reference to weight; and *this coat is lighter than even those spring pastels* is evidently a reference to color.

In isolation an utterance may have a number of "readings" (or meanings). For example, single words spoken in isolation may have numerous referents. A word such as *degree* may have the following meanings: (1) step or stage in an ascending or descending scale (*to the nth degree*), (2) measure of proximity in blood relationship (*he is two degrees removed*), (3) the 360th part of a complete angle or turn (*a 45-degree angle*), (4) a unit of measurement of temperature (*40 degrees centigrade*), (5) a geographical unit of measurement (*ten degrees east and thirty degrees north*), (6) relative measure of criminality (*first degree murder*), (7) an academic title (*a Ph. D. degree*), and (8) one of the three inflectional formations of adjectives and adverbs (*the comparative degree of fine is finer*). If, however, we use the word *degree* in a context, for example, *he has three degrees*, we can readily eliminate all the meanings except 4 and 7, and if we add, *but his temperature is not likely to rise*, we then have narrowed the meaning down to 4. Sometimes, of course, the clue to the proper meaning of a term is not to be found within the same sentence, but rather in the total discourse. For example, if the general subject matter is mathematics or insurance rates, then *table* will in all likelihood have quite a different meaning from what it would in a discussion of land reclamation and irrigation, where *table* would generally refer to surface features of the terrain (e.g. tableland) or the level of underground water resources (e.g. water table).

In general we assume that in the case of most messages the source of any utterance had one and only one intention in communicating. However, there are some types of messages which are purposely ambiguous (e.g. those of the famous Delphic oracle), and many literary works have more than one level of meaning—usually one overt level and one or more covert levels. Of course, many messages with multiple meanings are simply the result of imprecise handling of the language.

As noted in Chapter 4, some ambiguities in language result from the overlapping of grammatical structures, but these ambiguities are generally explicated by the context. In the Greek Gospels of the New Testament there are over 500 such grammatical ambiguities, but fully 90 per cent of these are resolved by the immediate context. In English the expression *I hit the man with a stick* is ambiguous, but the expanded form *I hit the man with a stick which I had picked up along the road* is not. Similarly *the fat major's wife* is ambiguous, but there is no such ambiguity in the fuller expression *the fat major's wife was always promising to diet but never kept at it.*

THE ESSENTIAL COMPONENTS IN A SEMANTIC THEORY

In the same way that a generative grammar requires an essential inventory of morphemes and a series of projection rules to state their patterns of occurrence, so a semantic theory requires a dictionary and a set of projection rules for describing the ways in which such lexical elements combine into meaningful expressions.

A dictionary is basic for three reasons. In the first place, we must be able to distinguish what is different in expressions which are grammatically the same and semantically diverse, e.g. *the girl hit him* and *the boy hit him*. The grammar cannot distinguish between *girl* and *boy*, but the dictionary must. Moreover, we need to know about expressions which are grammatically the same and morphemically different, but more or less semantically equivalent, e.g. *the cops shot him* and *the policemen shot him*. Similarly, we must be able to analyze the relationships between

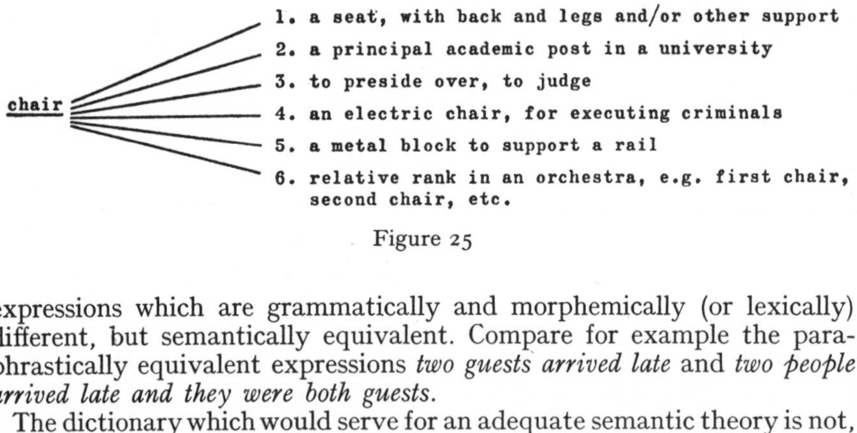

chair
1. a seat, with back and legs and/or other support
2. a principal academic post in a university
3. to preside over, to judge
4. an electric chair, for executing criminals
5. a metal block to support a rail
6. relative rank in an orchestra, e.g. first chair, second chair, etc.

Figure 25

expressions which are grammatically and morphemically (or lexically) different, but semantically equivalent. Compare for example the paraphrastically equivalent expressions *two guests arrived late* and *two people arrived late and they were both guests.*

The dictionary which would serve for an adequate semantic theory is not, however, merely some typical exhaustive dictionary, such as is commonly published today. For one thing, a semantic theory about the synchronic functioning of a language does not require information on pronunciation, etymology, and cognate relationships to words in other languages. What is required is a listing of all the meanings (linguistic, referential, and emotive) structured in such a way as to reveal the patterns of structural contrasts which form the framework of meaning. Unfortunately, in most dictionaries descriptions of meaning consist merely of lists of diverse usages, as in Figure 25.

Such a description of the meaning of *chair* is not too satisfactory, for there are obviously various degrees of relatedness between the diverse meanings.

This is very evident when in interpreting sentences using the word *chair* we discover that there are various types of ambiguity, which are resolved on different levels. For example, *he sat in the chair* can apply to meanings 1, 3, and 4. *He accepted the chair* may refer to 1, 2, 3, 5, and 6; *he was given the chair* may apply to 1 and 2; and *he had the first chair* may involve meanings 1 and 6. If we chart all of these patterns of real and potential ambiguity and determine the types of contexts which will resolve such ambiguities, we can diagram the semantic structure of *chair* in a more meaningful way, as in Figure 26.

There are several important features in the diagram of Figure 26.

1. The semantic markers enclosed in parentheses indicate the crucial points in the semantic structure, where potentially or actually ambiguous expressions are most economically differentiated.

2. The terms used in the semantic markers are merely convenient devices for signaling certain dominant features of the contrasts which exist between the sets of meanings. They are not all-inclusive in meaning nor necessarily always the most significant differentiations for all contexts. They should however be as relevant and as diagnostic as possible for the majority of contexts. The labels for the semantic markers are, of course, not as important as the recognition of the points of structural contrast.

3. The labels for parts of speech (N for noun and V for verb) are purposely placed at those points in the "tree" where they can most economically represent a part of the "linguistic meaning." For languages such as English, in which there is a considerable lack of parallelism between form classes and semantic functioning, it is not only more economical but also more valid to classify meanings in terms of their contrasting semantic functions first and then to label the particular grammatical functions which the lexical unit may have in such a semantic context.

4. The emotive meanings are symbolically indicated by plus or minus within { }. If there were sufficient space, one should provide an explanation as to the fact that terminal meanings 4-6 are generally characterized by favorable emotive meanings involving prestige, while terminal meaning 2 involves emotive meanings of disfavor and avoidance. The use of plus and minus is only the most general form for indicating positive and negative emotive reactions. Such symbols are, however, placed on the semantic tree, since they may be related to more than one terminal meaning. There are, of course, many emotive meanings which are not merely positive and negative. A full semantic theory would need to have a number of sets of symbols to mark such emotive meanings or to identify the fact that some significant emotive values are associated with certain meanings or groups of meanings, with fuller explanations given as "footnotes" to the tree of semantic structure.

5. The order of the terminal meanings is very important. For example, if we know from the context that the meaning of *chair* is object rather than role, then if there is no other identifying element in the context, we assume that the meaning is 1, namely, a piece of furniture. In other words, it is meaning 3 which needs to be specifically marked to indicate that it is a "chair for nonhuman use." If at the same time we know that *chair* is for human use, we assume that the meaning is number 1, unless the

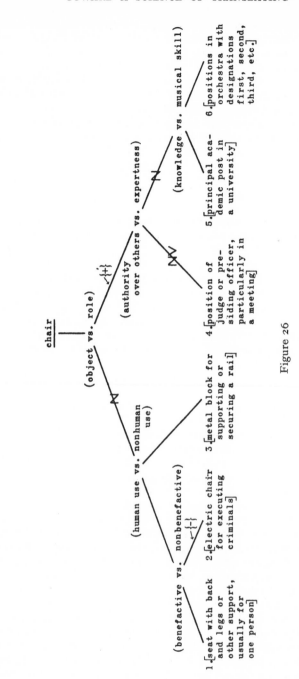

Figure 26

context specifically identifies meaning 2. On the other hand, if the context points to the meaning of *chair* as being a role rather than an object, then unless there is further specification of meaning we assume that the meaning is 4, namely, "presiding," "taking the chairmanship of a meeting," etc., rather than having the post of professor in a university or a position in an orchestra. This order of meaning is structurally important and provides the clue to the problem of "central vs. peripheral" meanings, for within the semantic structure there are several different grades of priority depending upon the complexity of structure in the semantic tree, and in each case the central meaning, having priority, need not be marked, while the peripheral meanings must be marked if we are to interpret the expression correctly.

6. The terminal meanings are not designed to describe all the features of the referents, but only those which distinguish the meanings from each other and from other lexical units which may overlap on the same referential domain. Greater specificity than is provided by the terminal meanings must be indicated by attributive expressions which further particularize the referent in question: e.g. (1) *the wobbly chair with the antique cane seat*, (2) *the huge sinister chair in the special room at the end of death row*, (3) *the iron chair which cracked from heat and the pounding of the freight trains*, (4) *despite extreme reluctance he agreed to chair the meeting*, (5) *he got the chair of philosophy only because his father had endowed the department*, and (6) *he played first-chair cornet with Sousa*.

There are several important factors which must be borne in mind when dealing with these classifications of meanings. In the first place, this is not an attempt to arrange the meanings of *chair* in any logical structure, based on shape, size, historical derivation, or similarities of form or function. We are only concerned here with the manner in which the language itself structures these meanings by resolving the ambiguities which may occur. Our first cut, division, or "node" is determined by the most significant high-level distinction which is signaled by the context, and each successive level is likewise determined by the degree of particularity in the context which identifies the alternative meanings.

One can be misled to some extent by the nature of the "semantic markers" which mark each node, for they would seem to be logically derived distinctions rather than merely labels for certain types of contextual cues which are significant in identifying the meanings involved. That is to say, the distinction of "object vs. role" is not based on any *a priori* logical system, but only on the fact that the most relevant types of contexts which distinguish potential ambiguities in the use of *chair* have words which signal whether the term is to be understood as being an object or a role. In other words, the classifications involved in these "tree structures" are not based upon any philosophical presuppositions, but are merely the results of examining various sets of ambiguities and noting the manner in which the language resolves them.

One could, of course, treat meanings in quite another way. For example, it would be possible to list all the various meanings of a term and then to list alongside of each meaning those particular types of contextual clues which help to identify the subdivisions in meanings. But to do this would inevitably involve one in a great deal of duplication. Moreover, certain cues or markers make very broad distinctions, while others are much more limited. Therefore, it seems only right that where such a hierarchical structuring exists it should be recognized, for such a method of dealing with the structure not only simplifies our understanding of the basic problems but also much more effectively explicates the relationships.

It is, however, most important to recognize at this point that speakers of a language may differ to some extent in their semantic classifications. This is not strange, for there are dialect differences on the levels of phonology and grammar, and it is therefore quite understandable that there should also be diversities of usage in semantics. A high percentage of these differences result from the fact that for a number of words many people have relatively specialized orientations. For example, some persons may not know the meaning of *chair* as a device for holding a rail. Others may make little or no use of the meaning of "first chair," "second chair," etc. In such instances we would merely have to describe the semantic structure of *chair* in a somewhat simpler way. On the other hand, one must also realize that practical circumstances as well as verbal signals may act as contextual conditioners of meaning. In a strictly academic setting, for instance, the mention of *chair* may imply a role, rather than an object, even though there is no verbal cue. In fact, when the situation of communication is highly precise, the addition of verbal cues seems unnecessary, if not pedantic. Certain of these problems of alternative structures and contextual conditioning will be even more evident in the treatment of the word *spirit*, as diagramed in Figure 27.

Figure 27, which provides a diagramatic sketch of the semantic structure of *spirit*, illustrates some of the more complex types of semantic relationships. Certain features of this analysis should be specially noted:

1. The diagram is purposely simplified by the elimination of the meaning of *spirit* as an event, e.g. *he spirited the corpse away*. The addition of this meaning would require a top-level distinction between object (and object-related features) vs. event. Similarly, we have omitted *spirits*, as used in the phrase *spirits of ammonia*.

2. Since all the uses of *spirit* in the diagram are nominal, the symbol N occurs at the top of the tree.

3. The same semantic marker may occur at various points in the tree, depending upon the complexity of the structure, e.g. *human vs. nonhuman*. It may be argued, of course, that one could employ the distinction *human vs. nonhuman* as the top-level dichotomy, since this distinction occurs in both branches. But if this is done, the resulting classifications do not reflect the most economical patterns of resolution of ambiguities. Moreover, the dichotomies *human vs. nonhuman* in these two positions in the semantic tree are not identical, for one distinguishes between objects having personality and those which do not, while the other distinguishes different types of character (in contrast with substance).

4. The order of left-hand and right-hand branching is presumed to reflect the unconditioned reaction of the average speaker. This could,

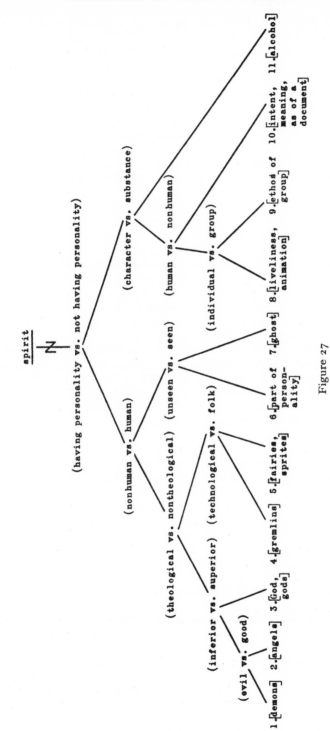

Figure 27

of course, be tested psychologically by getting informants to provide their ordered response to lexical symbols. Actually, of course, the order of 1, 2, 3, 4, 5, etc. throughout the series of terminal meanings is not what is important, except indirectly as it reflects marked and unmarked contexts higher up on the semantic tree. What is important is that without contextual evidence the average speaker is probably more likely to understand *spirit* in terms of something having personality or related to personality, rather than the opposite. Similarly, if the meaning is clearly indicative of personality, then the hearer is more likely to think of this in terms of nonhuman spirit rather than human, and so forth. Of course, some speakers of English can be so conditioned by their backgrounds and usage of their language that their semantic structuring of *spirit* may be different. For example, they may have used this word so much in contexts relating to human personality that for their speech the order of semantic contrasts is reversed, in which case the human meaning may be contextually unmarked while the nonhuman will require contextual marking. Actually, of course, in order to work out the details of this theory of semantic analysis, we would need a wide sampling of usage by the speakers of a language; and in the same way that dialectal differences are encountered on a formal level, one can expect to find equally important divergencies on a semantic level.

5. The terminal meanings in this diagram are only suggestive rather than being carefully descriptive.

6. The terminal meanings 8, 9, 10, and 11 may be illustrated by the following contexts respectively: *he really showed a lot of spirit, the college spirit was grand despite the defeat, the spirit of this law is certainly not vindictive,* and *a spirit lamp.*

7. The distinction *having personality* vs. *not having personality* applies to referents which are conceived of as possessing a separate personality or being a part of personality vs. those which are without individual personality, i.e. as a feature or characteristic of human activity or as a completely impersonal substance.

8. It is most important to note that in this treatment of the meanings of *spirit* we are not attempting to classify the referents themselves, but the concepts which speakers have about such referents and which are reflected in the uses of the term *spirit.* We are not concerned with the referents as such but with the manner in which language is used to speak about such referents.

9. It is easy to confuse the distinction between unmarked and marked order of sequence (as reflected in the left-hand and right-hand branches of the semantic tree) with differences of frequency. It is true that an unmarked meaning is often the more frequent, but our criteria for selecting the order of branching are not patterns of frequency but of contextual conditioning.

10. Some brief explanation of certain problems in the left-hand branch of this diagram below the label "nonhuman vs. human" may be relevant for our understanding of this approach to the structure of meaning. By means of the semantic marker "theological vs. nontheological" we

attempt to distinguish whether the context has serious religious content, or is on quite another level. It would have been possible to use the label "religious vs. nonreligious," but since there are so many controversies as to the meaning of "religious," it has seemed more satisfactory to use "theological," even though strictly speaking such a term would apply only to discussions of "God" and "gods."

If, however, the context indicates that the meaning is "nontheological", then the further distinction "technological vs. folk" is significant. For example, the use of the word *spirit* in speaking about machinery or airplanes can only mean a kind of "gremlin," while after a phrase such as *once upon a time* we expect to have the meaning of "fairy" or "sprite."

If the context is obviously "theological," there is a further distinction between superior power, which is marked, and an inferior power, which at this level may not be marked. Some such statements as "the Spirit which created the universe" or "the Spirit which controls the destinies of men" certainly point to a meaning of *spirit* which may be described as "God" or "gods." Even the use of capitalization is a clue to the right-hand meaning and an evidence that we feel the need of marking this meaning. On the other hand, if the term *spirit* identifies an inferior power, then there is usually some clue as to evil or good characteristics, e.g. "surrounded by protecting spirits" (i.e. angels), and "the spirits drove him mad" (i.e. demons). If, however, we know that the meaning is either "demons or angels," then it is the meaning of demons which is normally unmarked, and the meaning of "angels" which requires some contextual clue.

It is most important to realize that in this classification we are not attempting to classify demons, angels, God, gods, gremlins, fairies, etc., but only to distinguish the related meanings of *spirit* which may be identified roughly by these terminal meanings enclosed in brackets.

In contrast with some of the special problems of *spirit*, which involve referents for which there are so few perceptual models, a study of the word *rule* in Figure 28 provides a number of other important features.

Figure 28, which consists of a sketch of the semantic structure of *rule*, includes several features which should be specially studied:

1. The symbols V and N come at different points in the hierarchy on the basis of economy of representation. Such placements are, however, highly important for our appreciation of the relationships between formal and semantic structuring.

2. Some of the points of structural contrast, e.g. the distinction between meanings 7 and 8, are so trivial as not to require a dichotomous semantic marker. One could specify that 7 normally has a scale for measurement while 8 does not, but this is not sufficiently significant for our purposes. We may accordingly merely list both as being instruments, and let the terminal meanings specify the particular nature of the differences.

3. Semantic markers are primarily of two types: (1) those which mark positive-negative dichotomies, e.g. nonobject vs. object and verbal vs. nonverbal, and (2) descriptive contrasts, e.g. event vs. abstract, conceptual vs. behavioral, executive vs. judicial. In general there is a

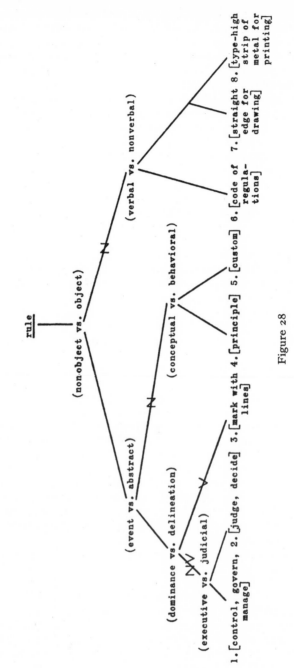

Figure 28

tendency for the positive-negative dichotomies to occur on higher levels, while the descriptive contrasts are more likely to occur on lower levels, but this is by no means always the case. By arranging for a number of added "steps" it might be possible to describe semantic structures by purely positive-negative dichotomies, but these would be unduly artificial and cumbersome. Though much of experience can be and is classified in popular usage by positive-negative binary contrasts, such a system is not universal.

4. There are certain relationships in meaning which are not indicated in this semantic diagram of structural contrasts. For example, meaning 6 is referentially related to 1 and 2 and meanings 7 and 8 show a relationship to 3. With a multidimensional diagram we could undoubtedly also plot some of these additional semantic relationships, but these are not the essential elements in our theory of semantic contrasts based upon patterns of ambiguity and points of resolution of such ambiguities.

SEMANTIC MARKERS

Though in the preceding sections we have discussed a number of features of semantic markers, it is important to summarize at this point some of the salient characteristics of these indispensable elements in the description of the semantic structure:

1. *Points of occurrence.* Semantic markers occur at those points in bifurcation of meaning which are "signaled" by the manner in which such ambiguities are resolved.

2. *Types of semantic markers.* The semantic markers are basically of two types: (a) positive-negative dichotomies and (b) descriptive contrasts. The choice of the particular type of semantic markers for any point depends upon the manner in which the language resolves the ambiguity. In other words, if the ambiguity can be resolved by a simple yes-no contrast, then the marker is positive-negative, but if the solution to the ambiguity consists in describing the respective areas of signification, then the marker must incorporate these descriptive contrasts. For the most part these differences are binary or dyadic, but they may be singular or multiple (or polyadic).

3. *Order of elements in the semantic markers.* The order is determined by the unmarked and marked features of the terminal usages. That is to say, the meaning which is most likely to be understood without contextual conditioning is regarded as unmarked, while the one which requires such contextual "strengthening" is marked. There are many instances, of course, in which there is no clear-cut distinction, since both meanings seem to be equally probable.

4. *Categories in semantic markers.* The possibilities for types of distinctions in semantic markers is theoretically unlimited. However, in the high-level distinctions one often finds such contrasts as object vs. event, event vs. abstract, object vs. abstract, human vs. nonhuman, animate vs. inanimate, natural vs. supernatural. In the low-level distinctions contrasts are often based on differences in sex, age, size, shape, time, space, value, and intensity.

It is important to note that the terms *object, event,* and *abstract* in their use in labels of semantic markers have a significantly different meaning from their usage in labels for features of linguistic meaning (see Chapter 4). As convenient devices for describing certain functions in the transformational structure these words designate only certain syntactic distributions. As elements in the labels for semantic markers, they specify certain significant contrasts in the concepts which speakers have of the referents themselves.

For each word of a language the order and type of categories expressed by the semantic markers depend entirely upon the semantic structure of the word in question, so that a category which is a high-level marker for one word may occur as a relatively lower-level distinction in another. However, for a language as a whole certain categories tend to cluster as high-level and others appear to be predominantly low-level.

Languages quite naturally differ as to the types and frequency of various categories. For example, in many languages shape and size are very important and are often signaled by the morphological structure itself. In other languages sex differentiation plays an important role, while in many languages animate vs. inanimate is a primary semantic category.

In the history of languages some of the semantic categories which are relevant for semantic markers have become overtly marked by morphological elements and in this way are often frozen into the word structures. For example, in many of the Bantu languages, the same root may occur with quite different prefixes, which immediately mark the term as to whether the referent is one of several classes, e.g. animate, inanimate, concrete, mass, individual, or collective. In Zulu the root *-ntu* may occur as *isintu* 'Bantu characteristics, culture, language'; *ubuntu* 'human nature, humaneness'; *uluntu* 'common people'; and *umuntu* (sing.) / *abantu* (pl.) 'person, African, Zulu tribesman'.

5. *Parallelism with formal structure.* Formal word classes and distinctions indicated by semantic markers are often parallel, as in the above data cited from Zulu and as indicated in Chapter 4, in which the formal word classes and the categories of objects, events, abstracts, and relationals were discussed. There is, however, always some lack of conformity, and often this nonconformity is very extensive. Accordingly, one is entirely unjustified in trying to force conformity upon the data, since the very lack of conformity is itself structurally significant.

It is very important not to confuse the use of similar categories on formal and semantic levels. For example, in English we may speak of sex (or gender) distinctions on a formal level by pointing out patterns of substitution for *he, she,* and *it* and *who* and *which.* This is, however, quite different from saying that a word such as *bachelor* generally means male, except in the meaning of "lowest of the academic degrees" (which includes no sex distinction) and that *prostitute* is female in unmarked contexts but may apply to males in marked contexts.

6. *Discovery procedures in determining semantic markers.* In general the most satisfactory discovery procedures for determining semantic

markers include the following: (1) list all the possible meanings of a word, (2) group these by setting up ambiguous contexts for the most inclusive to the least inclusive classes, (3) determine the manner in which such ambiguities are resolved, and (4) apply satisfactory labels to the points of division.

Though this discovery procedure is ideal, one can often short-circuit such a procedure by "hints" which come from (a) a componential analysis of meaning (important components may mark significant divisions), (b) grouping by context (following Joos's technique, as explained in this chapter), for the various sets of contextual conditionings almost always indicate significant groupings for semantic markers, and (c) substitution procedures (also discussed in this chapter), for differences which are discovered by comparing substitution potentialities usually coincide with important divisions in the "tree" structure.

7. *Labels for semantic markers.* As has been noted, the labels are not as important as the points of division. Moreover, the labels need not be exhaustive or determinative of the contrasts, so much as diagnostic. At times, the distinctions involved are actually too trivial (i.e. too low-level) to warrant marking. In other instances, the differences are so multidimensional (i.e. so extensive), that one must merely select one of the significant features of differentiation, rather than attempt to select some highly generic expression which will presume to include all the distinguishing features.

EMOTIVE MEANINGS

As implied in the previous discussions, emotive meanings are essentially different from referential ones, for they are not structured according to series of dichotomies or contrasts. Rather, emotive meanings consist of polar contrasts separated by a graded series with a high percentage of usages for most words clustering around the neutral position.

To measure the emotive meanings of a word we need a complex matrix for each word. The dimensions of such a matrix could include, for example, a ten-point graded series with such dimensions as good-to-bad, pleasant-to-unpleasant, favorable-to-unfavorable, happy-to-sad, lovable-to-hateful, beautiful-to-ugly, and acceptance-to-rejection. Such dimensions would change from word to word, depending upon patterns of applicability, but if we had the judgments of an adequate sampling of people's reactions to verbal symbols plotted on such a matrix we would have at least a profile of the major emotive features of such words. Obviously words such as *delicious, mother, honeymoon, cat, dog, whore, nasty,* and *bastard* would have quite different profiles.

To test the appropriateness of certain stylistic usages of these and similar words we could measure the match between the emotive values of the words and the types of discourse. For example, in so-called scientific writing we would expect a choice of words which would have a predominantly neutral or central profile. For expressive writing we would expect words which would fit the mood, e.g. *joyous* or *depressed.* For "slanted"

8

writing or speech we could judge the extent to which the profile of the words was in keeping with the intent of the message.

Some communications are, of course, purposely mixed in emotive meanings, as in the expression of irony and sarcasm, e.g. *charming rascal, damnably sweet,* and *deadly attractive.* Some communicators simply want to shock receptors, while others, including a number of existentialist novelists, communicate some of their theme of "absurdity" by the lack of match in the emotive meanings of words.

Within a particular language there are often quite radically different profiles for words, depending upon local usage and individual associations, e.g. *revolution, communism, Republican, Democrat, cotton-pickin',* and *beatnik.* Such differences must simply be treated as dialectal variants.

It is important to note that not all languages have the same dimensions for classification of emotive meanings. For example, in a number of languages in Latin America the distinction of *hot* vs. *cold* is a highly important dichotomy with important emotive overtones.

It must be recognized, of course, that languages tend to differ more radically in emotive meanings than in referential significations. In a number of areas in Africa, for example, there is very little taboo connected with the names of body parts and organic functions, while the names of certain animals, ancestors, and kin involve very heavy emotive significance. As noted in the study of hierarchical structures, the more languages depend upon perceptual models the greater is the agreement between them, and conversely the more they depend on conceptualization the greater are their differences. Patterns of emotive meaning, however, show even wider discrepancies than distinctions based on conceptualization.

Projection Rules

Having determined the linguistic, referential, and emotive potentialities in any combination of words, we are now obliged to set up a series of projection rules which will enable us to determine how the speaker generates and the receptor interprets the semantic elements of the utterance. These projection rules are somewhat similar to those used in describing the formal structures, but in the following analysis we are stating these rules in a highly simplified form so as to make them applicable to practical circumstances. It must be noted that these rules apply only to combinations of lexical units in actual utterances, for it is the meaning of words in context that is explicated by such projection rules.

In practical application the projection rules are essentially the following:

1. *Determine the appropriate linguistic meaning for each successive set of immediate constituents* (i.e. the linguistic meanings of the constructions are handled first). For example, in the two expressions *greenhouse* and *green house* we must first determine the differences of linguistic meaning. The phrase *green house* is obviously a nominal construction in

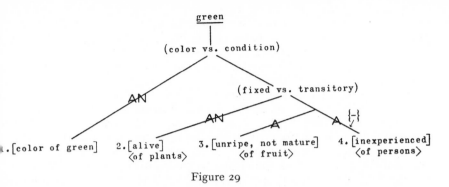

Figure 29

which the head word *house* is qualified in much the same way as it is in
the phrases *red house, white house, big house*, and *old house*. That is to say,
the attributive element (A) qualifies the head element (B). In *greenhouse*
the linguistic meaning of the construction is quite different, for *greenhouse*
occurs in a class of compound words such as *poorhouse* and *madhouse*,
with close structural analogies to other words such as *washhouse, storehouse*,
and *playhouse*. In these words the linguistic meaning is B is for A,
whether of objects which are characterized by a particular condition,
e.g. *poor* and *mad*, or of activities or events, e.g. *wash, store*, and *play*.

2. *Match the semantic structures of the lexical units so as to determine
the extent and types of agreement or parallelism.* If we set up the semantic
structures of *green* and *house* as in Figures 29 and 30, we must then
analyze the types and degree of "fit" for the two different constructions.

In Figure 29, it is important to note the three instances in which a
conditioning feature has been placed within wedges, namely, <of
plants>, <of fruit>, and <of persons>. That is to say, the meanings
of 'alive', 'unripe, not mature', and 'inexperienced' only apply if the
context specifies plants in the first instance, fruit in the second, and
persons in the third.

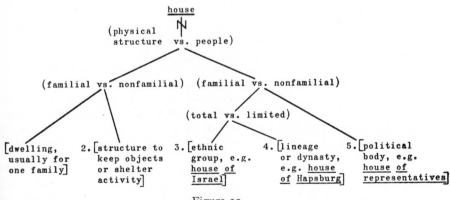

Figure 30

In applying the projection rule for the matching of the semantic structures of *green* and *house*, we first take up the structurally simpler phrase *green house*. On the basis of the linguistic meaning of this construction, namely, that A is attributive to B, our procedure is to match the structures beginning in each instance with the left-hand or unmarked branch to determine if the match is congruent or makes sense. If, for example, we select the first meaning of *green*, namely, a specification of color, and match it with the first meaning of *house*, we obtain a combination which makes sense, that is to say, the results are meaningful and the combination is possible within the limitations of meaning imposed by the construction. Moreover, there is no ambiguity of meaning. Unless the context should tell us something to the contrary, we must therefore assume that this is the proper meaning, for if there is to be a different meaning from this one, we would expect that the context would signal this fact overtly by some special element which would force us to accept one of the right-hand branches of the structure.

Our second task is to determine the meaningful structure of *greenhouse* by applying the projection rules. From the linguistic meaning of the construction we know that green is not attributive to *house*, but that it designates certain objects having a particular characteristic or condition. Our procedure, therefore, is to select the right-hand branch of the structure of *green*, which specifies a condition, rather than a color. Next, we tentatively select the left-hand branch, since in the meanings of 'unripe' and 'inexperienced' we expect some type of contextual marking. Having tentatively selected this meaning of green we then shift to the selection of an appropriate meaning for *house*. Without some marking which would specify the right-hand branch, we accept the left-hand branch, meaning physical structure, but at the juncture of familial vs. nonfamilial we take the right branch, for we earlier encountered no marker that specified the selection of *green* as applying to persons. We then end up with meaning 2 of *green* and meaning 2 for *house*. There is no special significance to the fact that in *green house*, the match is meanings 1 and 1, while in *greenhouse* the match is 2 and 2, except that without heavy contextual conditioning, left-hand meanings are of course more frequent than right-hand ones.

In the description of this selective process it would appear as though we make each selection in turn, beginning with the first lineal member of the utterance and then proceeding to the second, and so on. This, of course, is not true. In actual practice we work in both directions at the same time, and by means of mutual "re-enforcement" we arrive at solutions much more rapidly, for we constantly test possibilities of one meaning by seeing whether this makes sense from the standpoint of the range of meanings for the second element in any construction.

It can be argued that *greenhouse* is basically a single lexical unit, since this compound structure is not readily productive of new combinations. Of course, we could decide to consider *greenhouse* as a lexical unit and not bother with a statement of the semantic structures involved, but the procedures for the mutual delimitation of meaning in the semantic structures of *green* and *house* seem to be sufficiently evident as to warrant such a description. We have, however, excluded from this consideration the phrase *to have a green thumb,* since the meaning of this combination cannot be deduced from the meanings of the constituent parts.

3. *Add such emotive meanings as may be relevant to the interpretation of the utterance.* Normally, emotive meanings simply characterize the referential meanings, but in those instances in which emotive meanings within an utterance are of diverse types, one must suspect (a) shifts of intent, as in irony or sarcasm, or (b) shifts of actual referents, as in figurative language.

These three basic rules are, however, in many instances not sufficient to explicate the semantic structure. For example, in many circumstances ambiguity is not resolved within the construction in which the multiple meanings occur. For example, in the phrase *the lovely ball* we have no idea whether this is a pretty ball for a child to play with or a delightful social occasion, involving a dance. Even when we have the expression *the lovely ball was a huge...,* we are still in doubt, for *huge* could likewise apply to either meaning of *ball.* That is to say, the semantic structure of *huge* covers both terminal meanings of *ball.* If, however, we expand this expression into the form *the lovely ball was a huge success,* we then know that the meaning of *ball* is to be understood as a dance, rather than as a spherical object. A glance at the semantic structure of *ball,* as diagramed in Figure 31, will soon indicate the bases for the ambiguity and the manner in which a word such as *success* resolves the ambiguity by determining the choice of "event" rather than "object."

The clues for resolving a particular ambiguity may not exist within the sentence containing the ambiguity. In fact, they may be anywhere within the total discourse, including the title of the subject matter. To some extent the clues may even exist in the stylistic form, for in a highly poetic type of language we expect many nonliteral meanings. That is to say, the very specialization of form provides the basis for our choosing right-hand rather than left-hand branches in the semantic structure. In other words, we may say that the stylistic form serves as a marker to designate the right-hand alternatives.

The semantic analysis cannot, however, treat any feature which is not overtly present in the discourse. For example, the phrase *it is lighter* is structurally ambiguous. In a particular situation this sentence may be uttered in such a way as to make its meaning very evident to the source and receptor, but these nonlinguistic elements of the context are entirely outside the range of a linguistic theory of meaning. Resolving such an ambiguity depends upon cultural facts, not upon linguistic facts.

In analyzing the meaning of any combination of lexical units there are three possibilities: (1) that the result will equal 1, that is to say, one meaning and only one meaning (in which case the immediate problem is solved), (2) that the result will be more than 1, that is to say, 2, 3, 4, etc., representing various types of ambiguity (in which case, one must look further in the context to attempt to resolve the ambiguity), and (3) that the result will be 0, that is to say, the combinations will make no sense,

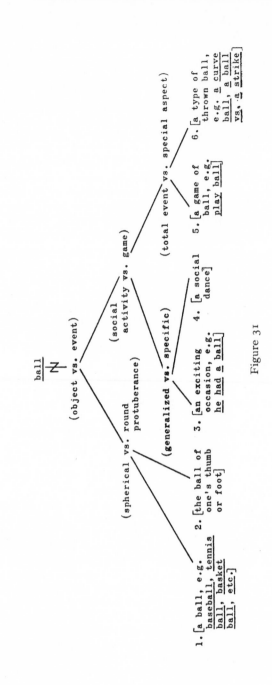

Figure 31

as in *whispering strawberries towered over delicious pine trees*. In a "null" utterance there simply is no congruence of structures and hence no meaning.

If we add together two elements which for the particular context have completely identical structures, the result is tautological. For example, *he is an unmarried bachelor* seems senseless, since in this context the semantic structure of *bachelor* includes the fact of not being married. Hence, the attributive *unmarried* adds nothing.

Synonymity is actually a measure of the extent to which the structures of two or more words are identical. For example, *oculist* and *eye doctor* agree almost completely in referential values. Similarly, *cop* and *policeman*, *joyful* and *glad*, *Negro* and *colored person*, and *dog* and *canis familiaris* may be regarded as referentially synonymous, since their referential structures are so similar.[1] On the other hand, the emotive profiles of *cop* and *policeman* are quite different. Compare also the substitution of *canis familiaris* for *dog* in the expression *love me, love my canis familiaris*.

---

[1] Note, however, that *Negro* and *colored person* are not referentially synonymous in South Africa.

CHAPTER SIX

THE DYNAMIC DIMENSION IN COMMUNICATION

Language consists of more than the meanings of the symbols and the combinations of symbols; it is essentially a code in operation, or, in other words, a code functioning for a specific purpose or purposes. Thus we must analyze the transmission of a message in terms of a dynamic dimension. This analysis is especially important for translating, since the production of equivalent messages is a process, not merely of matching the parts of utterances, but also of reproducing the total dynamic character of the communication. Without both elements the results can scarcely be regarded, in any real sense, as equivalent.

The Basic Factors in Communication

Five important phases of any communication must be considered by the translator: (1) the subject matter, i.e. the referents which are talked about; (2) the participants who engage in the communication (in speech these constitute the speakers and the hearers, but in written communication, the author and the widely scattered audience—both in space and time); (3) the speech act or the process of writing; (4) the code used, i.e. the language in question, with all its resources as a code, including symbols and arrangements; and (5) the message, i.e. the particular way in which the subject matter is encoded into specific symbols and arrangements.

Though the actual process of communication in any specific instance may be described on the basis of these five phases, it is also possible to treat communication as a procedure by which source and receptor are related through the instrument of a message. These three basic components of source, receptor, and message are related in rather complex ways, as Figure 32 suggests.

In Figure 32 S, M, and R stand for source, message, and receptor, respectively. The wavy line through the M suggests the acoustic transmission, while the printed form of M stands for a written communication. As appendages to the squares marked S and R there are sections labeled De and En, standing for "decoder" and "encoder," respectively.

Two types of feedback are suggested in this diagram: (1) the immediate type of monitoring feedback which everyone experiences when he hears himself talk (deaf people develop strange pronunciations partly because they lack this type of feedback); and (2) feedback which comes from the receptor during transmission, consisting either of visual feedback, e.g. gestures, facial expressions, nods of assent or disagreement, or verbal feedback, e.g. voiced agreement or disagreement. The feedback from receptor to source can be understood as a series of simultaneous messages going in the reverse direction. However, since these messages so intimately affect the form of the message being encoded by the source, they are most conveniently treated as feedback.

There is also a kind of forward feedback (technically called "feed-forward") or anticipatory feedback, an adjustment made in advance by the source to meet certain presumed objections. This anticipatory feed-back, a most important type of adjustment, is made by every good speaker or writer; otherwise he soon loses his audience. Such two-directional feedback is continuous, reciprocal, and mutually re-enforcing; for the source anticipates the reactions of the receptor, and hence makes certain adjustments, while the receptor presumes that certain adaptations have already been made, and hence responds in terms of what he judges to be the results of anticipatory feedback. The source is naturally aware of this calculation on the part of the receptor, and accordingly makes even further adjustments in the message.

The message, as diagramed by solid lines, represents the verbal elements which are communicated, and the message diagramed by broken lines symbolizes the nonverbal message which almost always accompanies

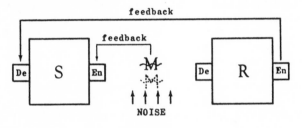

Figure 32

the verbal one. While a person is communicating a verbal message, he usually is simultaneously communicating nonverbal messages. For example, when he speaks, his appearance, degree of nervousness, stance, and gestures all tell us a good deal, not only about himself, but also about his attitudes toward the message in question. In printed communications, there are also many auxiliary accompaniments to the message, e.g. the style of type, format, the care taken to conform to orthographic standards, and the quality of paper. All these features are supplementary "messages." Such messages re-enforce the principal message, for nonverbal features, such as appearance and gestures, are supposed to "fit" the speech. When they do not, the receptor is either completely confused by such lack of agreement or assumes that there is some other element involved, e.g. irony, hypocrisy, or humor.

During the entire process of communication there is also a factor of "noise," to borrow a term from communications engineers, which enters into the process and tends to distort the message. In an actual speech event one always encounters physical noise, but in the transmission of printed communication there can also be a kind of "noise," e.g. an inadequate orthography, which cuts down on efficiency of transmission (the orthographic systems in some languages do not adequately represent the sounds and structure), mistakes in writing (e.g. misspellings), errors in copying, and deterioration of the medium (e.g. fading of ink and wearing out of paper).

In addition to these more obvious types of noise affecting spoken or written communication, we may also speak of psychological noise (Richards, 1953, p. 250), e.g. so-called Freudian slips (slips of the tongue or pen which indicate suppressed ideas), and distortions of the message caused by weariness and pain. Extreme examples of such distortion are associated with varying types of mental illness or failure of co-ordination. Similarly, in decoding it is possible that the physical condition or mental preoccupations of the receptor (including sympathy or antipathy for the source) will constitute serious psychological "noise" in the process of receiving the message.

Similar types of psychological noise may occur with written messages, e.g. slips of spelling or homeoteleuton (skipping of a line because two lines begin or end in the same sequence of letters), or substitution of a common word for a more difficult one. Though these instances of noise are largely nonpurposeful, there are instances of calculated noise, e.g. "jamming" of radio messages and altering of written messages by conscious changes designed to improve or to distort the original signal. Such "noise" is not uncommon in religious texts, for later copyists may suspect errors in what they are copying or set out to improve the original by what they regard as theologically justified editing.

In reality, the process of communication is considerably more complex than the diagram (Figure 32) and this brief explanation of it would imply. In the first place, the process of producing a message consists of three steps: (1) selection of a topic, i.e. the conception to be communicated; (2) the encoding of this conception into symbols and arrangement of symbols; and (3) the transmission of these symbols, i.e. the actual physical process of uttering or writing out the symbols. If this process is viewed from the standpoint of images and plans (Miller, Galanter, and Pribram, 1960), the topic may be viewed as the image, and steps 2 and 3 are two levels of plans.

The process of receiving a message likewise involves three different steps: (1) reception of the signal, either aurally, when it is heard, or visually, when it is read; (2) decoding of the signal, i.e. interpreting it, a kind of reversal of the process of encoding (this means extracting the image from the symbols in a manner analogous to that used by the encoder in selecting symbols to express the image); and (3) response.

We tend to think of the reception of a message as a relatively simple process, whereby a message is taken in and decoded, symbol by symbol, in a manner resembling the technique of a cryptanalyst, or in a process similar to that employed when we first studied Latin in high school. However, the decoding of a message in a language we know is far different from the process involved in figuring out the meaning of a signal in some purposefully obscured code or in a partially known foreign language. In fact, in spoken communication it often happens that the hearer is actually encoding a message on his own, which he presumes to be more or less parallel to what the speaker is saying. This is obviously true when, in a pause by the speaker, while he obviously seeks for just the right term, persons in the audience are at once able to supply the word, and sometimes do so, audibly. Not infrequently the hearer may actually be formulating several different possible messages, and he ascertains the source's intention by matching the communicated message with the closest corresponding message of his own. The fact that, in many instances, different hearers of a communication insist that quite different messages were communicated is further evidence that receptors often do not decode the actual message, but, rather, encode presumably equivalent messages which in the end may or may not be properly matched.

Written communication generally produces a rather different attitude toward decoding, for without the interpersonal give-and-take of speaker and audience there is much less tendency to encode a parallel message. The words are all there in fixed form, and hence the reader tends simply to take them in, either slowly or rapidly (depending upon the pace he sets), and interprets them, usually without much parallel encoding. Thus written communication often produces a less immediate effect upon the receptor, since he does not actively or vicariously participate in the formation of the message. Similarly, a speech read to an audience produces less effect than one spoken directly, since it discourages participation in the encoding process. Furthermore, really eloquent and successful speakers often introduce calculated hesitations to create an impression of not being quite sure at times of just the word to use, thus gaining the participation of a sympathetic audience. If a speaker is too smooth, he discourages audience participation.

The message itself consists of two different aspects: (1) the signal, including all the formal features of the message, and (2) the content, i.e. what the signal means. In the following discussions of communication, the word "message" is used to identify the formal aspects of the message, namely, the signal. Where the meaning is specifically involved, we shall speak of the content or meaning of the message.

In addition to these factors, we must also consider the channel, indicated in the diagram (Figure 32) by symbols to designate written or spoken forms of communication. The spoken channel is of course normally limited in both time and space (only recently has speech been able to overcome these limits, in space by electronic means and in time by various types of recording). The written channel, traditionally relatively unrestricted in time and space, has been the vehicle for man's most significant and lasting cultural accomplishments.

Linguists regard the written message as a secondary kind of symbolization; that is to say, writing puts into a different form what is essentially speech. As noted earlier, there are some obvious limitations in the written form of language, for most orthographies are not only inconsistent in the representation of sounds, but also consistently omit certain types of contrasts, or only partially represent them, e.g. stress groups, junctures, and intonational contours. The reader, however, tends to supply the missing elements on the basis of the clues which are available, and since many features of language are redundant he can succeed in this process to a marked degree. But the written form of a language is not the same as the spoken form, even apart from obvious orthographic deficiencies. Moreover, even within the spoken form of a language there are wide differences of style, e.g. casual vs. noncasual speech and serious vs. flippant utterances, which are parallel but not identical sets of contrasts. Furthermore, even in so-called primitive languages the noncasual speech of religion may differ appreciably from the noncasual speech of legal maxims.

In all literate societies the written form of language is different from either casual or noncasual speech, and the degree of difference depends upon the literary traditions of the people concerned. For example, in the Arabic-speaking world the written style is almost a different language from the colloquial; in fact, the written style has given rise to the formal style of speech of the educated person. But even with newly literate peoples the rapidly evolving written form of the language shows some rather marked distinctions from the spoken form. In the first place, the writing of a language tends to make it more systematic and more regular, with fewer anacoloutha (sentences which start out one way and end another), for writing introduces a conscious element into the process of communication. In the second place, the written form of a language is in many respects less verbose than the spoken language. It tends to be more concise and precise, more economical, and less cluttered with the extra particles which so readily flip in and out of colloquial speech.

A third characteristic of written style is its tendency to avoid certain typically colloquial forms, e.g. onomatopoeic particles, and to alter certain constructions which seem almost obligatory in colloquial speech, e.g. direct discourse. Onomatopoeic particles, which in many languages are so vivid and intimate a part of speech, just do not seem to fit in the written style of some languages. In certain languages where direct discourse is almost obligatory in the spoken language (i.e. in narrating a conversation the speaker takes the parts of the participants in question), the written style changes these direct forms to indirect ones. The very writing of a language seems to require some sort of shift in the liveliness of the account. Of course, this does not mean that translators working in a language which has recently acquired a written form should attempt to suppress onomatopoeic expressions, or alter direct to indirect discourse. Only the people themselves can judge what seems appropriate in the written style of their own language. On the other hand, it is a mistake for foreigners translating into such languages to attempt to resist certain changes in the written language which the people themselves wish to employ.

A fourth characteristic of written style is that it often involves the conscious introduction of colorful terms as a compensation for the failure to mark intonational features, or to symbolize accompanying gestures, tone of voice, and general animation—qualities that give the story told orally so much of its liveliness and color. A conscious literary artist will always try to make the written form of the language communicate the same basic message that the corresponding spoken form would convey. To do so he must use more attributive terms to characterize the activity, employ a higher percentage of action words to suggest a sense of motion and action, and introduce certain sound effects, e.g. alliteration and sound symbolism, thus compensating for the personal accompaniments of actual speech, i.e. the paralinguistic elements in language.

There are several reasons for the differences between the written style and spoken style of a language. For one thing, especially for the newly literate, the memory span in written style is shorter, for the material is produced and usually decoded at a slower rate. When, for example, an informant is asked to dictate a story as the linguist writes it down, rather than to tell it in a natural setting, the informant usually makes a considerable reduction in overall length, and if he himself is asked to write out a story, he often reduces it even further. In the second place, written style involves a more conscious effort than the spoken. As a result, greater attention is given to eliminating errors and to elaborating or beautifying some of its formal features. Since written language seems to require a more dignified form of expression and almost always carries greater cultural prestige than the spoken language, a casual form of language is considered unworthy of such a vehicle. Hence the written language tends more and more to accentuate certain aspects of non-casual speech. Furthermore, since writing usually implies a wider audience, both in time and space, there is a tendency to eliminate localisms and to concentrate on what is thought to be more generally understood and more widely acceptable.

This relationship between spoken and written language has never been so fully studied as it should be, especially in relation to societies which are only now becoming literate. However, there is abundant evidence that even in so-called primitive groups there exist the same pressures for special written-language forms as have been noted in varying degrees for languages with long literary traditions.

INFORMATION THEORY

Some very important insights for the translator have come from the science of cybernetics, which in its most specific application to translation is generally known as "Information Theory." [1] In terms of this theory it is possible to study the rate of flow of messages in a channel, for the number of messages which can be communicated is mathematically related to the number of signaling units. For example, if there is one such unit, which may be either "on" or "off," as in the case of any electronically controlled device, there are obviously two "messages" which can be communicated, but if there are two such signaling units, the number of messages, i.e. based on the number of combinations of on-off signals, is four. Similarly, with three such units, the number of messages is eight;

[1] For a clear and helpful explanation of certain aspects of Information Theory, see H. A. Gleason (1955), pp. 266-283.

with four units, sixteen; with five units, thirty-two, etc., following an exponential curve to the base 2. In the application of this theory to translation we cannot give precise mathematical formulations to our problems, [1] but we can obtain from some of the basic principles of information theory certain very important insights:

1. The "information" which is communicated by any message is a measure of the unpredictability of the signals which are given. In fact, information in this technical sense is largely equated with unpredictability. This implies, of course, that the more unpredictable the message the greater the channel which is required for the transmission and decoding of the message. In ordinary language this means that one can readily understand a message which is commonplace, but it takes much greater decoding effort to comprehend a message which is unusual, unpredictable, and strange.

2. In order to combine efficiency of communication with an effective guarantee against distortion by noise or other factors, languages tend to be about 50 per cent redundant. That is to say, they seem to reflect a kind of equilibrium between the unexpected and the predictable. Languages differ somewhat in the amount of redundancy they possess, but in formal as well as in semantic structure there seems to be a redundancy of about 50 per cent. [2]

Any message can be communicated through any channel, but it may be necessary to "lengthen" the message, that is, to take more time to communicate it if the channel is too restricted. If the receptive channel is very wide, the message can always be compressed, but if the channel is narrow, the message needs to be drawn out.

"Information" in cybernetics is not to be equated with meaning, but only with unpredictability. That is to say, in information theory we only determine the difficulties of communicating some message, not the relevance or value of the message to the receptors.

The relationship of information (in this technical sense) to unpredictability can be readily understood from a number of very practical situations. For example, if a person always declares that everything is "terrific," whether it is a meal, speech, dress, bouquet of flowers, ball game, movie, or a joke, the word *terrific* does not carry very much information, for it is largely predictable. Likewise, when an air raid siren goes off each Saturday at noon, it does not carry much information, for the noise is almost entirely predictable.

By saying that languages incorporate a great deal of redundancy into their structures, we are simply saying that languages reflect a good deal of predictability. For example, in the phrase *these men are...* we know from the sole occurrence of the plural form *these* that *men* and *are* will be employed rather than the singular forms *man* and *is*. Accordingly, we

[1] For further treatment of the more technical and mathematical aspects of Information Theory, see E. Colin Cherry (1957), F. H. George (1959), Norbert Wiener (1954), and Claude E. Shannon and Warren Weaver (1949).
[2] For important discussions of these problems, see J. H. Greenberg, C. E. Osgood, and S. Saporta (1954b), and Benjamin N. Colby (1958).

can say that the plural indicators in the forms *men* and *are* are redundant. Redundancy, however, is not repetition, for in a phrase such as *truly, truly, I say...* the adverb *truly* is repeated, but the second occurrence is not redundant, for it adds to the total meaning. One can also say *truly I say* or *truly, truly, I say*, and the second expression differs from the first in intensity. Nor is redundancy tautology, which in general usage (but not in logic) implies meaningless repetition, e.g. *he descended down*, in which case *down* is tautological to *descended*; but it is not so in the phrase *he climbed down*, for one can climb up as well as down.

Obviously, we must not confuse unpredictability (or information) with value, meaning, or relevance. One could say, for example, "This is a beautiful *pshlong*," in which *pshlong* would be highly unpredictable (and hence carry a great deal of information), but it has no meaning. On the other hand, a message with high unpredictability may have a great deal of meaning, but this depends upon the content of the message and not upon its formal unpredictability.

Before, however, we consider some of the other immediate relationships of information theory to problems of translation we must give further consideration to the redundancy which occurs in language, for only on the basis of a knowledge of such data can we evaluate the problems of impact and the capacity of the decoder to "take in" the message.

REDUNDANCY IN LANGUAGE

That languages incorporate a good deal of redundancy (i.e. raise the predictability of certain signals) into their structure is rather easily seen if we experiment with leaving out letters from words. For example, in the following partially written words the reader can usually supply the missing letters with considerable facility:

$$C— — \quad y— — \quad s— — \quad m— \quad d— \quad t— —s?$$

It does not take much puzzling with this series to recognize that the intended sentence is "Can you see me do this?" It should be noted that in this phrase the vowels are omitted more than consonants, for consonants are much less predictable than vowels, and hence more crucial for signaling what is meant. For this reason, in the abbreviation of words, as in telephone books, the general practice is to omit vowels rather than consonants.

Another readily recognized form of redundancy is the manner in which related grammatical forms signal the same types of information. For example, in Spanish the feminine gender is signaled four times in the phrase *una persona buena y capacitada*, 'a good, qualified person'. The four occurrences of the suffix *-a* are not theoretically required in order to signal feminine gender. One occurrence should be sufficient, but languages do not work this way. Rather, their systems employ a good deal of redundancy as a means of re-enforcing the signal.

In the selection of words within certain phrases there is often a high degree of redundancy. If, for example, one hears a sentence such as *he is down and* ..., there is no difficulty involved in supplying *out*, for *down and out* is a kind of set phrase. Similarly, such phrases as *everything in apple-pie order, seven come eleven*, and *love me, love my dog* all possess high degrees of predictability, and hence redundancy, for the final or near final elements.

Languages exhibit two rather opposite (though actually complementary) tendencies. One is to develop in the direction of automatization, with such fixed phrases as *how do you do, good-bye, take it or leave it, come what may*, and *once upon a time*. At the other extreme is a desire for novelty, which produces slang, jargons, and fresh figures of speech, especially prized for certain styles of writing, e.g. in English poetry and sports writing.

In general, redundancy is calculated as a "left-to-right" procedure; that is to say, the predictability of a following form is calculated upon the extent to which preceding forms determine its probability of occurrence. Thus if a particular term occurs after a series of delimiting or qualifying expressions, it is much more redundant than if it occurs first. For example, in the phrase *all these destitute, ragged X*, the final form can be filled only with some such word as *people, persons, waifs, orphans*; it cannot include such words as *animals, bushes, stones, squares, triangles*, and *happenings*. But if we use the expression *these X, who were destitute and ragged*, it is much more difficult to predict what *X* will be if we have only the preceding *these*. In actual speech, however, as well as in the understanding of written materials, persons do not decode merely from left to right. Rather, they take in what might be called "meaningful mouthfuls" and actually determine the meaning by two-directional decoding, so that redundancy must be calculated both lineally and structurally. Of course, if the preceding elements give almost all the required information, the last of the phrase is highly redundant. Moreover, some of the clues to the proper item in the first of a phrase may be supplied only at considerable length, e.g. *These X, who came to visit us last week, insisted that they be paid*.

Despite the relevance of two-way redundancy, we must recognize that in many senses spoken language and written language are different; for, especially in the case of new literates, reading proceeds rather painstakingly, syllable by syllable or word by word, and determining following words depends very much upon understanding and retaining preceding ones. Moreover, the memory span in such reading is shorter (in terms of words involved) than in normal speech, and this circumstance adds to the difficulty of decoding.

Though redundancy might theoretically seem to be a waste of effort, it actually fills a very important role in the efficiency of language, for by re-enforcing a communication by partially predictable signals one may overcome many of the hazards of "noise." For example, it is not necessary to hear every sound in order to determine what word is meant, and one need not identify all the words in a phrase in order to determine its meaning. Moreover, redundancy by grammatical agreement, government, and cross reference can serve to signal relationships between words.

INFORMATION AND IMPACT

Information, in the technical sense of unpredictability, quite naturally involves greater impact, for new expressions and fresh figures of speech have a much greater impact upon the receptor than old clichés and trite sayings. This greater impact based on unpredictability explains in some measure why congregations tend to be much more impressed with, though not necessarily more favorably disposed to, the reading of the Scriptures in some unfamiliar translation than in one which they know too well.

On the other hand, it would be wrong to assume that unpredictability is the only factor in impact. One must also reckon with "psychological distance." Something which is unusual has considerable impact, but if it occurs in one's own back yard, the impact is immeasurably greater than if it happens in some distant land, or even in a nearby town. This element of impact which is dependent upon distance is probably relatable to similar phenomena in merchandizing, in which it has been found that people's interest in a sale is inversely proportionate to the square of the distance. That is to say, a sale that is twice as far away will have only one-fourth of the interest.

In dealing with impact derived from distance we cannot, however, think merely in terms of physical distance, for it is psychological proximity which is important. For example, one may not be particularly interested in events in Japan until a member of one's family goes there to live. In such an instance, the geographical distance is no longer such a significant factor, for psychological interests overrule the physical element. Of course, one of the advantages, or curses, of present international communication is to make all events seem "psychologically close," for the broadcaster or reporter wants the audience to feel personally present.

It is quite true that greater impact, whether from more "information" or closer psychological distance, significantly increases the receptor's interest in decoding a message; but if the impact is too great, psychological proximity may also cause greater tensions, frustrations, and even rejection. Hence, impact can be a two-edged sword, to be used with considerable care.

THE DECODER'S CHANNEL

In any language it is possible to generate messages with a high communication load, though as indicated above, languages normally tend to produce messages of about 50 per cent redundancy. However, one can always contrive to exceed this limit of unpredictability by using rare forms of words, unusual syntax, strange combinations of words, and completely unfamiliar themes. This is unfortunately what happens so often in translated materials, when the translator unconsciously exceeds the normal limits by literally following the forms of the source language, with the result that unpredictability rises considerably above the 50 per cent level and conversely redundancy falls far below this limit. Of course, the language is always capable of being so organized as to contain

9

such "messages." Where the difficulty arises is in the capacity for the decoder to handle such communications. Furthermore, we must constantly be reminded that decoders differ appreciably in their capacities to deal with such messages, for there is a wide spread between the specialist and the new literate and between the well-educated adult and the partially educated adolescent. Hence, what may be quite simple for one person may prove utterly impossible for another, or what may be only moderately difficult for the instructed individual is hopelessly too hard for one without some background and training.

In order to understand how a relatively simple message in one language can be so difficult in another, we must consider two important sources of redundancy. First, there is the formal linguistic redundancy, whether of a formal or semantic nature, which is built into any normal message in a source language. But in addition to this regular form of linguistic redundancy, there is also a tremendous amount of cultural redundancy which is implicit in the communication event. For example, the original receptors were presumably acquainted with the source, knew something of his background, understood a good deal about the circumstances of the original message, and were full members of the linguistic and cultural community involved in the communication. No receptors for whom a translation is made can expect to be as completely informed of the circumstances of communication, and hence be in a position to appreciate the redundancy in the message which is known only from the cultural context. This means that in most instances any message in the source language will need to be filled out with at least some types of redundancy, so as to match the linguistic and cultural redundancy to which the original receptors had access.

From the standpoint of the average receptor a literal translation inevitably overloads the message, so that he cannot decode it with ease or efficiency. What may have been quite satisfactory in the source language needs to be "drawn out" in the receptor language if the two messages are to be equivalent in terms of information theory. Of course, one can usually argue the merits of a particular receptor-language rendering by insisting that "it can be said this way" and such may be true, but the real issue is whether it is normally and naturally said in such a manner and whether the implicit or explicit patterns of redundancy are in any way equivalent.

We may assume that in the case of an original message prepared specifically for a group of receptors there would be a considerable measure of "fit." That is to say, the form of the message would be constructed so as to fit the decoder's channel, as in Figure 33.

In the case of a literal translation, which attempts to pack the same amount of information into substantially the same length of message, it is inevitable that the linguistic awkwardness of the forms will increase the "communication load" or "information" in such a message. At the same time, the decoder's channel is inevitably narrower, since he lacks many of the cultural data which the decoder in the source language had, for he is not a part of the original communicative event. If we attempt

Original Communication

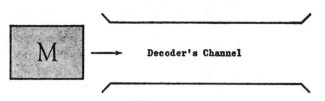

Decoder's Channel

Figure 33

to diagram this type of situation, we will inevitably find that the message is "wider" and the channel narrower, as in Figure 34.

If one is to produce an equivalent message, that is to say, one which is dynamically equivalent and which will fit the decoder's channel, which is restricted by lack of cultural awareness of the circumstances of the original communication, it is necessary to "draw out" the message by building into it the necessary redundancy, so as to make it equivalently meaningful. Such redundancy may be accomplished by a number of techniques, discussed primarily in Chapters 9 and 10, but the fact that

Literal Translation Into Receptor Language

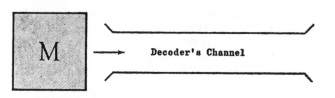

Decoder's Channel

Figure 34

this is necessary is confirmed not only by the obvious relevance of information theory but by the fact that almost all good translations tend to be appreciably longer than their originals. The relationship between this type of adjusted message and the corresponding decoder's channel may be diagramed as in Figure 35.

Without proper adjustments to the form of the receptor language an overloading of the message, in terms of the decoder's capacities, is almost inevitable. This does not mean, of course, that a decoder may not be able to figure out the message after long and arduous study, but a really

Adjusted Translation Into Receptor Language

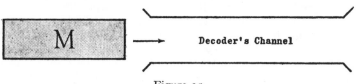

Decoder's Channel

Figure 35

satisfactory translation should not impose that sort of burden on the receptor. The message should not be appreciably harder for him to comprehend than it was to the original receptors. If it is too hard, he is likely to give up from discouragement or to feel that the results of his efforts are not proportionate to the investment of time and trouble. Of course, one can to some extent compensate for an inferior translation by placing great pressures upon the receptors to read and understand, but there is no real justification for this type of cultural bigotry or paternalism.

MESSAGE FEATURES TENDING TO OVERLOAD THE DECODER'S CHANNEL

Though normal language usage tends to center around 50 per cent redundancy, and thus provides a considerable "cushion" against noise and misunderstanding and keeps fatigue at a reasonable level, a translation often tends to overload the channel of communication simply because of its foreign background and content. These overloading features are basically of two types: (1) formal, and (2) semantic. The formal features may be subdivided into (a) orthography, (b) word formation, and (c) syntax; and the semantic features involve (a) words, (b) collocations of words, and (c) themes.

The orthographic overloading may result from a number of different causes: (1) the use of rare letters, such as may be introduced from borrowed words; (2) errors in the proper representation of verbal symbols (i.e. failure to conform to the orthographic system); (3) inadequacy of the orthographic system; and (4) inconsistency in the orthographic system.

Though rare letters and downright errors in the original transcription or in typography can be a problem, they are relatively less a factor in overloading the communication than are inadequacy and inconsistency of the orthographic systems themselves. Most orthographies tend to represent most of the segmental phonemes (i.e. the consonants and vowels), but a number of other features are often only partially represented, e.g. nasalized quality of the vowels, tonal distinctions, and length of vowels. In a practical alphabet it is not always necessary to represent all these features; indeed, in many instances their occurrence is highly redundant. For example, even though there may be tonal distinctions on the verbs to indicate tense, obligatory particles in the sentence may also signal corresponding tense differences, and thus provide a clue to the tonal contrasts occurring with the verbs. In such instances the tonal differences in the verbs usually need not be indicated. Similarly with such factors as length and quality of vowels. However, the accumulation of several inadequately marked distinctions may make the resultant orthographic system inadequate, since the communication load then carried by the rest of the symbols is simply too great.

Even when an alphabet represents most of the distinctions in a language, the inconsistent way in which these contrasts are indicated may complicate the orthographic system. For example, in one language in Central Africa there is a contrast between aspirated and nonaspirated consonants, but the nonaspirated types have been inconsistently represented, sometimes by the letters *p*, *t*, and *k*, and in other words by *b*, *d*, and *g*. The aspirated series has been represented in some words by *ph*, *th*, and *kh*, and in other words by *p*, *t*, and *k*. Moreover, the distribution of these distinctions in the orthography has been largely without rhyme or reason. The result has been a greatly "overloaded" system of spelling.

The general inadequacy and inconsistency of representation of sounds can be so extreme as to produce a complete breakdown in a program of written communication. In one instance a translator had so completely botched the job of producing an adequate orthographic system that ultimately only his principal helper succeeded in learning to read, and he was able to do so only because of his general familiarity with the content. However, even he had, first, to read over a passage, then listen to the way it sounded; finally, after "guessing" at its meaning, he repeated the entire expression in a form that would be intelligible.

Few orthographies fall into this category of "hopeless systems," but many of those worked out by persons untrained and inexperienced in the field have such serious limitations and involve so heavy a communication load that they tend to fatigue the reader unduly; thus ultimately they constitute an important factor in discouraging widespread literacy or developing a literature program.

Rare forms of words may also constitute serious obstacles to a proper communication load. For example, translators often find convenient formal parallels between constructions in the source and receptor languages, and, regardless of the relative frequency of such constructions in the languages concerned, endeavor to match the forms more or less automatically. Thus, both source and receptor languages may have passive forms of words, but in the source language they may be relatively frequent, while in the receptor language they are rare. If under these conditions one attempts to translate every source-language passive by a corresponding passive in the receptor language, the result will be an inevitable overloading of the communication, since the rarity of the passive in the receptor language means that it is relatively unpredictable, and thus carries a comparatively heavy communication load.

Another kind of verbal form which overloads the communication is the newly constructed term; this is so even when such a term is formed on the basis of models quite well known in the language. New combinations of forms on a syntactic level are to be expected in all languages, for they are characteristic of the syntactic level of structure. On the other hand, the morphological (or word-forming) level is generally characterized by much greater restriction in the facility with which new combinations can be coined. Such infrequency is a factor in greater unpredictability, and hence in the greater communication load involved. Such made-up words, often defensible on theoretical grounds (i.e. they conform to the grammatical requirements of the receptor language and thus are semantically justifiable), may meet with considerable resistance from receptors, or at least may cause hesitation, uncertainty, and, not infrequently, bewilderment. Languages, of course, differ in the degree to which they admit such new word formations; e.g. German employs new word formations to a much greater extent than does English. But in translations it is important not to overdo the number and frequency of such forms, or the resulting communication will inevitably be overloaded.

A communication is easily overloaded syntactically by the use of incorrect grammar, which immediately throws the reader off balance; but the use of unfamiliar forms is a more frequent error in translating. One may, for example, insist on using indirect quotations, when the receptor language almost always employs direct quotations. Or one may try to relate most clauses hypotactically, as in Greek, rather than paratactically, as is required in many languages. Similarly, there is a tendency for translators to render nouns by nouns and verbs by verbs, etc., when a consideration of communication load may require a complete revision of the sentence structure, so that, as in Zoque, spoken in Mexico, the Biblical expression "Perfect love casts out fear" becomes 'we do not fear when we truly love'.[1]

Within a single language there are different types of syntactic constructions, some of which carry proportionately heavier communication loads than others. Since these types are of great importance to the translator attempting to attain balance in the form of the message in a receptor language, they should be examined in some detail. They include features of (1) direction of attribution, (2) restricted vs. nonrestricted attribution, (3) terminal characteristics, and (4) total length.

If the order of attribution is from "left-to-right" (i.e. from preceding to following words), there is a much greater problem of immediate memory retention, for the entire series is structurally dependent upon a final head word. For example, the series *certainly not very well organized government* is almost a maximum left-right series (see Figure 36 for a diagramatic analysis of its structure):

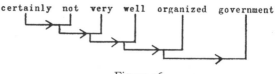

Figure 36

On the other hand, if the attribution is predominantly "right-to-left" (that is, from following to preceding), the structure can be almost unlimited, as in Figure 37, in which endocentric (attributive) structures are marked by arrows and exocentric structures by an ×.

One of the obvious contrasts in the structures diagramed in Figures 36 and 37 is the fact that in the phrase *certainly not very well organized government* there are no terminal points before the final head word is reached, while in *spoke to the man who asked him about the plane purchased by a mechanic*, there are several potential terminal points, namely, after *spoke, man, asked, him,* and *plane.* But quite apart from this feature of

---

[1]   See Wonderly, 1961, p. 393.

terminal potentiality, which we consider as a separate element at a later point, there is a sense in which left-to-right attribution involves a greater communication load, since after an attributive the range of possible head words is usually much greater than is the possible selection of an attributive once the head word has been given. This is simply because of the fact that for the most part an attributive may go with a wider range of head words than head words go with attributives.

A parallel to this problem may be noted in the contrast between Navajo and Quechua verb structure. In Navajo the prefixes constitute essentially attributive elements to the root, and in Quechua the suffixes are related to the root in somewhat analogous ways. However, in learning to read, Navajos in general have a much more difficult time than do Quechuas, and this difficulty cannot be explained solely on the basis of the more complex tonal contrasts and morphophonemic alterations in Navajo. The greater ease in the earlier stages in reading Quechua seems to be due in large measure to the fact that, once the verb root has been given, the selection of possible suffixes is more strictly determined than in Navajo,

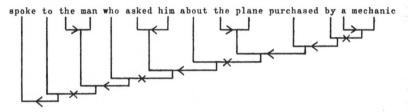

Figure 37

in which the prefixal formations do not, to the same extent, help the reader to predict either the sequence of prefixes likely to occur or the root likely to follow. This relationship can be easily stated in mathematical terms, for the prefixes, being strictly limited in number, go with many more different roots than roots go with prefixes.

Another important formal contrast involving varying degrees of communication load is the difference between restrictive and nonrestrictive attributives. At this point, however, a clear distinction must be made between formal and semantic characteristics. Since restrictive attributives are more intimately combined with the word they modify, they usually represent a heavier kind of construction, i.e. a more involved one, and hence tend to carry a greater formal communication load. Nonrestrictive attributives, on the other hand, can usually be omitted without impairing the basic sense of the expression. (Compare, for example, *John Baker, who was in the store, saw him* and *John Baker saw him*). We may say that, structurally, a restrictive attributive tends to pile up words into more elaborate and involved combinations, and thus formally carries a greater communication load. Nevertheless, on a semantic level this distinction between restrictive and nonrestrictive attribution is reversed, for nonrestrictive attributives may be of almost any semantic content, while restrictive attributives are far more conditioned by the context. Thus restrictive attributives tend to carry a heavier formal communication load, while nonrestrictive attributives usually carry a heavier semantic communication load.

The terminal potentialities existing within a series of words are also an important element in the communication load; for if the reader can stop at certain points in the sentence, without losing or distorting the sense which may be further expanded in the rest of the expression, obviously a minimum of memory retention is required. For example, in the expression *will drive him over there now* not only is the attribution from right to left, but there are potential terminal points after *drive, him, over,* and *there,* and at no point is the addition of the subsequent portion at variance with what has gone before. Such additive structures pose very few problems for the formal communication load, since all subsequent elements may be appended without complication to the existing utterance. This is not, however, always the case, for if *down* is added to *I'll run him,* the formal structure, and hence the semantic values, are radically altered, e.g. *I'll run him down.*

The contrast between the terminal and nonterminal character of a construction often involves a distinction between subordinate and co-ordinate constructions. For example, *after he had left, we distributed the gifts* cannot be meaningfully terminated until after the word *gifts,* but the co-ordinate arrangement of *he left, and then we distributed the gifts* does permit a potential termination after *left,* without prejudicing the meaning of what follows. Some languages employ such co-ordinate constructions more frequently than does English. In fact, to avoid overloading the communication in a receptor language one must often change a subordinate construction into a co-ordinate one.

The total overall length of a construction is also a determining factor in its formal communication load. Obviously shorter expressions involve much less formal structuring and embedding than longer ones, other things being equal. In many instances a very long sentence, even though having right-to-left attribution and with several potential terminal points, must be broken up into smaller segments to avoid formal overloading of the communication.

In order to reduce the load of otherwise heavy formal arrangements of words, languages employ three principal methods: (1) shifts of order, (2) discontinuous immediate constituents, and (3) constituent anticipators.

In English we are well aware of the principle of shifting order in placing attributives to the verbs. For example, the elements of verb, direct object, and "adverbial" attributive usually occur in just this sequence, e.g. *saw the man yesterday.* However, if the direct object has a heavy attributive and thus becomes a long expression, e.g. *the man to whom we had recently loaned money,* then *yesterday* is not in the second position following the verb but may be placed immediately before the verb, i.e. *yesterday saw the man to whom we had recently loaned money.*

In certain instances the placing of structurally related elements in juxtaposed positions results in very heavy constructions. For example, *as fine as you will ever find a person* is an exceedingly awkward arrangement, even though *as you will ever find* goes immediately with *as fine*, to which it is structurally related. However, such an involved and long attribution to *person* provides too heavy a structure, and hence *as fine* and *as you will ever find* are split, one before *person* and the other after, e.g. *as fine a person as you will ever find*.

The use of constituent anticipators is another device by which potentially heavy constructions can be lightened, e.g. *it is too bad that he...* and *there is no one who cannot learn to....* The use of *it* and *there* throws the topic of the sentence into the predicate position, where attributives can be attached one after another, almost without end, and without having to retain in the "temporary memory" the realization that a predicate must occur at the end. For example, instead of placing the topic of the sentence first, as in *That someone with his abilities and understanding of these intricate developments in nuclear physics should have to do this type of work is too bad*, a constituent anticipator, such as *it*, can be placed first, thus reducing the formal communication load. We then have: *It is too bad that someone with his abilities and understanding of these intricate developments in nuclear physics should have to do this type of work.*

Semantic features that overload the communication include rare words, rare collocations of words, and rare events or concepts. More often than not, the rare words which tend to overload translations are borrowed terms. [1] In many instances translators conclude that no equivalent exists in the receptor language and that the only practical solution is to borrow a word from the source language. The heavy communication load imposed by such borrowings can sometimes be reduced by the use of "classifiers." For example, if in a translation of the Scriptures one feels obliged to borrow such words as *silk, ruby, camel,* and *Pharisees*, one can in some contexts add certain classificatory terms to make these meaningless foreign words somewhat more intelligible, and thus reduce their communication load. For example: 'cloth silk', 'valuable stone called ruby', 'animal camel', and 'religious group Pharisees'.

The difficulty of decoding a message is related not only to the rarity of certain words, but also to that of certain combinations of words. For example, in Keats's poem "Fancy," most of the words are well known, but some combinations of words, as in the following passage, are so unusual as to carry a relatively heavy communication load:

> Autumn's red-lipp'd fruitage too,
> Blushing through the mist and dew,
> Cloys with tasting:

[1]   It is important to distinguish between words borrowed for the purpose of the particular message and those which have been assimilated into the receptor language and have acquired wide usage. In the latter case, they must be judged on the same basis as any word of native origin, namely, in terms of frequency of use, correctness of area of meaning, and appropriateness of occurrence in such a context (i.e. stylistic "fit").

and

> White-plum'd lillies, and the first
> Hedge-grown primrose that hath burst;
> Shaded hyacinth, alway
> Sapphire queen of the mid-May;

Similarly heavy communication loads are to be found even in some of the more readily interpreted poems of Robert Browning. The following lines from "The Last Ride Together" are typical:

> My soul
> Smoothed itself out—a long-cramped scroll
> Freshening and fluttering in the wind.

and

> And so, you, looking and loving best,
> Conscious grew, your passion drew
> Cloud, sunset, moonrise, star-shine too,
> Down on you, near and yet more near,
> Till flesh must fade for heaven was here!

Of course, part of the heavy communication load of these lines from Keats and Browning is due to the formal features of order and the imposed limitations of the rhythmic pattern. But there are also semantic features which contribute to the load, namely, the rare collocations of words and the obviously unusual themes—which are in a certain sense the essence of poetry. Thus a heavy communication load is not an evil in itself, and such a load in the source language is generally matched by a correspondingly heavy load in the receptor language.

The second way in which the semantic communication load may be greatly increased is by lack of correspondence between the linguistic order of words and the nonlinguistic order of events. For example a number of passages in the New Testament provide considerable difficulty in some languages, and especially in those which tend to preserve considerable parallelism between linguistic and temporal sequences. Such problems may be illustrated by Mark 6:16-18, which in the Revised Standard Version reads:

> But when Herod heard of it he said, 'John, whom I beheaded, has been raised.' For Herod had sent and seized John, and bound him in prison for the sake of Herodias, his brother Philip's wife; because he had married her. For John said to Herod, 'It is not lawful for you to have your brother's wife.'

In this passage there are several principal events, referred to in the following linguistic order: (1) Herod's hearing about Jesus, whom he assumed to be John; (2) the beheading of John; (3) the seizure and imprisonment of John; (4) Herodias' responsibility for the arrest; (5) the fact that Herodias had been Philip's wife; (6) Herod's marriage to Herodias; and (7) John's denunciation of Herod. The actual historical order of events, however, is quite different: 5, 6, 7, 4, 3, 2, 1. In some languages the translation must follow the historical order if the message is not to be overloaded.

In order to reduce somewhat the unduly heavy communication load which results from unusual combinations of words and lack of correspondence between linguistic and historical orders of events, one can always (1) introduce a degree of redundancy, so as to prepare the receptor for the meaning of a term, and (2) change the linguistic order so that it will match the historical order of events.

Redundancy can be introduced by adding words, if they are obviously implied in the context (see the discussion of techniques of adjustment in Chapter 9), or rearranging the sequences of words in order to place the redundancy before, rather than after, a word. For example, as Wonderly (1961, p. 394) has pointed out, the sentence *The town had a kermess in honor of the new governor* leaves *kermess* as a very improbable transitional possibility, if one considers only the information which precedes. Moreover, if a person did not know what a *kermess* was, he could guess almost anything at this point, e.g. flood, fire, riot, or epidemic. However, the words *in honor of the new governor* help to make the term *kermess* somewhat more redundant, for at least it seems to be something which is culturally approved and socially acceptable. If, however, the sentence is turned around so that it reads, *In honor of the new governor the town had a kermess*, then the final word *kermess* is much more redundant in its occurrence, for the preceding expressions have helped to define, at least to some extent, the area of meaning implied by such a word.

By providing formal clues, languages tend to take away some of the shock of rare sequences, especially those requiring interpretation as exocentric combinations. For example, the fact that certain combinations occur in a poetic structure, with rhyme and rhythm, alerts us to the likelihood of finding a number of unusual sequences. Being thus forewarned, we can usually take such combinations in our stride. Similarly, in many languages the stylistic structure of proverbs is highly specialized, thus providing important clues to the fact that they are not to be understood as normal, endocentric expressions.

In discussing the semantic features that appreciably add to the communication load, one must not overlook the aspect of total content or theme; for, even though the words themselves may be well known and the sequences not disturbingly unfamiliar, the total concept may be so new as to make decoding a very real problem. For example, the following sentence contained in Louis de Broglie, *The Revolution in Physics* (p. 267): "Paul's exclusion principle is therefore expressed analytically in wave mechanics by admitting as wave functions of systems containing electrons only wave functions antisymmetric with respect to all electron pairs." But relatively rare concepts are not restricted to books on contemporary developments in nuclear physics. The introduction to the Gospel of John contains an even more difficult theme: "In the beginning was the Word, and the Word was with God, and the Word was God." To many people these words are just as difficult to comprehend as anything written by the most abstruse philosophers or mathematicians. But even such abstract concepts are not the only ones which result in a high communication load because they are difficult to comprehend. For the Kakas of the Cameroun one of the most difficult stories of the entire Bible to "decode" is the one concerning Lot's daughters, giving birth to sons who became heads of important nations, for the Kakas are convinced that the offspring of incest never live to adulthood.

In some languages the strangeness of certain themes is often reduced through the use of certain anticipatory cues. For example, *once upon a time* in English immediately signals the fact that the story to follow is likely to be fantastic, and is certainly not to be interpreted literally. Even the introductory phrase *have you heard this one?* immediately helps the receptor to know that, not a personal account, but a joke or a folk story is coming.

TECHNIQUES FOR ANALYZING THE COMMUNICATION LOAD

To make a complete analysis of the communication load of any message one of two methods can be employed: (1) the setting up of elaborate scales of the frequency of occurrence of various sequences in a language (something which does not exist for any language), and the measurement of the transitional probabilities of each sequence, counting both from left to right and from right to left; or (2) the employment of native speakers of the language (who possess a kind of built-in "feeling" for such transitional probabilities by virtue of their speaking of the language) and getting them to "systematically guess" the form of a message. This latter technique would be an elaborate extension of the "20 questions" game, but it has been used in preliminary types of calculations of communication load.

Theoretically significant as these approaches to the problem of communication load may be, they are practically quite impossible to use in most situations. Accordingly, one must use simpler devices which will give a basis for comparative analysis, even though they may not provide comprehensive and exact data. To fulfill this purpose the so-called "cloze technique" is highly useful (W. L. Taylor, 1953, 1954, 1956). In this method, every fifth or tenth word of a message is deleted and the reader is asked to fill in the word which seems to fit the context most satisfactorily. The ease and accuracy with which the average reader can do this is a measurement of certain aspects of the communication load; for if the reader finds it difficult to select the proper word to fill the blank, or if the choice is in many instances wrong, it is evident that the transitional probabilities are very low; in other words, the sequences are highly unpredictable.

Another method of judging communication load is to measure the hesitations and mistakes in oral reading. This method is not so "objective" or so subject to correct measurement as the cloze technique, but in practical situations it is often very useful; for if those points at which the average reader hesitates or makes an incorrect choice of a word are carefully observed, it is very likely that these points mark an abrupt rise in communication load. Such hesitations or mistakes may, of course, mark an incorrect grammatical form—which produces a high formal communication load. They may, however, mean that the word chosen simply does not fit the context, in which case the reader is puzzled. A still further problem may be introduced by virtue of the rarity of the theme or concept described. Whatever the reason, the fact of a high communication load is signaled by consistent hesitations and mistakes in oral reading.

Another type of test involves having persons read over a message or listen to its being read, and then having them report what they have read or heard. If they tend more or less consistently to distort the account, to have difficulty in explaining certain features, or to omit significant details, it is probable that at these points the account carries too heavy a communication load; for the tendency of hearers is to reduce the communication load in retelling, either by reinterpreting what they have heard in a form more predictable, in terms of their experience, or by omitting elements difficult to understand.

BALANCING OUT THE COMMUNICATION LOAD

In any message the various features which contribute to the communication load have different peaks and troughs. A wave of formal communication load might have the contours shown in Figure 38.

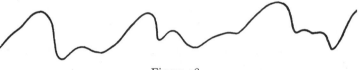

Figure 38

On the other hand, the semantic features of the communication load might have the series of peaks and troughs shown in Figure 39.

The various features which combine to make up the total communication load produce a composite wave which may have any number of different forms. Such a composite wave, in which various features would

Figure 39

be weighted as to relative importance, would always have marked variations; for no sameness of communication load can be maintained, and, if it could, it would most certainly not be desirable to do so. We would expect, therefore, that the total communication load might vary as shown in Figure 40.

Obviously it is unwise to devise a message with an exceedingly high level of communication load, for the receptor would soon become fatigued. Similarly a consistently low level would result in the receptor's becoming bored. What one must strive for is a communication load sufficiently challenging to appear relevant and interesting, but not so heavy as to be fatiguing.

To accomplish this goal it is important to bear in mind the possibility of balancing out the communication load. If both the formal and the semantic features of a message pile up a heavy communication load at the same point, the decoding of such a portion may require entirely too much work; that is to say, the receptor will feel that the energy expended is entirely out of proportion to the results. On the other hand, if, at a point of heavy semantic load, one lightens the formal load, and the converse, it is possible to balance out the factors, and thus attain a higher level of overall proficiency.

The practical application of this principle may be seen in a comparison

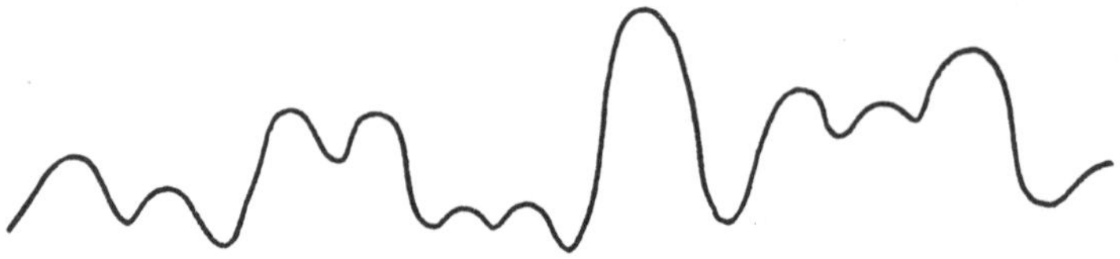

Figure 40

of the Gospel of Mark with the Epistle to the Ephesians. Both in formal and semantic communication load Mark is much less heavy than Ephesians. As a result, even awkward and literal translations of Mark may be relatively intelligible to receptors. In Ephesians, however, both the formal and semantic loads are so great that a literal rendering is often quite useless as a vehicle of communication. Of course, by virtue of the basic differences in theme and content it is impossible to reduce Ephesians to the same average communication load as Mark. However, much can be done to make Ephesians more understandable by: (1) substituting easier for more difficult formal arrangements of words; and (2) building in considerable redundancy to make the combinations of words more readily intelligible. This is precisely what J. B. Phillips has done; for in his *Letters to Young Churches* (covering the New Testament Epistles) he has taken proportionately far greater liberties than in his translation of the Gospels. Such measures were necessary if the same approximate level of communication load was to be maintained for all the books of the New Testament (1961). The results depart rather widely from traditional tendencies in translation, but they do result in much greater communication, for they are more in conformity with balanced communication loads.

DIFFERING RECEPTOR CAPACITIES FOR DECODING MESSAGES

It is obvious that different receptors (i.e. people who receive a message, whether written or spoken) have quite different capacities for decoding messages. Except for individual differences in intelligence such diverse capacities are due to two principal factors; (1) formal education, involving at least three principal levels: (a) the specialist, (b) the well-educated adult, and (c) the adult with relatively limited education; and (2) informal education (or general experience), usually expressible in terms of age, and involving three principal levels: (a) adult, (b) adolescent, and (c) children. Of course, it must be recognized that many adults have relatively narrow experience, while some children are unusually perceptive and have been exposed to a wide variety of learning experiences. Individual differences within the categories are accordingly even greater than the averages of the classes. Nevertheless, one must recognize that these different basic capacities are of great importance in the preparation of any literature or translations for a specific receptor audience. One of the most serious mistakes made is to equate adults in other cultures (especially members of primitive societies) with children in our own, and to prepare messages for them of a type appropriate to children in our society. Even in the most primitive society, adults acquire a great deal of information by means of informal education, and their inexperience or deficiency in literacy does not by any means place them in the category of school children in our society.

The ability to decode a particular type of message is constantly in process of change, not only as the result of an increase in general education, but especially through specific acquaintance with the particular type of message. For example, at first a new reader of the Scriptures is obviously confronted with a very heavy communication load, but as he becomes familiar with certain words and combinations of words, the communication load is reduced. Obviously, then, the communication load is not a fixed characteristic of a message in and of itself, but is always relative to the specific receptors who are in the process of decoding it.

Because of this shift in communication load, we are faced with two alternatives: (1) changing the receptors, i.e. giving them more experience, and (2) changing the form of the message, i.e. providing different forms of the message for different grades of receptors. In the past the tendency was to insist on educating the receptors to the level of being able to decode the message. At present, however, in the production of all literature aimed at the masses the usual practice is to prepare different grades of the same message, so that people at different levels of experience may be able to decode at a rate acceptable to them. The American Bible Society, for example, is sponsoring three translations of the Bible into Spanish: one is of a traditional type, aimed at the present Evangelical constituency; another is of a more contemporary and sophisticated character, directed to the well-educated but nonchurch constituency; and a third is in very simple Spanish, intended especially for the new literate, who has usually had a minimum of contact with Protestant churches. Communist propagandists, it may be noted, have engaged in a similar scaling of translations of Lenin and Marx, making important adaptations for various grades of background and educational experience.

If the communication load is generally too low for the receptor, both in style and content, the message will appear insipid and boring. The failure of Laubach's *The Inspired Letters* (a translation of the New Testament Epistles from Romans through Jude) is largely due to this fact. It is possible, of course, to combine a low formal communication load with a relatively high semantic load (especially by the inclusion of allusions) and to produce thus a very acceptable piece of literature or translation. The Kingsley-Williams translation of the *New Testament in Plain English* is an example of a translation which purposely employs a limited vocabulary and simple grammatical constructions, but in which the semantic content is not watered down or artificially restricted. In the field of literature, *Alice in Wonderland* and *Winnie the Pooh*, and, in contemporary cartoon strips, *Pogo* and *Peanuts*, provide examples of quite low formal communication loads combined with high semantic loads. On the highest level, the power of Jesus' teaching by means of parables exemplifies this combination of low formal communication load with superbly challenging semantic content.

It is possible to produce a very acceptable translation while combining high formal and semantic communication loads, as has been done in the New Testament of the New English Bible—an outstanding work of translation. From time to time any good literary production must of necessity pierce the upper limit of ready decodability; but again it must also drop below this limit in order to adjust to the periodicity which is a part of all normal human activity.

A really successful translation, judged in terms of the response of the audience for which it is designed, must provide a challenge as well as information. This challenge must lie not merely in difficulty in decoding, but in newness of form—new ways of rendering old truths, new insights into traditional interpretations, and new words in fresh combinations.

CHAPTER SEVEN

THE ROLE OF THE TRANSLATOR

No discussion of the principles and procedures of translation can afford to treat translating as something apart from the translator himself. Nor should the poor translator be dragged in at the end of the discussion, with the admonition to follow the prescribed law of the Medes and Persians. Since the translator himself is the focal element in translating, and thus there cannot be any completely impersonal objectivity in his work—since he is a part of the cultural context in which he lives—his role is central to the basic principles and procedures of translating. We cannot, however, fully appreciate his role without having first analyzed certain basic formal and semantic elements of the translation process.

For the most part the translator's lot has been one of little thanks, poor pay, and plenty of abuse. Sir John Denham describes the average translator in such lines as,

> Such is our pride, our folly, or our fate
> That few, but such as cannot write, translate. [1]

But, difficulties and thanklessness notwithstanding, if the translator is to produce an acceptable translation he must have an excellent background in the source language and at the same time must have control over the resources of the language into which he is translating. He cannot simply match words from a dictionary; he must in a real sense create a new linguistic form to carry the concept expressed in the source language.

MODEL OF THE TRANSLATOR'S ROLE

We actually do not know precisely what takes place in the translator's mind when he translates, for psychologists and neurologists do not know the manner in which language data are stored in the brain. The fact that in some brain injuries the capacity of bilingual persons has been reduced to the speaking of one language and not the other has led to the belief that there may be compartmentalization in the brain. However, this hypothesis has been generally rejected.

One argument against any strict compartmentalization is the fact that a person who knows several languages is not always aware of the language in which certain concepts were communicated to him. However, a person who has, for example, studied mathematics in German, music in French, and science in English seems to retain a good deal of this compartmentalization in his participation in such activities. At the same time, merely having a knowledge of two languages is no guarantee that a person can function as a translator; for in certain individuals there

[1] Cited by Tytler, 1790, p. 5.

seems to be no connection between the two sets of experiences which provide the cultural contexts for the use of the two languages. If a person is to serve as a translator, and especially if he is to be an interpreter of continuous discourse (simultaneous interpreting), he must have had a good deal of experience in language switching. Moreover, some bilingual persons are good in translating from one of their languages into the other, but cannot easily reverse the roles. Before we can actually understand the psychological basis of translating, a great deal of research must be done.

Fortunately, however, for the purpose of our study of the translator's role, we need not have a comprehensive understanding of the psychological processes involved. These we shall simply have to take for granted. More important for us is a careful analysis of the larger cultural context into which the translator's activity fits.

In contrast with the relatively simple model of one-language communication (see Figure 32), the translator's activity is obviously complex, as the diagram in Figure 41 attempts to show.

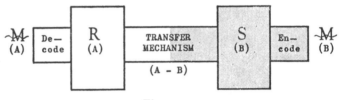

Figure 41

In this model a message in language A is decoded by the receptor into a different form of language A. It is then transformed by a "transfer mechanism" into language B, and the translator then becomes a source for the encoding of the message into language B. If we understood more precisely what happens in this transfer mechanism, we should be better able to pinpoint some sources of the difficulty persons have in interpreting from one language to another. One thing we do know, however— that the translator must not only discover corresponding symbols with which to communicate the message in B, but must also organize these symbols in the form required by language B. Basically we may describe translating as a process in which the concept is transferred possibly in essentially "kernel" form, and then the corresponding utterance in language B is generated. Some descriptions of the translational process would seem to imply that the procedure consists merely in matching successive corresponding symbols and grammatical structures of the two languages. In some artificially simple situations this may be true, but it is much more likely that the message of language A is decoded into a concept, and that this concept then provides the basis for the generation of an utterance in language B.

In terms of a psychology employing the image-plan model (Miller, Galanter, and Pribram, 1960), we could say that the transfer takes place at the level of the image, not at some stage of the plans. If the transfer occurs on the level of plans, especially on the lower hierarchical levels, the resulting translations will inevitably be awkward and artificial. Persons with a good deal of experience in simultaneous translating may become so expert in "matching" that they tend to short-circuit this transfer on the image level by selecting certain frequently recurring correspondences on the level of plans (before the conceptual image is complete). Careful literary translating must be concerned with "meaningful mouthfuls" (i.e. with reasonably whole images) and with translating entire concepts, not merely series of words or isolated fragments.

Anyone experienced in translating from one particular language to another does tend to speed up the process of transfer by anticipating in the decoding something of the encoding process. But if there is too much automatic or mechanical adjustment, there is likely to be severe distortion, for each language must be treated as a system in and of itself.

ETHNOLINGUISTIC MODEL OF TRANSLATION

As already stated, even more important than what takes place inside the translator's brain is what takes place in the total cultural framework in which the communication occurs. Moreover, in an attempt to describe these interlanguage and intercultural factors, we must reckon with differences of time (i.e. translations from ancient texts, often in languages now extinct) and differences of culture. There are always cultural differences between societies widely separated in time, and there are radically different degrees of cultural diversity in contemporary societies.

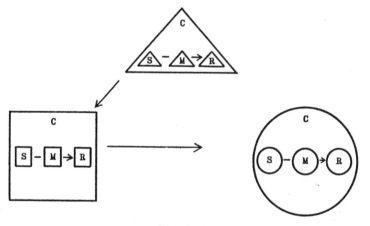

Figure 42

Figure 42 diagrams the typical situation in which an English-speaking translator tries to render the Biblical message (whether from Greek or Hebrew) into some present-day non-Indo-European language.

Certain features of Figure 42 should be especially noted:

1. The S, M, and R stand for Source, Message, and Receptor.
2. The large triangle, square, and circle, marked C, represent the total cultural contexts in which the communications take place.
3. The larger arrows indicate the translational process, first from Greek or Hebrew into English, and then into a third language.
4. The small triangles, squares, and circles enclosing the S, M, and R in each instance are designed to point out the manner in which participants and message reflect the total cultural context in which the communication takes place.
5. The vertical dimension represents temporal differences, while the placement of the square and the circle on the same level indicates that they are contemporaneous.
6. The differences in shape are designed to highlight the overall cultural differences. In many respects, however, some so-called aboriginal cultures of today are closer to the culture of Biblical times than to our own highly technological society, so that the contrastive shapes in the diagram are not entirely justified.

One might argue that the proper procedure for a Bible translator would be to take the text in Greek and render it directly into the final language, rather than filter it through his own English-language background. Theoretically this is the ideal procedure. In general, however, this is by no means the practice, for few English-speaking persons have so perfect a control of the original source language that they translate directly. Moreover, what is even more important to realize is that almost all the knowledge the average English-speaking translator has acquired of the Greek or Hebrew text has come through dictionaries and grammars written in English. Thus the mediating language is bound to be of great influence, regardless of the translator's wish to avoid such "linguistic contamination."

Moreover, it is questionable whether it is wise for a translator to try to escape from his own cultural context. Richmond Lattimore (1959, p. 54) insists that: "No translator can escape being colored by his own time, and it is wrong to try too hard to cut free from this influence. One can not translate in a vacuum."

One important element in this ethnolinguistic model of translation is the nature of the response implied. The receptors in each instance can only respond to the message as communicated to them in their own language, and can only express this response behaviorally within the cultural context in which they live. This means that basically the receptor must be able to respond to the message within the context of his own culture, and to do so he need not become a kind of pseudo-receptor of the triangle culture. Stated in theological terms, this means that a person need not be a member of a "New Testament Church" in order to be a Christian, any more than he needs to know Greek in order to understand the meaning of the New Testament. Fundamentally it means that in this type of communication we are not concerned with the formal matching of the message in the circle culture with the message in the triangle culture, but with the dynamic relationship of the various receptors to the respective messages. Stated as a kind of formula, we may say that for the type of message contained in the New Testament, we are concerned with a relationship such as can be expressed in the following equation:

$$\left(\text{R}:\text{M}\right) \text{C} \; :: \; \left(\text{R}:\text{M}\right) \text{C}$$

That is to say, the receptor in the circle culture should be able, within his own culture, to respond to the message as given in his language, in substantially the same manner as the receptor in the triangle culture responded, within the context of his own culture, to the message as communicated to him in his own language.

RELATIONSHIP OF TRANSLATOR TO SOURCE AND RECEPTOR LANGUAGES

Ideally, a translator should be completely bilingual in source and receptor languages, and should be translating into his mother tongue. But this ideal is rarely realized. Instead, there are various levels of compromise in which the translator's role is adjusted in various ways to the languages concerned. For example a person from a "square" language-culture attempting to translate into a "circle" language-culture might be represented as in Figure 43.

Figure 43

But this type of representation is really not accurate; rather, in his double role the translator becomes, not something entirely different but actually a dual or even a multiple person, participating at the same time in more than one linguistic and cultural world.

If we represent the mother language of the translator by a solid line and the acquired language by a broken line, we can diagram a number of different combinations (Figure 44), using a square to represent the source language and the circle to stand for the receptor language.

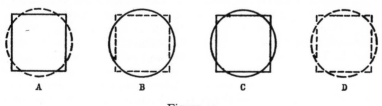

Figure 44

A then represents translating from one's mother tongue into an acquired language; *B*, translating from an acquired language into one's mother tongue; *C*, translating from one mother tongue to another (complete bilingualism); and *D*, translating from one acquired language into another acquired language.

Of the four possibilities listed, *A* is typical of most missionary translating; *B* is of course a decidedly preferable procedure. The circumstances of *C* can be almost as good as *B*, though there is a tendency for some translators in this category to mix their usage and thus not be stylistically

Figure 45

as acceptable as they should be in the receptor language. The circumstances of *D*, though quite common, are the least satisfactory. In fact, in most Bible translating, where a three-language arrangement is usual, the type of relationship between original, mediating, and final languages is that shown in Figure 45.

BASIC REQUIREMENTS FOR THE TRANSLATOR

The first and most obvious requirement of any translator is that he have a satisfactory knowledge of the source language. It is not enough that he be able to get the "general drift" of the meaning, or that he be adept in consulting dictionaries (this he will have to do even at best). Rather, he must understand not only the obvious content of the message, but also the subtleties of meaning, the significant emotive values of words, and the stylistic features which determine the "flavor and feel" of the message.

Even more important than knowledge of the resources of the source language is a complete control of the receptor language. A certain amount of data on the source-language message can usually be secured from dictionaries, commentaries, and technical treatises, but there is no substitute for thorough mastery of the receptor language. Certainly the most numerous and serious errors made by translators arise primarily from their lack of thorough knowledge of the receptor language.

It is one thing, however, to know a language in general and another to have a special knowledge of a particular subject. For example, one may be generally familiar with a language and still know nothing about nuclear physics or organic chemistry. Such a general knowledge is quite inadequate as a background for translating technical materials in such fields. In other words, in addition to a knowledge of the two or more languages involved in the translational process, the translator must have a thorough acquaintance with the subject matter concerned (Limaye, 1955).

Even if the translator possesses all the necessary technical knowledge, he is not really competent unless he has also a truly empathetic spirit. Basil Anderton (1920, p. 66) compares this empathy of the translator for the original author with that of the good actor, able to "feel" his part: "The words which he is to employ are set down for him. These words he has to interpret into the language of movement and gesture, of voice, of facial expression: in a word, he must translate them into visible and audible human emotion; he must impersonate the characters." Similarly, the translator must have the gift of mimicry, the capacity to act the author's part, impersonating his demeanor, speech, and ways, with the utmost verisimilitude (Nabokov, 1941).

Justin O'Brien (1959, p. 85) states the case thus: "One should never translate anything one does not admire," and if possible, "a natural affinity should exist between translator and translated." In addition to this affinity, O'Brien argues that the translator should also have something of the same cultural background as that of the author he is translating. If such is not the case, "the translator should be willing and readily able to make up for this deficiency." At the same time, a translator must be content to be like his author, for it is not his business to try to excel him.

Even thorough knowledge of the languages and the subject matter, combined with empathy, will not suffice to guarantee really effective translating unless the translator also has a capacity for literary expression. Nabokov (1941) contends that ultimately the fully effective translator should have as much talent, or "at least the same kind of talent, as the author he chooses." [1] Tytler (1790, p. 204) earlier stated this same requirement, saying that, "The genius of the translator should be akin to that of the original author," and that "The best translators have shone in original composition of the same species with that which they have translated."

A. J. Arberry (1946, p. 240) presents somewhat this same point of view in his discussion of the Persian poet Ḥāfiẓ: "No translation, however learned, is of any value that does not give at least some of the joy to the reader that was given by its original. Ḥāfiẓ has for centuries been one of the great literary joys of the Orient. Is it good translating to turn what is such pleasure for the East into such positive pain for the West?" To reproduce something of the charm and excellence of Ḥāfiẓ' style requires, however, real stylistic gifts in the translator. As L. Portier (1926, p. 457) says in describing the translations of Giacomo Zanella: "One does not render a poet as, with a compass, one measures and tells the dimensions of a building," but rather in the way in which "one reproduces some beautiful music upon a different instrument"—a procedure which requires genuine skill of performance and sensitivity to artistic style.

---

[1]   See also Edward Roditi (1942) and Ervino Pocar (1956).

The translation of highly "personal messages," as in lyric poetry, calls for an even greater degree of combined empathy and stylistic excellence than does prose. J. M. Cocking (1949, p. 318) describes the successful translation of lyric poetry as "a lucky coincidence of mood and experience with the original poet at the period of creation." But he insists that, in the stylistic adjustments that are necessary in translating a poem from one language to another, the translator must be fully conscious of the technical problems and limitations involved, for only then can "he make the inevitable sacrifice with his eyes open and make no more than the inevitable."

In translating the Bible, most outstanding translators have also insisted upon a further requirement, namely, a devout recognition of dependence upon divine grace. This element has been repeatedly noted in the attitudes of such translators as Jerome, Wycliffe, Luther, and Tyndale, and is expressly set forth as a prerequisite by Frederick C. Grant (1950, p. 149): "The translator should not only make use of the best scientific philology and exegesis, but also invoke and rely upon divine grace for the fulfilment of his task."

The Motives of the Translator

Perhaps the motives or combinations of motives of translators are as varied and numerous as translators themselves. Undoubtedly there are few instances of completely unmixed motives in this field. Nevertheless, some principal motives which both enter into the translator's work and in various ways influence the results can be discerned and sorted out.

A purely monetary motivation is rare, but where it exists it results in the typical "hack job," with words thrown together, ideas strung along, and an absence of sensitivity to the real message and spirit of the original work. But since pay for translating is notoriously poor, few persons engage in it merely for monetary reward. Certainly, when the work is at all outstanding, other and much more important considerations are present; for example, the challenge of solving a puzzle in communication, a vicarious participation in some great creative work, or a desire to gain some distinction at least on the periphery of *belles lettres*. A translator may also be motivated by a sincere humanitarian purpose, namely, to convey an important message in an intelligible form. Such a motivation has certainly been dominant in the history of Bible translating, and is similarly evident in the dedicated efforts of early scholars who reproduced the classics in modern European languages, as well as in those of many present-day translators who strive to translate scientific texts into languages in which the terminology of Western science is strange and new.

Various combinations of experience and motivation produce different types of translators. They can probably best be summarized in three principal categories, as Nabokov (1941, p. 161) has done: (1) the scholar, who certainly commits fewer blunders than the drudge, but who must have, in addition to learning and diligence, some imagination and style if he is to do a good job; (2) the well-meaning hack, who laboriously strings words, phrases, and sentences together in intelligible, but stylistically barren, ways; and (3) the professional writer, who, on the one hand, may miss the point in his translation because he lacks the scholar's insight, or, on the other, may tend to dress up the real author to look like himself.

THE TRANSLATOR AS PIONEER, MIDWIFE, OR TEAMMATE

To summarize, the ideal role of the translator calls for a person who has complete knowledge of both source and receptor languages, intimate acquaintance with the subject matter, effective empathy with the original author and the content, and stylistic facility in the receptor language. However, such an ideal set of abilities is rarely found, and therefore the essential elements in the role of the translator must often be distributed among several persons in various ways. Particularly must such a division of labor be made in situations in which a translator is attempting to reproduce a message in a source language with which he is not fully acquainted, or over which he has not complete linguistic control. In such circumstances the translator's function may be characterized in one of three principal ways: (1) as pioneer, (2) as midwife, and (3) as teammate.

When functioning as a "pioneer," the translator hammers out the basic form of a translation, largely without the help of others, even though he may have less than complete mastery of the lexical and syntactic resources of the language. He then reads this type of translation to various persons, and on the basis of their responses proceeds to change the selection of words, modify the word order, and in various ways polish up his work. This "pioneer" role is characteristic of missionaries who have gone into areas where there is as yet no written language or literary tradition. In order to translate a text into such a language, the missionary has to take the full responsibility for both preliminary drafts and the task of polishing. In such a situation he succeeds in his task when he knows the indigenous language well and is sensitive to native-speaker criticism, itself frequently not easy to interpret.

The "midwife" role is of quite a different type. In these circumstances the so-called translator serves primarily as a specialist in exegetical and linguistic matters, and native speakers of the language themselves do the actual translating. In many instances of Bible translating, for example, the missionary restricts himself primarily to the tasks of: (1) explaining carefully what the text means; (2) indicating something of the type of communication involved, e.g. conversation, exposition, or narrative; (3) writing down what his helpers suggest as appropriate ways of rendering such passages; and (4) bringing to the attention of his helpers certain obvious semantic and grammatical problems. In this process, the translator is a kind of resource person who, though he may suggest possible ways of rendering the message in the receptor language, relies almost entirely upon his informants for the actual form of the translation. He may do a great deal to prune the message, eliminate obviously extraneous elements, correct evident errors, and even polish the form, but the informants supply the actual forms of expression. In the final analysis they pass judgment on all basic problems of word selection, intelligibility, and style. In such circumstances the missionary translator functions as a kind of technical assistant.

In the "teammate" role, the translator may share more or less equally with others the responsibility for the form of the message in the receptor language. For example, one person may interpret the meaning of the source-language message, another may suggest the equivalent rendering in the receptor language, and a third may be responsible for style. A number of translation committees are set up in this way: one may be an expert on text, another on exegesis, a third on indigenous religious beliefs, a fourth on lexical and grammatical structures in the receptor language, and a fifth on style. However the total responsibility is divided, the resulting procedures are essentially the same, namely, a division of responsibility for various aspects of the total work. At the same time, however, some committees are formed, not on the basis of complementary responsibilities, but with each person theoretically as proficient as any other in all aspects of the work. Such circumstances, though seeming to be ideal, are in practice not only unworkable, but actually undesirable; for it is much better for members of a committee to have related and complementary qualifications recognized by all, rather than for each to be presumably equally expert in all fields. Where there is truly a team, the teammates can be expected to help one another; where too many wish to be prima donnas, certain persons tend to cancel out the others. The "translator-reviser" system so widely used in most of the linguistic services of international organizations is an apt example of teammate role in translation.

Dangers of Subjectivity in Translating

No translator can avoid a certain degree of personal involvement in his work. In his interpretation of the source-language message, his selection of corresponding words and grammatical forms, and his choice of stylistic equivalents, he will inevitably be influenced by his overall empathy with author and message, or his lack of it. It is quite understandable that the behavioral and intraorganismic meanings employed by the author will affect and be affected by the translator's corresponding values—which in no instance will be exactly the same as the author's. Intellectual honesty requires the translator to be as free as possible from personal intrusion in the communication process. The translator should never tack on his own impressions or distort the message to fit his own intellectual and emotional outlook. At the same time, the human translator is not a machine, and he inevitably leaves the stamp of his own personality on any translation he makes. This being the case, he must exert every effort to reduce to a minimum any intrusion of himself which is not in harmony with the intent of the original author and message.

When a translator intrudes in the transmission process, his behavior may be accounted for in various ways. At times a translator has purposely·

and consciously attempted to change a message in order to make it conform to his own political, social, or religious predilections. For this type of willful distortion there is no real cure. But most instances of undue alteration of an original are not the result of any conscious desire to modify or to distort the message, but rather of unconscious personality traits which influence a person's work in subtle and seemingly innocent ways. These are particularly evident when a translator feels inclined to improve on the original, correct apparent errors, or defend a personal preference by slanting his choice of words.

The dangers of subjectivity in translating are directly proportionate to the potential emotional involvement of the translator in the message. For scientific prose such involvement is usually at a minimum, but in religious texts it may be rather great, since religion is concerned with the deepest and most universal value systems. In some instances it is the translator's own sense of insecurity which makes it difficult for him to let the document speak for itself, and in other instances a lack of humility may prompt him to translate without consulting the opinions of those who have studied such texts more fully than himself.

At times the translator may be misled by his own paternalistic attitude into thinking that the potential receptors of his translation are so limited in understanding or experience that they must have his "built-in" explanations. Or he may believe that their language is so deficient that only by certain "improvements" (often arbitrary and artificial) can he communicate the message.

Perhaps the translator's greatest danger in religious translating is simply his not recognizing that sincerity alone may not be enough, for he must not only be competent in the languages involved, well acquainted with the subject matter, adept in the use of words, but also fully aware of himself—his weaknesses, strengths, and potentialities. For the translator "Know thyself!" has unusually applicable significance.

To summarize: The translator's task is essentially a difficult and often a thankless one. He is severely criticized if he makes a mistake, but only faintly praised when he succeeds, for often it is assumed that anyone who knows two languages ought to be able to do as well as the translator who has labored to produce a text. But even if his work is rarely rewarded by the praise of others, the task itself has its own rewards, for successful translating involves one of the most complex intellectual challenges known to mankind. Moreover, in our present world the need for extensive, accurate, and effective communication between those using different languages gives the translator a position of new and strategic importance.

CHAPTER EIGHT

PRINCIPLES OF CORRESPONDENCE

Since no two languages are identical, either in the meanings given to corresponding symbols or in the ways in which such symbols are arranged in phrases and sentences, it stands to reason that there can be no absolute correspondence between languages. Hence there can be no fully exact translations. The total impact of a translation may be reasonably close to the original, but there can be no identity in detail. Constance B. West (1932, p. 344) clearly states the problem: "Whoever takes upon himself to translate contracts a debt; to discharge it, he must pay not with the same money, but the same sum." One must not imagine that the process of translation can avoid a certain degree of interpretation by the translator. In fact, as D. G. Rossetti stated in 1874 (Fang, 1953), "A translation remains perhaps the most direct form of commentary."

DIFFERENT TYPES OF TRANSLATIONS

No statement of the principles of correspondence in translating can be complete without recognizing the many different types of translations (Herbert P. Phillips, 1959). Traditionally, we have tended to think in terms of free or paraphrastic translations as contrasted with close or literal ones. Actually, there are many more grades of translating than these extremes imply. There are, for example, such ultraliteral translations as interlinears; while others involve highly concordant relationships, e.g. the same source-language word is always translated by one—and only one—receptor-language word. Still others may be quite devoid of artificial restrictions in form, but nevertheless may be overtraditional and even archaizing. Some translations aim at very close formal and semantic correspondence, but are generously supplied with notes and commentary. Many are not so much concerned with giving information as with creating in the reader something of the same mood as was conveyed by the original.

Differences in translations can generally be accounted for by three basic factors in translating: (1) the nature of the message, (2) the purpose or purposes of the author and, by proxy, of the translator, and (3) the type of audience.

Messages differ primarily in the degree to which content or form is the dominant consideration. Of course, the content of a message can never be completely abstracted from the form, and form is nothing apart from content; but in some messages the content is of primary consideration, and in others the form must be given a higher priority. For example, in the Sermon on the Mount, despite certain important stylistic qualities, the importance of the message far exceeds considerations of form. On the other hand, some of the acrostic poems of the Old Testament are obviously designed to fit a very strict formal "strait jacket." But even the contents of a message may differ widely in applicability to the receptor-language audience. For example, the folk tale of the Bauré Indians of Bolivia, about a giant who led the animals in a symbolic dance, is interesting to an English-speaking audience, but to them it has not the same relevance as the Sermon on the Mount. And even the Bauré Indians themselves recognize the Sermon on the Mount as more significant than their favorite "how-it-happened" story. At the same time, of course, the Sermon on the Mount has greater relevance to these Indians than have some passages in Leviticus.

In poetry there is obviously a greater focus of attention upon formal elements than one normally finds in prose. Not that content is necessarily sacrificed in translation of a poem, but the content is necessarily constricted into certain formal molds. Only rarely can one reproduce both content and form in a translation, and hence in general the form is usually sacrificed for the sake of the content. On the other hand, a lyric poem translated as prose is not an adequate equivalent of the original. Though it may reproduce the conceptual content, it falls far short of reproducing the emotional intensity and flavor. However, the translating of some types of poetry by prose may be dictated by important cultural considerations. For example, Homer's epic poetry reproduced in English poetic form usually seems to us antique and queer—with nothing of the liveliness and spontaneity characteristic of Homer's style. One reason is that we are not accustomed to having stories told to us in poetic form. In our Western European tradition such epics are related in prose. For this reason E. V. Rieu chose prose rather than poetry as the more appropriate medium by which to render The Iliad and The Odyssey.

The particular purposes of the translator are also important factors in dictating the type of translation. Of course, it is assumed that the translator has purposes generally similar to, or at least compatible with, those of the original author, but this is not necessarily so. For example, a San Blas story-teller is interested only in amusing his audience, but an ethnographer who sets about translating such stories may be much more concerned in giving his audience an insight into San Blas personality structure. Since, however, the purposes of the translator are the primary ones to be considered in studying the types of translation which result, the principal purposes that underlie the choice of one or another way to render a particular message are important.

The primary purpose of the translator may be information as to both content and form. One intended type of response to such an informative type of translation is largely cognitive, e.g. an ethnographer's translation of texts from informants, or a philosopher's translation of Heidegger. A largely informative translation may, on the other hand, be designed to elicit an emotional response of pleasure from the reader or listener.

A translator's purposes may involve much more than information. He may, for example, want to suggest a particular type of behavior by means of a translation. Under such circumstances he is likely to aim at full intelligibility, and to make certain minor adjustments in detail so that the reader may understand the full implications of the message for his own circumstances. In such a situation a translator is not content to have receptors say, "This is intelligible to us." Rather, he is looking for some such response as, "This is meaningful for us." In terms of Bible translating, the people might understand a phrase such as 'to change one's mind about sin' as meaning "repentance." But if the indigenous way of talking about repentance is "spit on the ground in front of," as in Shilluk,[1] spoken in the Sudan, the translator will obviously aim at the more meaningful idiom. On a similar basis, "white as snow" may be rendered as 'white as egret feathers', if the people of the receptor language are not acquainted with snow but speak of anything very white by this phrase.

A still greater degree of adaptation is likely to occur in a translation which has an imperative purpose. Here the translator feels constrained not merely to suggest a possible line of behavior, but to make such an action explicit and compelling. He is not content to translate in such a way that the people are likely to understand; rather, he insists that the translation must be so clear that no one can possibly misunderstand.

In addition to the different types of messages and the diverse purposes of translators, one must also consider the extent to which prospective audiences differ both in decoding ability and in potential interest.

Decoding ability in any language involves at least four principal levels: (1) the capacity of children, whose vocabulary and cultural experience are limited; (2) the double-standard capacity of new literates, who can decode oral messages with facility but whose ability to decode written messages is limited; (3) the capacity of the average literate adult, who can handle both oral and written messages with relative ease; and (4) the unusually high capacity of specialists (doctors, theologians, philosophers, scientists, etc.), when they are decoding messages within their own area of specialization. Obviously a translation designed for children cannot be the same as one prepared for specialists, nor can a translation for children be the same as one for a newly literate adult.

Prospective audiences differ not only in decoding ability, but perhaps even more in their interests. For example, a translation designed to stimulate reading for pleasure will be quite different from one intended for a person anxious to learn how to assemble a complicated machine. Moreover, a translator of African myths for persons who simply want to satisfy their curiosity about strange peoples and places will produce a different piece of work from one who renders these same myths in a form acceptable to linguists, who are more interested in the linguistic structure underlying the translation than in cultural novelty.

---

[1] This idiom is based upon the requirement that plaintiffs and defendants spit on the ground in front of each other when a case has been finally tried and punishment meted out. The spitting indicates that all is forgiven and that the accusations can never be brought into court again.

Two Basic Orientations in Translating

Since "there are, properly speaking, no such things as identical equivalents" (Belloc, 1931a and b, p. 37), one must in translating seek to find the closest possible equivalent. However, there are fundamentally two different types of equivalence: one which may be called formal and another which is primarily dynamic.

Formal equivalence focuses attention on the message itself, in both form and content. In such a translation one is concerned with such correspondences as poetry to poetry, sentence to sentence, and concept to concept. Viewed from this formal orientation, one is concerned that the message in the receptor language should match as closely as possible the different elements in the source language. This means, for example, that the message in the receptor culture is constantly compared with the message in the source culture to determine standards of accuracy and correctness.

The type of translation which most completely typifies this structural equivalence might be called a "gloss translation," in which the translator attempts to reproduce as literally and meaningfully as possible the form and content of the original. Such a translation might be a rendering of some Medieval French text into English, intended for students of certain aspects of early French literature not requiring a knowledge of the original language of the text. Their needs call for a relatively close approximation to the structure of the early French text, both as to form (e.g. syntax and idioms) and content (e.g. themes and concepts). Such a translation would require numerous footnotes in order to make the text fully comprehensible.

A gloss translation of this type is designed to permit the reader to identify himself as fully as possible with a person in the source-language context, and to understand as much as he can of the customs, manner of thought, and means of expression. For example, a phrase such as "holy kiss" (Romans 16:16) in a gloss translation would be rendered literally, and would probably be supplemented with a footnote explaining that this was a customary method of greeting in New Testament times.

In contrast, a translation which attempts to produce a dynamic rather than a formal equivalence is based upon "the principle of equivalent effect" (Rieu and Phillips, 1954). In such a translation one is not so concerned with matching the receptor-language message with the source-language message, but with the dynamic relationship (mentioned in Chapter 7), that the relationship between receptor and message should be substantially the same as that which existed between the original receptors and the message.

A translation of dynamic equivalence aims at complete naturalness of expression, and tries to relate the receptor to modes of behavior relevant within the context of his own culture; it does not insist that he understand the cultural patterns of the source-language context in order to comprehend the message. Of course, there are varying degrees of such dynamic-equivalence translations. One of the modern English translations which, perhaps more than any other, seeks for equivalent effect is J. B. Phillips' rendering of the New Testament. In Romans 16:16 he quite naturally translates "greet one another with a holy kiss" as "give one another a hearty handshake all around."

Between the two poles of translating (i.e. between strict formal equivalence and complete dynamic equivalence) there are a number of intervening grades, representing various acceptable standards of literary translating. During the past fifty years, however, there has been a marked shift of emphasis from the formal to the dynamic dimension. A recent summary of opinion on translating by literary artists, publishers, educators, and professional translators indicates clearly that the present direction is toward increasing emphasis on dynamic equivalences (Cary, 1959b).

Linguistic and Cultural Distance

In any discussion of equivalences, whether structural or dynamic, one must always bear in mind three different types of relatedness, as determined by the linguistic and cultural distance between the codes used to convey the messages. In some instances, for example, a translation may involve comparatively closely related languages and cultures, e.g. translations from Frisian into English, or from Hebrew into Arabic. On the other hand, the languages may not be related, even though the cultures are closely parallel, e.g. as in translations from German into Hungarian, or from Swedish into Finnish (German and Swedish are Indo-European languages, while Hungarian and Finnish belong to the Finno-Ugrian family). In still other instances a translation may involve not only differences of linguistic affiliation but also highly diverse cultures, e.g. English into Zulu, or Greek into Javanese. [1]

Where the linguistic and cultural distances between source and receptor codes are least, one should expect to encounter the least number of serious problems, but as a matter of fact if languages are too closely related one is likely to be badly deceived by the superficial similarities, with the result that translations done under these circumstances are often quite poor. One of the serious dangers consists of so-called "false friends," i.e. borrowed or cognate words which seem to be equivalent but are not always so, e.g. English *demand* and French *demander*, English *ignore* and Spanish *ignorar*, English *virtue* and Latin *virtus*, and English *deacon* and Greek *diakonos*.

When the cultures are related but the languages are quite different, the translator is called upon to make a good many formal shifts in the translation. However, the cultural similarities in such instances usually

[1] We also encounter certain rare situations in which the languages are related but the cultures are quite disparate. For example, in the case of Hindi and English one is dealing with two languages from the same language family, but the cultures in question are very different. In such instances, the languages are also likely to be so distantly related as to make their linguistic affiliation a matter of minor consequence.

provide a series of parallelisms of content that make the translation proportionately much less difficult than when both languages and cultures are disparate. In fact, differences between cultures cause many more severe complications for the translator than do differences in language structure.

DEFINITIONS OF TRANSLATING

Definitions of proper translating are almost as numerous and varied as the persons who have undertaken to discuss the subject. This diversity is in a sense quite understandable; for there are vast differences in the materials translated, in the purposes of the publication, and in the needs of the prospective audience. Moreover, live languages are constantly changing and stylistic preferences undergo continual modification. Thus a translation acceptable in one period is often quite unacceptable at a later time.

A number of significant and relatively comprehensive definitions of translation have been offered. Procházka (Garvin, 1955, pp. III ff.) defines a good translation in terms of certain requirements which must be made of the translator, namely: (1) "He must understand the original word thematically and stylistically"; (2) "he must overcome the differences between the two linguistic structures"; and (3) "he must reconstruct the stylistic structures of the original work in his translation."

In a description of proper translation of poetry, Jackson Mathews (1959, p. 67) states: "One thing seems clear: to translate a poem whole is to compose another poem. A whole translation will be faithful to the *matter*, and it will 'approximate the form' of the original; and it will have a life of its own, which is the voice of the translator." Richmond Lattimore (1959, in Brower, 1959, p. 56) deals with the same basic problem of translating poetry. He describes the fundamental principles in terms of the way in which Greek poetry should be translated, namely: "to make from the Greek poem a poem in English which, while giving a high minimum of meaning of the Greek, is still a new English poem, which would not be the kind of poem it is if it were not translating the Greek which it translates."

No proper definition of translation can avoid some of the basic difficulties. Especially in the rendering of poetry, the tension between form and content and the conflict between formal and dynamic equivalences are always acutely present. However, it seems to be increasingly recognized that adherence to the letter may indeed kill the spirit. William A. Cooper (1928, p. 484) deals with this problem rather realistically in his article on "Translating Goethe's Poems," in which he says: "If the language of the original employs word formations that give rise to insurmountable difficulties of direct translation, and figures of speech wholly foreign, and hence incomprehensible in the other tongue, it is better to cling to the spirit of the poem and clothe it in language and figures entirely free from awkwardness of speech and obscurity of picture. This might be called a translation from culture to culture."

It must be recognized that in translating poetry there are very special problems involved, for the form of expression (rhythm, meter, assonance, etc.) is essential to communicating the spirit of the message to the audience. But all translating, whether of poetry or prose, must be concerned also with the response of the receptor; hence the ultimate purpose of the translation, in terms of its impact upon its intended audience, is a fundamental factor in any evaluation of translations. This reason underlies Leonard Forster's definition (1958, p. 6) of a good translation as "one which fulfills the same purpose in the new language as the original did in the language in which it was written."

The resolution of the conflict between literalness of form and equivalence of response seems increasingly to favor the latter, especially in the translating of poetic materials. C. W. Orr (1941, p. 318), for example, describes translating as somewhat equivalent to painting, for, as he says, "the painter does not reproduce every detail of the landscape"—he selects what seems best to him. Likewise for the translator, "It is the spirit, not only the letter, that he seeks to embody in his own version." Oliver Edwards (1957b, p. 13) echoes the same point of view: "We expect approximate truth in a translation . . . . What we want to have is the truest possible *feel* of the original. The characters, the situations, the reflections must come to us as they were in the author's mind and heart, not necessarily precisely as he had them on his lips."

It is one thing, however, to produce a generalized definition of translating, whether of poetry or prose; it is often quite another to describe in some detail the significant characteristics of an adequate translation. This fact Savory (1957, pp. 49-50) highlights by contrasting diametrically opposed opinions on a dozen important principles of translating. However, though some dissenting voices can be found on virtually all proposals as to what translating should consist of, there are several significant features of translating on which many of the most competent judges are increasingly in agreement.

Ezra Pound (1954, p. 273) states the case for translations making sense by declaring for "more sense and less syntax." But as early as 1789 George Campbell (1789, pp. 445 ff.) argued that translation should not be characterized by "obscure sense." E. E. Milligan (1957) also argues for sense rather than words, for he points out that unless a translation communicates, i.e. makes sense to the receptor, it has not justified its existence.

In addition to making sense, translations must also convey the "spirit and manner" of the original (Campbell, 1789, pp. 445 ff.). For the Bible translator, this means that the individual style of the various writers of the Scriptures should be reflected as far as possible (Campbell, 1789, p. 547). The same sentiment is clearly expressed by Ruth M. Underhill (1938, p. 16) in her treatment of certain problems of translating magic incantations of the Papago Indians of southern Arizona: "One can hope to make the translation exact only in spirit, not in letter." Francis Storr (1909) goes so far as to classify translators into "the literalist and the spiritualist schools," and in doing so takes his stand on the Biblical text, "The letter killeth but the spirit giveth life." As evidence for his thesis,

Storr cites the difference between the Authorized Version, which he contends represents the spirit, and the English Revised Version, which sticks to the letter, with the result that the translation lacks a *Sprachgefühl*. The absence of literary stylists on the English Revised Committee was, however, corrected in the New English Bible (New Testament, 1961), in which one entire panel was composed of persons with special sensitivity to and competence in English style.

Closely related to the requirement of sensitivity to the style of the original is the need for a "natural and easy" form of expression in the language into which one is translating (Campbell, 1789, pp. 445 ff.). Max Beerbohm (1903, p. 75) considers that the cardinal fault of many who translate plays into English is the failure to be natural in expression; in fact, they make the reader "acutely conscious that their work is a translation . . . . For the most part, their ingenuity consists in finding phrases that could not possibly be used by the average Englishman." Goodspeed (1945, p. 8) echoes the same sentiment with respect to Bible translating by declaring that: "The best translation is not one that keeps forever before the reader's mind the fact that this is a translation, not an original English composition, but one that makes the reader forget that it is a translation at all and makes him feel that he is looking into the ancient writer's mind, as he would into that of a contemporary. This is, indeed, no light matter to undertake or to execute, but it is, nevertheless, the task of any serious translator." J. B. Phillips (1953, p. 53) confirms the same viewpoint when he declares that: "The test of a real translation is that it should not read like translation at all." His second principle of translating re-enforces the first, namely a translation into English should avoid "translator's English."

It must be recognized, however, that it is not easy to produce a completely natural translation, especially if the original writing is good literature, precisely because truly good writing intimately reflects and effectively exploits the total idiomatic capacities and special genius of the language in which the writing is done. A translator must therefore not only contend with the special difficulties resulting from such an effective exploitation of the total resources of the source language, but also seek to produce something relatively equivalent in the receptor language. In fact, Justin O'Brien (1959, p. 81) quotes Raymond Guérin to the effect that: "the most convincing criterion of the quality of a work is the fact that it can only be translated with difficulty, for if it passes readily into another language without losing its essence, then it must have no particular essence or at least not one of the rarest."

An easy and natural style in translating, despite the extreme difficulties of producing it—especially when translating an original of high quality—is nevertheless essential to producing in the ultimate receptors a response similar to that of the original receptors. In one way or another this principle of "similar response" has been widely held and effectively stated by a number of specialists in the field of translating. Even though Matthew Arnold (1861, as quoted in Savory, 1957, p. 45) himself rejected in actual practice the principle of "similar response," he at least seems to have thought he was producing a similar response, for he declares that: "A translation should affect us in the same way as the original may be supposed to have affected its first hearers." Despite Arnold's objection to some of the freer translations done by others, he was at least strongly opposed to the literalist views of such persons as F. W. Newman (1861, p. xiv). Jowett (1891), on the other hand, comes somewhat closer to a present-day conception of "similar response" in stating that: "an English translation ought to be idiomatic and interesting, not only to the scholar, but to the learned reader . . . . The translator . . . seeks to produce on his reader an impression similar or nearly similar to that produced by the original."

Souter (1920, p. 7) expresses essentially this same view in stating that: "Our ideal in translation is to produce on the minds of our readers as nearly as possible the same effect as was produced by the original on its readers," and R. A. Knox (1957, p. 5) insists that a translation should be "read with the same interest and enjoyment which a reading of the original would have afforded."

In dealing with translating from an essentially linguistic point of view, Procházka (in Garvin, 1955) re-enforces this same viewpoint, namely, that "the translation should make the same resultant impression on the reader as the original does on its reader."

If a translation is to meet the four basic requirements of (1) making sense, (2) conveying the spirit and manner of the original, (3) having a natural and easy form of expression, and (4) producing a similar response, it is obvious that at certain points the conflict between content and form (or meaning and manner) will be acute, and that one or the other must give way. In general, translators are agreed that, when there is no happy compromise, meaning must have priority over style (Tancock, 1958, p. 29). What one must attempt, however, is an effective blend of "matter and manner," for these two aspects of any message are inseparably united. Adherence to content, without consideration of form, usually results in a flat mediocrity, with nothing of the sparkle and charm of the original. On the other hand, sacrifice of meaning for the sake of reproducing the style may produce only an impression, and fail to communicate the message. The form, however, may be changed more radically than the content and still be substantially equivalent in its effect upon the receptor. Accordingly, correspondence in meaning must have priority over correspondence in style. However, this assigning of priorities must never be done in a purely mechanical fashion, for what is ultimately required, especially in the translation of poetry, is "a re-creation, not a reproduction" (Lattimore, in Brower, 1959, p. 55).

Any survey of opinions on translating serves to confirm the fact that definitions or descriptions of translating are not served by deterministic rules; rather, they depend on probabilistic rules. One cannot, therefore, state that a particular translation is good or bad without taking into consideration a myriad of factors, which in turn must be weighted in a number of different ways, with appreciably different answers. Hence there will always be a variety of valid answers to the question, "Is this a good translation ?"

Principles Governing a Translation Oriented toward Formal-Equivalence

In order to understand somewhat more fully the characteristics of different types of translations, it is important to analyze in more detail the principles that govern a translation which attempts to reproduce a formal equivalence. Such a formal-equivalence (or F-E) translation is basically source-oriented; that is, it is designed to reveal as much as possible of the form and content of the original message.

In doing so, an F-E translation attempts to reproduce several formal elements, including: (1) grammatical units, (2) consistency in word usage, and (3) meanings in terms of the source context. The reproduction of grammatical units may consist in: (a) translating nouns by nouns, verbs by verbs, etc.; (b) keeping all phrases and sentences intact (i.e. not splitting up and readjusting the units); and (c) preserving all formal indicators, e.g. marks of punctuation, paragraph breaks, and poetic indentation.

In attempting to reproduce consistency in word usage, an F-E translation usually aims at so-called concordance of terminology; that is, it always renders a particular term in the source-language document by the corresponding term in the receptor document. Such a principle may, of course, be pushed to an absurd extent, with the result being relatively meaningless strings of words, as in some passages of the so-called Concordant Version of the New Testament. On the other hand, a certain degree of concordance may be highly desirable in certain types of F-E translating. For example, a reader of Plato's Dialogues in English may prefer rigid consistency in the rendering of key terms (as in Jowett's translation), so that he may have some comprehension of the way in which Plato uses certain word symbols to develop his philosophical system. An F-E translation may also make use of brackets, parentheses, or even italics (as in the King James Bible) for words added to make sense in the translation, but missing in the original document.

In order to reproduce meanings in terms of the source context, an F-E translation normally attempts not to make adjustments in idioms, but rather to reproduce such expressions more or less literally, so that the reader may be able to perceive something of the way in which the original document employed local cultural elements to convey meanings.

In many instances, however, one simply cannot reproduce certain formal elements of the source message. For example, there may be puns, chiasmic orders of words, instances of assonance, or acrostic features of line-initial sounds which completely defy equivalent rendering. In such instances one must employ certain types of marginal notes, if the feature in question merits an explanation. In some rare instances one does light upon a roughly equivalent pun or play on words. For example, in translating the Hebrew text of Genesis 2:23, in which the Hebrew word *isshah* 'woman' is derived from *ish* 'man,' it is possible to use a corresponding English pair, *woman* and *man*. However, such formal correspondences are obviously rare, for languages generally differ radically in both content and form.

A consistent F-E translation will obviously contain much that is not readily intelligible to the average reader. One must therefore usually supplement such translations with marginal notes, not only to explain some of the formal features which could not be adequately represented, but also to make intelligible some of the formal equivalents employed, for such expressions may have significance only in terms of the source language or culture.

Some types of strictly F-E translations, e.g. interlinear renderings and completely concordant translations, are of limited value; others are of great value. For example, translations of foreign-language texts prepared especially for linguists rarely attempt anything but close F-E renderings. In such translations the wording is usually quite literal, and even the segments are often numbered so that the corresponding units may be readily compared.

From what has been said directly and indirectly about F-E translations in preceding sections, it might be supposed that such translations are categorically ruled out. To the contrary, they are often perfectly valid translations of certain types of messages for certain types of audiences. The relative value and effectiveness of particular types of translations for particular audiences pose another question, and must not be confused with a description of the nature of various kinds of translations. At this point we are concerned only with their essential features, not with their evaluation.

Principles Governing Translations Oriented toward Dynamic Equivalence

In contrast with formal-equivalence translations others are oriented toward dynamic equivalence. In such a translation the focus of attention is directed, not so much toward the source message, as toward the receptor response. A dynamic-equivalence (or D-E) translation may be described as one concerning which a bilingual and bicultural person can justifiably say, "That is just the way we would say it." It is important to realize, however, that a D-E translation is not merely another message which is more or less similar to that of the source. It is a translation, and as such must clearly reflect the meaning and intent of the source.

One way of defining a D-E translation is to describe it as "the closest natural equivalent to the source-language message." This type of definition contains three essential terms: (1) *equivalent*, which points toward the source-language message, (2) *natural*, which points toward the receptor language, and (3) *closest*, which binds the two orientations together on the basis of the highest degree of approximation.

However, since a D-E translation is directed primarily toward equivalence of response rather than equivalence of form, it is important to define more fully the implications of the word *natural* as applied to such translations. Basically, the word *natural* is applicable to three areas of the communication process; for a *natural* rendering must fit (1) the receptor language and culture as a whole, (2) the context of the particular message, and (3) the receptor-language audience.

The conformance of a translation to the receptor language and culture as a whole is an essential ingredient in any stylistically acceptable rendering. Actually this quality of linguistic appropriateness is usually noticeable only when it is absent. In a natural translation, therefore, those features which would mar it are conspicuous by their absence. J. H. Frere (1820, p. 481) has described such a quality by stating, "the language of translation ought, we think, . . . be a pure, impalpable and invisible element, the medium of thought and feeling and nothing more; it ought never to attract attention to itself . . . . All importations from foreign languages . . . are . . . to be avoided." Such an adjustment to the receptor language and culture must result in a translation that bears no obvious trace of foreign origin, so that, as G. A. Black (1936, p. 50) describes James Thomson's translations of Heine, such renderings are "a reproduction of the original, such as Heine himself, if master of the English language, would have given."

A natural translation involves two principal areas of adaptation, namely, grammar and lexicon. In general the grammatical modifications can be made the more readily, since many grammatical changes are dictated by the obligatory structures of the receptor language. That is to say, one is obliged to make such adjustments as shifting word order, using verbs in place of nouns, and substituting nouns for pronouns. The lexical structure of the source message is less readily adjusted to the semantic requirements of the receptor language, for instead of obvious rules to be followed, there are numerous alternative possibilities. There are in general three lexical levels to be considered: (1) terms for which there are readily available parallels, e.g. *river, tree, stone, knife*, etc.; (2) terms which identify culturally different objects, but with somewhat similar functions, e.g. *book*, which in English means an object with pages bound together into a unit, but which, in New Testament times, meant a long parchment or papyrus rolled up in the form of a scroll; and (3) terms which identify cultural specialties, e.g. *synagogue, homer, ephah, cherubim*, and *jubilee*, to cite only a few from the Bible. Usually the first set of terms involves no problem. In the second set of terms several confusions can arise; hence one must either use another term which reflects the form of the referent, though not the equivalent function, or which identifies the equivalent function at the expense of formal identity. The basic problem is treated later in this chapter. In translating terms of the third class certain "foreign associations" can rarely be avoided. No translation that attempts to bridge a wide cultural gap can hope to eliminate all traces of the foreign setting. For example, in Bible translating it is quite impossible to remove such foreign "objects" as *Pharisees, Sadducees, Solomon's temple, cities of refuge*, or such Biblical themes as *anointing, adulterous generation, living sacrifice*, and *Lamb of God*, for these expressions are deeply imbedded in the very thought structure of the message.

It is inevitable also that when source and receptor languages represent very different cultures there should be many basic themes and accounts which cannot be "naturalized" by the process of translating. For example, the Jívaro Indians of Ecuador certainly do not understand 1 Corinthians 11:14, "Does not nature teach us that for a man to wear long hair is a dishonor to him?", for in general Jivaro men let their hair grow long, while Jivaro adult women usually cut theirs rather close. Similarly, in many areas of West Africa the behavior of Jesus' disciples in spreading leaves and branches in his way as he rode into Jerusalem is regarded as reprehensible; for in accordance with West African custom the path to be walked on or ridden over by a chief is scrupulously cleaned of all litter, and anyone who throws a branch in such a person's way is guilty of grievous insult. Nevertheless, these cultural discrepancies offer less difficulty than might be imagined, especially if footnotes are used to point out the basis for the cultural diversity; for all people recognize that other peoples behave differently from themselves.

Naturalness of expression in the receptor language is essentially a problem of co-suitability—but on several levels, of which the most important are as follows: (1) word classes (e.g. if there is no noun for "love" one must often say, 'God loves' instead of 'God is love'); (2) grammatical categories (in some languages so-called predicate nominatives must agree in number with the subject, so that 'the two shall be one' cannot be said, and accordingly, one must say 'the two persons shall act just as though they are one person'); (3) semantic classes (swear words in one language may be based upon the perverted use of divine names, but in another language may be primarily excremental and anatomical); (4) discourse types (some languages may require direct quotation and others indirect); and (5) cultural contexts (in some societies the New Testament practice of sitting down to teach seems strange, if not unbecoming).

In addition to being appropriate to the receptor language and culture, a natural translation must be in accordance with the context of the particular message. The problems are thus not restricted to gross grammatical and lexical features, but may also involve such detailed matters as intonation and sentence rhythm (Ezra Pound, 1954, p. 298). The trouble is that, "Fettered to mere words, the translator loses the spirit of the original author" (Manchester, 1951, p. 68).

A truly natural translation can in some respects be described more easily in terms of what it avoids than in what it actually states; for it is the presence of serious anomalies, avoided in a successful translation, which immediately strike the reader as being out of place in the context. For example, crude vulgarities in a supposedly dignified type of discourse are inappropriate, and as a result are certainly not natural. But vulgarities are much less of a problem than slang or colloquialisms. Stanley Newman (1955) deals with this problem of levels of vocabulary in his analysis of sacred and slang language in Zuñi, and points out that a term such as *melika*, related to English *American*, is not appropriate for the religious atmosphere of the kiva. Rather, one must speak of Americans by means of a Zuñi expression meaning, literally, 'broad-hats'. For the Zuñis, uttering *melika* in a kiva ceremony would be as out of place as bringing a radio into such a meeting.

Onomatopoeic expressions are considered equivalent to slang by the speakers of some languages. In some languages in Africa, for example, certain highly imitative expressions (sometimes called ideophones) have been ruled out as inappropriate to the dignified context of the Bible. Undoubtedly the critical attitudes of some missionary translators toward such vivid, but highly colloquial, forms of expression have contributed to the feeling of many Africans that such words are inappropriate in Biblical contexts. In some languages, however, such onomatopoeic usages are not only highly developed, but are regarded as essential and becoming in any type of discourse. For example, Waiwai, a language of British Guiana, uses such expressions with great frequency, and without them one can scarcely communicate the emotional tone of the message, for they provide the basic signals for understanding the speaker's attitude toward the events he narrates.

Some translators are successful in avoiding vulgarisms and slang, but fall into the error of making a relatively straightforward message in the source language sound like a complicated legal document in the receptor language by trying too hard to be completely unambiguous; as a result such a translator spins out his definitions in long, technical phrases. In such a translation little is left of the grace and naturalness of the original. *see tPt p91 & BT17*

Anachronisms are another means of violating the co-suitability of message and context. For example, a Bible translation into English which used "iron oxide" in place of "rust" would be technically correct, but certainly anachronistic. On the other hand, to translate "heavens and earth" by "universe" in Genesis 1:1 is not so radical a departure as one might think, for the people of the ancient world had a highly developed concept of an organized system comprising the "heavens and the earth," and hence "universe" is not inappropriate. Anachronisms involve two types of errors: (1) using contemporary words which falsify life at historically different periods, e.g. translating "demon possessed" as "mentally distressed," and (2) using old-fashioned language in the receptor language and hence giving an impression of unreality.

Appropriateness of the message within the context is not merely a matter of the referential content of the words. The total impression of a message consists not merely in the objects, events, abstractions, and relationships symbolized by the words, but also in the stylistic selection and arrangement of such symbols. Moreover, the standards of stylistic acceptability for various types of discourse differ radically from language to language. What is entirely appropriate in Spanish, for example, may turn out to be quite unacceptable "purple prose" in English, and the English prose we admire as dignified and effective often seems in Spanish to be colorless, insipid, and flat. Many Spanish literary artists take delight in the flowery elegance of their language, while most English writers prefer bold realism, precision, and movement.

It is essential not only that a translation avoid certain obvious failures to adjust the message to the context, but also that it incorporate certain positive elements of style which provide the proper emotional tone for the discourse. This emotional tone must accurately reflect the point of view of the author. Thus such elements as sarcasm, irony, or whimsical interest must all be accurately reflected in a D-E translation. Furthermore, it is essential that each participant introduced into the message be accurately represented. That is to say, individuals must be properly characterized by the appropriate selection and arrangement of words, so that such features as social class or geographical dialect will be immediately evident. Moreover, each character must be permitted to have the same kind of individuality and personality as the author himself gave them in the original message.

A third element in the naturalness of a D-E translation is the extent to which the message fits the receptor-language audience. This appropriateness must be judged on the basis of the level of experience and the capacity for decoding, if one is to aim at any real dynamic equivalence. On the other hand, one is not always sure how the original audience responded or were supposed to respond. Bible translators, for example, have often made quite a point of the fact that the language of the New Testament was Koine Greek, the language of "the man in the street," and hence a translation should speak to the man in the street. The truth of the matter is that many New Testament messages were not directed primarily to the man in the street, but to the man in the congregation. For this reason, such expressions as "Abba Father," *Maranatha*, and "baptized into Christ" could be used with reasonable expectation that they would be understood.

A translation which aims at dynamic equivalence inevitably involves a number of formal adjustments, for one cannot have his formal cake and eat it dynamically too. Something must give! In general, this limitation involves three principal areas: (1) special literary forms, (2) semantically exocentric expressions, and (3) intraorganismic meanings.

The translating of poetry obviously involves more adjustments in literary form than does prose, for rhythmic forms differ far more radically in form, and hence in esthetic appeal. As a result, certain rhythmic patterns must often be substituted for others, as when Greek dactylic hexameter is translated in iambic pentameter. Moreover, some of the most acceptable translating of rhymed verse is accomplished by substituting free verse. In Bible translating the usual procedure is to attempt a kind of dignified prose where the original employs poetry, since, in general, Biblical content is regarded as much more important than Biblical form.

When semantically exocentric phrases in the source language are meaningless or misleading if translated literally into the receptor language, one is obliged to make some adjustments in a D-E translation. For example, the Semitic idiom "gird up the loins of your mind" may mean nothing more than 'put a belt around the hips of your thoughts' if translated literally. Under such circumstances one must change from an exocentric to an endocentric type of expression, e.g. 'get ready in your thinking'. Moreover, an idiom may not be merely meaningless, but may even convey quite the wrong meaning, in which case it must also be modified. Often, for example, a simile may be substituted for the original metaphor, e.g. "sons of thunder" may become 'men like thunder'.

Intraorganismic meanings suffer most in the process of translating, for they depend so largely upon the total cultural context of the language in which they are used, and hence are not readily transferable to other language-culture contexts. In the New Testament, for example, the word *tapeinos*, usually translated as 'humble' or 'lowly' in English, had very definite emotive connotations in the Greek world, where it carried the pejorative meanings of 'low', 'humiliated', 'degraded', 'mean', and 'base'. However, the Christians, who came principally from the lower strata of society, adopted as a symbol of an important Christian virtue this very term, which had been used derisively of the lower classes. Translations of the New Testament into English cannot expect to carry all the latent emotive meanings in the Greek word. Similarly, such translations as 'anointed', 'Messiah', and 'Christ' cannot do full justice to the Greek *Christos*, which had associations intimately linked with the hopes and aspirations of the early Judeo-Christian community. Such emotive elements of meaning need not be related solely to terms of theological import. They apply to all levels of vocabulary. In French, for example, there is no term quite equivalent to English *home*, in contrast with *house*, and in English nothing quite like French *foyer*, which in many respects is like English *home*, but also means 'hearth' and 'fireside' as well as 'focus' and 'salon of a theater'. Emotively, the English word *home* is close to French *foyer*, but referentially *home* is usually equivalent to *maison*, *habitation*, and *chez* (followed by an appropriate pronoun).

Areas of Tension between Formal-Equivalence and Dynamic-Equivalence Translations

In view of the fact that F-E and D-E translations represent polar distinctions, it is quite understandable that there are certain areas of tension between them. The problems are not too acute in dealing with distinctly contrastive types of translations, but when the principles governing some particular translation are about halfway between the extremes, the conflicting factors produce real difficulties. Under such circumstances the three principal areas of tension may be described as: (1) formal and functional equivalents, (2) optional and obligatory equivalents, and (3) rate of decodability.

In three principal situations a conflict occurs between formal and functional equivalents. First, there may be no object or event in the receptor culture which corresponds to some referent in the source text, but the equivalent function is realized by another object or event. For example, people may have no experience of snow, and hence no word for it, but they may have a phrase such as 'white as kapok down' which is functionally equivalent to 'white as snow'. Similarly, some people may not be able to understand a phrase such as 'wagging their heads' as a sign of derision, since for them this function is expressed by 'spitting'. Secondly, one may find that the receptor culture does possess almost the same object or event as is mentioned in the source message, but in the receptor culture it may have an entirely different function. In Western European languages, for example, we use the 'heart' as the center of the emotions and as the focal element in the personality; but in many other languages the 'heart' may have nothing to do with the emotions. Rather, one must speak of the 'liver', 'abdomen', or 'gall'. Again, in some instances one finds no equivalent, either formal or functional. Some of the Indian tribes in South America, for example, know nothing of gambling, and hence have no words for objects with which to cast lots or even for the process of selecting by chance. In other areas there are no such objects as crowns, and nothing that parallels either the victor's wreath or the ruler's diadem.

There are four principal means of dealing with problems arising out of conflicts between formal and functional equivalents. First, one may place a term for the formal equivalent in the text of the translation and describe the function in a footnote—a characteristic procedure in an F-E translation. Second, one may place the functional equivalent in the text, with or without identifying the formal referent in the margin—the usual procedure in D-E translations. Third, one may use a borrowed term, with or without a descriptive classifier. *Pharisees*, for example, may be borrowed from the source language, but an added word such as 'sect', to be employed in a phrase such as 'sect called Pharisees', helps to provide a clue to the meaning of the borrowed word. One may also borrow so-called common nouns and add classifiers, e.g. 'jewel ruby', and 'cloth linen'. Fourth, it is possible to use descriptive expressions employing only words of the receptor language, so that a term such as *phylacteries*, in place of being borrowed (as it is so often in F-E translations), is rendered by a descriptive equivalent, e.g. 'small leather bundles with holy words in them', as is done in Navajo.

The principles governing the choice of one or another of these alternatives depend upon a number of factors. For one thing, the degree of sophistication of the receptors influences the extent to which one can use functional equivalents. In this connection it is important to note that so-called primitive peoples, whom we would regard as entirely unsophisticated, are usually quite ready to accept radical departures in the direction of functional rather than formal equivalents. Similarly, highly educated people in the Western world will gladly accept such far-reaching alterations. But partially educated persons, whether in folk or civilized societies, appear to have difficulty with anything but the most literal renderings, for their newly acquired respect for "book learning" seems to prejudice them against real comprehension and in favor of literalistic obscurantism. A little education can be a dangerous thing!

Whether one adopts borrowed words or not also depends very largely upon the cultural traditions of the receptors. In some societies it is taken for granted that one will usually borrow foreign words for new things, as in English, while in others one finds that the people usually attempt to make up descriptive equivalents, based on their own models of words or phrase formation, as in German.

A people's cultural security also influences the extent to which they may prefer one or another solution to the problems of formal vs. functional equivalence. If, for example, the people are insecure, they often insist on borrowed words which they do not understand; they will not find acceptable any attempt to substitute more meaningful functional equivalents from their own language. On the other hand, some peoples express their grave cultural insecurity by refusing to admit any borrowed terms. In fact, to preserve their ethnic identity they feel called upon to purge their language of any foreign traces and to keep it pure. Apparently they believe that only in this way can they maintain themselves against foreign cultural domination.

The second area of tension between F-E and D-E translations involves optional and obligatory elements. At this point translators encounter some of their most difficult problems, for languages differ most in what they *must* convey, not in what they *may* convey (Jakobson, 1959b, p. 236). That is to say, the obligatory categories of various languages give them their distinctive character, and at the same time impose serious restrictions on the extent to which corresponding expressions can be made fully equivalent. For example, in Campa, a language of Peru, one must always specify the positional relationship of the grammatical subject to the event by indicating whether the person is already on the scene, has just arrived, or is passing by or leaving the scene. Such specifications of position are obligatory, and the translator cannot avoid them. On the other hand, the tense-aspect suffixes obligatory in Greek have no immediately corresponding equivalents in Campa, and all such features of an event are optionally given, if at all. Similarly, Guaica, a language of southern Venezuela, requires each sentence to indicate whether the event described has been personally witnessed by the speaker, has been told to him by others, or is legendary; but Guaica makes no such tense distinctions as we make in English. Nor are the obligatory or optional features of a language restricted to so-called morphological categories, such as tense, aspect, voice, number, gender, animate-inanimate, and alive-dead. They may also involve any formal element of the language, e.g. word order, number and arrangement of attributives, and overt specification of all possessive relationships. For example, in many languages one cannot say merely 'son', but must say 'son of so-and-so'.

When a particular feature is obligatory in the receptor language, the translator really has no alternative to employing it, for the first requirement of any adequate translation, whether F-E or D-E, is that it conform to the obligatory formal features of the receptor language. The real difficulties for the translator are to be found in dealing with the optional features. Here he is not compelled by any evident "rules," but is free to choose between alternatives, which in varying degrees reflect proximity to the source message.

The criteria which determine how to handle optional elements in the translation involve primarily the principle of "communication load," for these optional elements are significant in the maintenance of the proper "flow" of the message. Here sensitivity to style, insight into the intent of the author, and empathy with the receptors are essential if an adequate D-E translation is to be achieved.

The serious problems posed for the translator by the existence of obligatory elements in source and receptor languages occur in general under three sets of circumstances. First, there are situations in which one must indicate in the receptor language something nonexistent in the source message. For example, a category of repetitive vs. nonrepetitive action may require one to specify whether, in Mark 1:21, Jesus had ever before visited the city of Capernaum. Presumably he had, but there is no evidence in the source message to this effect.

Second, one must frequently specify in the receptor language something only poorly defined (i.e. ambiguous, obscure, or merely implicit) in the source message. For example, a language may employ an elaborate system of honorifics which tend to classify all speakers and participants in any event; but when this system is applied to the New Testament there are many areas of doubt. One does not know in what manner the prestigeful Pharisees should be represented as speaking to Jesus, for they probably regarded him as an upstart, though he was accepted by some as a Rabbi.

Third, it is not uncommon to find that what is explicit in the source message text cannot, or should not, be expressed in the receptor language. In some of the Indian languages of Peru, for example, there are no polite vocatives of direct address. The use of a name in speaking directly to a person is either a means of summoning him from a distance or of showing contempt for him. Similarly, pluralization, which is obligatory in Greek, may be entirely out of place if used to the same extent in another language. In Bolivian Quechua, to cite an instance, the plurality of participants in an event may be indicated once, but it is quite wrong to continue specifying this plural feature by tacking on a suffix every time the equivalent plural form occurs, as in Spanish, English, or Greek.

Though one does not and should not carry everything over from one language to another in the process of translating, there is a tendency, nevertheless, toward gain in linguistic forms and loss in meaning. The gain results from the fact that we normally assume that everything in the original must be rendered in some way or another, and also because, in addition to what occurs in the source text, certain obligatory features of the receptor language must be introduced. Furthermore, while the original author can assume a good deal of background information on the part of his audience (for they are presumably full participants in the culture in which the communication is made), the translator cannot make the assumption, since the audience receiving the translation more often than not represents a very different cultural setting. Accordingly, if the message is to be meaningful, a certain number of semantic elements must be added to provide a message with a roughly equivalent communication load. That is to say, some redundancy must be built into the message. Thus the form of the original message is almost always expanded, both as the result of differing patterns of obligatory features and because of cultural diversity. Even so, there is an almost inevitable loss of meaning, for a translator can rarely do complete justice to the total cultural context of the communication, to the emotive features of meaning, and to the behavioral elements, for a shift of setting provides a widely varying range of consequences to any communication. However, this almost inevitable loss in total meaning does provide justification for a certain amount of expansion in the formal elements of the translation. Its precise extent depends upon a great variety of considerations, including such matters as the nature of the message, types of receptors, setting of the communication, and purpose of the publication.

The third area of tension between F-E and D-E translations involves the rate of decodability, for one must consider the rate at which the message is both transmitted and decoded. In a sense we have anticipated this problem in discussing the need for expansion of the message because of cultural diversity. It is clear that unless the receptors can be provided with a text involving a satisfactory basis for decoding the message at an appropriate rate, they will soon become weary, bored, or perplexed.

As noted in an earlier chapter, the degree of decodability is dependent upon the communication load, consisting of both formal and semantic elements. In contrast with an F-E translation, a D-E translation aims at a higher degree of decodability, even if it involves a rather extensive redundancy, which expands the translation in order to make it relevant to a contemporary setting, e.g. J. B. Phillips' translation of the New Testament. In a typical F-E translation, on the other hand, little or no attention is paid to the speed with which the receptor can decode. One may argue, for example, that in Huichol, a language of Mexico, the closest equivalents to English *love*, *joy*, and *peace* are three nouns constructed from corresponding verbal forms, and capable of being used syntactically in essentially the same types of constructions as the English nouns occur. Formally, this is true. Dynamically, however, it is far from being true; for though in English *love*, *joy*, *peace* may be used as nouns, without specification as to the participants involved, the situation is otherwise in normal Huichol discourse. Accordingly, in Huichol one must use corresponding verb forms, specify the persons involved, and indicate the tense, aspect, and mode of the action. A good example of a translation which is not concerned with the rate of decodability is the American Standard Version, which in Romans 5:12-13 reads as follows:

> Therefore, as through one man sin entered into the world, and death through sin; and so death passed unto all men, for that all sinned: —for until the law sin was in the world; but sin is not imputed when there is no law.

J. B. Phillips, aiming at a dynamic equivalence decodable by the average individual without special recourse to background study or supplementary information, translated the passage as follows:

> This, then, is what has happened. Sin made its entry into the world through one man, and through sin, death. The entail of sin and death passed on to the whole human race, and no one could break it for no one was himself free from sin.
>
> Sin, you see, was in the world long before the Law, though I suppose, technically speaking, it was not "sin" where there was no law to define it.

Some persons may object to such a free rendering of these verses, but whether Phillips' translation of this passage is the best way of rendering these difficult verses is not the question at this point. We are simply concerned with the fact that his approach is directed toward greater decodability.

RESTRICTIONS ON THE PERMISSIBLE DEGREE OF DYNAMIC EQUIVALENCE IN TRANSLATING

Certain serious restrictions of a linguistic and a cultural nature immediately confront anyone who undertakes to produce a translation with a considerable degree of dynamic equivalence. The linguistic restrictions involve both the literary forms (poetry, narration, proverbs, etc.) and the vehicle used as an accompanying instrument of transmission of the message, e.g. song or motion picture. The cultural restrictions involve attitudes about so-called "faithfulness" in translating, the pressures exerted by already existing translations, and the diversity of dialects in the receptor language. A still further type of restriction is imposed by diglot publication.

The influence of literary forms is found in two principal areas: (1) the occurrence of sound effects, e.g. puns, acrostic series, and rhyming and alliterative sequences, and (2) rhythmic speech utterances, whether rhymed or not.

As noted in previous sections of this chapter, there is little possibility of reproducing various types of sound effects; for languages differ in the types of sounds they use and the values they tend to attach to these uses, and it is largely a matter of chance if a sound effect in one language can be duplicated by an equivalent, though not identical, sound effect in another. When languages are closely related, as German is to English and Hebrew to Arabic, one can sometimes hit on a useful parallel in sound; but even in closely cognate languages sound effects can rarely be adequately translated with much formal similarity.

As already indicated, the translation of a poem in verse really involves "composing another poem" (Mathews, 1959, p. 67). When one must organize a message into periodic units, as the composition of poetry requires (Stankiewicz, 1960b, p. 77), only rarely can the content be translated by the customary equivalents. Horace sensed this problem centuries ago and warned translators against any word-for-word kind of rendering (*Nec verbum verbo curabis reddere, fidus interpres*).

Perhaps the secret to understanding the underlying problem involved in translating poetry is the fact that, as Mukařovský (in Garvin, 1955) has said, poetic language is the systematic violation of the language norm, or perhaps more rightly, the superimposition of one set of constraints upon another. However, since this poetic superstructure is so diverse in different languages, it is understandable that formal agreement is rare. Therefore, in the translation of poetry one must abandon formal equivalence and strive for dynamic equivalence. Moreover, the very purpose of poetry is to a large extent the communication of feeling, not everyday facts, and hence the translator must take the liberty of "composing another poem" capable of eliciting similar feeling.

However, the translator of poetry without musical accompaniment is relatively free in comparison with one who must translate a song—poetry set to music. Under such circumstances the translator must concern himself with a number of severe restrictions: (1) a fixed length for each phrase, with precisely the right number of syllables, (2) the observance of syllabic prominence (the accented vowels or long syllables must match correspondingly emphasized notes in the music), (3) rhyme, where required, and (4) vowels with appropriate quality for certain emphatic or greatly lengthened notes. Obviously the translator of song "toils in a strait jacket," as Peyser has rightly said (1922, p. 359). [1]

Because of the severe restrictions form places upon the song translator, he must make certain adjustments in order to accomplish anything at all. For one thing, he may take the theme of a song or hymn and adapt it to other music, as John Wesley did in translating thirty-three hymns from German into English. These hymns in German represented twenty-nine different meters, but Wesley used only six. As Henry Bett (1940, p. 290) says, "John Wesley was enough of a poet to know that many of the German metres could not be imitated successfully in English, and so he did not attempt it." But John Wesley's approach to German hymns, though certainly the simpler way of dealing with the problem, is not the usual one, for in general it is the music that is preserved, and not the words or theme. Accordingly, since the form must be maintained, the translator must make certain sacrifices in content. This he does by radical alterations in arrangement of themes, omission of certain elements and addition of others, and even alteration of the themes themselves. All this is quite proper, if words and theme are to fit the music. One requirement, however, is essential in any lyric, namely, that the words be completely natural. Nothing so completely spoils the charm of a song as awkward words or unnatural grammar. But these adjustments, which are perfectly possible in individual songs, cannot be employed in the same way in opera, in which the dramatic sequences and the total plot usually demand much greater conformity to the musical vehicle.

Translating Motion Pictures

If the translator of poetry or songs is hemmed in by the limitations of the communication medium, the translator for motion pictures is subject

[1] For further significant articles on the special problems of song translating see: A. H. Fox-Strangways, 1921; Carl F. Price, 1944-45; E. J. Dent, 1921; Sigmund Spaeth, 1915; Jacob Hieble, 1958; and Elaine T. Lewis, 1960.

to restrictions sometimes even more severe. Some persons regard translating for the cinema as peripheral and not too important. However, as
Pierre-François Caillé (1960a, p. 110) has shown, in interlingual communication film translating probably surpasses book translation in total
impact. Successful motion picture translating is increasingly vital to the
cinema industry, for at least three-fourths of the receipts from a foreign
film depend upon its being adequately translated.

There are two types of translating for motion pictures. First, there are
the "titles," reproduced along with the picture sequence, and usually
exhibited immediately below the picture itself. Consisting of a précis of
the words spoken by the actors, they are run at a maximum speed of
eight syllables per second for reading time, and, as far as possible, are
synchronized with the action.

The translation of titles is no great task, but "dubbing," the replacement of one language with another in live sound, is difficult and complicated. In this type of translating there are several important factors:
(1) timing, both of syllables and breath groups; (2) synchronization of
consonants and vowels with obvious lip movements by the actors ("lip
sync"); (3) words appropriate to the gestures (some words just do not
fit a shrug of the shoulders); (4) characteristic differences of dialect in the
various actors; and (5) timing of humor or expressions which produce
special responses from other actors. To make matters even more difficult,
there is an increasing tendency to shoot close-ups of the actors. In fact,
during almost three-fourths of speaking time the camera comes in close,
thus making any lack of synchronization very conspicuous. Moreover,
it is necessary to keep the synchronization within a range of one-fifth of
a second for general purposes. Though some translations of films do not
attain this standard, it is a necessary standard for satisfactory results.

In making a translation of a motion picture, the first step is simply to
translate meaningfully and idiomatically the speaking-script, with some
general attention to overall corresponding length. This translation is then
carefully edited by checking it against the film as it is being shown. The
translation is then written out on film, which is synchronized with the
picture, and the person who is doing the foreign-language dubbing speaks
as he reads and watches the picture being shown.

This type of translating obviously requires the closest possible attention
to a number of formal restrictions, while at the same time reproducing the
substance of the story; otherwise the acting would become meaningless.
Of course, it is possible to make a number of formal adaptations without
destroying the meaningful content. For example, Caillé (1960a, p. 118)
cites the instance of a French film in which *l'Amérique du Sud* was translated into English as *in Mexico*. The substitution of this phrase permitted
a very close parallelism of lip movement, timing of stressed syllables, and
overall similarity in total speed of utterance. [1]

---

[1] For a series of special articles on the problems of translation in motion
pictures, see *Babel*, Vol. 6, No. 2, 1960.

PRESSURES FROM TRADITION

No one who undertakes to translate in a language with a literary tradition is completely free to do what he likes, for the historical background always tends to dictate the extent to which receptors will accept a particular translation as "faithful," "accurate," or "effective." Moreover, at different periods in the literary history of any language community there are differences of taste in translating which must be considered if the translator is to produce something acceptable at the time.

The pressures from tradition become even greater when the translator's task is to revise a work that already exists in the language. The translator is then confronted, not only by general pressures for conformance to certain acceptable standards, but also by the immediate necessity of making the revision acceptable to those already acquainted with an earlier translation. Perhaps Scripture translating elicits the most acute form of such pressures, for the very nature of religious belief in historical revelation makes immediately suspect any attempt at radical modification. For the most part receptors do not object strongly to syntactic alterations—though strong traditionalists often prefer archaisms, which seem not only to strengthen historic associations, but also to heighten the mystery of religious expression. What most people object to most strongly are exegetical and textual alterations. Even lexical changes can be made acceptable if the meanings of the words are a distinct improvement and have already gained some currency in ecclesiastical usage, e.g. the use of *love* in place of *charity*. The average person is in no position to judge the validity of exegetical and textual changes, but, even so, he usually objects to both with equal force, since such alterations seem to be tampering with "God's Word," by which he really means "God's words."

The principal factors which enter into the receptor's objections to revision are: (1) the extent to which a translation has already been widely used, especially if large portions have been committed to memory or are extensively employed in liturgy; (2) devoted attachment to the translation or the translator (e.g. the German Lutheran church has greater difficulty in revising the Luther text than the English-speaking church has in altering the King James Version); and (3) the extent to which there are "theological tensions" within the receptor group. If, for example, there are deep-seated tensions within any receptor group, a revision is likely to be made the focal symbol of the conflict, and thus only rarely will it be judged with any objectivity.

The introduction of revisions is essentially a matter of education. A church that has used a traditional text of the Scriptures for several generations will obviously not find immediately acceptable a radically different translation, reflecting contemporary insights into text, exegesis, and lexicon. Rather, it is necessary to prepare a whole series of such revisions, with definite grades of adjustment to the theoretical goal. Thus, over a period of some twenty to fifty years the people may become better prepared to accept what is more nearly accurate and meaningful. Since in some measure it is the textual and exegetical alterations that are most strongly resisted, it is very important that any revision provide certain compensations for these changes. If there are to be changes in actual meaning, one must also introduce some obvious improvements in general clarity; for example, by eliminating evident obscurities, misleading archaisms, and stilted expressions. In the absence of such compensations, the receptors are quite unlikely to accept the exegetical improvements. This is precisely what happened with the English Revised Version (1885) and the American Standard Version (1901). Though 17th century English was purposely retained in both, neither gained wide acceptance, for no improvements were made to compensate for the obvious alterations in the direction of greater accuracy. The truth of the matter is that when dealing with religious writings people are generally far less concerned with accuracy than with traditional expression, familiar through long use.

DIALECTAL DIFFERENCES

Dialectal problems also constitute restrictions upon the form of a translation. They are of two distinct types, (1) external, and (2) internal. The external problems involve competing dialects and the inevitable difficulties of trying to determine just how to accommodate these complex linguistic facts. The internal problems are those posed by dialectal variations in the text itself. For example, in rendering Steinbeck's *Grapes of Wrath*, Procházka (in Garvin, 1955, p. 126) describes the problem of reproducing in Czech the Okie speech used by some of Steinbeck's characters. To do so he chose an Eastern Bohemian dialect, the speakers of which are regarded as "a little clumsy, a little slow-thinking, but thoughtful and honest."

The "external" dialects are of two principal types, (a) geographical, and (b) social, with usually a good deal of overlapping, for some geographical dialects (e.g. those of the cultural centers) have a good deal more social status and prestige than others. The social dialects are basically those of the class structure, and often they are quite highly and overtly structured, as in Japanese and Thai.

In dealing with the problem of competing "geographical" dialects, one of three courses can be followed: (1) employ the leading dialect of the cultural center, with the assumption that ultimately the other dialects will gradually conform (this has been the history of almost all national languages); (2) follow primarily the leading dialect, but make concessions from time to time to usage in other dialects, especially if these are known in the leading dialect (this is the usual procedure where a so-called primitive language may consist of a number of related dialects); or (3) construct a composite language by selecting certain features from the different dialects, thus forming a "union dialect." This last solution is the one often advocated by colonial administrators, for it seems a natural type of "compromise." If there is a strong educational policy to enforce the use of this dialect for a number of years, there is some chance of a modicum of success. Essentially, however, this compromise approach to language development is both artificial and ill advised, for "nobody speaks that way."

To a considerable extent the problems of social dialects are even more complex than those of geographical ones. In Thai, for example, there are three social dialects: a colloquial standard employed by the average uneducated man, a socially "correct" speech of the educated person, and an elevated speech of the nobility. A translation in the colloquial style of the uneducated man would be considered vulgar by the educated person, while a translation in the speech of nobility would be quite unintelligible to the common person. Similarly, a translation in the correct speech of the educated person would be too high for the uneducated or partially educated individual, while it would be judged undignified by the nobility. Similar types of problems exist in the Arabic-speaking world, where the literary language is quite different from colloquial speech, and where even within the literary language there are a number of grades, ranging from Koranic usage to modern newspaper and radio styles.

In view of such differences in social dialect, it is often necessary to produce more than one translation. In Arabic, for example, the Christian Scriptures have been traditionally published in colloquial as well as literary form. However, since anyone who is literate has learned to read the literary standard, not the colloquial, it has seemed preferable to concentrate on two levels of Arabic—one, a so-called Modern Standard Arabic and another, a simpler form of literary language. For Haiti, the Scriptures are published in Haitian Creole, which is essentially a colloquial dialect of French, and in two forms of French, standard and simplified. In the simplified form of French the grammatical forms and lexical usages are not incorrect; they are merely simplified. The same procedure is now being carried out in Spanish for Latin America and in English for such regions as Liberia.

Diglot Publication

Diglot publication also places certain restrictions on the translator, posed by the reader's ready access to a corresponding text, whether on an opposite page, in a parallel column, or at the bottom of the page.

In polyglot publications intended for scholars, little attention need be paid to the difficulties of correspondence, since the scholar understands the basis for nonconformity. But the average diglot translation is produced primarily for those who, though their knowledge of one of the languages is good, have only a limited understanding of the second language. Moreover, in many instances it is the second language which has cultural prestige. For example, in diglot publications in Latin America, in which an Indian language text is accompanied by the Spanish equivalent, the Spanish obviously has greater prestige than the Indian language can ever have. Moreover, the Indians are likely to feel culturally quite insecure, and hence insist that their own language must conform in so far as possible to Spanish. Furthermore, their knowledge of Spanish is usually so imperfect that they fail to recognize idiomatic usages, and hence assume that whatever is said in Spanish must be reproduced word for word in their own language; otherwise, the translation is regarded as incorrect.

Accordingly, to deal with the limited linguistic backgrounds of the typical receptors of diglot publications, the translator must follow the prestigeful language with a greater degree of conformity than he otherwise would. However, this pressure for agreement between two languages in diglot publications must not persuade the translator to make artificial adjustments or adaptations in the form of the less prestigeful language; for it is desirable that receptors recognize the idiomatic divergences between languages. But in matters of text and interpretation, especially in translating the Bible, it is important that there be substantial agreement. Otherwise the reaction will be unfavorable, since such receptors are seldom persuaded that the text in their own language is as valid as the one in the national language.

CRITERIA TO BE USED IN JUDGING TRANSLATIONS

Since different principles apply to different types of F-E and D-E translations, it is not easy to judge the relative merits of two or more translations. However, three fundamental criteria are basic to the evaluation of all translating, and in different ways help to determine the relative merit of particular translations. These are: (1) general efficiency of the communication process, (2) comprehension of intent, and (3) equivalence of response.

The efficiency of a translation can be judged in terms of the maximal reception for the minimum effort of decoding. In a sense, efficiency is closely related to Joos's "first law of semantics" (Joos, 1953), which may be stated simply: "That meaning is best which adds least to the total meaning of the context." In other words, the maximizing of redundancy reduces the work of decoding. At the same time, redundancy should not be so increased that the noise factor of boredom cuts down efficiency. Perhaps the factor of efficiency may be restated thus: "Other things being equal, the efficiency of the translation can be judged in terms of the maximal reception for the minimal effort in decoding." Because of the diversities in linguistic form and cultural backgrounds, however, translations are more likely to be overloaded (and hence inefficient in terms of effort) than so redundant that boredom results.

The second criterion in judging translations, comprehension of the original intent (or, stated in other terms, the accuracy with which the meaning of the source-language message is represented in the translation), is oriented either toward the source culture (a formal-equivalence translation) or toward the receptor culture (a dynamic-equivalence translation). In an F-E translation, the comprehension of intent must be judged essentially in terms of the context in which the communication was first uttered; in a D-E translation this intent must be understood in terms of the receptor culture. The extent to which intent can be interpreted in a cultural context other than the one in which the message was first given is directly proportional to the universality of the message. Aristophanes' play *The Clouds* obviously does not lend itself so well to comprehension of intent in different cultures as does the Book of Job.

This criterion of "comprehension of original intent" is designed to cover what has often been traditionally spoken of as "accuracy," "fidelity," and "correctness." Actually, one cannot speak of "accuracy" apart from comprehension by the receptor, for there is no way of treating accuracy except in terms of the extent to which the message gets across (or should presumably get across) to the intended receptor. "Accuracy" is meaningless, if treated in isolation from actual decoding by individuals for which the message is intended. Accordingly, what may be "accurate" for one set of receptors may be "inaccurate" for another, for the level and manner of comprehension may be different for the two groups. Furthermore, comprehension itself must be analyzed in terms of comprehending the significance of a message as related to its possible settings, i.e. the original setting of the communication and the setting in which the receptors themselves exist. This second criterion (i.e. comprehension of intent) is in no sense designed to sidestep the issues of accuracy and fidelity, but to place them in their right perspective—in terms of a total theory of communication.

The third criterion in judging translations, equivalence of response, is oriented toward either the source culture (in which case the receptor must understand the basis of the original response) or the receptor culture (in which case the receptor makes a corresponding response within a different cultural context). The extent to which the responses are similar depends upon the cultural distance between the two communication contexts.

In this description of the various criteria involved in the judging of translations, intent and response have been isolated from each other. But actually such isolation is impossible; for the nature of the response is closely tied to intent, presumed or actual, and any final judgment of translations must deal with both interrelated elements. At the same time, this formulation implies that the orientation can be to either the source or the receptor context, while in actual practice no either/or distinction can be made; rather, various grades of mixture or interpenetration must be dealt with. The either/or distinction is primarily a matter of principal focus of attention, or of priority of concern. In the same way, no judgment on translations can completely isolate the source context from the receptor one. Nevertheless, though the three criteria of efficiency, comprehension of intent, and similarity of response cannot be fully isolated from one another, they are all basic to an understanding and evaluation of different translations.

Though there is a relatively wide range of possible legitimate translations beginning with somewhat literal F-E (Formal Equivalent) renderings to rather highly D-E (Dynamic Equivalent) ones, there are certain points on both ends of this scale at which extremely F-E or D-E translations fall off rapidly in efficiency, accuracy, and relevance. On the F-E end of the scale a translation which is exceedingly literal, contains numerous awkward expressions, and is hence "overloaded" as far as the prospective receptors are concerned, is obviously far below legitimate standards. At the other end of the scale, a D-E translation may likewise fail to come up to a valid standard, if in the translator's concern for the response of the receptors he has been unfaithful to the content of the original message.

F-E translations which fall below standard are generally more common than correspondingly inadequate D-E translations, for the gross errors in F-E translating arise primarily out of ignorance, oversight, and failure to comprehend the true nature of translating. On the other hand, mistakes in D-E translations are generally less numerous, for they are usually made with the translator's eyes wide open. In a sense, renderings which err in being too far in the direction of a D-E translation may be more dangerous, particularly if a translator is clever in concealing his "slanting." But the mistakes resulting from filling a translation with renderings which are too much in the direction of F-E translating are more ruinous, for the translation is usually so overloaded that it is unlikely to be used with any great effectiveness, except where there is an unusual amount of incentive and cultural pressure.

ANALYSIS OF DIFFERENT TYPES OF TRANSLATIONS

Anyone who has dealt with a variety of translations has little difficulty in appraising some of the major characteristics of translations, and can easily classify such translations into various groupings, e.g. literal, paraphrastic, archaizing, free, or stiff. However, it is not always easy to specify precisely those features of the translation which give it these characteristics. Accordingly, before discussing the types of correspondences between source and receptor languages and the kinds of adjustments to be made in the process of translating, it is important to consider certain techniques to be used in describing the exact differences between translations. The following methodology has been worked out primarily by my colleague, William L. Wonderly.

An effective way to describe the differences between translations is to set up a series of three stages of translation. The first is a *literal transfer*, which is almost a word-for-word and unit-for-unit "transliteration" of the original into corresponding lexical units in the receptor language. In such a transfer there are no obligatory alterations of order, constructions, or parts of speech. The results of such a transfer are scarcely intelligible. They do, however, provide a descriptive base for calculating the types of changes to be made in the second stage of the process, when a minimal number of grammatical and lexical modifications are introduced. This second stage, which may conveniently be called a *minimal transfer*, represents only those alterations from stage 1 which are necessary if the translation is to conform to the obligatory categories of the receptor language. The third stage may be regarded as a *literary transfer*. A number of different forms of translation may represent this third stage; for, while the second stage is controlled by obligatory alterations, the changes from stage 2 to stage 3 are optional, and may thus be quite diverse. If we are to sort out the obligatory and optional modifications, we must therefore set up these three stages of literal, minimal, and literary transfers, and then calculate the differences between literary translations on the basis of the minimal transfers. In other words, the analysis of different literary translations starts from the minimal, obligatory alterations incorporated into stage 2; these alterations must underlie all literary translations. [1]

The procedures involved in setting up a three-stage descriptive analysis of translation include: (1) the numbering of the lexical units of the source-language text (these numbers are carried through the entire sequence); (2) the use of asterisks, italics, and small capitals to identify, respectively, omissions, additions, and structural modifications (with the exception of changes of immediate constituent structure, which are generally identified by numerical sequences).

It is possible to elaborate the system considerably by identifying certain other features. For example, the functionally significant semantic elements (objects, events, abstracts, and relationals, marked by O, E, A, and R, respectively) can be traced throughout the three stages of translation. However, for the sake of simplicity of presentation, we have here chosen to use a more limited system.

The practical and theoretical implications of this approach will become more obvious as we illustrate its application to a very simple passage of the New Testament, John 1:6-8, beginning first with the Greek text (Nestle's 24th edition), and then continuing with literal and minimal stages, before illustrating the literary level by means of the American Standard Version (1901), the Revised Standard Version (1946), the New English Bible (1961), and Phillips' New Testament in Modern English (1958), abbreviated, respectively, as ASV, RSV, NEB, PME.

JOHN 1:6-8

Greek:

[1]egeneto [2]anthrōpos, [3]apestalmenos [4]para [5]theou, [6]onoma [7]autō [8]Iōannēs; [9]houtos [10]elthen [11]eis [12]marturian, [13]hina [14]marturēsē [15]peri [16]tou [17]phōtos, [18]hina [19]pantes [20]pisteusōsin [21]di' [22]autou, [23]ouk [24]ēn [25]ekeinos [26]to [27]phōs, [28]all' [29]hina [30]marturēsē [31]peri [32]tou [33]phōtos.

---

[1] This use of three descriptive levels is somewhat similar to Voegelin's "Multiple Stage Translation" (Voegelin, 1954b). Though Voegelin is concerned primarily with special problems of translating texts dictated by informants, much of his discussion is of interest to anyone analyzing literary translations. However, a three-level approach, less rigid and compartmentalized than Voegelin's eight stages, seems to be sufficiently detailed for our purposes, and at the same time is much easier to apply.
   A multiple stage approach to translation has been employed with varying degrees of exactitude by a number of persons, and in some instances has even been used as a pedagogical device. For example, Mabel C. Daggett (1926-27) has advocated a three-step technique for teaching English to French-speaking persons, who use word-for-word translations as an intermediate stage in developing idiomatic control of English.

Literal transfer (stage 1):

> [1]became/happened [2]man, [3]sent [4]from [5]God, [6]name [7]to-him [8]John; [9]this/the-same [10]came-he [11]into/for [12]testimony/witness, [13]that/in-order-that [14]testify/witness-might-he [15]concerning/of/to [16]the [17]light, [18]that/in-order-that [19]all [20]believe-might-they [21]through [22]him. [23]not [24]was [25]he/that-one [26]the [27]light, [28]but [29]that/in-order-that [30]witness-might-he [31]concerning/of/to [32]the [33]light.

Here alternative lexical equivalents are marked by slant lines, and translations requiring more than one word are joined together by hyphens, to indicate that they correspond to a single unit in the source text. The *literal transfer* of stage 1 cannot be regarded as in any sense a translation. Rather, it is a kind of rewriting of the original, with corresponding lexical items from the receptor language.

In stage 2, the *minimal transfer*, the material of stage 1 is adjusted to the obligatory grammatical and lexical structures of the receptor language. In this stage some items are inevitably lost; an asterisk marks the fact that there is no corresponding element for such items in the receptor rendering. (In the particular passage treated here such losses occur only in stage 3.) Other elements have to be added; these are indicated by *italics*. Some items in the source message must be altered, either grammatically or lexically; these are marked by SMALL CAPITALS. Any changes of order are indicated by the retention of the original number of items, but in nonnumerical sequences. A minimal transfer of this same passage follows:

Minimal transfer (stage 2):

> *There* [1]CAME/WAS *a* [2]man, [3]sent [4]from [5]God, [7]WHOSE [6]name *was* [8]John; [9]HE/the-same [10]came [11]for [12]testimony/witness, [13]that *he might* [14]witness [15]of/to [16]the [17]light, [18]that [19]all *might* [20]believe [21]through [22]him. [25]He [24]was [23]not [26]the [27]light, [28] but *came* [29]that *he might* [30]witness [31]of/to [32]the [33]light.

As indicated earlier, a minimal transfer may be regarded as a translation, at least of sorts; but it is certainly not a fully acceptable type of rendering, since it involves only the modifications obligatory if the text is to make sense. Such a minimal transfer provides a second level of rendering, on the basis of which various types of literary transfers may be made.

The following literary transfers represent four different and progressive levels of modification from the stage of minimal transfer.

ASV:

> *There* [1]CAME *a* [2]man, [3]sent [4]from [5]God, [7]WHOSE [6]name *was* [8]John. [9]The same [10]came [11]for [12]witness, [13]that *he might* BEAR [14]witness [15]of [16]the [17]light, [18]that [19]all *might* [20]believe [21]through [22]him. [25]He [24]was [23]not [26]the [27]light, [28]but *came* [29]that *he might* BEAR [30]witness [31]of [32]the [33]light.

RSV:

> *There* [1]WAS a [2]man [3]sent [4]from [5]God, [7]WHOSE [6]name *was* [8]John. [9]He [10]came [11]for [12]testimony, [13]TO BEAR [14]witness [15]to [16]the [17]light, [18]that [19]all *might* [20]believe [21]through [22]him. [25]He [24]was [23]not [26]the [27]light, [28]but *came* [29]TO BEAR [30]witness [31]to [32]the [33]light.

NEB:

> *There* [1]APPEARED a [2]man [6]NAMED [7]* [8]John, [3]sent [4]from [5]God; [9]he [10]came [11]AS *a* [12]WITNESS [13]TO [14]testify [15]to [16]the [17]light, [18]that [19]all *might* BECOME [20]BELIEVERS [21]through [22]him. [25]He [24]was [23]not *himself* [26]the [27]light; [28]* *he came* [29]TO BEAR [30]witness [31]to [32]the [33]light.

PME:

> [1]* *A* [2]man [6]NAMED [7]* [8]John WAS [3]sent [4]BY [5]God [9]* [10]* [11]AS *a* [12]WITNESS [13]* [15]to [16]the [17]light, [18]SO that [19]ANY MAN WHO [21]HEARD [22]HIS [14]TESTIMONY *might* [20]believe *in the light.* [25]THIS MAN [24]was [23]not *himself* [26]the [27]light: [28]* *he was* SENT *simply* [29]AS *a personal* [30]WITNESS [31]to [32]THAT [33]light.

Even a quick glance at the markings of these four literary transfers will indicate that there are four distinct types or degrees of departure from the minimal transfer of stage 2. We can, however, make some statistical comparisons of the various types of alterations from stage 2 to stage 3. (There is no need to compare stage 3 with stage 1, since certain basic alterations are obligatory, and thus are irrelevant in comparing various literary transfers.) These comparisons are shown in Table 2.

TABLE 2

Types of changes	ASV	RSV	NEB	PME
1. Changes in order			2	4
2. Omissions (asterisks)			2	6
3. Structural alterations (small capitals)	2	4	9	18
4. Additions (italics)			3	10

This statistical summary indicates clearly that the ASV is very close to a minimal transfer. This is, of course, precisely what the translators attempted to make it—that is, as close to the Greek as was possible and still make the passage intelligible in English. In this particular passage, the RSV as well shows little more than minimal transfer changes. The NEB, on the other hand, has more than twice as many structural alterations, while introducing the other types of changes as well. Phillips obviously has the greatest number of changes of all types.

In a sense this type of summary is misleading, for the various changes are by no means of the same weight or importance. For example, the changes of order cannot all be equated in judging how "free" a translation might be; for some of the shifts of order are within the same phrase, others involve transpositions of entire phrases, while still others entail the shifting of immediate constituents. It is therefore important to set up a numerical value for such differences and to weight them. This may be done by assigning the value of 1 to the simplest change in order, the value of 2 to the second type (transposition of phrases), and the value of 4 to a shift of order involving significant grammatical relationships. The geometric proportion in 1, 2, 4 is a more valid weighting than a mere arithmetical progression, since it more accurately reflects the relative differences of impact. Similarly, if we classify structural changes, whether lexical or grammatical, we likewise have three major types. In certain instances the differences between such a verb expression as *witness* and such a verb-noun phrase as *bear witness*, or the distinction between *that* and *to* as indicators of purpose, are quite minor; they should be rated merely as 1. (In fact, they might even be considered as legitimate alternatives in a minimal transfer, in which case they would not be counted at stage 3.) A more complex change would involve a shift of word classes, e.g. *whose name was* to *named*, or phrase structure, e.g. *came for witness* to *came as a witness*. This type of change may be given a value of 2. A radical change of structure, e.g. *believe through him* to *heard his testimony might believe*, would then have the value of 4, following the same system of geometric proportion.

Omissions and additions may also be classified into three levels: (1) those which are more or less expected, such as implicit additions, e.g. the introduction of *he* as the subject of a verb; (2) those which are radically different, e.g. the use of *personal* as an attributive to *witness*; and (3) those which lie somewhere between, e.g. *simply*. Omissions show similar differences. The omission of item 13 in PME is a more or less expected omission, while the omission of 1 is a rather radical change. Omissions such as 9 and 10 fall somewhere between.

From the standpoint of Information Theory, however, additions should be given considerably more weight than omissions, for the impact of what is lost is not so great as the effect of what is added. Furthermore, additions which are not obligatory (i.e. introduced in the minimal transfer stage) would seem to be twice as important from the standpoint of the communication load as are either alterations of order or shifts in lexical or grammatical structure. Accordingly, for the purposes of this rough calculation we would seem justified in rating the various grades of omission as 1, 2, and 4 (as we have done for changes of order and structure) and regard additions as having the values of 2, 4, and 8, respectively. The statistical comparison of the four translations then becomes quite different, as shown in Table 3.

Though the numerical values assigned to the various factors cannot be completely justified statistically, one's impression of reading the ASV, RSV, NEB, and PME tends to confirm this type of evaluation; namely, that the total impact of the differences is greater than the mere sum of the various types of modifications.

In a sense, the passage from John is hardly representative of what one finds in a fuller comparison of the ASV, RSV, NEB, and PME. Hence it

TABLE 3

Types of changes	ASV	RSV	NEB	PME
1. Changes in order			3	10
2. Omissions			2	14
3. Structural alterations	2	4	14	31
4. Additions			8	36
	—	—	—	—
Totals	2	4	27	91

may be useful to provide a summary of the differences which have been found for 2 Corinthians 3:10-11:

Greek:

¹kai ²gar ³ou ⁴ dedoxastai ⁵to ⁶dedoxasmenon ⁷en ⁸toutō ⁹tō ¹⁰merei ¹¹eineken ¹²tes ¹³huperballousēs ¹⁴doxēs. ¹⁵ei ¹⁶gar ¹⁷to ¹⁸katargoumenon ¹⁹dia ²⁰doxēs, ²¹pollō ²²mallon ²³to ²⁴menon ²⁵en ²⁶doxē.

Literal transfer (stage 1):

¹indeed/verily ²for ³not ⁴made-glorious/glorified-has-been-it ⁵the/that-which ⁶made-glorious/glorified-has-been ⁷in ⁸this ⁹the ¹⁰case-respect ¹¹on-account-of/by-reason-of ¹²the ¹³surpassing ¹⁴glory/splen/dor. ¹⁵if ¹⁶for ¹⁷the/that-which ¹⁸passes-away/fades-away ¹⁹through/with ²⁰glory/splendor, ²¹much ²²more ²³the/that-which ²⁴remains ²⁵in/with ²⁶glory/splendor.

Minimal transfer (stage 2):

²for ¹indeed/verily ⁵that-which ⁶has-been-made-glorious/has-been-glorified (⁴)has ³not ⁴been-made-glorious ⁷in ⁸this ⁹* ¹⁰case/respect ¹¹on-account-of/by-reason-of ¹²the ¹³surpassing ¹⁴glory, ¹⁶for ¹⁵if ¹⁷that-which ¹⁸passes-away/fades-away *was* ¹⁹with ²⁰glory/splendor, ²¹much ²²more ²³that-which ²⁴remains *is* ²⁵in/with ²⁶glory.

Literary transfers (stage 3):

ASV:

²For ¹verily ⁵that which ⁶hath been made glorious (⁴)hath ³not ⁴been made glorious ⁷in ⁸this ⁹* ¹⁰respect, ¹¹by reason of ¹²the ¹⁴glory THAT ¹³SURPASSETH. ¹⁶For ¹⁵if ¹⁷that which ¹⁸passeth away *was* ¹⁹with ²⁰glory, ²¹much ²²more ²³that which ²⁴remaineth *is* ²⁵in ²⁶glory.

RSV:

¹Indeed ²* ⁷in ⁸this ⁹* ¹⁰case, ⁵WHAT *once* ⁶HAD SPLENDOR (⁴)HAS COME TO HAVE ³NO ⁴SPLENDOR *at all*. ¹¹BECAUSE OF ¹²the ¹⁴splendor THAT ¹³SURPASSES *it*. ¹⁶For ¹⁵if ¹⁷WHAT ¹⁸faded away CAME ¹⁹with ²⁰splendor, ²³WHAT ²⁴IS PERMANENT *must* ²⁵HAVE ²¹much ²²more ²⁶splendor.

NEB:

[1]Indeed, [2]* THE [6]SPLENDOUR [5]THAT *once* ([6])WAS IS *now* [3]NO [4]SPLEN-DOUR *at all* [7-10]*; [11]* *it* [13]IS OUTSHONE BY [12]A [14]splendour ([13])GREATER STILL. [16]For [15]if [17]that which ([18])WAS *soon* [18]TO fade ([19])HAD *its moment* [19]OF [20]splendour, *how* [21]much [22]GREATER *is* THE [26]SPLENDOUR [25]OF [23]that which [24]ENDURES.

PME:

[2]AND *while it is* [1]TRUE *that* [5]THE ([3-4])FORMER *temporary* [6]GLORY HAS BEEN *completely* [13]ECLIPSED [11]BY [12]THE [14]LATTER, [7-10]*, [15-16]* *we do well to remember that* [17] IT [18-20]IS ECLIPSED *simply because* [23-24]THE PRESENT PERMANENT PLAN IS *such* A *very* [21]much [22]more GLORIOUS THING *than the old*.

The analysis of changes in such a passage are not easy to classify or to evaluate. Certain semantic components are spread out over several different words, and again, what might appear to be pure and simple additions are really structural modifications on a semantic level, thus requiring certain added words, e.g. *the, a,* and *that.* Moreover, in PME the entire semantic structure is so altered that it is difficult to determine the precise manner in which the corresponding parts are related to one another. In the numbering of orders it is necessary in several instances to indicate splits by placing the numerical designation of a dependent item in parentheses, but in others two or more items in the minimal transfer have coalesced; a hyphen is employed between numerals to designate this development.

One cannot determine with any degree of certainty the order of omissions. Unless, therefore, the translation is quite a literal rendering, the ordered arrangements of omissions cannot be counted. As the original message is expanded in such translations as the NEB and PME, a number of words occur without numbering.

Rather than number each component of an expanded phrase by the same number repeated for each word, it is to be assumed that a number applies to all following words until another number is encountered. By implication, any added word (term in italics) is also a part of this same expanded phrase. But added terms are obviously not so easily related to the original text as are words in small capitals, which represent more obvious semantic or grammatical restructuring. However, despite the great number of complications and the indeterminate character of many borderline cases, one can nevertheless obtain something of a quantitative view of the differences between these various literary transfers. Such an analysis is given in Table 4, which lists, first, the number of changes in each category and then gives the numerical evaluation, based on the scale cited.

Thus, the ASV is shown to be almost as close as possible to a minimal transfer. The RSV in this instance is appreciably different from the ASV, but certainly not so "free" as the NEB or PME. In any comparison of the NEB and PME it should be noted that, though the total number of

TABLE 4

Types of Changes	ASV		RSV		NEB		PME	
	no.	val.	no.	val.	no.	val.	no.	val.
1. Changes of order	1	1	3	7	6	10	4	13
2. Omissions			2	3	4	4	5	5
3. Structural alterations	2	2	19	21	22	41	22	65
4. Additions			5	10	9	24	19	58
Total	3	3	29	41	41	79	50	141

changes in the two translations is not appreciably different, i.e. 41 vs. 50, the quality of changes is quite diverse; for the value of the changes in the NEB is only about twice the number of modifications, while the value of the changes in the PME is almost three times the number of modifications.

In this preceding analysis of F-E and D-E translations we have been measuring only the degree of formal differences and have not attempted any evaluation, even though it may have appeared from the description that the greater the number of D-E characteristics the better the translation. This is not automatically the case, for an evaluation of a translation depends upon a great many other factors, including type of audience, purpose of the translation, nature of the message, and existing sociolinguistic pressures. It would be convenient if we could construct some formula which would assign numerical values to these different factors and provide some more or less mechanical means by which we might rate different translations. This, however, would be impossible, for the diverse factors are too complex, too multidimensional, and to a large extent incommensurate.

In attempting to measure purely formal differences between F-E and D-E translations we have not included a consideration of so-called mistakes in translating, but have assumed that all the renderings fell within a satisfactory range of "accuracy." Of course, in judging a translation one must consider the problem of mistakes, but these are of two quite distinct types. First, there are the errors which arise because the translator has misinterpreted the intent of the author or because he has carelessly overlooked or misconstrued some element. Such mistakes can be equally numerous in any and all types of translations, whether F-E or D-E. Errors of this kind are not, however, to be confused with those which result from the translator's selecting a less appropriate interpretation out of several possible renderings (i.e. a forgivable failure in judgment concerning ambiguities). The second type of errors occur because of the use of certain kinds of formal features which tend to obscure the meaning of the original. For example, a translation which consists strictly of F-E renderings tends to distort the meaning of the original because of its very rigid formal equivalence. At the same time, a D-E translation which goes to the opposite extreme will likewise obscure the intent of the original, for the very freedom of form tends to distort the intent. The fact, however, that the extremes of F-E and D-E translating skew the message does not mean that the best translation is necessarily at a halfway point between the two extremes. Actually there is a relatively wide band in F-E and D-E translations in which the formal differences in and of themselves do not necessarily distort the message. It is when one reaches the extremes that serious damage is done to the message by the formal features.

In practice F-E translations tend to distort the message more than D-E translations, since those persons who produce D-E translations are in general more adept in translating, and in order to produce D-E renderings they must perceive more fully and satisfactorily the meaning of the original text. For the most part a translator who produces D-E renderings is quite aware of the degree of distortion, and because of greater conscious control of his work is able to judge more satisfactorily whether or not the results seem to be legitimate. On the other hand, a translator who produces strictly F-E renderings is usually not conscious of the extent to which his seemingly "faithful" translations actually involve serious distortions. This lack of awareness in F-E translating as to what is happening results in far more serious skewing than is generally the case with D-E translating.

CHAPTER NINE

TYPES OF CORRESPONDENCES AND CONTRASTS

Correspondences and contrasts between source and receptor languages are of two major types: (1) structural and (2) dynamic. Structural features are, again, of two types: (a) formal, comprising problems of phonology, morphology, and syntax (from phrase to discourse); and (b) lexical, involving both single words and semantically exocentric phrases. Dynamic features are likewise of two types: (a) formal and (b) lexical. In dynamic correspondences, however, the problems are related, not to specific units, but to the communication load carried by such units.

PHONOLOGICAL CORRESPONDENCES AND CONTRASTS

Phonological correspondences between source and receptor languages are of three major types: (1) transliteration of borrowed lexical units; (2) plays on words which are phonologically similar; and (3) patterns of form-sound style, involving (a) alliteration (the beginning of two or more stressed syllables of a word group by the same sound or combination of sounds), (b) rhyme, and (c) acrostic arrangements, i.e. a composition, usually verse, in which the initial letters of the successive lines have some special significance.

Transliteration

The most common phonological problems encountered by translators involve transliteration, especially of proper names; such words must usually be borrowed. Since no two languages have exactly the same sounds, it is inevitable that carrying over a word from one language to another will involve some type of adjustment. This adjustment may be based on the sounds involved, or it may be merely a type of transcription of the letters used to identify the names. For example, in reproducing certain texts from ancient languages, e.g. Hittite, Sumerian, and Mycenaean Greek, in which in many instances we do not know the precise character of the sound, it is the general practice to transcribe more or less letter for letter. Even in New Testament Greek we employ a transcription which, though it identifies the principal orthographic contrasts, certainly does not represent what we know to have been the pronunciation. Otherwise we would be obliged to transliterate Greek *oi, ei, i, u,* and *ê* (omicron-iota, epsilon-iota, iota, upsilon, and eta) all as /i/, since by New Testament times all these vowel sounds had fallen together.

In borrowing from one living language into another, however, the general practice is to base the transliteration on the spoken form of the language, with results which often seem far from the graphic form of the original. For example, in Miskito, a language of Nicaragua and Honduras, one encounters the following transliterations: Ilaidya (Elijah), Sairus (Cyrus), Ilai (Eli), and Retsel (Rachel). However, since the Miskito structuring of sounds (both of types and sequences) is not very different from that in English, these transliterations are not strikingly different. In Shilluk, on the other hand, one encounters the following transliterations, which represent rather radical adjustments to the sound structure of the receptor language: *Jidhath* (Jesus), *Krayth* (Christ), *Thiopilath* (Theophilus), *Ilidhabeth* (Elizabeth), *Ilaja* (Elijah), and *Aydhaya* (Isaiah).

The problems of borrowing and transliteration are often complicated by the fact that the receptor language may have already borrowed some source-language terms, which in turn have undergone considerable change. For example, in Conob, a Mayan language of Guatemala, a number of Biblical proper names were introduced soon after the Spanish Conquest. As a result, there is a series of well-disguised proper names: *Mic* (Santiago), *Luin* (Pedro), *Xuni* (Juan), *Malin* (Maria), and *Kuxin* (Markos). In translating the Scriptures, however, these early borrowings, which have now acquired more or less the status of nicknames, are not regarded as acceptable. Hence, one must use a more contemporary adaptation.

When a language has a literary tradition, even of relatively short duration, one often finds a considerable inconsistency in transliteration; for some translators may have based the transcription on one source language, some on another. Moreover, some have tried to follow spelling; others to reproduce the corresponding sounds. Even in adjustment to sounds there are several grades of correspondence, since alternative adaptations may be quite permissible within the phonological structure of the receptor language. As a result, there may be a bewildering array of alternatives. Thus, for example, the name Bartholomew has been variously transliterated into Swahili as *Baritholomi, Bartolomayo, Bartholomayo, Baritolomayo, Baritholomayo, Bartolomeo*, and *Balutolomayo* (Dammann, 1954, p. 81).

Practical solutions to the problem of transliteration of proper names are of three types: (1) complete adaptation of the sound of the borrowed word to the phonological system of the receptor language; (2) simple borrowing of the orthographic form of the proper name from the source language, without reference to the sounds or the orthographic "strangeness" in the receptor language; and (3) a compromise. A compromise involves a distinction between well-known names and those which are unfamiliar. Familiar names are written as pronounced in the receptor language if there is no literary tradition, and, if there is one, are written as in the receptor language, often with considerable deference to the orthographic tradition of the source language if the people are linguistically insecure. Proper names that are unfamiliar in the receptor language are usually adjusted to the phonological patterns of the language.

It is almost impossible to reproduce a play on words. Nevertheless, in some rare instances it is possible to approximate the patterning, though not the sounds, of an original phonological correspondence. Thus Buber and Rosenzweig translate as *Irrsal* and *Wirrsal* the Hebrew *tohu* and *bohu* 'waste and void' (Genesis 1:1). Usually, however, the plays on words which are so important a part of certain elaborate styles are simply lost in translation. However, if the sense of a passage depends on the play on words, as for example with several proper names in Genesis (e.g. Eve, 3:20; Cain, 4:1; Peleg, 10:25; and Abraham, 17:5), the names must be translated, either in the text or in a footnote.

Even more difficult to represent are whole series of form-sound patterns. Psalms 111 and 112 consist of acrostic poems in Hebrew, for each line in order begins with a successive letter of the Hebrew alphabet. Psalm 119 also has an acrostic structure, but in this poem each set of eight lines begins with the same letter of the alphabet, and the sets are arranged in the order of the Hebrew alphabet. Lamentations 3 has a similar structure, but there are only three lines for each letter of the Hebrew alphabet. These patterns, based on phonological features of the source language, simply cannot be reproduced in a receptor language, unless a formal correspondence is introduced by some radical distortion of the meaning.

Metrical and rhyming structures must almost always be altered, for phonological correspondences between languages are so diverse as to make any one-for-one patterning impossible. Although all languages have metered expression and can employ rhymed series of lines, the ways in which such forms are used do not correspond closely from language to language, especially when language structures and literary traditions are quite diverse.

MORPHOLOGICAL CORRESPONDENCES AND CONTRASTS

The formal correspondences between word structures of different languages involve three principal features: (1) the relative complexity of word formation; (2) differences of word classes, especially as these formal classes are related to different functional types (i.e. objects, events, abstracts, and relationals); and (3) categories expressed by various classes of words.

Complexity of Word Formation

When one translates from a highly inflected language, such as Greek, into a more or less isolating language, such as Chinese or Lahu, a gain in the number of words involved is inevitable. In Greek, the verb specifies not only the particular action, but also such features as actors, time, and aspect. In an isolating language, one must usually reproduce all these elements as separate words; that is, by verbs, particles, and pronouns. Though this process involves an obvious gain in the number of words involved, i.e. in the forms written as separate units, there is no gain in the total information carried by the message; the units have merely been redistributed in different ways.

On the other hand, some languages, e.g. Quechua, Aymara, Ilocano, and Eskimo, include much more in the verb than is included in a Greek verb. A Quechua verb, for example, often incorporates within its structure a number of diverse semantic elements, e.g. 'coming', 'going', 'up', 'down', 'helping', 'for someone's benefit', 'just', 'here', 'about to', 'please', 'right away', and 'ought'. In addition, one may also include in the verb direct and indirect object pronouns.

In such a situation a comparison of the total number of words in the texts of source and receptor languages necessarily shows a reduction; but again, this reduction is relatively meaningless, for the same basic semantic components are all there—they have simply been redistributed in other combinations.

Word Classes

Not only do languages differ radically in the number of different principal word classes (anywhere from three to eight, in most instances); they are just as diverse in the semantic content, which also may be expressed by such classes. For example, the meaning rendered in English by such adverbs as *recently, not yet, quickly, earnestly,* and *always,* is in Ngok Dinka rendered by auxiliary verbs. But one cannot generalize and say that all adverbial "ideas" are verbs in Ngok Dinka, for English *slowly* is rendered by an adverbial particle, not by a verb, as is *quickly.* In Navajo both *broad* and *road* are essentially verbs, so that *broad is the way* (Matthew 7:13) becomes literally 'being-broad it-roads', a sequence of two verb expressions. Moreover, the problems of word classes involve not only words indicating objects, events, and abstracts, but also relationals. For example, in Maya the words which correspond to the English conjunctions *and, in order that,* and *because* turn out to be possessed nouns.

Since languages differ extensively, not only in the number and semantic content of word classes, but also in the way in which such classes may be combined, translators must often completely reorganize the formal and semantic structure of a message in adapting it to the requirements of the receptor language. For example, the clause "there is no fear in love" (1 John 4:18) has been recast in Mazatec to read 'he who really loves forgets to be afraid'. The concepts of love and fear must be expressed by verbs, not nouns, and hence an actor must be expressed. Furthermore, the relationship indicated by English *in* must be radically altered, for though *in* can express the relationship of objects to each other in Mazatec, it does not show the relationship of events, as it does in English.

MORPHOLOGICAL CATEGORIES

In some respects the proper handling of categories expressed by languages is even more difficult than the complexity of word formations or the diversity of word classes. In treating such categories as number, person, tense, mode, gender, and voice, there are three types of problems: (1) their obligatory or optional character, (2) their range of occurrence, and (3) their frequency of selection.

Though languages differ more radically in what they *must* say than in what they *can* say—that is, the obligatory features of languages distinguish them more decisively than their optional ones—nevertheless, the optional features of language produce the greatest difficulties for the translator. If, for example, a language simply does not have a passive voice, as in the Zacapoastla dialect of Aztec, then, to translate adequately, all passives in the source language must be changed into actives. This may not be easy, but there is no question that it should be done, for adjustment is obligatory. The real difficulty occurs with an optional category, e.g. plurality in Quechua, which may be required by the sense of the passage, but is not obligatory; the real problem here is to determine just when to use such optional categories so that they will seem entirely natural in the translation.

If the range of a category is widespread in a language, e.g. singular vs. plural in English, one usually has little difficulty in dealing with it, for its all-pervasive character generally leaves no doubt as to what forms should be used. In certain relatively limited structural patterns one encounters greater difficulty. For example, in English there is a contrast between personal and nonpersonal, e.g. *who* vs. *which* and *he* and *she* vs. *it*. In expressions such as *this is the group of people which came* or *this is the group of people who came*, an English speaker may be puzzled about which form to use. Normally he would say *people who* but *group which*, but in the phrase *group of people*, the optional choice of *who* or *which* constitutes a problem.

The frequency of selection of a particular category is a further factor in judging whether or not such a form should be employed. This frequency factor may be related to the two parts of a pair, e.g. active vs. passive; or it may concern only the frequency of occurrence of a single category, contrasting, not with some opposite feature, but, optionally, with zero. The problem of contrasting pairs is illustrated by the use of active and passive verb forms in some Nilotic languages, in which passive forms are usually preferred; that is to say, they occur with much greater frequency. Thus, even though an active form in the source language can often be translated by a corresponding active in such a receptor language as Shilluk, it is preferable to shift to the passive, which is much more frequently employed in normal speech. On the other hand, in Bolivian Quechua the plural suffix *-runa*, which contrasts with zero (i.e. with a significant absence of the suffix), is strictly optional, and though it can be used for any plural in Spanish or English, it is certainly not used with anything like the frequency with which Spanish or English would use plural formations. A Quechua text full of words ending in *-runa* could be judged as grammatically correct—that is, there would not be any word which was grammatically wrong; nevertheless, the total effect of the sentence would be bad.

The principle of frequency of selection applies to all analogical formations. Though it is perfectly possible, and even easy, to construct a host of new words in some languages, such formations are not so acceptable as some translators have considered them to be. The forms may be correct, but the frequency of selection is not, and thus the communication channel is overloaded.

Obviously it is impossible to treat here all the morphological categories which occur in languages throughout the world. However, it has seemed useful to select at least several categories, e.g. number, tense, aspect, voice, mode, condition, gender, and person, as illustrative of the types of difficulties encountered in dealing with the range of correspondences between languages.

Number

The question of number offers difficulties to the translator because it is obligatory in some languages, as in Hebrew and the Indo-European languages, while in many other languages it is optional. It also presents problems because of: (1) its arbitrary values, (2) the exacting nature of some distinctions, and (3) the necessity of different treatments within specific contexts.

As with any semantic component, number is essentially arbitrary. In English, for example, we generally employ a singular form for generic number, e.g. "love your neighbor as yourself," but in Shilluk, Nuer, and Anuak one must use the plural, 'love your neighbors as yourselves'. In a sense, of course, the plural is more logical, for more than one person is obviously involved.

In some languages number becomes a rather exact feature. For example, in Pame, spoken in Mexico, one cannot speak of the "string of his sandals" (Mark 1:7). Rather, one must say 'strings', for each sandal has a string. Similarly, in Kizanaki, spoken in Tanganyika, the phrase *this people's heart* (Matthew 13:15) must be rendered as 'these persons' hearts', for several persons, and hence several hearts, are involved.

In the use of number in a sequence the translator finds further problems. In the Old Testament, for example, the Hebrew often shifts back and forth from singular to plural in a single sentence. In a language such as Loma, spoken in Liberia, it is impossible to duplicate these sequences. Even in a passage such as John 3:7, 'Do not marvel that I said to you, You must be born anew', the Greek text, which uses the singular in the first clause and the plural in the second, cannot be reproduced in Loma, for either the singular or the plural must be used throughout. Modern English avoids this problem by the use of the pronoun *you*, which can be either singular or plural, but in so doing fails to make a distinction clearly marked in Greek.

Tense

Tense, which marks the relative time of events, is generally accepted as given by those who speak an Indo-European language, for such distinctions as past, present, and future are considered to be a basic ingredient in any verbal expression. Actually, the expression of tense, even in a language such as English, is by no means clear-cut. For example, a so-called present-tense form may indicate a variety of relative times, e.g. the verb *comes* in the following expressions: *if he comes, we will help him* (future), *after that he comes and hits him, while everyone was staring right at him* (past), and *he comes every day at ten o'clock* (past, present, and future). In place of past, present, and future we should often speak of prior, contemporaneous, and subsequent, but even these distinctions do not cover all the problems of tense in English.

Other languages, on the other hand, employ quite a different basis for distinctions in tense. In Loma, tense is divided into two principal categories: (1) past leading into the present, and (2) present carrying into the future. Cashibo, a language of Peru, has three basic distinctions: (1) potential action, (2) future action, and (3) a series of completed actions—in the present, the immediate past, the past of this morning, the past of yesterday, the past of yesterday-to-remote, and the distinctly remote past. Though some languages also have a number of different futures, past tenses are almost always more elaborate than those indicating the future. This difference is understandable, for past actions are obviously more readily classifiable as to relative time than are future contingencies.

When translating from one language to another, it is necessary not only to adjust to quite a different system, but also to reckon with the special restrictions which may exist within such a system. For example, in Navajo there is no present or imperfect form of the verb meaning 'to forget'; that is to say, Navajo regards 'forgetting' as a completed process.

In some languages tense distinctions may occur with nouns, something which we ourselves do rather unsystematically in speaking of an ex-president and a president-elect. In Ngbandi, a language of northern Congo, tense distinctions are generally indicated by tonal differences on the subject pronouns, while aspectual differences are signaled by differences of tone on the verbs.

Regardless of the formal or semantic differentiations made in the tense system, the important fact is that no two systems are in complete agreement. Even in languages as close as French and Spanish, there are important differences. French, for example, has almost given up the use of the preterit tense, except in strictly literary style, and has substituted the perfect tense, using the auxiliary verb *avoir*. However, Spanish still employs the preterit as the regular form for past actions.

Aspect

Aspect, which defines the nature of the action, is a much more frequently used grammatical category than tense. Even within the Indo-European languages it was at one time more significant than at present. As a description of the kind of action involved in the verb, aspect serves to differentiate a number of contrasts, of which some of the most common are: (1) complete vs. incomplete, (2) punctiliar vs. continuous, (3) single (or simulfactive) vs. repetitive, (4) increasing vs. decreasing, (5) beginning vs. ending, and (6) single vs. habitual or customary.

In ancient Greek, aside from the indicative, the different so-called tense forms primarily signify distinctions in aspect; thus an aorist negative command indicates that one should not do something in the future (punctiliar aspect), while a present negative command specifies that one should cease doing what one is presently doing (continuative aspect). For this reason we know that in John 20:17 one should not translate 'do not touch me' (following the King James Version) but rather 'do not keep holding on to me'. In Hebrew the basic distinctions in the verb are fundamentally aspect, not tense; however, they are often treated as tense distinctions for the sake of those who speak such a language as English. In the Old Testament, however, the differences between the Hebrew completive and incompletive forms are essentially contrasts between kinds of action; for this reason one finds such apparently anomalous features as the prophets, using the same verbal forms to describe past action and to predict future events. Thus, one is not always certain whether a saying is to be understood in a prophetic sense or as a description of a past event. On the other hand, this use of the completive forms of the verb by the prophets is neither linguistic juggling nor word magic. Rather, it means that the prophets regarded such events as so certain of fulfillment as to be "theologically completed."

Hebrew is not the only language with its own peculiar method of handling aspectual contrasts. In Navajo, where there is a distinction between single and repeated action, it is still not easy to translate James 5:15, "if he has committed sins, he will be forgiven." At first glance one would assume that the repetitive aspect of the verb 'forgiven' would be required, for God obviously is willing to forgive more than once. On the other hand, the repetitive form of 'to forgive' implies extreme indulgence on the part of God, and hence conveys the impression that there is complete license to sin. In the Villa Alta dialect of Zapotec there is also a distinction between repetitive and nonrepetitive action, but the repetitive form of the verb 'to come' means to 'return home', and hence cannot be used for the second coming of Jesus Christ; for if the abode of Jesus Christ is considered as being in heaven, then the repetitive form would mean to return to heaven, not to return to earth. This same dialect of Zapotec has an important aspectual distinction between (1) congenital disability and (2) disease which occurs later in life. This means that in any New Testament passage which deals with disease or healing, the translator must specify whether the infirmity in question was congenital or not.

Voice

Voice specifies the relationship between the participants and the event indicated in the verb; e.g. active (*he went*), passive (*he was hit*), middle (*do it to* or *for oneself*), reflexive (*hit himself*), reciprocal (*hit each other*), benefactive (*worked for him*), transitive (*hit him*), intransitive (*he came*), instrumental (*did it by means of something*), agentive (*did it through someone*), and causative (*caused it to happen*, or *caused him to do it*). It constitutes one of the most extensive problems for the translator, since the shifting of the relationship of the participants to the action often requires complete recasting of the grammatical structure.

The most frequent problems of translation involving voice include difficulties of (a) active vs. passive forms and (b) causatives. Some languages have a definite preference for passive forms, even in the case of verbs not regarded by English speakers as capable of passive relationships. For example, "I went to him" would normally be rendered in Shilluk as 'he was gone to by me'. In certain other languages there are simply no passive forms, and all passives in the source language must be changed to actives. Such a shift is no problem as long as the agent of the action is clearly specified, for *Bill was hit by John* can be readily transformed back into *John hit Bill*. However, when no agent is expressed, the shifting of a passive to an active is not always easy, though some languages leave no alternative but to make such a change. Accordingly, an expression such as "Judge not that you be not judged" (Matthew 7:1) must be translated 'Do not judge so that God will not judge you', assuming that the appropriate subject, as implied by the context, is God, and not merely one's fellow citizens.

However, the most serious difficulties with active and passive contrasts are not the obvious ones, in which the verb expression is clearly marked; they occur, rather, with verbal derivatives which have no such evident specification. For example, possessive verbal noun expressions such as "(consider) your calling" (1 Corinthians 1:26), "(bearing) his reproach" (Hebrews 13:13), and "(not for) your destruction" (2 Corinthians 10:18) are passive, even though there is no marker of passive form. In a language which requires such events to be expressed by full, active verb forms, one must obviously introduce certain radical adjustments in grammatical structure; e.g. 'consider how God called you' or 'consider how you were when God called you'; 'while people reproach us as they reproached him'; and 'and not that we should destroy you'.

The problems of causative voice are somewhat more subtle than those of active and passive voice. Especially is this so for those who are unfamiliar with the requirement of some language structures, namely, that one specify clearly whether a person performs an action himself, or causes another person or object to perform or undergo the action. Accordingly, in Mark 6:16 it is impossible in many languages to translate literally Herod's words, "John, whom I beheaded," unless one wishes to imply that Herod himself was the executioner—something which is explicitly denied later in the same chapter. Accordingly, one must render this passage as 'John whom I caused to be beheaded'.

Mode

Mode (or mood), which defines the psychological background of the action, involves principally such categories as possibility (probable, possible, conditional, potential), necessity (imperative, hortatory, jussive, obligatory), and desire (desiderative, optative, and petitive). Because of the subjective nature of such concepts, the categories of mode are undoubtedly the most difficult of all to deal with in translating. Particularly is it true of the modal concepts of necessity, which are poorly defined in some languages. Generally the imperative forms, direct commands in the second person, are widespread, but in some languages one must often use some sort of auxiliary, such as 'ought' or 'must'. A hortatory, e.g. 'let us do it', may be entirely absent in some languages, with the only close parallel being 'we ought to do this'. The jussive, namely, a third person imperative, 'let him suffer' (not permission but command), is highly ambiguous in English, and in some languages is only translated as 'he must', 'he should', or 'he ought to'.

Some modal expressions have been translated by highly idiomatic expressions. For example, Greek *mê genoito*, an optative negative of the verb 'to become', has been variously translated into English, e.g. "God forbid!" (King James Version), "By no means!" (Revised Standard Version), "Never!" (Moffatt), "Certainly not!" (New English Bible), and "Of course not!" (Phillips).

Condition of Objects

In some languages the objects which participate in events are elaborately classified by such categories as animate vs. inanimate, alive vs. dead, honored vs. common, and shape and size. In English we have a very limited category of animate vs. inanimate in the use of *who* vs. *which* and *what*, and in *he* and *she* vs. *it*. However, in some languages, e.g. various Algonkian dialects, this distinction runs throughout the structure. In the Villa Alta dialect of Zapotec a categorical distinction is made between persons who are dead and those who are alive, thus posing some real problems in speaking of Jesus Christ after his resurrection. In Rawang, a language of Burma, a somewhat similar distinction between dead and alive is employed, but with special restrictions. In the Gospel of Mark, for example, it is necessary at first to specify that John was no longer alive at the time of the writing of the book, but from there on it is possible to use grammatical forms identical with those employed of any person who is alive.

Honorifics, referred to at several points in preceding chapters, produce some of the most complex problems faced by translators in some areas of the world, for honorific language may consist of wide differences in vocabulary items, as in Ponapean, spoken in Micronesia; or it may involve both vocabulary and grammatical forms, as in Japanese, Korean, Balinese, and Thai. Moreover, languages may specify not merely two grades of honor, i.e. those with honor and those without, but often three or more classes, depending upon various status levels. In Balinese (Swellengrebel, 1950a), for example, there are four pronouns of the third person, two of which are used of more honored persons, and two of which are used for those on the same grade as the speaker or beneath him; but in the second set, one pronoun is used to refer to such a person in a familiar way, while another implies a polite attitude toward him. It would not be too difficult to apply such a system to a text coming from a source language, were it not for the fact that status levels are often reinterpreted, irrespective of the actual historical circumstances. To illustrate, it is quite unthinkable that the Pharisees would address the upstart young Rabbi Jesus of Nazareth in honorific terms, but a contemporary Balinese Christian audience insists upon what may be regarded either as an anachronistic reinterpretation of honorific titles or an adherence to the viewpoint of the "secondary source" (namely the attitude of the Biblical writer), so that Jesus can always be addressed in terms befitting their present-day high regard for him.

Not infrequently honorific expressions cause ambiguity; for example, in Moré, a language of the Haute Volta, all honorifics are plurals (the so-called plural of majesty). The resulting translation can be seriously ambiguous unless sufficient redundancy is built in to make it quite clear that the plural is merely an honorific, not a specification of plural participants.

Extensive categories of shape and size, e.g. long, short, slender, stout, thin, thick, fat, round, stiff, supple, leaflike, stonelike, etc. are found in a number of languages, especially in South America. However, some languages of Southeast Asia incorporate certain distinctions as to shape and size into their numerical systems. That is to say, there are various sets of numeral forms, depending upon what is being counted.

Gender

Gender distinctions, which identify grammatical classes of words within groups of words, i.e. the so-called "parts of speech," serve to set off such important groupings as masculine-feminine-neuter in many Indo-European languages, as well as the various concord classes in various Bantu languages. Within the Indo-European languages the distinctions between masculine, feminine, and neuter have some basis in nonlinguistic phenomena, i.e. words for males are usually placed in the masculine class; for females, in the feminine class; and for things, in the neuter class. But there are hundreds of obvious exceptions, as when German *Frau* 'woman, wife' is feminine, but *Fräulein* is neuter; or when English *ship* can be spoken of as either *it* or *she*. In Bantu languages some classes have certain semantic components, e.g. many personal terms are in the first or *mu-/ba-* class, and certain diminutives are often in special prefixal classes; but basically, gender classes are not groupings according to sex, shape, size, or condition, but according to grammatical usage.

Though such gender classes may be quite a nuisance for the translator, since they require careful attention to grammatical detail, they are in most cases the least of his worries; for they are essentially so arbitrary and all-pervasive in the linguistic system that alternatives are rarely permitted. In other words, the syntactic rules of the language are usually so explicit in the matter of gender that one can rarely make a mistake without its becoming quite obvious. Moreover, few associated meanings cluster about these gender distinctions, for the meanings of such forms are usually strictly linguistic.

Case

Case distinctions serve to mark the relationships between words within constructions, e.g. subject, object, indirect object, location, and instrument. In many Indo-European languages, case is a very conspicuous part of the grammatical signaling system. In most languages, however, cases do not exist, and relationships are likely to be signaled merely by order or by particles.

In many languages of the Philippines a syntactically significant set of phonologically dependent particles is employed to mark some important relationships between words (Waterman, 1960a). Basically, these particles serve to identify the topic (or subject) in contrast with the comment (or predicate), so that almost any feature of a sentence may be highlighted by making it the significant element of the expression. This system of marking the significant parts of the sentence by particles seems to be much more widespread than is the case system typical of Indo-European languages.

Person

Pronouns are usually spoken of as first, second, and third person, by which we usually mean the speaker (and those associated with him, if plural), the one or ones spoken to, and the one or ones spoken about. The nomenclature of "first," "second," and "third" comes from the traditional order of such pronouns in Greek and Latin.

Even within such a relatively neat system as three persons, singular and plural, certain serious complications can arise. Thus, some of the forms may be ambiguous, as they are in English, where *you* serves for both singular and plural. Again, there may be alternative forms for certain persons, e.g. Spanish *Usted* and *Ustedes*, in contrast with *tu* and *vosotros* (formal vs. familiar discourse). Furthermore, such formal vs. familiar discourse is not so easily defined as one might at first think; for though *tu* may be used in familiar home situations and between close friends, it is also employed in speaking to God in very formal discourse. *Vosotros*, which can likewise be a symbol of familiarity in certain situations, may also be a sign of formal oratorical style. Within each system, therefore, one must expect to find numerous and subtle distinctions, which cannot easily be reduced to readily manipulatable rules.

Two serious problems result in considerable ambiguity and obscurity in translating from certain Indo-European languages. First, some languages do not employ a so-called editorial first person plural, e.g. "we think," or "we believe," when the real subject is only the speaker himself. Such "editorial we's" must be shifted to 'I' if they are to be intelligible in some languages. Second, the use of a third person reference for the first person is relatively rare in languages, so that such epistolary introductions as occur in the Pauline letters, "Paul . . . to the church . . ." must be changed to read, 'I, Paul, write to the church . . .'. Similarly, in the Gospels it is impossible to have Jesus speak of himself purely in the third person as 'the Son of man', unless one is to assume that Jesus never identified himself as the Son of man. Accordingly, most translators use 'I, who am the Son of man'.

There are two elaborations of the basic first-second-third person pronominal structure: (1) the addition of a fourth person, and (2) the distinction between inclusive and exclusive first-person plural. The fourth person, i.e. an additional third person, is a relatively rare type of distinction, but it is a very handy device for systematically distinguishing two different third-person referents. The inclusive-exclusive first-person contrast, a widespread feature of languages, gives rise to many problems in translating from a source language which does not make this distinction. For example, in Galatians 2:15 there is a troublesome passage for which the selection of an inclusive or exclusive form is highly debatable. The preceding sentence is obviously a part of direct discourse; but what are we to understand by the words "we ourselves, who are Jews by birth and not Gentile sinners"? Is Paul here continuing to represent what he said in Antioch in opposition to Peter, or is he merely arguing a general position with the Galatian church audience to whom he is writing? If one assumes that Paul is still addressing the assembly in Antioch, and Peter in particular, then the inclusive form is required; but if the words are directed to the church in Galatia, obviously one should employ the exclusive. Scholars are by no means agreed on this point, for the Greek text itself is obscure. Apparently there is a gradual shift from the specific situation which involved Peter to a general statement of the gospel as it is related to the Galatian church. The translator who is rendering this passage into a language with an inclusive-exclusive distinction cannot, however, retain this obscurity. He must specify clearly by the very forms he uses whether or not this sentence is to be regarded as a part of the direct discourse.

In some instances a contextually fitting interpretation of the inclusive-exclusive contrast actually does violence to the historical facts of a situation. For example, in John 8:33 the Jewish leaders are quoted as saying to Jesus, "We are descendants of Abraham," by which they repudiate his statement that only by accepting the truth can the Jews be made free. If one were to use the inclusive first-person pronoun, which would thus include Jesus as a Jew, the results would be equivalent to 'we all, including you, are the descendants of Abraham'; but it was just this contrast between Jesus and the Jewish leaders which this statement is supposed to emphasize. Accordingly, in order to fit the social facts of the circumstance, and thus to be in accord with the spirit of the context, it is necessary to use 'we (exclusive) are the sons of Abraham', even though this statement is not in accord with the genealogical facts of the case.

Possession

It is often assumed by translators that possession is possession in any language. Nevertheless, there are certain important differences which result in significant problems of correspondence. Thus some languages have two types of possession, often called intimate and nonintimate. For example, 'his bone' as intimate possession would mean the bone of one's own body, but 'his bone' with a nonintimate form would designate a bone, perhaps of some animal, which the person has in his possession.

Languages also differ as to obligatory features of possession. For example, in many languages some words must be possessed under all circumstances, e.g. 'father', 'son', 'mother', 'daughter', 'wife', 'husband', 'heart', 'soul'. A word such as 'son' seems meaningful in such a language only when it is related to some person; for, after all, a person who is a son is only such in relationship to some particular person or persons. Accordingly, in translating the Scriptures it is impossible to talk about "the Son" as in John 5:19-23. Rather, one must say 'his Son', referring to God as the referent of 'his'. Likewise, in this same passage, 'Father' must be possessed, but since in many languages God as Father is always spoken of as 'our Father', one may use this general designation rather than make the possession refer only to 'the Son'.

In certain languages some types of possession simply cannot be used. For example, in Hopi one cannot speak of 'my God', for God cannot be possessed. One must say, 'the God in whom I believe'.

CORRESPONDENCES AND CONTRASTS IN SYNTACTICAL STRUCTURES

Errors in syntactic correspondence undoubtedly account for the largest number of mistakes in translating, though not necessarily the most serious ones. Anyone who has examined a word-for-word translation into any language cannot but be impressed by the incredible number of syntactically weird combinations which result. Of course, at times these combinations make no sense at all, and sometimes they give precisely the wrong meaning. For example, in one language a translation of the phrase "grace for grace" (John 1:16) resulted in an expression meaning 'favor for favor', or in other words, 'if you help me, I will help you'—precisely the opposite meaning of the passage in question. Similarly, the Semitic expression "blessing I will bless" (Hebrews 6:14) was rendered literally in another language, with the resultant meaning of 'if you bless me, then I will bless you'.

It is clearly impossible within the scope of this volume to classify all, or even a relatively small proportion, of the total types of syntactic correspondences between languages. Rather, the discussion must be limited to pointing out some of the constructions on the various levels of phrase, clause, sentence, and discourse which tend to produce special problems. Moreover, in this analysis no attempt is made to follow a rigidly defined distinction among all the various levels. Rather, all structurally significant combinations of words are classified in three major groupings: (1) phrase, (2) clause and sentence, and (3) discourse. Within each of these, some of the structures which frequently give rise to special difficulties are indicated.

Phrase Structure

Of the scores of different types of phrase structures in languages, some of the most troublesome consist of: (1) co-ordinate expressions; (2) words related to each other by some syntactic marker, e.g. case ending or particle, which may have a wide range of meanings; (3) so-called prepositional relationships; and (4) comparative expressions.

Co-ordinate phrases, such as "God and Father," (2 Peter 1:11) "answered and said," and "sat and begged" (John 9:8) can all produce certain complications, since they are formally co-ordinate but semantically not so. For example, "God and Father of our Lord Jesus Christ," if translated literally into some receptor languages, would mean that God was not the Father of Jesus Christ, since the co-ordinator 'and' would imply two persons, not one. Accordingly, in such languages one must change this type of co-ordinate structure into an appositional one, e.g. 'God, Father of . . .' or 'God who is Father of . . .'.

"Answered and said" may be equally difficult in some languages, simply because this type of Semitic co-ordination is supplementary, while in many languages the literal equivalent is contradictory. The question is put by the speaker of such a language, "What did he do, answer or speak?" Therefore, rather than being "additive," in some languages the use of these two verbs is "subtractive." Accordingly, the translator must choose one or the other.

In the expression "sat and begged" as rendered into Tau Sug, a language of the Philippines, one must specify one of these actions as primary and the other as secondary, for the blind man did one while doing the other. Accordingly, one must say 'he sat begging' or 'he was begging while he sat'. Otherwise, the two events combined by this co-ordinator would appear to be sequential. Thus any expression in the source language which is formally co-ordinate, but semantically appositional, contradictory, contemporaneous, or subordinate, should be immediately suspect, and hence subjected to careful scrutiny and possible adaptation.

In translating from Greek or English, the two most complex series of difficulties arise respectively from the genitive case form and the preposition *of*, for these are the forms in the corresponding languages which cover the widest range of meaningful relationships between words. Earlier, in Chapter 5, several of the problems relating to the use of "of" were discussed. Here we can only illustrate some of the more common ways in which certain of these problems may be resolved. In the following list, classified on the basis of the meaningful relationship between components A and B, which respectively precede and follow *of*, a number of different possible solutions are illustrated. In each instance the receptor-language adaptation is reflected in a relatively literal back-translation, with a language in which such a rendering has been noted indicated in most instances. One must not assume, however, that the interpretation followed in each case is the only legitimate one, nor that the particular form of expression is the most felicitous possible.

1. B is associated with A: *day of wrath*, 'day which will bring wrath' (Romans 2:5, Cakchiquel); *furnace of fire*, 'furnace that has fire' (Matthew 15:42, Panayan); *cup of the Lord*, 'the cup by which we remember the Lord' (1 Corinthians 10:21, Cakchiquel).
2. A is associated with B: *the door of faith*, 'how they could believe' (Acts 14:27, Mazatec).
3. B qualifies A: *Father of glory*, 'glorious father' (Ephesians 1:17, Aymara); *hearing of faith*, 'hear and believe' (Galatians 3:2, Zoque); *kiss of love*, 'loving one another, kiss' (1 Peter 5:14, Navajo).
4. A qualifies B: *wisdom of words* (KJV), 'well arranged (i.e. wise) words' (1 Corinthians 1:17, Cakchiquel); *error of (his) way*, 'road of mistakes' (James 5:20, Navajo).

5. B is the goal of A: *knowledge of God*, 'to know God' (Colossians 1:10, Aymara); *love of the Father*, 'love (our) Father' (1 John 2:15, Mazatec).
6. A is the goal of B: *object of his desire*, 'that which he desires'; *sons of wrath*, 'those against whom God is angry'.
7. A is the causative subject of B: *God of peace*, 'God who gives peace' (Philippians 4:9, Navajo); *spirit of infirmity*, 'spirit which causes sickness' (Luke 13:11, Huanuco Quechua); *bread of life*, 'bread that causes to live' (John 6:35, Zacapoastla Aztec).
8. A is the direct subject of B: *man of sin*, 'one who sins'; *sons of disobedience*, 'those who disobey'.
9. B is the direct subject of A: *love of God*, 'God loves'; *the work of evil men*, 'what evil men do'.
10. A is the causative goal of B: *the peace of God*, 'the peace (or reconciliation) which God causes'.
11. B is in apposition with A: *temple of his body*, 'temple which was his body' (John 2:21, Guajiro); *gift of the Spirit*, 'gift which is the Spirit' (Acts 2:38, Aymara).
12. A is related to B: *I am of Paul*, 'I walk behind Paul' (1 Corinthians 1:12, Navajo).
13. A is from B: *Jesus of Nazareth*, 'Jesus who comes from Nazareth'.
14. A is a part of B: *heart of man*, 'heart in a man'; *city of Galilee*, 'big town in Galilee country'; *wilderness of Judea*, 'uninhabited region in Judea'.
15. B possesses A: *the house of Philip*, 'the house Philip owned' (or 'where Philip lives').

Prepositional phrases, e.g. *in the house* and *with John*, may be difficult to translate, simply because in some languages the concepts expressed in English by such prepositions as *in* and *with* are indicated by words of a different structure. For example, in some Mayan languages *in* corresponds to a possessed noun, literally 'stomach', so that *in the house* is 'its stomach the house'. Similarly, *with John* becomes 'his withness John'. In east Toradja, spoken in Indonesia, 'they mentioned his-he-ness' is a way of rendering "they spoke about him."

A special difficulty encountered in translating from an Indo-European language is that many languages have not quite so neat a formula for expressing comparison. For example, in a number of African languages comparison must be expressed by a verb meaning 'to surpass'. In Yipounou, a language of the Gabon, "it will be more tolerable for Tyre . . . than for you" (Matthew 11:22) becomes 'it will surpass in being well to Tyre . . . and not to you'. In a number of languages comparison is expressed by straightforward positive-negative contrasts. "My father is greater than I" (John 14:28) becomes in Zacapoastla Aztec simply 'My father is really great, I am not very great'. If understood in a literal way, this rendering would involve a serious theological problem; but comparison can be expressed only in this way in this language, and it is properly understood as comparison, not as negation. In still other languages one finds such expressions as 'he is behind' or 'he is ahead of'.

Clause Structure

Correspondences in clause structure normally involve the following types of difficulties: (1) significance of the order of component parts, (2) type of clause, and (3) the way in which clauses are combined.

In English the usual order of the principal units in a transitive clause is subject, verb, object, but in some languages this is by no means the order followed. For example, in Mazahua the normal order is verb, object, and subject, but the object may be placed in an emphatic initial position by the order object-verb-subject; similarly, the subject may be made emphatic by the order subject-verb-object. Any literal word-for-word reproduction of English order would therefore distort the Mazahua clause patterns.

All languages have a variety of so-called clause types, e.g. equational (*he is rich*), intransitive (*he works hard*), and transitive (*he saw him*); but in English all these are combined under what we call the subject-predicate type of construction, which is the major sentence type. There are, however, certain minor types in English, e.g. aphorisms (*the more the better*, and *love me love my dog*), exclamatives (*Fire!*, *Police!*, *Ouch!*), and supplementives, e.g. running comments or answers to questions. In some languages the closest equivalent to the subject-predicate clause type may be better designated as topic-comment. All languages, of course, make use of minor clause types, but not necessarily of the same types as in English. In fact, a number of languages seem to have considerably more minor types than are normally used in English. Obviously, no translator can do an acceptable piece of work until he has ascertained precisely what clause types exist in the receptor language concerned, as well as how frequently they occur, for an unusual disparity in frequency is bound to distort the communication load.

The most acute problem in clause correspondences occurs when a clause type that is important in the source language simply does not exist in the receptor language. Rhetorical questions, for example, are nonexistent in a number of languages. In Matthew 12:48, for example, Jesus is recorded as saying, "Who is my mother? And who are my brethren?" In a language which has no rhetorical questions, this type of question is utterly misleading. Jesus was certainly not asking for information, for the people had just finished telling him that his mother and brethren were outside the door. One way of handling these questions is to include them as a question within a question, e.g. "Do you ask me, Who is my mother and my brothers?", for then Jesus proceeds to answer the principal question. The question may also be framed as, "Do you wish to know who is my mother and who are my brothers?"

Clauses are combined by three principal methods: (1) parataxis, (2) hypotaxis, and (3) prostaxis. Under parataxis are classified those combinations of clauses which are closely related semantically, but which have no formal markers, at least those of a segmental type, i.e. conjunctions, enclitics, or particles (e.g. *and*, *but*, *since*, *when*), which show

14

that they are combined. [1] Such paratactic combinations are found frequently in the Old Testament, for Hebrew had a characteristically paratactic type of interclause structure. In the first verse of Psalm 23, for example, the two clauses are obviously paratactic, for the real meaning is: "Since the Lord is my shepherd, I shall not be in need."

Hypotaxis is a term used to describe elaborate systems of grammatical subordination, the type of structure so highly developed in literary Greek, and reflected in varying ways in a number of Indo-European languages. Though many complex systems of dependency marked by means of conjunctions and special forms of the verbs are found in various languages throughout the world, it is true that by and large most languages seem to prefer parataxis or prostaxis to hypotaxis. As a result, one must often take the highly involved sentences of the source language and break them up into paratactically combined units. For the Bible translator this is especially necessary in the case of certain passages in the Pauline Epistles.

Prostaxis is here used to identify a particular way of combining clauses into long strings of relatively co-ordinate expressions. In Chuj, a Mayan language of Guatemala, for example, a text normally consists of a long series of more or less co-ordinate clauses combined by means of particles which mean something equivalent to 'and then'. Formally these clauses are combined by conjunctions, but these continuative particles are really not the equivalent of *and* in English. In fact, instead of combining clauses, these conjunctions serve to mark the divisions between clauses. They function more like periods than conjunctions. For this reason this type of structure cannot be regarded as either parataxis (for there are formal markers) or hypotaxis of a co-ordinating variety (for the markers divide rather than unite). The overall significance of such prostactic particles is, however, more like parataxis than like hypotaxis. There is, however, a parallel to prostaxis in Old Testament Hebrew and in the Semitic Greek of the New Testament. In Hebrew the clause initial *waw* is often merely a signal of a clause beginning, and does not really link the clause in any co-ordinating way to the previous clause. Similarly, in the first chapter of Mark the string of *kai* 'and' forms does not make a single sentence out of the many clauses. Rather, these forms mark the syntactic units by separating clauses from each other. Accordingly, this type of structure can also be regarded as prostactic.

Discourse Structure

Formal structuring in language does not, of course, end with the sentence. The speaker of a language does not simply put together any combination of sentences he pleases, without regard to their interrelation-

---

[1] Though paratactically combined clauses have no combinative forms consisting of segmental phonemes, they usually are marked in spoken language by certain types of intonational contours and nonfinal junctures. In some instances the two clauses may be combined within a single overarching intonational pattern.

ships. Rather, any discourse is in many respects quite highly structured (Harris, 1952).

Any language has several different types of discourse, e.g. narrative, conversation, exposition, declamation, and poetry, but the formal features which characterize these diverse types in various languages are often strikingly different. For example, in Shilluk the traditional narrative style calls for a long series of verb expressions which dramatically tell the story in fast-moving sequences. In a number of other languages most narratives are characterized by many ideophones, highly onomatopoeic expressions.

All languages possess two major types of speech, formal and informal, or, as one may prefer to classify them, noncasual and casual (Voegelin, 1960a). Conversation, of course, is primarily casual, while poetry is usually very noncasual, since it is highly structured. However, a narrative discourse may be either casual or noncasual. In some languages personal narratives are usually casual, while tribal narratives (i.e. legends) are highly structured. Because of the emphasis placed upon correct communication with and about the supernatural world, religious discourse is in some languages the most highly structured and formally elaborated of all types of discourse. At times this type of discourse is the result of a long religious tradition which has preserved many archaic forms and obsolete expressions. On the other hand, religious functionaries often create artifically "mysterious" language and formal structure to heighten the feeling of awe experienced by the receptors.

If all languages were in agreement on the characteristics of casual and noncasual forms of discourse, the translator's task would be greatly simplified. Of course, from time to time there are certain fortunate correspondences. For example, in some Indonesian poetry there is a marked tendency toward parallelism of formal structure and semantic content in succeeding pairs of lines. Thus in translating Old Testament poetry (H. van der Veen, 1952b) many serious difficulties are resolved by this similarity in style. However, in most parts of the world no such poetic parallelism exists, and receptors are often irked by what they regard as obnoxious repetition and tautology in Semitic poetic forms.

Though it is impossible to describe here all the important discourse types, five features can be singled out which are particularly relevant to the translator's task, and which form the basis for a high proportion of the problems of correspondence. These are: (1) sequences of sentence and clause types; (2) markers of sequences; (3) temporal features of sentence and clause sequences; (4) spatial features of sentence and clause sequences; and (5) formal and semantic "carry-overs" from one sentence or clause to another.

Problems of direct and indirect discourse constitute the most common difficulties involving sequences of sentence and clause types. In English we are well acquainted with direct and indirect discourse, though we recognize that for lively narrative the direct forms are preferable. In some languages, however, almost all indirect discourse must be shifted into a direct form. Even such an expression as "declaring themselves to be wise" (Romans 1:22) must be recast as 'they said, We are wise'. Such a shift from direct to indirect discourse involves a number of radical adjustments in form, including shifts of tenses, pronouns, and usually order of words and phrases.

The markers of sentence sequences may consist of: (a) transitional conjunctions or adverbs, e.g. *therefore, moreover, furthermore, then*; (b) special forms of the verbs, to indicate that the clause in question is dependent upon some other clause or sentence; and (c) pronominal forms, which indicate that the subject or object person involved is the same as, or different from, the corresponding form in a preceding or following sentence.

The temporal factors of a narrative are often highly important in the discourse structure, for in some languages the linguistic order of words and the historical order of events must be parallel. That is to say, one cannot use a form such as 'we put him out because he refused to agree'. Rather, one must change the order to read, 'he refused to agree, and therefore we put him out' or 'because he refused to agree, we put him out'. One often finds that a sequence of verb forms, such as immediate past followed by remote past, cannot be preserved unless there is some specific marker of time which orients the receptor to the temporal features of the two events.

Spatial features of sentence and clause sequences are also an important part of discourse in some languages. For example, in some languages the spatial point of view for any action is the position of the narrator at the time of speaking, and therefore all expressions for 'coming' and 'going' or 'here' and 'there' are dependent upon the "author's standpoint." Some languages shift the point of view to accord with the position of the focal personality in the narrative, or the presumed relationship of the narrator to the events in which he participates, either personally or vicariously (by identification with the "viewpoint character"). In many languages spoken by primitive peoples, the expressions for spatial orientation are precise and highly structured—far more so than the terms for time. By comparison, Indo-European languages pay less attention to spatial sequences. As a result, the translator from an Indo-European language to a language which has a tightly organized spatial structure finds it necessary to make a number of adaptations.

Clause and sentence "carry-overs" are common in relating semantic features and pronominal references from one sentence to another, helping to orient the receptor to a series of events and the persons participating in them. At the same time, some languages demand that, instead of referring twice to the same object or event by a single word, a close synonym must be used to avoid repetition. This kind of reversed "carry-over" is a common feature of languages with an established literary tradition. Nevertheless, in some receptor languages such a shifting of terms may lead merely to confusion; for such a language may require that the same object be referred to always by the same word, especially in immediately contiguous sentences—precisely what we usually attempt to avoid in English. Of course, this stylistic characteristic of avoiding repetition often leads to ambiguity, not only in a receptor language, but also in the source language. For example, a serious problem in the exegesis of the Gospel of John results from what may or may not be a tendency for John to substitute near synonyms, rather than continue to use the same word. Most scholars, for example, feel that this is the problem involved in the famous shift between *agapaō* and *phileō*, two words for 'love' (John 21:15-17).

A number of languages repeat part of a previous sentence at the beginning of an immediately following one to accomplish a transition. For example, instead of translating simply 'Jesus went to the other side of the Sea of Galilee, and a multitude followed him', one must in such languages translate thus: 'Jesus went to the other side of the Sea of Galilee. While he was going a multitude followed him'. Here the phrase *while he was going* marks the linkage between elements in the discourse.

Formal carry-overs are of two principal types: (a) metrical or rhyming features of sequences, and (b) parallel or chiastic arrangements of units. Once one has adopted a particular poetic structure, the sequences must, of course, be adjusted to such a formal arrangement. Whether one maintains a parallel or chiastic arrangement depends largely upon whether such literary devices are easily recognizable. For example, the following passage is probably chiastic: "Do not give dogs what is holy; and do not throw your pearls before swine, lest they trample them underfoot and turn and attack you" (Matthew 7:6), for the criss-cross arrangement combines *dogs* with *turn and attack* and *swine* with *trample underfoot*. Such a chiastic arrangement may be shifted into a parallel structure if required for intelligibility.

Where there is semantic parallelism in poetry, both semantic and formal carry-overs are involved.

Lexical Correspondences

The basic problems of lexical correspondences discussed in Chapter 5 are here supplemented by notes on certain problems that pose special difficulties to the translator.

Any study of lexical correspondences between languages highlights three negative aspects of the problem, namely, that: (1) literal correspondences are often dangerously misleading; (2) ,,manufactured'' expressions are often not correct correspondences; and (3) borrowings are often deceptive.

Literal Correspondences

Though the misleading nature of literal correspondences should be evident to anyone engaged in translating, serious errors continue to be made because translators are not fully aware of the folly of translating word for word. For example, in one language 'to receive the Kingdom of God' meant, in literal translation, nothing else than to rebel against God and to take over his rule. In another language, the phrase 'opens the womb' in "Every male that opens the womb shall be called holy to the

Lord" (Luke 2:23) was understood in the sense of sexual intercourse, not of being born.

All translators tend to make up receptor-language constructions on the model they find in the source language. This practice can be dangerous. Greek *metanoeō* 'repent' means literally 'to change the mind', but a translational correspondence made up on this model usually means little more than to have another idea about something. In some instances, translators attempt to make up equivalents by constructing descriptive names, e.g. 'long-eared-animal' for "donkey," only to discover, as happened in one language, that this expression was understood by receptors to mean a rabbit.

The borrowing of foreign-language words is often regarded as a safer practice than manufacturing terms with indigenous lexical components, but such borrowings, especially if they are already used, must be carefully scrutinized. For example, the Spanish term *seguro* 'certainly' is borrowed into several Philippine languages with the meaning of 'perhaps', and Spanish *ángeles* 'angels' is understood in some Indian languages of Latin America as referring to dead children, who are often buried with paper wings as a symbol of their presumed status after death. In the process of borrowing, terms are always subject to change in meaning, often with quite drastic reorientations. For example, Spanish *río* 'river' is borrowed by Trique, a language of Mexico, with the meaning of 'boat'.

Though it is useful to study the negative aspects of correspondences in lexical structure, it is essential to consider as well the positive features underlying the bewildering array of disparate elements in languages. Thus, one must recognize that usage in the receptor language determines the validity of a translation, even though that usage may seem (1) completely contradictory to what occurs in a source language, (2) meaningless from the standpoint of the source language, or (3) out of keeping with the context, as judged by the source-language usage.

Contradictory usages are found in comparing any source and receptor languages. For example, Conob, a Mayan language of Guatemala, employs the phrase 'to say silence' in place of "keep quiet." The use of 'say' appears to us to be contradictory to the concept of silence, which implies not saying anything. Nevertheless, the Conob idiom is a perfectly valid one. In Moré, a language of the Haute Volta, one says 'thirst has me', rather than *j'ai soif* 'I have thirst' as in French. In Shipibo, a language of Peru, one must use the phrase 'she left the fever' (Mark 1:31) rather than "the fever left her."

To the translator, certain receptor-language expressions may appear meaningless, as, for example, when stars are called 'head-chickens' in Mixteco, or when, as in Bambara, a language of West Africa, the right hand is the 'rice hand' and the left hand the 'nose hand'. Again, in Kiyaka, a language of Congo, the right hand is the 'father's hand', and the left hand is the 'mother's hand', while in Pidgin English of West Africa the right hand is the 'man hand' and the left hand is the 'woman hand'.

An expression in the receptor language may in some instances appear entirely inappropriate to the context. For example, the word for "thank-you" in Maya is literally 'May God pay you', but this expression can also be used in speaking to God. Such a usage would appear impossible to the person oriented solely toward the source language, but is quite acceptable to those who use this receptor expression as a semantically exocentric phrase.

The cultural circumstances which validate the usage of any receptor language are the result of historical developments; accordingly, expressions which may at first seem inappropriate may come to be fully acceptable. For example, the regular word for 'to pray' in Tarascan means literally 'to say poor', but the literal significance of the term is not an active element in the meaning of the word, just as the underlying meaning of 'boast' in Greek *euchomai* 'pray' is not a relevant feature of New Testament usage. In Bassa, a language of Liberia, the English phrase *hell of a* has been borrowed through Pidgin English as an attributive meaning 'tremendous, great, and important', so that a Bassa churchgoer can quite appropriately tell the pastor that his latest message was 'a *helava* sermon'.

But if historical developments can make a word or expression appropriate, they can also result in its becoming unacceptable. For example, in Spanish the verbs *cojer* 'to take' and *parir* 'to give birth to' have recently been largely eliminated from a revision of the Scriptures, for *cojer* has acquired the connotation of sexual intercourse and *parir* applies only to the birth of animals. In Bolivian Quechua a very good term for Lord, *Apu*, has been abandoned in certain contexts because in the object form it must occur with the suffix *-ta*, resulting in the form *Aputa*. But the Spanish word *puta*, a vulgar term for 'whore', is also widely used, and because of its resemblance to *Aputa* the latter has become unacceptable.

These problems occur in all areas of vocabulary and on all levels of usage. Moreover, the problems are especially acute on the higher hierarchical levels of generic vocabulary, where distinctions in meaning are more dependent upon conceptualization than upon perception. Furthermore, lack of correspondence is much greater in the symbolic segment of the vocabulary, which corresponds in large measure to phenomena not present to the senses, as is true of most of the religious vocabulary.

Within the scope of this treatment it is impossible to include examples of the entire range of lexical correspondences. There are, nevertheless, certain limited areas which illustrate problems of cultural specialization. These can be briefly summarized under: (1) the meanings of single terms, and (2) the use of semantically exocentric phrases.

Problems in the Meaning of Single Terms

In the following series of correspondences, involving primarily single terms, the purpose is to indicate the range of semantic areas involved, the types of difficulties encountered, and the basic principles applicable to the adjustments required to produce equivalent expressions. In this way some of the problems treated in the following chapter, on Techniques of Adjustment, can be anticipated. [1]

Certain problems relating to terms for ecology serve to illustrate some basic difficulties in finding adequate lexical correspondences. For those living in the temperate zone of the northern hemisphere, the north wind means cold weather, and the south wind indicates warm weather, an east wind is normally associated with rain, and a west wind with clearing skies. This pattern does not hold throughout the world, however, for in the northern hemisphere prevailing winds follow a clockwise motion, and in the southern hemisphere a counterclockwise motion. Moreover, the associations of cold and warm are completely reversed in countries below the equator. Furthermore, there are many local variations which make it necessary to incorporate a number of radical adjustments in any reference to winds, especially if connotative inferences are involved.

In the Scriptures the "four winds" often refer merely to directions, and this use only complicates what is often a difficult system at best, namely, the specification of directions. In general, directions have three types of orientation: (1) local geographical objects, e.g. 'toward the mountains', 'beyond the river', 'by the sea', 'toward the desert', etc.; (2) nearby ethnic units (indicated often by naming the land of the tribe or the chief in question); and (3) astronomical features, usually the sun, e.g. 'toward the setting sun', 'toward the rising sun', 'at the right hand of the rising sun', and 'at the left hand of the rising sun' (the latter two expressions referring to south and north, respectively). In many instances, expressions which have arisen because of some local circumstance can be transferred to another region, where the literal description does not fit. In some Guaica dialects of Venezuela, for example, the directions of north and south are described in terms of upstream and downstream, even though such terms do not always fit the region where the tribe is located.

Certain problems relating to words for fauna also illustrate basic difficulties in lexical correspondences. When there is no immediately corresponding animal in the receptor culture, there are usually three possible kinds of correspondences, e.g.: (1) a descriptive expression, using a generic name plus some distinguishing characteristic, e.g. 'big-humped animal' as a name for "camel" in Barrow Eskimo; (2) a descriptive expression employing a specific name plus some identifying characteristic, e.g. 'cotton deer' for "sheep" in Maya; and (3) the use of a specific term, (a) with a "cue" term, e.g. 'animal like a horse' for "camel" in Loma, or (b) without such a built-in cue as to an extension of meaning, e.g. Maya *tsimin*, extended from 'tapir' to 'horse'.

Terms associated with social culture pose numerous problems, not only because the basic systems are often so different, but also because the extensions of meaning appropriate to one system rarely work in another. In Isthmus Zapotec, to cite an example, it is impossible to translate English "sister" and "brother" by immediately corresponding terms. Rather, one must adjust to quite a different system, which

[1] For a more comprehensive treatment of a wide range of lexical problems in translating, see Nida, 1947a.

employs three different terms: (1) a male sibling of the same sex, (2) a female sibling of the same sex, and (3) a sibling of the opposite sex. But even more complicated than the basic kinship systems are certain metaphorical extensions. To illustrate, in Mark 5:34 Jesus addressed a mature woman as "daughter." In Shipibo such a word could only be used of a girl before puberty or of one's own daughter. The only equivalent in Shipibo is 'old lady', even though the woman may not have been aged. In the Villa Alta dialect of Zapotec, this same passage would have to be translated as 'my child', for daughter would be understood in a literal sense. Later, in the same passage, when Jesus speaks to Jairus' daughter as "little girl" (Mark 5:41), the appropriate equivalent in Trique is 'niece'.

Such Biblical metaphorical expressions as "children of Israel" and "daughter of Zion" must in many languages be radically altered; for, in the first instance, receptors may get the impression that God's concern for mankind in the Old Testament was principally focused on small children, since they are so frequently called 'children of Israel'. Moreover, 'daughter of Zion' is often understood only as a single individual, rather than as a title for the women of Jerusalem and, by extension, the Jewish people.

Because of vast differences in the technologies of different peoples, the corresponding terms for this area of human experience are often quite diverse. Moreover, within the range of vocabulary for technology, words used for weights, measures, and currencies produce possibly the most acute problems. Currencies obviously present special difficulties, because of great differences in buying power. For example, a Greek denarius of New Testament times had a silver content equal to about 17 cents in present U.S. currency, but the buying power of this coin was evidently much greater, for it was the standard daily wage of the unskilled worker. A further difficulty in attempting to translate currency equivalents is the extent to which precision is required. For example, if one reduces 300 denarii (Mark 14:5) to 51 dollars, the precision implied is entirely unfitting in this type of context, where a general figure is called for. To illustrate, in the story of Peter's obtaining money from the fish's mouth in order to pay taxes for himself and Jesus, one certainly should not translate the tetradrachma as '64 cents'. An ancient talent was worth, in silver content, about 960 dollars, but the man who received five talents should not be recorded as getting 4,800 dollars, but rather 'five thousand', if one is going to make an adjustment in currency.

When a precise measurement would be misleading, or an equivalent in a modern language would be so anachronistic as to be out of keeping with the context or style of the message, there are two possible solutions: (1) the use of a relatively equivalent receptor-language expression, e.g. Navajo 'step' for the Biblical "cubit" and Shipibo 'large cooking pot' for "bushel" (Matthew 5:15); or (2) a borrowed word, e.g. denarius, talent, shekel, etc., identified in terms of buying power on some easily calculable base. This may be done, for example, by relating all Biblical currencies to the denarius and explaining the denarius as equal to one day's wage of a common laborer.

Problems of time present fewer difficulties than weights and measures. Nevertheless, there are idiomatic types of divergences to be reckoned with. The languages of primitive peoples often possess quite a full system of time measurements. Uduk, for example, identifies a number of relatively precise periods: early morning ('when the eye springs out'); about ten o'clock ('the sun eats'); noon ('the sun is in the middle'); about two o'clock ('the sun arrives at the side'); about four o'clock ('the sun stretches out his arm'); sunset ('the sun goes in the hole'); and midnight ('the time of the middle of the eye'). The same period may be spoken of in very different ways in diverse languages; e.g. the Biblical "tenth hour" (or 4 P.M.) is called 'the sun is about to die' (Kabba-Laka), 'the sun is astride the mountain' (Tzotzil), and 'time for untying the oxen' (Bolivian Quechua).

One problem of temporal reckoning is posed by the fact that different languages select different elements to be counted. In some languages years are reckoned by the number of summers, in others, by winters. In the tropics some languages count by wet seasons, and others by dry seasons. In Hebrew one can even speak of "the days of the years," meaning the number of years. But even the way of counting the total number of units may be different. For example, in English, Wednesday is regarded as the second day after Monday, but in ancient Greek it would be the third day. Here, of course, is the age-old problem of interpreting the phrase "on the third day he will rise" (Luke 18:33, and parallels). In some languages two weeks are reckoned as fourteen days, but in others as fifteen days, since both the first and the last day are counted.

In some instances a precise number, though in a sense a more accurate correspondence, is really quite out of place. To illustrate, in speaking of the 5,000 men, not counting women and children, who were fed by Jesus (Mark 6:44), one could render this literally in Uduk by a very long and complex expression calculated on a basic unit of twenty; but the Uduks simply do not use their numerical system for such large numbers. Accordingly, it is actually better to use an expression such as 'people like grass', with a footnote, if it seems necessary, to provide the literal equivalent.

As noted earlier, terms for psychological experiences exhibit a number of special problems of correspondence; for languages often select quite different organs as centers or seats of various psychological states or responses, e.g. heart, liver, abdomen, gall, and kidneys. Moreover, different languages describe such experiences by quite different series of attributes or attendant circumstances. Almost all languages make certain important distinctions in the localities of psychological states or responses. In Shilluk, the various parts of the total personality are described in terms of: the *pyeth* 'heart', *cwiny* 'liver', *del* 'body' (none of which experience life after death); *wey* 'spirit' (the indestructible part of the personality which lives on after death); and *tipa* 'ghost, shadow' (the "half-life" which continues for a time after death, but gradually disintegrates and fades). Each one of these entities in the personality is regarded as the center for certain psychological experiences, and more often than not the distinctions appear to be quite arbitrary.

Contrastive qualities or activities present a special problem. In English we have scores of polar contrasts; for example, hot/cold, short/long, easy/difficult, full/empty, good/bad, believe/doubt. In some languages, however, these pairs do not exist. Rather, one finds negative-positive series, e.g. in Cuna 'shallow' and 'not-shallow '(i.e. 'deep'), 'cold' and 'not-cold' (i.e. 'hot'), and 'doubt' and 'not-doubt' (i.e. 'believe'), 'difficult' and 'not-difficult' (i.e. 'easy'). Some persons have regarded 'not-doubt' as an entirely inadequate equivalent for "believe" or "to have faith," but in terms of the Cuna lexical structure, the negative expression 'not-doubt' is every bit as valid as our corresponding English expression.

Problems in the Use of Semantically Exocentric Expressions

The correspondences involving semantically exocentric expressions, i.e. idioms and figures of speech, are best classified in terms of types of necessary adaptations, e.g. metaphors to metaphors, metaphors to similes, metaphors to nonmetaphors, and nonmetaphors to metaphors.

With an obvious metaphor, e.g. *Adam's apple*, it is clear that some adjustment in lexical form is inevitable, especially in regions where apples are unknown and no one has ever heard of Adam. In Uduk, for example, this anatomical feature becomes 'the thing that wants beer'. However, correspondences between metaphors may involve rather similar areas of meaning. In Lahu, a language of Burma and Southwest China, one cannot translate literally the hymn "Stand up, stand up, for Jesus" without being somewhat silly, for Lahus simply do not 'stand up' for their leaders. On the other hand, one can say 'to stand firm', and this is the expression used. Similarly, in Loma the expression 'withered hand' (Mark 3:3) does not make sense, for hands do not 'wither' as plants do. However, one can speak of a 'dead hand', and make perfectly good sense.

The metaphors in a language are often closely related to the actual experience of the people. In Valiente, a language of Panama, a proper translation of the line "Just as I am, though tossed about" (which begins the second stanza of a famous hymn) is 'just as I am with a swollen spleen'. The basis of this metaphor is the fact that persons who have chronic malaria normally have swollen spleens, and they are also frequently beset by constant worry and mental turmoil.

If semantically exocentric expressions in the source language are translated literally, they are generally interpreted as endocentric (i.e. more or less literally), unless practical or linguistic clues signal that the expression used involves an unusual extension of meaning. For this reason one often finds that a simile is the most effective way of rendering a metaphor. Words such as 'like' and 'as' immediately cue the reader to the fact that the words in question are to be taken in a special sense. In the Trique translation of Mark 4:20, accordingly, one does not say that some of the persons 'bear fruit thirtyfold', but 'some are like seeds that increase to thirty'. By means of the term 'like' one indicates that the people are like seed which grows up and produces thirty grains to a plant. Without this shift from metaphor to simile the passage can be very confusing. Likewise in Navajo one cannot speak of people 'being hungry and thirsty for righteousness' (Matthew 5:6). On the other hand, one can say 'like hungering and thirsting, they desire righteousness', in which case a simile proves to be the real equivalent of the metaphor.

Metaphors, however, must often be translated as nonmetaphors, since the particular extensions of meaning which occur in the source language have no parallel in the receptor language. This is even true in such a relatively simple expression as 'his countenance fell' (Mark 10:22), which in Subanen, a language of the Philippines, must be translated simply as 'he became sad'. Under certain circumstances one would naturally expect metaphors to be rendered by nonmetaphors. If, for example, there is no feature in the receptor culture corresponding to the referent in the source language, one must make some radical adjustment, usually from metaphor to nonmetaphor, as when "they were reputed to be pillars" (Galatians 2:9) must be translated in Zoque as 'they were said to be the big ones'. When one finds a so-called mixed metaphor, the chances of necessary alteration are likewise very high. The phrase "uncircumcised of heart" (Acts 7:51) must, of course, be radically altered in a number of receptor languages, as it has been in Cakchiquel, 'with your hearts unprepared'. When two or more elements of a figure of speech involve extensions of meaning, there is also a high probability that extensive adjustments must be made; for example, such an expression as "fruit of his loins" (Acts 2:30) is rarely acceptable in another language. Hence, as in Mazatec, it may often be translated simply as 'his child'.

Some persons object to any shift from a metaphor to another metaphor, a metaphor to a simile, or a metaphor to a nonmetaphor, because they regard such an alteration as involving some loss of information. However, the same persons usually do not object to the translation of a nonmetaphor by a metaphor, for such a change appears to increase the effectiveness of the communication. In other words, most people do not object to a profit in making a transfer from one language to another, but they do feel that a loss is reprehensible, especially when a sacred text is involved, though there are, of course, some persons who object strongly to any "heightening" of meaning. If a new figure of speech in the receptor language appears to be appropriate, it is usually approved readily by outside critics, either out of sheer delight and curiosity, or perhaps because of certain unrecognized paternalistic attitudes toward the receptor culture. At any rate, even though a Kapauku speaker in New Guinea has to refer to something of great importance as 'being carried on the end of the nose', such an idiom is generally regarded as quite acceptable, for it implies a gain in information.

There are, however, two types of shifts from nonmetaphor to metaphor which involve certain problems and reservations. First among these are instances in which a figure of speech is based upon an indigenous mythology which is thought to be out of keeping with the source-language message. The Miskito Indians, for example, speak of the eclipse of the moon as 'the moon has caught hold of his mother-in-law'. In general, however, such expressions are not taken literally, just as our own unscientific statements that the "sun sets" and the "sun rises" are not so taken.

The second class of dubious correspondences involve indigenous religious beliefs which impinge upon those of the source language. For example, in Shilluk the only way to speak of sickness is to say 'he is taken by God', but this use of *Jok* 'God' in such a highly idiomatic phrase is not interpreted by the people endocentrically. Thus it has proved to be a fully acceptable equivalent, despite the apparent impingement of indigenous beliefs upon Christian ones.

Psychological states of being, as suggested previously, involve a number of instances in which nonmetaphors must be shifted to metaphors, often with specializations of meaning which are not formally equatable between source and receptor language. In Maya, for example, one says 'he has a hot head' to mean that the person in question is insane. Such a phrase has no relationship to anger or temper, as it has in English.

Some shifts from nonmetaphors to metaphors introduce semantic elements which, though inappropriate in the source language, are entirely acceptable in the receptor-language context. For example, in Black Thai the regular way of saying that a man is stingy is to declare 'his purse is constipated'.

Problems of Correspondence Related to Style

In the analysis of all these formal correspondences, whether grammatical or lexical, we have been dealing essentially with the ingredients of style, though not entirely under this heading. At this point it is important to consider certain overall features of style which play an essential role in the process of translation. For besides attention to isolated transfers of a formal feature in the source language to a corresponding feature in the receptor language, the total effect of the numerous formal elements which combine to make up various styles must be considered.

The importance of stylistic sensitivity is never more evident than when it is lacking. An anonymous New Testament translation of 1729, for example, contains such high-flown and ill-fitting phrases as "vented his divine enthusiasm" for "filled with the Holy Spirit" (Luke 1:67), "collector-general of the customs" for "tax collector" (Luke 19:2), and "Lord of the celestial militia" for "Lord of hosts" (Hebrews 7:22) (cited by Campbell, 1789).

Everyone recognizes a number of different styles of speech, e.g. telegraphic, rambling, slangy, reasoned, legal, journalistic, literary, baby-talk, pidgin, and subculture jargon. Albert Guerard (1947) has attempted to classify styles on ten levels, from the automatic reflex of a groan or cry, through various stages of conscious ordering of language expression, to a final level of silence, the language of the mystic. Karl Thieme (1955) distinguishes four practical levels or types, priestly, official, literary, and commercial, each with its special problems of translation.

The use of one or another style of language depends upon a number of factors, which can usually be summarized in terms of subject matter, audience, and circumstances of communication. Religious communication, however, involves certain special difficulties, since it appears to require language having a solemn or esoteric flavor. Such a flavor is often developed by means of archaisms, which, by virtue of their antique appearance, seem to provide the text with a temporally derived authority.

In some languages an important and obligatory ingredient of style is the clear representation of the speaker's or narrator's attitude toward what is being communicated. In Waiwai, for example, the text must be filled with modal particles which constantly inform the audience of the precise attitudes of the participants—whether, for example, they are amused by the incident they are relating, treat it with suspicion, feel that it is ironic, or regard the theme as sorrowful.

Style may be defined technically as "the message carried by the frequency of distributions and transitional probabilities of its linguistic features, especially as they differ from those of the same features in the language as a whole" (Bloch, 1953). Accordingly, though style depends upon grammar, or the formal structure of the language, it is essentially different from grammar; for while grammar is predictive (i.e. describes what can be said), style is classificatory and dynamic (Saporta, 1960, p. 93).

Certain major differences in style are related to various levels of human experience, of which three are basic to our consideration: (1) experience taken for granted, not consciously recognized, and not talked about; (2) experience overtly recognized, understood, and discussed, but in a nontechnical way; and (3) experience which consists of analyzing and describing experience. The third level is the metalevel of existence, in which men consciously attempt to formulate abstractions about what may be called the technical and scientific level of experience.

These three levels may be illustrated by the experience of "hate." On the first level it is impulsive, immediate, and heavily intraorganismic. On the second level, it may consist of an organized campaign of hate through well-contrived propaganda. On the third level "hate" may be a technical study of psychological reactions exhibited during certain types of experiences. In its customary and normal usage, language is related primarily to the second level, where it may be either (1) random and casual, or (2) structured according to certain esthetic norms, in which case we regard it as stylistically pleasing.

Scientific and technical language, however, is a specialized development in societies which have become intellectually aware of their own experience (activities, perceptions, and conceptions). Such societies attempt to classify their experience systematically (including the world around them) and to relate their observations to wider and wider laws (or descriptions) of continually expanding relevance. On this level of language there is a great deal of high-level vocabulary (both generic and abstract), systematic classifications (differing greatly from folk taxonomies), and styles of communication which fit generalizations rather than specific occurrences. In fact, such a style, especially as exemplified in many contemporary textbooks, seems to aim at calculated dullness. Nevertheless, as Machine Translating has indicated, this level of language is in some ways easier to translate from one language to another, provided of course that the two languages share more or less the same "scientific outlook." This level of language, experientially so lifeless, is linguistically very manipulable. For to the extent that language can be separated from the unique qualities of experience and can be made a kind of linguistic mathematics, its units can easily be arranged and rearranged with little interference from the cultural context.

If, however, the translation of scientific texts from one language to another participating in modern cultural development is not too difficult, it is not surprising that the converse is true—that translating scientific material from a modern Indo-European language into a language largely outside the reach of Western science is extremely difficult. This is one of the really pressing problems confronting linguists in Asia today.

The other side of this coin is that the Judeo-Christian Scriptures can be translated with relative ease in most languages; for they share with many cultures, and therefore languages, certain basic religious and social concepts, e.g. holiness of taboo, kinship revenge, sacrificial offerings, tribal organization, nomadic or agricultural life, a person-centered concept of history, and awareness of spirit beings (God, demons, spirits, angels, etc.). On the other hand, it is not easy to translate the Bible into contemporary European languages; for, though the words and the style of language of the Bible are not meaningless to the twentieth century, there is nevertheless so wide a gap between the real experiential perception of "then" and "now" that the correspondences are basically deceptive.

DYNAMIC CORRESPONDENCES AND CONTRASTS

By implication we have already touched on a number of problems relating to the dynamic correspondences between texts in source and receptor languages. However, certain formal and lexical features of correspondences should be briefly noted in relation to the accompanying dynamic elements.

Formal dynamic correspondences include phonological, morphological, and syntactic features.

Phonological Features

The phonological features involve two special problems: (1) the relative adequacy of the receptor-language alphabet, and (2) the attitudes of receptors toward the incorporation of foreign sounds or symbols from the source language. When an orthographic system is deficient in necessary contrasts (i.e. when it does not distinguish the phonemes adequately), obviously the communication load will be increased; for the sequences are not so predictable as when the orthography more fully reflects the actual spoken form of language. Accordingly, if the orthographic system of the receptor language imposes a heavy communication load on the decoding process, the possibility of compensating at other points, e.g. in the morphological and syntactic structures, should be explored, in order to provide as much balance as possible in the total load. Of course, the communication load of an orthography is not the same for all readers, for some become expert in its use, while others never achieve efficient control. For those who lack efficient control, a translation in quite simple language is the closest dynamic equivalent, since for such readers much of the communication load has already been pre-empted by orthographic difficulties.

Languages differ greatly in the extent to which they admit the incorporation of foreign words, exotic spellings, and unusual sounds or combinations of sounds. In English, for example, we readily accept such orthographic novelties, and in translations of the Bible people seem to accept as a matter of course the very unusual spellings of proper names, apparently because many English names are spelled in nonphonemic ways. In Spanish, however, the presence of strange combinations of sounds and letters in the Bible has been a major obstacle to ready acceptance. Hence, in Spanish there has been great pressure to recast such names into common orthographic forms.

Morphological Features

Dynamic correspondences related to the morphological structure, i.e. the word forms, include two basic problems: (1) the tendency for translators in highly synthetic languages (those which incorporate into the verb structure, for example, a great many different semantic components) to include entirely too much in the word structure, simply because it is theoretically possible; and (2) the practice of constructing words on the basis of models which, though possible, are not highly probable. The fact that a receptor language has a verbal structure in which object, subject, indirect object, tense, aspect, direction, mode, and condition can all be expressed does not necessarily mean that all the information available in the source-language text must be made explicit. Actually, an examination of source-language texts often shows that many features are left implicit. If this is the case, the translator should attempt to parallel such structures, rather than try, in a spirit of faithfulness to the original, to include every possible element in the receptor language. At the same time, it is important to recognize that, though some word formations are quite possible—that is to say, they are built on viable models—they may not be very probable. Such formations tend to increase the communication load very appreciably, and hence call for simplification or compensation.

Syntactic Features

Dynamic correspondences on a syntactic level include general stylistic comparability and certain adjustments in specific structures. As noted earlier, the literal translation of all Greek conjunctions in an English text may transform a dignified Greek style into a "babyish" English style. The appropriate dynamic correspondences demand, therefore, that not everything that exists in one language (i.e. the presence of numerous conjunctions) should necessarily be duplicated in the other. For example, the piling up of largely synonymous phrases in the Pauline Epistles, not without a number of anacolutha, serves in Greek to give the impression of profound spontaneity—a man who finds himself overwhelmed with the grandeur of his theme and his own deep emotional involvement; but when this form of expression is translated more or less literally into English, the result may be an impression of muddy verbosity. To do justice to the dynamic qualities of Paul's style, one must sometimes use quite different formal correspondences.

Three types of formal features, all of which are discussed in Chapter 6, are principally involved in dynamic equivalences: (1) the total number of units in any expression (i.e. the length of the sentences); (2) the arrangement of the parts, in terms of: (a) depth (the number of layers of immediate constituents), (b) direction of attribution (preposed elements generally involve more communication load than postposed ones), and (c) the potential terminal character of the sequence (i.e. whether the expression can be stopped, and at the same time make sense, or whether something else is needed to complete it); and (3) the ways in which the arrangements are signaled, whether by (a) order of words, (b) affixes of case and concord, and/or (c) intonational contours, most of which are unmarked in the average orthography.

Due consideration of the values of dynamic correspondence in formal features means that the translator is not content merely to select for A, a particular grammatical feature of the source language, a corresponding formal feature, a, in the receptor language. Such a feature, though the closest formal equivalent, may not necessarily be the closest dynamic correspondence. Hence, the source-language construction A may be paralleled in some contexts by receptor-language form x, in others by y, and in only a few situations by a.

If considerations of dynamic correspondence are important on the strictly formal level, they are even more so on the lexical level. This is true, not only because translations tend to incorporate a number of relatively rare semantic features, e.g. borrowings, rare combinations of words, and new themes and ideas; but also because the lexical structure of the source-language text presupposes that the original receptors brought to the decoding process a good deal of background information which decoders in a second language cannot be expected to have, especially if the languages represent widely different cultural contexts. Thus correspondences must take into consideration the need for calculated redundancy—a technique well demonstrated by Phillips in his translation of the New Testament. Furthermore, it must be recognized that in the process of translation a good deal of the original sparkle and luster of language is usually lost. Accordingly, if a translation is to be anything but a pale reflection of a brilliant original, it must have certain compensating correspondences which reflect a dynamic concept of translating. It is not impossible, however, for a translation to outdo or to improve on an original.

CHAPTER TEN

TECHNIQUES OF ADJUSTMENT

In previous chapters the principles underlying translating and the types of correspondences between languages have been discussed. The present chapter deals with the techniques of adjustment used in the process of translating. Here we are concerned, therefore, not with *why* the translator does one thing or another, but with *what* he does, in terms of additions, subtractions, and alterations.

Such terms to some degree distort the picture of the translation process, making it appear that the translator himself performs these operations on the material in question. In point of fact, what he really does, or should do, is to select in each instance the closest natural equivalent. But if the corresponding forms in the source and receptor languages are compared after such equivalents have been selected, it will be found that they conveniently fall into such classes of modification as can be described by these terms: additions, subtractions, and alterations.

Before considering the techniques of adjustment, it is important to indicate the essential purposes of these techniques. Briefly, they are designed to produce correct equivalents—not to serve as an excuse for tampering with the source-language message. For example, the Hebrew text of Genesis 5:22, 24 states quite clearly that "Enoch walked with God." But this type of anthropomorphism was apparently not in keeping with the theological presuppositions of the translator of this book in the Septuagint, who made it read: "Enoch pleased God." This reading then provided the source of the wording in Hebrews 11:5. The techniques discussed here are not designed to justify such a modification of the source-language message, but to facilitate its reproduction in a different form, and in its fullest and most accurate sense.

The purposes of these techniques are essentially as follows: (1) permit adjustment of the form of the message to the requirements of the structure of the receptor language; (2) produce semantically equivalent structures; (3) provide equivalent stylistic appropriateness; and (4) carry an equivalent communication load. To fulfill these purposes, numerous minor alterations in form must be made; but radical changes are not to be made merely for the sake of editorial improvement or at the translator's whim or fancy. The translator's basic task is to reproduce what he has been given, not to improve it, even when he thinks he can do so. However, there are two situations which require certain radical types of changes, namely: (a) when a close formal equivalent is utterly meaningless, and (b) when it carries a wrong meaning.

The extent to which adjustments should be made depends very largely upon the audience for which the translation is designed. For example, if it is to be used by those who have little or no background in the subject matter and relatively little experience in "decoding" such texts, a greater degree of redundancy must be built into the translation. Accordingly, there will not only be more adjustments, but the adjustments made will be far-reaching. Moreover, the nature of the audience determines to a large extent whether these adjustments are to be reflected in the text of the message or in accompanying explanations, e.g. marginal notes.

Though the illustrative examples cited in this chapter deal almost exclusively with Biblical materials, the techniques are equally applicable to all types of translating.

ADDITIONS

Of the many types of additions which may legitimately be incorporated into a translation, the most common and important are: (a) filling out elliptical expressions; (b) obligatory specification; (c) additions required because of grammatical restructuring; (d) amplification from implicit to explicit status; (e) answers to rhetorical questions; (f) classifiers; (g) connectives; (h) categories of the receptor language which do not exist in the source language; and (i) doublets. Many of these additions are actually a part of the process of structural alteration, so that one technique cannot be rigidly isolated from another.

a. *Filling out elliptical expressions.* Though ellipsis occurs in all languages, the particular structures which permit such "omitted" words are by no means identical from language to language. Accordingly, in an expression almost obligatorily elliptical in one language, an ellipsis may not be permitted in another. Hence, a clause such as "he is greater than I" may require expansion into 'he is greater than I am great'. Where there is obvious parallelism in structure, there are relatively few problems in determining the exact words to be added. When ellipsis is not based upon parallel structures, however, the difficulties of adjustment are obviously greater. Such nonparallel structures may be formulaic, and hence lend themselves to ready adjustments, as in the translation of epistolary formulae. In the New Testament Epistles of Paul, for example, one may translate as 'Paul...writes to...', though the word 'writes' is not in the source language. In other circumstances, the nonparallel ellipsis is a much less evident element. For example, in a series such as occurs in Philippians 3:4-5, "If any other man thinks he has reason for confidence in the flesh, I have more: circumcised on the eighth day, of the people of Israel, of the tribe of Benjamin, a Hebrew born of the Hebrews," many languages require not only the filling out of the obvious parallel ellipsis, but the addition as well of some subject and verb elements in the list of evidences cited, e.g. 'If any other man thinks he has reason to be confident because of his personal qualifications, I have even more reason to be confident, for I was circumcised on the eighth day, I was born a member of the tribe of Benjamin, which is a part of the nation of Israel. I am a Hebrew-speaking person, born of Hebrew-speaking parents'.

b. *Obligatory specification*. The specification required in some translations results from one of two reasons: (1) ambiguity in the receptor language formations, and (2) the fact that greater specificity may be required so as to avoid misleading reference. In Mazatec a literal translation of 'they tell him of her' (Mark 1:30) would be in a form which could have thirty-six different meanings, since there is no indication in such a Mazatec verb of differences in number and gender of the pronominal affixes (Florence H. Cowan, 1950). If one is to render such a passage correctly and unambiguously, it is necessary to say, 'the people there told Jesus about the woman'. In other instances, a third person reference, such as 'Paul...to the church at...' would imply that some Paul other than the writer is being spoken of, since, if the writer is the same individual as is mentioned in the salutation, it is necessary to add 'I', e.g. 'I, Paul, am writing to the church at...'.

c. *Additions required by grammatical restructuring*. Almost any type of restructuring of a source-language expression can result in some lexical additions. However, perhaps the most common instances which require amplification are (1) shifts of voice, (2) modification from indirect to direct discourse, and (3) alteration of word classes.

When a passive expression, e.g. "he will be condemned" (Mark 16:16), is changed to an active one, as many languages require, it is obviously necessary to insert the agent, in this instance 'God', so that the translation reads, as in Zacapoastla Aztec, 'God will condemn him'.

When indirect discourse, whether explicit or implicit, is changed into direct discourse, a number of elements must often be added. This is especially so when the discourse is largely implicit. "Glorified God" (Mark 2:12) becomes in Huichol 'said to God: You are of good heart' and in Amuesha 'said: God is great'. "To confess sins" (Mark 1:5) becomes in Shipibo 'to say, It is true we have sinned'.

Probably the most frequent additions must be made when there is a shift in word classes. A change from nouns to verbs produces some of the most radical additions, since with verbs it is usually necessary to specify the participants. Accordingly, in Navajo, "...consolation of love" (Philippians 2:1) becomes 'if by loving your minds can be put to that place of refuge'. It must be noted, however, that this same expression in Greek may be understood as "incentive of love," which is rendered by Phillips as "if...love means anything to you."

An adjective may, of course, be shifted into another class of words, so that, in Luvale, spoken in Angola, the phrase "false prophets" becomes 'those who pretend the work of a prophet'. Similarly, concepts expressed in Greek by prepositions may be carried by verbs in other languages, as when "he that is not against us is for us" (Mark 9:40) becomes, in Totonac, 'he who does not fight-against me stands-up-with us' (i.e. as a companion).

d. *Amplification from implicit to explicit status*. Important semantic elements carried implicitly in the source language may require explicit identification in the receptor language. Such additions are of many types, but the following examples illustrate their range and variety. In Trique, for example, "said to her, *Talitha cumi*" (Mark 5:41) would be entirely misleading unless the verb of 'saying' were amplified by the phrase 'in his language', so that the following Aramaic words would be accepted as forms the Trique receptor was not expected to understand.

A phrase such as "queen of the south" (Luke 11:31) can be very misleading when neither 'queen' nor 'south' is familiar in the receptor language, and when the combination is likewise obscure. Accordingly, in Tarascan one must say 'woman who was ruling in the south country'. Thus the word "queen" is expanded into a phrase identifying an object and an event, and the word "south" is expanded, by means of a classifier, to specify the type of object referred to. All this information, implicit in the source-language phrase, must be made explicit in many receptor languages.

The clause "as it is written in Isaiah the prophet" (Mark 1:2) can be quite misleading, since the proper name of a person (identified as such by the use of the word 'prophet') is usually not associated with the name of a book. The implicit elements of this phrase may be clarified by such an expansion as, 'as it is written in the book containing what Isaiah the prophet said'. In some languages "book of Isaiah" would mean simply 'a book Isaiah possessed'. (Rather than expand this clause by spelling out the implicit elements, it is possible to alter the structure, e.g. 'as Isaiah the prophet wrote', a type of modification treated later in this chapter).

In some instances phrases represent compact semantic relationships, with many of the finer distinctions left to the context. Literal transfers of such phrases may, however, result in ambiguity, and hence may require amplification. "Field of blood" (Acts 1:19) and "God of peace" (Philippians 4:9) are two such phrases. The first may require such an expansion as 'field where blood was spilled' (or 'shed') or 'field that reminded people of blood' (the context provides two quite different possible interpretations). A literal transfer might carry the meaning that the field itself consisted of blood, an obviously misleading rendering. The phrase "God of peace" must usually be amplified in such a way as to indicate, not 'a peaceful God', but 'God who gives peace' or 'God who causes peace'.

In some languages it seems impossible to compress certain actions into a limited number of more or less general symbols, so that "taken in adultery" (John 8:3) requires definitive expansion in some languages, e.g. 'taken when sleeping with a man who was not her husband' (Zacapoastla Aztec).

e. *Answers to rhetorical questions*. In some languages rhetorical questions always require answers. Such a series of questions as that in Matthew 11:7-9 is especially difficult to translate, for three of the questions are expanded by immediately appending supplementary questions, but the full answer is not given until the middle of verse 9:

> "What did you go out into the wilderness to behold? A reed shaken by the wind? Why then did you go out? To see a man clothed in soft raiment? Behold, those who wear soft raiment are in kings' houses. Why then did you go out? To see a prophet? Yes, I tell you...."

In languages which require answers to such questions, it is possible so to combine certain of the questions as to provide a fitting answer, e.g.: 'Did you go out into the wilderness to look at a man who was like a reed shaken by the wind ? No! Then, did you go out to see a man wearing fine luxurious clothing ? No, indeed! Those who wear fine clothes are in kings' courts. Did you, then, go out to see a prophet ? Yes! And I tell you....'.

f. *Classifiers*. Classifiers provide a convenient device for building meaningful redundancy into an overloaded text, especially in languages which readily employ such terms to identify proper names and borrowed terms, e.g. 'river Jordan', 'city Jerusalem', 'building synagogue', 'cloth linen', 'jewel ruby', and 'sect Pharisees'. Such classifiers need not be used in all passages where such a proper name or borrowed word occurs, but their employment at strategic points in the translation can reduce appreciably the excessive communication load.

g. *Connectives*. Transitionals, which consist of the repetition of segments of the preceding text, are widely used in many languages. In place of saying literally, 'He went up to Jerusalem. There he taught the people', some languages require the equivalent of, 'He went up to Jerusalem. Having arrived there, he taught the people'. Such transitionals appreciably increase the total volume of the text, but do not add information. They serve merely to orient the reader constantly to the sequences of events and the precise relationships between events.

h. *Categories of the receptor language*. When a receptor language has certain categories, obligatory or optional, which do not exist in the source-language text, it is obviously necessary to add the obligatory categories and to weigh the desirability of adding the optional categories. In Campa, a language of Peru, for example, a category of benefaction is obligatory. Thus in Mark 1:34 the text must specify for whom the demons were driven out, and accordingly will read, 'he cast out many demons for them' (i.e. for the people). In languages having many optional categories the translator must judge where their absence will be stylistically noticeable. In Piro, for example, there are a number of verbal affixes: quotatives, assertives, duplicatives, intensifiers, correlatives, progressives, hortatives, etc., all of which add important aspects to the narration, and without which a text seems thin and strange. Accordingly, a translator must employ a number of these optional categories, and in doing so make explicit what is often implicit in the source language.

i. *Doublets*. A number of languages, including Biblical Hebrew and Greek, make frequent use of semantic doublets, i.e. two semantically supplementary expressions in place of one, e.g. 'answering, said', 'asked and said', or 'he said...said he' (as in English folk tales). In some languages such doublets are almost obligatory in certain types of contexts, for in marking direct discourse they function almost like quotation marks. In such circumstances the translator must introduce the appropriate supplementary expression into the receptor text.

Although we may describe the above techniques as involving "additions," it is important to recognize that there has been no actual adding to the semantic content of the message, for these additions consist essentially in making explicit what is implicit in the source-language text. Simply changing some element in the message from implicit to explicit status does not add to the content; it simply changes the manner in which the information is communicated.

SUBTRACTIONS

Though, in translating, subtractions are neither so numerous nor varied as additions, they are, nevertheless, highly important in the process of adjustment. They include primarily the following types: (a) repetitions, (b) specification of reference, (c) conjunctions, (d) transitionals, (e) categories, (f) vocatives, and (g) formulae. At this point, correspondences which simply reflect multiple-to-one semantic equivalents are not considered. The fact that "brother and sister" in the source language becomes 'siblings' in the receptor language is purely a matter of semantic correspondence, and does not represent any basic adjustment in the translational process, for the single word meaning 'siblings' covers roughly the same semantic area as the two words "brother and sister." In the present treatment of subtractions only those adjustments which involve certain structural losses, but which, however, are advisable because of the grammatical or semantic patterns of the receptor language are considered.

a. *Repetitions.* Semantic doublets such as "answering, said," "asked and said," or "he said, said he," may be quite acceptable in some languages; in fact, they are required in certain instances, as noted above. In other languages, however, they may be not only tautological, but even misleading. Hence, one of the pair must be omitted.

Not all repetitions consist of doublets. Some are repetitions for the sake of emphasis, e.g. "verily, verily" or "blessing I will bless." Nevertheless, in many languages one of these repeated lexical items must be omitted, or, in some cases, replaced by a term that intensifies the expression in question. In other instances epic style often calls for the piling up of roughly synonymous expressions, e.g., "I will kill him with my weapon, I will slay him with my sword." But the equivalent of this parallelism is in many languages merely 'I will certainly kill him with my sword', for a literal transfer of the repetition in the receptor language might imply something oddly whimsical or strangely unreal. If, of course, a repetition adds strength to the resultant expression, its close translation is justified; but if it proves to be nothing more than a misleading tautology, it should be eliminated.

b. *Specification of reference.* More often than not, a transfer from source to receptor language requires the addition of elements which serve to make the reference to participants more exact and explicit. However, the reverse situation also occurs, for reference is not expressed in the same way in all languages. In some languages, for example, the repetition of a proper name in two closely related sentences may be misleading; thus, in some languages the name Lazarus in John 11:2 must be omitted, since this person is clearly identified in the first verse. The occurrence of the word "God" 32 times in the first chapter of Genesis, which contains only 31 verses, proves to be stylistically inappropriate and syntactically confusing in some languages. For that reason pronominal reference may be used, or the word may be omitted if the relationships are unmistakable.

A shift of word classes may also result in the loss of words indicating reference; for just as the change from a noun to a verb tends to add words for participants in the action, a shift from a verb to a noun will eliminate such units.

c. *Conjunctions.* Two principal types of conjunctions are lost, namely: (1) those associated with hypotactic constructions (and hence lost when the structure is shifted from hypotactic to paratactic sequences); and (2) those which link co-ordinates, elements often combined without conjuctions, either in appositional relationships, e.g. "God and Father" becomes 'God, Father', or in a series, e.g. "John and Bill and Jim" becomes 'John, Bill, Jim'.

d. *Transitionals.* Transitionals differ from conjunctions in that, instead of combining two formally related units, they serve merely to mark a translation from one unit to another. In the New Testament, for example, there is a Greek form *egeneto* (which corresponds to a common Semitic transitional) usually translated in the King James Version as "it came to pass." On occasion this transitional may be rendered effectively as "then," "now," or "after that," but in many contexts it is better simply to omit it.

The Gospel of Mark employs a very frequent Greek transitional *euthus*, which means literally "straightway" or "immediately." It may in certain cases be so translated as to indicate the immediacy of the subsequent event, but in many contexts the omission of such a transitional is a closer equivalent.

e. *Categories.* The insistence of some translators that all categories in the original be fully reflected in the receptor-language text has resulted in some very awkward translations. For example, a language may have a category of plural, but only as an optional set of forms; thus in a translation such forms should be employed only in the same types of situations, and with approximately the same frequency, as in a receptor-language text. Of course, when the receptor language simply has no corresponding category the translator has no problem. He is simply obliged to omit such references, or to express them in entirely different ways; e.g. past tense in the verb may be represented by some appropriate adverbial expression of time. Such losses must not be regarded as a violation of the principle of fidelity; rather, not to omit such categories would be a real violation of the principle of accurate correspondence.

f. *Vocatives.* All languages have ways of calling to people, but in some languages there is no means by which one may directly address another in a polite form. The use of the name or a title in a direct form may imply either that the person was at some distance or that he was being roundly denounced before others. For example, instead of "Peter said to Jesus: Teacher, it is well that we are here" (Mark 9:5), one must sometimes translate, 'Peter said to Jesus, his teacher: It is well that we are here'. In this situation the vocative is shifted into a nearby clause; however, in many instances such vocatives must simply be omitted if the total impact of the passage is not to suffer serious distortion of intent and meaning.

g. *Formulae.* A number of formulae in source languages are relatively meaningless in receptor languages. For example, in the Scriptures the phrase *in his name* or *in the name of the Lord* is in some contexts more adequately expressed simply as 'by him' or 'by the Lord', since in some societies the term 'name' is in no sense a symbolic substitute for the individual.

As in the case of additions, these subtractions do not actually alter the total content of the message. They may change some features from explicit to implicit status, but this does not substantially lessen the information carried by the communication. In fact, these subtractions are justified primarily on the basis that they result in a closer equivalence than would otherwise be the case. That is to say, by subtracting certain formal elements one can preserve a greater degree of correspondence than would otherwise be true.

ALTERATIONS

Any satisfactory translation must mean inevitably a "new birth in the new tongue," for the form of the original can never be fully retained (Petersen, 1926). Accordingly, the entire text must be subjected to a series of changes, involving not only additions and subtractions, but also alterations, some of them relatively radical. Alterations may, of course, be of all types, from the simplest problems of correspondence in sounds to the most complicated adjustments in idiomatic phrases. However, in general, alterations can be treated under the following classes: (a) sounds, (b) categories, (c) word classes, (d) order of elements, (e) clause and sentence structures, (f) semantic problems involving single words, and (g) semantic problems involving exocentric expressions.

a. *Sounds.* Even the most consistent system of transliteration may occasionally produce a severe difficulty, since the resulting form may have another meaning in the receptor language. In Loma, for example, straightforward transliteration of *Messiah* turns out to mean 'death's hand', and hence the transliteration has to be altered to the form *Mezaya*, so that it will not be a misleading form. [1]

Since proper names often have etymological meanings in the source languages, e.g. *Christ* 'anointed', *Peter* 'rock', *Bethlehem* 'house of bread', *Jerusalem* 'city of peace', and *Israel* 'prince of God', some translators have considered it advantageous to translate the names, especially in languages

[1] For a number of significant problems relating to transliteration, see Seely, 1957, pp. 59-60.

in which the corresponding names might have readily recognizable meanings. However, such a procedure is usually unwise; for, though the derivation of names may be ascertained in many instances, the forms serve as symbols for unique objects, and except for certain rare contexts do not carry with them the significance of the constituent parts.

b. *Categories*. Alterations of categories include not only shifts of forms within categories, but also the employment of expressions which have no corresponding function in the source language. A singular expression, especially if it is generic in meaning, may be readily altered to a plural, as in the expression in Mark 4:25, "for to him who has will more be given," which becomes in Trique, 'because to those who have...'. Similarly, a past tense may be changed to a future, as in the clause (Mark 13:20), "if the Lord had not shortened the days," which in Isthmus Zapotec must be rendered as a future, since the event has not yet taken place. Shifts from active to passive or passive to active also involve similar alterations of categories.

In certain instances the shift of categories seems somewhat more radical, especially if the equivalent concept is expressed by a different class of word forms into adverbial expressions, e.g. 'then', 'later', 'earlier', 'before that', 'yesterday', 'tomorrow', etc. In other cases a category of possession may be modified because typical interpersonal relationships are expressed in quite different ways. In Kijita, a language of Tanganyika, one would not speak of "your father" (Genesis 31:6, 7, 9), but rather 'my father-in-law'.

c. *Word Classes*. In previous sections the principles and procedures governing the shifts from one class of words to another have been dealt with. At this point it is necessary only to list some of the more typical kinds of alterations. Undoubtedly the shift from event nouns to verbs is the most common. In Shipibo, for example, words such as "theft," "murder," "coveting," "deceit," "slander," "foolishness" (Mark 7:21-22) are all translated by corresponding verbal forms: 'they steal', 'they kill people', 'they go crazy for things', 'they deceive', 'they slander people', and 'they are without minds'. In some instances a noun may involve not only an event, but a causative component as well, so that "I am the resurrection" (John 11:25) becomes 'I am the one who causes people to live again'. When two closely combined nouns are shifted into verbs, the resulting expression may appear quite altered, as when "the voice of your greeting" (Luke 1:44) becomes in Tagalog 'when I heard you greet me'.

All other word classes may also be subject to alteration, as when prepositions correspond to verbs; e.g. "from death to life" (1 John 3:14) may be rendered as 'leave death and come to life' (Mazatec), or "he who is not against us" (Mark 9:40) may become 'he who does not look mean at us' (Kekchi). In other instances, an attributive may be changed into a parenthetical expression, e.g. "about two thousand" (Mark 5:13) becomes 'two thousand, I believe' (Piro).

Where greater specificity of identification is required by the grammatical or semantic structure, pronouns often correspond to nouns, and determiners, such as *the* or *a*, are altered to expressions meaning 'this same', 'some', 'any', etc.

d. *Order.* The necessity for adjustments in the order of words seems so obvious as scarcely to require mention. However, there are certain situations in which the shifts of order may not seem so vital, but in which they are nevertheless important, if the translation is to be natural. In one language of Central Africa there is a regular pattern of placing the negative particle at the end of the clause, rather than juxtaposed to the particular elements which are semantically negated. Some translators have attempted to recast the language into the Indo-European mold, with unfortunate results. Of course, one can often force a language into a particular pattern without completely destroying the meaning. For example, even though Tarahumara normally permits only one adjective immediately attributive to a noun head, while setting off the others in postposed dependent phrases, it is possible to make sense by translating Spanish, or even English, word order more or less literally. However, the process produces a bad Tarahumara style.

When the order of an expression is obviously complicated, as in Mark 15:21, which even in the RSV is rendered as, "And they compelled a passerby, Simon of Cyrene, who was coming in from the country, the father of Alexander and Rufus, to carry his cross," it is not surprising that a drastic alteration takes place in word order in translation, e.g. 'Simon of Cyrene, who is the father of Alexander and Rufus, was coming in from the country. The soldiers ordered him to carry Jesus' cross'.

In some receptor languages vocative expressions must be placed at the beginning of a direct discourse, rather than imbedded within the introductory expressions, as they are in good Greek style (cf. Luke 1:3 and Acts 26:2).

Obligatory adjustments in order may result in very severely altered expressions, as for example, in Kaka, in which all interrogatives are final rather than initial to clauses, e.g. 'The people of God, they who?' 'The churches, they how many?' or 'The believers in Christ, how?' However, for the translator, these obligatory modifications are ultimately not so much a problem as are the optional variants in order, which serve to highlight emphatic elements in the sentence, provide a pleasing rhythm, or adjust the linguistic to the historical order of events.

e. *Clause and sentence structure.* Undoubtedly the most serious problems of alteration in clause and sentence structure are found in shifts between hypotactic and paratactic formations, with or without additions or subtractions of lexical elements. Fang (1953, p. 121) says that one of the principal tasks of the translator from Chinese into English is to render "the predominantly paratactical structure of Chinese texts" into equivalent hypotactic structures. However, to those accustomed to hypotactic organization of lexical units, paratactic structures often seem to be an utterly inadequate means of expression. In Chol, for example, the expression "be transformed by the renewal of your mind" (Romans 12:2) is accurately rendered as 'make yourselves good; make your hearts new'. Even though the logical connection of goal and means in these two expressions is not explicitly marked, as it is in English by means of the preposition "by," nevertheless, the meaningful relationship is quite clear in Chol. An even more evident departure from English practice may be seen in the Kaka rendering of a question from the catechism, "What things keep us from being Christians?" Such a question must be translated by two paratactically combined phrases, to which is added a question intonation, 'Things that trouble us; we live like God's people?'

Two other important alterations in clause and sentence structure involve: (1) shifts from questions to statements, when, for example, rhetorical questions do not occur in the receptor language, and (2) changes from indirect discourse to direct, or vice versa. In some languages certain special complications affect the use of direct and indirect discourse. In Waiwai, a language of British Guiana, indirect quotation is preferable when the writer is understood not to have been present, direct quotation when he is presumed to have been at the scene. This type of distinction poses certain major problems of interpretation in the treatment of the four Gospels, for according to early tradition Matthew was present to hear many of the statements of Jesus, but Mark and Luke were not. On the other hand, this early tradition is not in accordance with most contemporary scholarly judgments on the literary sources of the Matthaean record. Hence a difficulty exists for the translator in many receptor languages.

f. *Semantic problems involving single words.* By no means do all the semantic problems involving single words arise from distinctions in hierarchical status. Nevertheless, a number of the most important alterations in meaning do involve such structuring. Accordingly, alterations of this type may be classified on the basis of whether the lexical elements in question are of a lower rank, of a higher rank, of a higher rank plus qualifiers, or of the same rank but shifted in position.

The translator is often forced by the semantic structure of the receptor language to select a term lower in hierarchical rank, since no equivalent high-level term is available. In Villa Alta Zapotec, for example, it is not possible to translate the words of Salome to her mother Herodias, "What shall I ask?" (Mark 6:24), without further specifying that: (1) Salome already knew what she herself wanted, (2) she did not know what she should ask for, (3) she had forgotten what she had been told, or (4) she had forgotten some details. This greater specificity means lower hierarchical rank.

Similarly, a translator may be required to employ words with a higher hierarchical value, as when terms such as 'hour' and 'day' are rendered by 'time' and 'occasion'.

A very common practice is to translate a lower level term in the source language by a higher level term plus a qualifier, which tends to bring the more generic term down to the appropriately corresponding level. In Luvale, for example, "wolf" becomes 'hunting dog', in which 'dog' is the higher generic term, but by means of the qualifying term 'hunting' (not at all equivalent to the connotations in English *hunting*) the expression indicates a wild kind of predatory canine.

By the use of certain widely employed attributives one can deal with whole series of words—first, by selecting more highly generic expressions, and then by shifting them to their proper corresponding level through the use of these attributive elements. For example, in Shilluk a number of religious terms are constructed by adding 'of God': 'message of God' (for "gospel"), 'declare the word of God' (for "preach"), 'speak to God' (for "pray"), 'day of God' (for "Sabbath"), and 'building of God' (for "temple").

A shift may also be necessary when a word that seems to be of the same hierarchical level as the source-language word actually occupies a different position because of cultural differences. The word "wolves," for example, as used in "wolves in sheep's clothing," is rendered in Bulu as 'leopards'. A more nearly accurate way of describing such a shift would be to say that, though the referential meanings of the two terms reflect different positions in the lineal series, the functional meanings are the same.

Descriptive equivalents are deliberate attempts to produce satisfactory equivalents for objects, events, attributes, and relationals for which no regular term exists in the receptor language. They often involve an entire recasting of the semantic elements in the source-language word. The most common types of descriptive equivalents involve: (1) objects largely unknown in the receptor culture, e.g. 'house where law was read' for *synagogue* (Maya), 'thing that makes bread rise' for *leaven* (Loma), and 'metal worn on the chest for protection' for *breastplate* (Luvale); and (2) attributes or processes which have no ready lexical parallel, e.g. 'desire what another man has' for *covetousness* (Maya), and 'those that praise themselves, saying: We are better' for *the proud* (Shipibo).

g. *Semantic problems involving exocentric expressions.* Undoubtedly the principal difficulty of the translator in dealing with exocentric expressions is that he tends to overlook their exocentric character. In the Bible many figurative extensions of meaning which relate, for example, to light and truth, the human body and the church organization, marriage and fidelity to God, and body and soul, are so much a part of the Scripture message that they seem, to the reader familiar with them, quite matter-of-fact statements, and not, as they are, exocentric idioms. For these reasons some Bible translators have completely missed the point by rendering literally such phrases as 'sat at table' (implying that the people were merely sitting there and not eating), 'under the law' (suggesting the meaning illegal and contraband), 'dead to sin' (suggesting that people were killed by sin), and 'with sins covered' (implying that even God did not discover their evil deeds).

The necessity for certain thorough alterations of exocentric expressions has always been recognized by good translators. Thus such idioms as German *Mit Wölfen muss man heulen* (literally, 'one must howl with wolves') may be rendered in English as 'when in Rome do as the Romans'; the French phrase *ventre à terre* (literally, 'belly to the ground') may be rendered variously as 'as quickly as possible', 'at full stretch', and 'hell for leather' (Savory, 1957, p. 16); and Spanish *rasgarse la barriga* (literally, 'to scratch one's belly') becomes 'to twiddle one's thumbs'. It has been traditional in D-E translations to render classical idioms by corresponding idioms in modern languages. A Latin phrase such as *manibus pedibusque* (literally, 'with hands and feet') becomes 'tooth and nail', and *rem acu tetigisti* (literally, 'you touched the thing with a needle') is rendered as 'you have hit the nail on the head'.

When there is no readily corresponding idiom in the receptor language, a slight adjustment in the source-language expression may make it acceptable in the receptor language. In Uduk, for example, "walk in the Spirit" (Galatians 5:15) is quite meaningless, but 'let the Spirit lead you in the way' is a close parallel. Similarly, a literal equivalent of "crown of life" (James 1:12) is hopeless in Navajo, but an adjustment to 'the life-way prize' preserves the basic meaning of the original and fits the indigenous concepts very well.

Whether certain metaphors will be considered appropriate by receptors is sometimes unpredictable. However, certain features of the receptor language, e.g. a widespread practice of creating new metaphors, a readiness to adopt foreign figures of speech, and the existence in it of metaphors of the same types as those of the source language, are favorable indications that a particular figure of speech will be readily received and properly understood. In Ecuadorian Quechua the Biblical idiom "heap coals of fire on his head" seemed to offer no special difficulties, though in many languages it does, while "to drink of one spirit" proved quite impossible to carry over. The only certain way to determine whether an idiom will be acceptable in a receptor language is to try it out on a representative audience.

THE USE OF FOOTNOTES

When a literal or close rendering would result in a meaningless expression, or wrong interpretation, the necessary adjustments are usually made in the text. However, there are circumstances in which more or less literal renderings are preserved in the text, and the required adjustments are explained in marginal notes or footnotes. For example, in the production of an F-E translation, or when a modification of the text would seem to introduce anomalies not in keeping with the temporal or cultural distance between source and receptor languages, one may be justified in retaining a more or less literal equivalent in the text, and explaining it in a footnote.

Basically, in a translated text footnotes have two principal functions: (1) to correct linguistic and cultural discrepancies, e.g. (a) explain contradictory customs, (b) identify unknown geographical or physical objects, (c) give equivalents of weights and measures, (d) provide information on plays on words, (e) include supplementary data on proper names (e.g. *Pharisees, Sadducees, Herodians*); and (2) to add information which may be generally useful in understanding the historical and cultural background of the document in question.

These notes may be placed on the page where the object or event is spoken of, or the substance of such notes may be summarized in the form of tables or glossaries, placed at the back of the book. However, tables and glossaries are usually intended to help rather sophisticated readers.

Some translations are published with relatively extensive notes. In such instances they are usually classified as commentaries. Such commentaries are often based on traditionally translated texts.

ADJUSTMENTS OF LANGUAGE TO EXPERIENCE

In general we regard translation as more or less a single act, without recognizing that a translation, especially one of the Bible, is usually the result of a number of years' work, during which time not only the translator or translators, but also the people for whom the translation is being prepared, have contributed extensively to the form of the translation as the result of their own experiences.[1] Moreover, particularly in the case of the Bible, translating is rarely regarded as complete for all time, for any document designed to serve the continuing needs of a living community must be constantly revised. Accordingly, the language of one translation inevitably affects the usage of a revision, as the wording of the first interacts in the experience of the receptors.

The adjustment of language to experience is readily recognized when new cultural events take place within a society. Among the Tzeltals in southern Mexico, the coming of missionaries and the initial presentation of the Christian message resulted in the conversion of many hundreds of persons, who responded, in their eagerness to describe their spiritual experiences, by creating many new phrases. Thus they used such expressions as 'to turn one's heart toward God' ("to trust God"), and 'to be sad before God' ("to feel convicted of sin"). The use here of the productive element *ta stojol Dios*, meaning 'at, in, of, toward God', constituted an important adjustment of language to experience. All the words used in these phrases had existed in the language, but the new combinations and specialization of their use in these phrases constituted an adjustment of language to the experience of the people.

At the same time, the Tzeltal people were undergoing certain adjustments of experience to new elements of language, for the introduction of such Spanish terms as *templo* 'temple', *ministro* 'minister', *anciano* 'elder', and *diacono* 'deacon', and the accompanying features of Protestant worship and organizations, served to provide a basis for adjustment of experience to language.

The interplay between language and experience in any evolving lan-

---

[1] For an important article on this matter, see Marianna Slocum (1958).

guage-culture situation largely determines the direction and nature of any revision. In fact, it is almost impossible to speak of a completely "new translation" of any culturally important document, for if the earlier renderings have had any effect upon the experience of the people, it is inevitable that many of the most important lexical usages will be already determined in advance. Furthermore, the very demand for a revision is in itself evidence of an important interaction between the language of the document in question and the response of the receptors. One cannot be divorced from the other.

CHAPTER ELEVEN

TRANSLATION PROCEDURES

In preceding chapters the principles underlying translating have been outlined. We must now consider some of the fundamental procedures relevant to the actual performing of the task. They can be divided roughly into two categories: (1) technical, and (2) organizational. Technical procedures concern the processes followed by the translator in converting a source-language text into a receptor-language text; organizational procedures involve the general organization of such work, whether in terms of a single translator or, as is true in many instances, of a committee.

TECHNICAL PROCEDURES

Technical procedures consist essentially of three phases: (1) analysis of the respective languages, source and receptor; (2) careful study of the source-language text; and (3) determination of the appropriate equivalents.

Analysis of Source and Receptor Languages

In general it is assumed that the translator will have a complete command of the source and receptor languages, as a bilingual and possibly bicultural participant in the respective speech communities. Unfortunately, such comprehensive knowledge is more often the ideal than the actuality. Moreover, even when the translator has a relatively high degree of practical competence, he may lack certain specific types of knowledge which are of strategic importance.

He should in the first place have a good grasp of the linguistic structures of the two languages, not only in terms of the usual types of transfers from one language to another, but also and more specifically in terms of the types of transforms which occur within a specific language. That is to say, he must know how the language in question "generates" sentences and how these structures are related to one another, for it is this kind of knowledge which makes it possible to manipulate the structures readily and effectively. Moreover, it is essential that he be fully acquainted with the meanings of syntactic structures; it is in this particular area that translators often show their greatest weakness. Though they may understand quite well the meaning of individual words and phrases, they are often woefully lacking in fundamental appreciation of the meanings of constructions.

In the second place, the translator must have a complete understanding of the meaning of lexical elements, whether endocentric or exocentric. Competence in this respect implies not only an appreciation of the contemporary cultural relevance of expressions, but also of their historical background and traditional usage. Of course, no person has a complete knowledge of the total lexical resources of any language, nor can one have a comprehensive understanding of all the areas of human knowledge or activity contained in most source-language texts. Accordingly, translators must specialize, e.g. in commercial, literary, legal, religious, or technical subjects. Within these limitations, however, it is nevertheless essential that the translator have a complete grasp of all the semantic equivalences within the area of his chosen work.

Thirdly, the translator must be both sensitive to and capable of producing an appropriate style, whether in spoken or written form. A language which has only recently been reduced to writing will offer considerable difficulty; one with traditional styles to be observed demands that the translator become fully acquainted with these styles, both in theory and in practice. One who cannot himself write acceptably is rarely able to translate well.

Analysis of the Source-Language Text

Analysis of a source-language text is a more complicated task than it is often assumed to be. If the text is oral, all the phonemic factors are present, e.g. intonation, junctures, terminal contours, and often as well such important supplementary features as gesture, tone of voice, and hesitations. When all the relevant features are present, there is still the problem of rapid analysis of an ongoing, fleeting text. If the text is a written one, either the so-called "autograph" or a reasonably close approximation, the translator must attempt to reconstruct certain features present in a transcription in which all the phonemic elements of speech would be included. That is to say, he must make up for the deficiencies of the orthographic system. A further problem exists in a message which is obviously not the original document, and which has presumably been altered at various points, either intentionally or unintentionally. Intentional modifications may have resulted from either hostility or sympathetic interest. Sympathetic alterations are usually the most difficult to detect, for they seem to accord well with the intent of the document; hostile changes are usually manifest distortions.

When important problems of textual criticism are involved in the analysis of the form of the source-language message, the principle of communication load is generally the most relevant factor in determining the original readings; for unintentional changes are usually directed toward reducing the communication load. Accordingly, the harder reading is more likely to be the original one. Other, more mechanical, factors—such as haplography, dittography, itacism, and homoeoteleuton —enter into the difficulty of textual criticism, but they are beyond the scope of this analysis. Anyone concerned with serious textual problems must either undertake to study the factors of internal and external evidence in considerable detail, or be prepared to follow the expert opinion of textual editors who have made a careful analysis of the source-language text.

Once the correct form of the text has been determined, its meaning must be studied. This procedure can be conveniently described in terms of several stages, but in actual practice it involves continuous inter-dependence of insights gained from the various levels of analysis. Basically, these stages of semantic analysis can be described as: (1) lexico-grammatical features of the immediate unit, (2) discourse context, (3) communicative context, (4) cultural context of the source language, and (5) cultural context of the receptor language.

a. *Lexico-grammatical features of the immediate unit.* In analyzing the meaning of a particular unit, usually a long sentence or a short paragraph, one must determine all the semantic elements: syntactic, referential, and emotive. As a matter of useful procedure, the translator may "decompose" them into their simplest forms and introduce the most explicit statement of interrelationships. In treating such lexico-grammatical features, both form and content must be dealt with, since special forms, e.g. poetry, liturgy, parables, proverbs, epigrams, and epistolary formulae, are all important factors in determining meaning. In fact, as a general principle one must recognize that in proportion as the stylistic forms become more "demanding" (i.e. restrictive and limiting), by that same degree can one discount the meaning of the individual lexical items; for under such circumstances the selection of particular symbols is dictated more and more by the formal requirements of the style, and less by the extent to which such symbols denote precisely the range of actual experience.

b. *Discourse context.* The meaning of a particular unit, regardless of its extent, must be analyzed in terms of the wider context of the total relevant discourse, whether this unit is a paragraph, section, chapter, or book. In other words, the immediate unit selected for analysis cannot be treated as a separate element; it must be considered as an integral part of the total discourse. Furthermore, the meaning of the discourse as a whole must be analyzed in terms of both content, i.e. the subject matter of the message, and form, e.g. epic poetry, legendary narrative, exposition, or apocalyptic literature. In the book of the Revelation, for example, the interpretation of particular parts is greatly influenced by the elaborate structure of the entire book, since the final section of a particular series often serves merely to introduce a following series, so that there are sequences within sequences—an important literary device of apocalyptic "wheels within wheels."

c. *Communicative context.* The meaning of a message cannot be adequately analyzed without considering the circumstances involved in the original communication, including such matters as time, place, author, audience, intent, and recorded response. In studying the relationship of the source to the message, we analyze such factors as: (1) the background of the source (knowing something about the author is of great importance in attempting to decode his message); (2) the particular manner in which he produced his message, e.g. dictated, written by hand, written and then edited, or dictated and then corrected by some amanuensis; (3) the factual background of the message, e.g. personal experience, data gathered from others, oral and/or written sources; and (4) the circumstances in the life of the source which prompted this particular communication.

In studying the role of the original receptors of a message in order to determine something of the meaning of the text, we must analyze: (1) the background of the intended receptors (e.g. the evident differences between the audiences for the Gospel of Matthew and the Gospel of Luke); (2) the manner in which the message was actually received, e.g. heard or read, as liturgy, a letter, or a study document; (3) the behavior of the receptors which may have "provoked" such a message; and (4) the manner in which the receptors may have responded to the message.

In analyzing the meaning of a narrative message, however, there are often two sets of sources and receptors to be considered. For example, in the case of the Gospels one must deal not only with the statements of Jesus, as messages from a particular source, and directed to the receptors he addressed, whether the multitudes or his disciples; but also with the Gospels as accounts prepared by later writers, and addressed primarily to the church, either for their edification or as tools of evangelism. The meaning of a particular parable must then be analyzed, not only in terms of what Jesus himself probably meant when he addressed a particular audience, but also in terms of what the Gospel writer was trying to communicate in the selection and arrangement of this parable in the larger context of the Gospel. Accordingly, one must be concerned not only with the primary source and receptors, but also with secondary ones. [1]

d. *Cultural context of the source language.* The larger cultural context is of utmost importance in understanding the meaning of any message; for words have meanings only in terms of the total cultural setting, and a discourse must be related to the wider sphere of human action or thought. Therefore, in determining the exegesis of a message we must look to the larger cultural context for important clues to interpreting the significance of the text. For example, in the exegesis of the Old Testament, it is important to understand such features as: covenant relationships, Semitic tribal organization, the customs of revenge and retaliation, the ecstatic behavior of the prophets, polygamy among commoners and royalty, patrilineal descent, and male dominance. It is necessary also to understand the Hebrew view of human personality, e.g. the range of meanings of *nephesh* 'breath', 'respiration', 'life', 'soul', 'spirit', 'mind', 'living being', 'creature', 'person', and 'self'; and of *leb* 'heart', 'life', 'seat of emotions', 'way of thinking and acting', 'seat of purpose' (will, and determination), 'understanding', 'intelligence', 'wisdom', 'middle', and 'midst'. For the New Testament, it is essential to know something of the Greek "divisions of personality," Neoplatonic use of such expressions as

---

[1] Form criticism, as related to exegesis and exposition of the Scriptures, studies the effect of this secondary source-receptor relationship upon the form and meaning of the message.

"dominions, powers, authorities, thrones," the mystery religions, and organizational developments in the early church.

e. *Cultural context of the receptor language.* In analyzing the meaning of a source-language text, one would suppose the cultural context of the receptor language to be largely irrelevant; but this is not so in the case of messages which have already been communicated in the receptor culture. For example, except for strictly pioneer work, no translator of the Bible can completely overlook the way in which certain expressions in Scripture have already come into use in the receptor language. In certain instances the correspondences may not be too satisfactory, but their widespread use tends to condition their being employed in a translation, even in one which aims at the greatest possible fidelity to the form, content, and spirit of the original message.

Determination of Equivalence

The process by which one determines equivalence between source and receptor languages is obviously a highly complex one. However, it may be reduced to two quite simple procedures: (1) "decomposition" of the message into the simplest semantic structure, with the most explicit statement of relationships; and (2) "recomposition" of the message into the receptor language, in such a way as to employ those correspondences which (a) conform to an F-E translation, a D-E translation, or a compromise translation, and (b) provide the most appropriate communication load for the intended receptors.

ORGANIZATIONAL PROCEDURES

The technical procedures apply to any and all types of translating, but there are different types of procedural problems, owing to the diverse ways in which a translation process may be organized. There are naturally many varieties of such organization, as implied elsewhere in the description of the pioneer, midwife, and split-personality types. Moreover, revisions are in some ways a good deal more difficult than original translations, and hence often involve very complex procedures, usually because of vested interests.

On the other hand, it is possible to exaggerate the differences between translation and revision. Hence, in the following outline of organizational procedures, no attempt is made to distinguish between the two processes. By implication, certain important distinctions between translating by a single person and by a committee can be attributed to the fact that revisions are most often done by committees—usually because they involve a larger constituency and more numerous vested interests. Under these conditions there are more persons who must be consulted, or who think they should be consulted.

Translation by One Person

It is obviously impossible to describe the wide range of circumstances under which individual translators work, or to define adequately all the variety of procedures they employ for different types of translations. However, some of the principal steps in procedure employed by a competent translator can be outlined, as follows:

1. *Reading over the entire document.* Before actual translating can be started, or even a preliminary background study can be undertaken, it is essential to read the entire "message."

2. *Obtaining background information.* It is important that the translator obtain all information available about the document in question, including the circumstances of its writing, publication, and distribution, its relationship to other documents of a similar type (whether coming from the same source or not), and any detailed studies of the document by competent scholars. For the Bible translator, this means a thorough acquaintance with the opinions of leading commentators on the Scripture text in question.

3. *Comparing existing translations of the text.* A translator should not be guilty of merely copying the work of others, but by studying what others have done he has a greater chance of profiting by their experience as well as avoiding the errors they may have made.

4. *Making a first draft of sufficiently comprehensive units.* No translation should proceed word by word or even phrase by phrase, but should take as a minimal unit the longer sentences or shorter paragraphs. In writing out or dictating such units, the translator should not hesitate to employ boldness and freedom of expression. Moreover, the first draft should aim at fullness of expression, rather than a bare minimum of equivalence.

5. *Revising the first draft after a short lapse of time.* It is important that a first draft be left "to cool" at least for a day or so, so that one can return to the work with a greater objectivity and detachment. During the process of revision one can (a) prune out unnecessary words, (b) rearrange the component parts, (c) correct errors in meaning and style, and (d) give special attention to the connection between basic units.

6. *Reading aloud for style and rhythm.* Because of the primacy of oral over written forms of language, it is essential that the form of a translation be read aloud in order to test its style and rhythm.

7. *Studying the reactions of receptors by the reading of the text by another person.* The reactions of receptors to the hearing of a text are important indicators of the validity of the overall impression of a translation. The translator himself can note the points at which the reader hesitates (often marking awkward style or overly heavy communication load due to word choice), as well as expressions of comprehension or misunderstanding in the hearers. Moreover, the translator can question hearers about matters which may not have been clear and items which could lead to misunderstanding. This may be done by direct questions about content or by asking certain persons to explain the substance of what they have heard.

8. *Submitting a translation to the scrutiny of other competent translators.* Such persons may be either stylists in the receptor language or experts in the meaning of the source-language document.
9. *Revising the text for publication.* This last step in procedure involves not only attention to comments made by others, but should include very close attention to orthographic detail, in order to avoid extensive modifications in the printer's proofs.

In many instances certain obvious changes must be made in these steps. For example, many professional translators need not employ steps 7 and 8; other translators find it necessary to expand them into an extensive series of checks of usage, with many informants coming from various dialectal areas. For certain "pioneering" situations there are, of course, no existing translations to compare; step 3 then becomes irrelevant. Moreover, when there are no other translators who are particularly competent in the style of the receptor language, only certain limited aspects of step 8 can be followed. Nevertheless, in so far as these nine steps can be applied to a particular situation, they are fully justified and are highly recommended to the translator.

Translation or Revision by a Committee

Translations of important documents having significant bearing upon the traditions and practices of large constituencies are almost always entrusted to committees, since there is not only safety in numbers, but also greater balance of decision—though often less creativity—in corporate activity. In such committee work the individual members may employ a number of these steps of procedure recommended for individual translators. However, for the corporate work of the group there are certain problems of constituencies and procedures which should be noted.

Types of Committees

In group translations or revisions there are usually three types of committees, or at least three types of functions which are distributed in various ways. These may be conveniently described in terms of (1) editorial, (2) review, and (3) consultative committees. It is the Editorial Committee which actually does the work of getting out the basic draft. The Review Committee consists of persons who provide a considerable amount of expert opinion, and whose suggestions influence the translation in an appreciable way. The Consultative Committee is made up of persons needed to provide a kind of representative blessing on the work. In other words, they approve what has been done, but do not themselves participate to any considerable extent in the translating.

In actual matter of fact, there are in many translation programs only two recognized committees—one presumably charged with doing the work, and another which puts its stamp of approval on the job. Moreover, within the so-called "working committee" there is usually a small core of persons who actually do most of the work, while the other members serve to guide and review the project, rather than contribute appreciably to the work of the undertaking. Increasingly, however, there is a tendency to recognize formally the three levels of work, either by naming three different committees or by setting up two—an Editorial Committee and a Consultative Committee—and appointing certain persons to serve as "special consultants" to the Editorial Committee.

1. *The Editorial Committee.* The Editorial Committee should be as small as practicable (from three to five) to get the work done. Certainly, the mere adding of members is no guarantee of finishing the job sooner, since the length of time required to complete such a task is often geometrically proportionate to the number of persons working. It is of utmost importance that the members of the Editorial Committee be of relatively equal competence, since a fair sharing of responsibility and mutual respect are essential ingredients in any co-operative undertaking. At the same time, it is useful if the members of this committee have complementary abilities, since in this way they tend to supplement, rather than compete with, one another. Almost more important than any other factor is the capacity to work together.

2. *The Review Committee.* The Review Committee should be limited to about 10 persons, chosen for their special abilities; they should have either stylistic competence in the receptor language or expert knowledge of the source language. The extent to which such persons participate in discussions with the Editorial Committee depends largely upon the relevance of what they have to say and their capacity to work in the team. In general, however, the suggestions of the Review Committee can be handled most expeditiously through correspondence.

3. *The Consultative Committee.* The Consultative Committee may number from 25 to 100 persons, depending upon the practical requirements of the situation. They should make their contributions through correspondence, except when some major issue may require the presence of an unusually representative body. The members of a Consultative Committee are chosen for a variety of reasons: political, geographical, dialectal, etc., and though they may not have much time to give to the enterprise in question, their relationship to such a project is important in obtaining final approval and acceptance by the constituency for which the translation or revision is being prepared.

A Clear and Detailed Statement of the Principles of Translation

In any committee undertaking it is essential that the principles to be employed in the work be carefully and fully worked out. Of course, many of the principles must of necessity be broad in their implications, e.g. avoidance of obsolete grammatical forms, elimination of meaningless figures of speech, indentation of poetic lines, and contemporary spelling of proper names. However, it is also important that the principles be as extensive and explicit as practicable, for they perform a very important function in any committee undertaking.

First, such principles provide a basis for consistency in the work of different members of the Editorial Committee; they also guide the range and type of suggestions made by members of the Review and Consultative Committees. Moreover, such principles tend to avoid needless discussion, for problems can then be treated in terms of principles agreed upon, rather than as new and unique difficulties. Such principles also serve to prevent personal antagonism, for the members of the committees can argue against or for the principles, rather than against one another. Furthermore, if and when principles are changed during the course of a project, the committee will know exactly what portions must be redone in order to conform to the altered or expanded principles.

The development of principles to govern a committee translation or revision can best be done in five stages: (1) by careful consultation with the constituency for which the translation is being prepared (i.e. by wide solicitation of suggestions from all those willing to respond); (2) by thorough study of such suggestions in the light of expert opinion; (3) by tentative formulation of the most essential principles and application of them to a series of representative passages; (4) by the modification and elaboration of principles in the light of such "test cases"; and (5) by careful revision during the entire process of translation.

An important element in any statement of principles and procedures must be the assigning of ultimate responsibility for the work. In general, the tendency is to claim that the ultimate responsibility rests with the Consultative Committee, which presumably has the greatest "political power," while in actuality, except for certain limited issues, the real responsibility rests with the Editorial Committee. In many instances there seems to be good reason to make the real and the ideal lines of authority agree, and thus to give to the Editorial Committee the final authority, provided of course that the members of this committee have been carefully selected and are both competent and sensitive to the criticisms and suggestions of others. Such a procedure produces results that are much more rapid, and usually more consistent and acceptable.

Procedures in Committee Work

Translation procedures particularly applicable to committee work, and based upon the three-committee arrangement, are described below. For a project as extensive as translating the entire Bible, these steps in procedure are not carried out completely, one after another. Rather, the procedures are begun with some limited portion, and as this portion is being carried through the various stages of review and revision, another portion is started. Thus, one portion after another is started on its way, and in successive "waves" the whole task is at last completed.

1. *Dividing the work among members of the Editorial Committee.* Various portions of any large undertaking are usually distributed on the basis of the members' individual interests or competence.
2. *Translating of assigned portions by members of the Editorial Committee.* In carrying out this work the translator may employ a number of the procedural steps suggested for work done by individual translators.

3. *Submitting the work to other members of the Editorial Committee.* As each member completes his work, he submits it to other members of the committee, to be read over and corrected, or to have questions or issues raised.

4. *Studying of these suggestions by the translator.* If the first translator agrees completely with the suggestions made by other members of the Editorial Committee, he merely incorporates them into his basic draft. All other points are discussed by the Editorial Committee as a group.

5. *Submitting the resultant draft to the Review Committee.* The members of the Review Committee are expected to study the translation with care and to propose any changes they regard as necessary or helpful. When such suggestions do not accord with the principles agreed upon, the person making such a suggestion should note the fact and attempt to state just why an exception to the original principles should be made in this instance. In general, the contributions of members of the Review Committee are made through correspondence, but at times some member of this committee may be of sufficient value to the Editorial Committee discussion to warrant his personal participation in some sessions.

6. *Studying all changes and suggestions made by the Review Committee.* Either the original translator or an "editorial secretary" should go over all comments and classify all suggestions coming from members of the Review Committee. All suggestions which reflect evident oversights (orthographic or stylistic) can be automatically adopted; others can be treated according to the kind of problem involved.

7. *Preparing a revised draft by the Editorial Secretary.* If members of the Editorial Committee are not to be burdened with too much time-consuming detail in preparing preliminary and final drafts, it is important that the committee be provided with competent editorial assistance. Such a person can take major responsibility for checking the consistency of spelling of proper names, cross references, parallel expressions and passages, and orthographic detail.

8. *Submitting a revised draft to members of the Consultative Committee.* The members of the Consultative Committee are expected to go over the translation as it comes to them, in order to give their general evaluation and, when necessary, to make suggestions for further modification. All their work, however, is done by correspondence, unless some member proves to be so useful as to warrant his participation in some sessions of the Editorial Committee.

9. *Studying all suggestions made by the Consultative Committee.* The changes suggested by the Consultative Committee should be studied in the same manner as those made by the Review Committee. The extent to which these suggestions are adopted depends largely upon the degree to which the committee may be presumed to have final authority. However, only rarely does such a large committee reach

full agreement on any very controversial issue; hence, more often than not the final decision-making power must rest with the Editorial Committee.

10. *Preparing a final draft.* The responsibility for preparing a final draft for the printer should be the main task of an Editorial Secretary, who may, of course, be a member of the Editorial Committee. This final draft must be carefully checked for completeness, consistency, and correctness.

11. *Publishing tentative editions of limited portions.* The testing of a major translation or revision by publishing tentative editions is highly recommended, though in certain circumstances special factors make it advisable to complete an entire work before submitting portions to the public.

12. *Studying public reaction to limited portions.* The reaction of the public should be not only overtly sought, but carefully studied by interviews and observation.

13. *Polishing of the final draft.*

14. *Publishing of the complete translation.*

15. *Incorporating postpublication corrections into subsequent printings.* Within six months to a year it is important to introduce into subsequent editions any necessary corrections. In general, it is preferable to collect all corrections as may be noted by readers, to have these studied by the Editorial Committee, and to make all the changes at one time.

16. *Postpublication revision of the text.* Within not less than five years, and not more than ten years, it is important to consider making certain significant improvements in a translation. More than mere corrections of obvious errors and inconsistencies of rendering, such improvements constitute a revision of the translation embodying desirable changes noted by scholars or suggested by readers.

CHAPTER TWELVE

MACHINE TRANSLATION

Machine translation is treated in this final chapter only after a consideration of the total range of translational problems as they occur in their more traditional forms; for the difficulties and potentialities of machine translating cannot be fully appreciated without a grasp of the complexities involved in the more familiar procedures. Furthermore, even though machine translation has important theoretical implications for all types of translating, nevertheless, its full potential is far from actual realization. Much practical and theoretical work must be done before it can be expected to resolve the major problems of interlanguage communication.

It is unfortunate that MT (standard abbreviation for machine translation) has been overpublicized, perhaps giving the impression that machines will soon be doing all types of translating—not only more rapidly, but even better than human beings. Of course, MT does capture the imagination, especially of the gadget-minded public. The idea that machines can perform what is presumably a distinctively human function has a romantic appeal which sometimes prompts reporters and public relations experts to describe fancy as fact, and to speak of theoretical designs as functioning machines.

The actual application of MT to practical translation problems has been limited so far to very brief passages—a few sentences to a brief article, with the subject matter usually carefully restricted to one area of discourse; for example, nuclear physics, mathematical procedures, or chemical processes. Furthermore, in order to produce anything fully usable by a reader unfamiliar with the source language or document, some appreciable postediting has been necessary. This editing often equals the time it takes for a competent person to translate the document in the traditional manner. Nevertheless, despite a rather general disillusionment, a realistic appraisal shows that three important facts have emerged from research on MT: (1) machine translation is possible for certain restricted types of documents dealing with limited subject matter treated in a relatively simple manner; (2) with present technical developments in the "hardware" (i.e. the computer machines) presently or soon to be available, machine translation of a "rough and ready" type and for semantically and stylistically limited texts is practically attainable at an economically feasible price; and (3) important theoretical considerations in machine translation throw considerable light on problems of traditional translation, and are proving highly stimulating to various developments in linguistic theory.

Though machine translating can be useful for certain types of texts, there are certain theoretical limitations of machine translating which make its use for literary translating an impossibility. It is simply not feasible nor possible to put into a machine sufficient background data to permit the machine to resolve the numerous formal and semantic problems which in certain situations depend upon an almost unlimited knowledge of the universe. The programing of machine procedures so as to handle the syntactic structure of a language would be complicated enough, particularly when one realizes the fact that language is capable of generating an infinite number of previously unheard utterances. But if we were to add to this the capacity to resolve all the semantic problems, so many of which depend upon highly specialized cultural settings, we would completely overload any known or theoretically conceivable computer.[1] This does not mean that certain machine translating is not useful nor practicable, since for a limited range of materials it can no doubt make an important practical contribution, but much of the earlier enthusiasm for MT has now been sobered by the realities of deeper insights. Though a number of persons continue to be keenly interested in MT, both from a practical as well as theoretical standpoint, some of the more significant results for translation theory have come as a by-product of research in MT, rather than as a direct result of computer analysis and functioning. In the first place, MT has stimulated a demand for more explicit descriptions of linguistic processes. Since any procedure in MT must be "fed into the machine" in a detailed and orderly manner, linguists in this field are required to be explicit about certain linguistic operations and exact in handling exceptions. In the second place, theoretical work on MT has highlighted a need for constant reference to language structure, for a machine cannot be told how to deal with an infinite number of diverse combinations; rather, it can deal only with structurally related sets of combinations. In the third place, the need for "generating" sentences in MT has undoubtedly been an important factor in the appeal of Chomsky's "new look" for many linguists. MT has quite naturally stimulated concern also for a more adequate statistical treatment of language patterning, not merely in terms of word frequencies, but also in terms of sequential probabilities, i.e. the probability that a particular type of form will follow another. All these developments have important theoretical and practical implications for traditional translating.

Work on Machine Translating

Though scholars in many parts of the world have become interested in both the practical and theoretical implications of MT, substantial progress has been made primarily in three countries: Russia, Great Britain, and the United States.

In Russia a large number of persons are engaged in MT research (Harper, 1961)—probably more than in all other countries combined. But so far as one can judge, a good deal of the work of compilation is being done by hand, since adequate machines are apparently not available. Furthermore, the very limited glossaries available there suggest that

[1] See Bar-Hillel, 1953c and 1955a.

Russian researchers do not contemplate using large or sophisticated machines within the near future. Much of the work seems to be on a purely empirical basis, with the rules made up to fit the texts in question and expanded as exceptions and additional problems arise—the "trial and error" approach.

In Great Britain a good deal of interesting lexical work has been done, with special emphasis upon semantic analysis, including concern for multiple meanings and keys to the determination of the related correspondences in other languages.

In the United States work on MT has been undertaken on a broad front in a number of universities and research centers, e.g. Harvard University, Massachusetts Institute of Technology, Georgetown University, Ramo-Wooldridge Laboratories, IBM Research Center (Yorktown, New York), University of California at Berkeley, the Rand Corporation, and Wayne State University. A distinguishing feature of MT in the United States is the diversity of approach and the resulting variety of creative insights, despite some overlapping and duplication of effort.

BASIC APPROACHES TO MACHINE TRANSLATION

In general there are two major approaches to the problems of machine translating (Miller, Galanter, and Pribram, 1960, pp. 52-55). In the first approach, the attempt is to develop the simplest possible program which will take care of the immediate problems. With the aim of getting at least some results from the materials in hand, a series of simple instructions to the machine is worked out, involving transposition of order, choice of meanings, omission of words not required for the translation, and insertion of words necessary in the receptor language. When a new expression cannot be handled by such a series of instructions, certain modifications are made so that the materials "come out right." By adding rules here and there to "turn the trick," the results are made to appear relatively satisfactory for the limited type of material being translated. But even though these rules contain many important principles of transfer and correspondence, they are nevertheless a kind of impromptu scaffolding erected to fit the particular building.

In another approach to the problems of MT, an attempt is made to set up a series of integrated rules (in the form of instructions to the machine) which will theoretically be able to deal with any and all types of structure. Such rules are ultimately intended to be sufficient to analyze and "generate" all kinds of sentences and utterances, and thus provide a framework for setting up comprehensive procedures which will make possible all types of transfers from the structure of one language to that of another. These rules aim at something more than merely "doctoring up" MT results which do not come out right. Rather, they seek to determine the types of connections which are involved when a human translator actually transfers material from one language to another. This second approach is of much greater theoretical interest for the scientist than is the first. However, it is still only in its preliminary stages, for the linguistic analysis which must precede any comprehensive programing of MT has still to be done.

The empirical approach to MT, in which the researcher engages in a trial-and-error series of corrections and expansions of rules, may be regarded as a "cyclic approach," with presumably an ever-increasing degree of accuracy and range of relevance. Such a procedure is not without value, for it often and quickly exposes real "holes" in the structural analysis. On the other hand, such an approach may also cover up deficiencies which do not show up because the data in question do not provide a crucial case of overlapping or inconsistency with the rules. For this reason a number of scholars prefer to make a thorough linguistic analysis before attempting to undertake serious machine translating.

Another basic problem in MT procedures concerns the extent to which the language data are to be synthesized. For example, one can build into a machine a number of relatively elaborate rules to take care of such inflected forms as verb endings, e.g. *ride, rides, rode, ridden,* and *riding.* In such a system one "lists" the stem only once, and then works out "rules" by which the stems occur with various inflected endings, with or without certain accompanying changes in the stems. But one can also provide the machine with all five forms intact, and with instructions as to when the combinations are to be used. In dealing with a machine with a relatively limited "memory," it is obvious that providing the stems plus the required rules will be more economical than giving all the forms in full. For such a language as Russian, which has a number of inflected forms of the verbs and several case endings on nouns (most of which carry important distinctions in meaning), the abstracting of the inflectional affixes is very important, but not without numerous complications.

The solutions to such problems are constantly influenced by developments in engineering. At present certain technological improvements are producing almost fantastic machine capabilities. For example, one machine developed by IBM is capable of handling 32 disc files, each with a capacity of more than 4 million "machine words." High-speed magnetic tapes have a transmission rate of over 10,000 words per second, and a total of over 130 million machine words. The main magnetic-core memory consists of 262,000 words of 64-bits each, and has a potential translation rate of about 3 million text words per hour (Blickstein, 1961, p. 489).

In view of such remarkable possibilities in the machine, it would seem that the more work one could make the machine do, the better. However, even with the most efficient machine operation, at least 90 per cent of the work in any overall program of translation consists of linguistic analysis, and only 10 per cent of programing the results for the machine to use (Lamb, 1961a, p. 140). In other words, even bigger and better machines cannot do the basic linguistic analysis on which a program of machine translation must depend.

THE TURNING OF LETTERS INTO NUMBERS

Digital computers, as their name implies, are based upon numbers, and anything fed into them must be turned into some aspect of mathematics.

The computer cannot, of course, "think," as some persons have implied it could. It can only give back what has been fed into it in terms of original data and the operations the machine has been instructed to perform on such data.

Since the machine is an electrical device, it can only record positive and negative impulses and open or closed circuits. In other words, all the data must in some way or other be reducible to a kind of "yes-no" alternative, so that even numbers are ultimately reduced to such positive-negative contrasts, and language must be handled similarly.

Because of the positive-negative nature of electrical impulses, it is evident that a binary system of contrasts can best be employed; and if a number of different signs are needed to identify the elements of a language, e.g. all the letters of the alphabet, space between words, etc., it is convenient to set up a system based on at least 32 different possibilities or five positions of contrast, i.e. five bits (Log$_2$ 32 = 5). If we permit 1 to represent a positive charge and 0 a negative one, the alphabet could then be symbolized as follows:

A	00001	E	00101	
B	00010	F	00110	
C	00011	G	00111	
D	00100	H	01000	etc. [1]

Thus, in this type of system, there are for each letter of the alphabet five positions, which must be properly coded as positive or negative; thus a word of five letters would require a total of 25 marked positions. This would seem to imply stretching out words to unwieldy lengths, but data can be stored away on discs or tape in which the positions are measured in mere thousandths of an inch. However, once the linguistic symbol has been turned into this kind of plus-minus (or positive-negative) codification, it can be manipulated by the machine in the same way as any other kind of unit, e.g. it can be stored, transferred from one position to another, erased, or retrieved.

This type of 5-bit code is a very simple one—in fact, too simple to avoid some complications, for a certain amount of redundancy must be built into codes if they are to be "safe," that is, reasonably free from mistakes. Accordingly, some systems use groups of 6 or 7 bits as the fundamental units in the code. This makes it possible to use at least one of these bits as a "check bit," just to be sure some obvious error has not occurred in the encoding process. One of the most common computer units is a grouping of six of these 6-bit groups into a 36-bit "machine word."

The type of encoding which is used in turning letters into a binary code of 0's and 1's must, of course, be capable of being "transliterated" into various media. For example, electrical impulses on a tape must be reproducible as holes in a card, or positive and negative charges on a disc, or photosensitive contrasts on a photoscopic plate. Moreover, these

[1]   See Booth, Brandwood and Cleave, 1958b, p. 37.

same impulses must in some way be translatable back into letters, so that the impulses on a tape can be printed in words again, allowing the material to be read. This means that a computer must have a number of components, all of which are closely related.

BASIC ELEMENTS IN A COMPUTER MACHINE

There are three major parts in a computing machine: (1) the input, (2) the main storage and processor, and (3) the output. The input machine receives data as they are fed into it, e.g. from punched cards or electronic tape. The requirement of feeding specially coded material into the machine has in the past constituted one of the principal bottlenecks to efficient and practical translating; for a text must be turned into punched cards or in some way changed from letters into binary-code numerals before it can be fed into the machine. The time and cost required by this process of preparing the text for the machine have been almost as great as for traditional translating. However, at present automatic print readers can handle as many as 1,000 characters per second, with the possibility of even more rapid scanners in the future. In this process an electronic eye passes over the letters, sorts out the distinguishing features, and translates this information into binary-code units.

A computer machine uses two kinds of material: (1) the background data which are stored in the machine, whether in the main core memory or in some supplementary storage, and (2) instructions on what the machine is to do with the information coming into the machine from the input. In a simple operation such as payroll calculations, the input machine feeds in data about the name of the person and the number of hours worked, while the computer has instructions to bring from the memory data about hourly rate and types of deductions on which the salary is computed. The machine then makes a series of simple comparisons and calculations and sends the results to an output component, which makes out the checks. As the following sections show, even the simplest translating is by no means so easy a task. Nevertheless, it is based essentially on these same fundamental operations—receiving of data, looking up relevant stored information, making such calculations and adjustments as are required by the two sets of information, and feeding the results to the output machine.

Despite the complexity and sophistication of computer machines, they are nevertheless "robots." That is to say, they can only do what they have been told to do, though they do it with fantastic speed. One may say that they do "mental work," but they do not "think." They can only carry out processes in a particular order and mechanically "spell out" the results. In some machines certain very simple procedures for "learning from mistakes" have been incorporated, and in some instances the machine itself can indicate just where the programing went wrong. In short, the computer is certainly a most remarkable machine, but it has no brain. The creative brainwork must be done by the linguist and the programer if the end results of even very simple MT translating are to be intelligible.

17

Basic Divisions in Machine Translation Procedure

There are two fundamentally different aspects of MT: (1) the stored data, including, for example, the dictionaries of the two languages (source and receptor); and (2) the processing of the text, including such procedures as the identification of words and meaningful combinations of words and the generating of a corresponding message in the receptor language.

As is evident in these two aspects of storage and processing, there are actually three major stages: (a) analysis, (b) comparison, and (c) synthesis, in each of which storage and processing are important. When the source-language text is fed into the computer, the analysis stage must identify the semantic units and analyze the structural patterns. This can only be done, of course, as the input text is compared with information already stored in the machine. However, as the data are analyzed both semantically and structurally, certain "specifiers" can be associated with the elements in question, as tags of identification. In the comparison stage, the specifiers of the source-language text are matched with specifiers of the receptor language, so that the corresponding semantic and structural elements are properly identified. Such a comparison quite naturally involves the two fundamental aspects, (1) the stored data and (2) the intricate system of instructions for matching specifiers (or labels). In the synthesis stage, the computer must take the semantic and structural specifiers in the receptor language and "generate" the appropriate sentence which is the closest approximation of which the machine is capable. In such a generation of sentences there are again two aspects: (1) the stored data, including the semantic units, words and idioms, and the grammatical rules which govern their usage, and (2) the ordered procedures by which such data can be assembled into meaningful utterances. [1]

Methods of Linguistic Analysis

Though a machine can do only what it has been told precisely to do, nevertheless, it must be capable of analyzing word combinations which it has never met before; otherwise, it would be utterly useless as a translator. Though the linguist himself actually performs the basic analysis of the source and receptor languages, the machine must be able to make discriminating decisions about language structure, for it must translate, not a string of words, but a structure. Moreover, to do so it must be able to identify the borders of constructions and the key words around which the parts of the sentence may be said to pivot.

This need for a technique for determining structure has resulted in two quite different ways of treating language sequences: (1) the phrase structure approach, and (2) the predictive method, based on sequential probabilities.

[1] In the outline of these fundamental aspects and stages of MT, we have followed the procedures suggested by Victor Yngve (1961c, pp. 127-128).

The phrase structure may be analyzed in two slightly different ways: (a) by determining sets of immediate constituents and (b) by lining up patterns of dependencies. An analysis based on IC (immediate constituents) structure implies a layering of the data, as represented in the analysis of *the man went home*, where the ultimate structural components are diagramed either as hierarchical levels or as "trees" (Figure 46).

Or, such a sentence can be described in terms of the presumed sets of dependencies; in this case, by making the subject and predicate dependent upon the verb, which may be said to serve as the fulcrum of the sentence. Such a dependency structure would be diagramed as in Figure 47.

What is fed into the machine is, of course, not marked as to layers or dependencies. The machine itself must have built-in instructions by which it can identify such units and relate them. Such instructions can follow

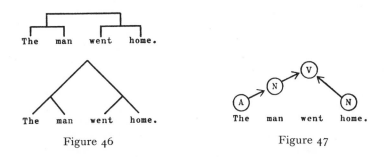

Figure 46   Figure 47

several different patterns of procedure, but in any event the sentence in question must "pass" several times through the analyzer, in order that successively more detailed and/or comprehensive comparisons can be made with data stored in the memory. The analytical procedures can be based upon several different approaches. For example, the analyzer can attempt to discover first the biggest units and then, on each succeeding pass, break these units down into smaller components. Or the analyzer can begin with the smallest units, and build these up to larger and larger combinations. It is possible for the machine to begin each search at the beginning of words and phrases and go "from left to right"; or exactly the reverse process may be used, with the machine working backward through the sentence, picking up the related components in reverse order. This kind of "pass procedure" is essentially the linguist's view of the structure, for he sees it in ordered layers.

In contrast with this pass procedure is a "predictive method" (Oettinger, 1961b, pp. 363-365), which more closely represents the mathematician's view of the language structure—one based on the expectations of what is to follow. For example, an initial word such as *the* immediately suggests a substantive to follow, with or without an intervening attributive, which will be dependent not upon the *the* but upon some following expression. Theoretically, if a machine has a permanent memory of the types of sequences which occur, the ability to identify units and handle the probabilities in question (while retaining in the temporary memory all that is required until the entire construction is completed, i.e. until there is nothing left to depend on it), it would be possible for it to analyze the meaningful combinations and set up the necessary "specifiers," so that corresponding features of the receptor language might be produced.

Whether one uses the "pass" or the "predictive" technique, there are still two types of information essential for the proper identification of grammatical combinations of words: (1) the degree of cohesiveness between words; and (2) the types of dependencies involved, in terms of agreement (e.g. gender and number), government (e.g. case endings required by certain grammatical positions), and cross reference. Though the "pass" method may appear to be more analytic, since it more readily reflects the type of procedure a translator normally employs in dealing with a printed text, the "predictive" technique has some highly significant practical and theoretical values, which parallel rather closely what happens in simultaneous interpreting.

THE ESSENTIAL FUNCTIONS IN MACHINE TRANSLATION

One of the most obvious requirements in a machine designed to translate from one language to another is a bilingual dictionary, providing a means by which the input of words in one language can be transformed into an output of words in another language. At first this requirement did not seem to involve too great a problem, since word counts carried out by Bell Laboratories had indicated that in English 500 words accounted for fully 77 per cent of the words used in writing and 93 per cent of the words used in speaking (Harkin, 1957). If all these words represented any kind of possible one-to-one correspondence between source and receptor languages, the working out of lexical transfers would be relatively easy. However, the fact that these very common words are precisely those which have multiple areas of meaning and thus give rise to the most numerous correspondences in other languages is the crux of the difficulty in translating.

As noted above, most work on MT at the present time is restricted to the translation of texts in which words have relatively limited and well-defined areas of meaning. In some scientific texts, for example, there are somewhat fewer possibilities for one-to-multiple meanings than in general literary texts, since the topic under discussion is usually more well defined and the comments made about it are strictly descriptive or explanatory, rather than metaphorical, lyrical, or affective. Nevertheless, even technical terms may have more than one area of meaning. For example, Spanish *radio* may be equivalent to English *radio*, *radius*, or *radium*. In order to know what term in English to choose, it is essential to learn from the context what meaning is involved. If the subject relates to broadcasting, *radio* is the obvious choice; if the context contains words involving geometry or anatomy, the equivalent is *radius*; but if chemistry is being discussed, then *radium* may be the correct equivalent. The only way by which the machine can determine the correct alternative is to identify certain diagnostic words in the context which point to the topic of discourse. Setting up an adequate dictionary for MT is thus no simple task, for the different meanings of a form must be carefully classified, and various types of cue words must be listed with each term, so that the proper equivalent may be selected.

A further problem in producing a dictionary for a computer is the fact that both meaning and structure must be constantly considered together, since (1) different forms may be functionally equivalent, e.g. the suffixes *-s*, *-en*, and *-i* in such words as *boys*, *oxen*, and *alumni*, and (2) identical forms may be semantically different, e.g. *light* (vs. *darkness*) and *light* (vs. *heavy*). All languages have many homographs, and these add difficulties to the already complex problems of multiple meanings.

An MT dictionary must take into account not only referential and emotive meanings but also structural data. For example, one may list all words as complete free forms, that is, with each inflected form given as a separate entry; the dictionary will then be very large and will contain many related forms having essentially the same meanings. Or one may list stems and affixes separately, thus reducing the number of entries, but also complicating the rules for determining which combinations occur and what they mean in combination. Even a rule to list only complete words is not sufficient, for genuine idioms, e.g. *bats in the belfry*, *pain in the neck*, and *polishing the apple*, must be listed as units, for their meanings are not determined by adding up the meanings of the component parts, but by knowing the range of occurrence of the phrase as a whole. Furthermore, even if one says that stems and affixes are to be listed separately, one does not thereby resolve all the difficulties; for though in most instances inflectional suffixes are abstracted from stems, one is not always certain of the extent to which derivational affixes are to be separated. There is obviously little point in listing separately the *re-* which occurs with *-ceive* and *-mit* in the words *receive* and *remit*, but one cannot treat as insignificant the productive prefix *re-* occurring with such words as *reconstitute* and *re-employ*, for this prefix produces many formations. In fact, if one does not list some of the more productive affixes, e.g., in English, *un-*, *-ness*, and *-ee*, there will be some expressions which a machine cannot readily translate.

Whether one is to list whole words or not depends a good deal upon the structure of the language in question. For example, in German new compound formations are readily made, and to limit a dictionary to those already in traditional use would result in a complete breakdown in translating certain types of texts. To illustrate, in scientific German fully 40 per cent of the compounds do not occur in the usual technical dictionaries (Edmundson, ed., 1961, p. 344).

Though the listing of word units by their component parts does present certain important advantages, especially in the case of new formations, the problems resulting from such a listing are not easily handled; for combinations do not always have predictable types of meanings, e.g. compare *upset* with *setup* and the use of *-y* in such words as *ratty*, (vs. *rat*), *icy* (vs. *ice*) and *mommy* (vs. *mom*).

One of the compensations in MT dictionaries is the remarkably short time required to "look up" words. Using an IBM 704, it is possible for the machine to look up a word in a dictionary accommodating a vocabulary of up to 500,000 words in only 8 milliseconds per word, or at the rate of 125 words per second (Lamb, 1961c, p. 341).

MULTIPLE MEANINGS

As already indicated, one of the principal sources of difficulty in translating arises from the multiple meanings of words. To resolve such problems there are two initial approaches, one grammatical, the other semantic. The word *man*, for example, has quite different meanings when used as a noun (*the good man*) and as a verb (*they will man the ship*). Thus by determining the grammatical function of a particular word one may in many instances appreciably narrow down the number of meanings.

In most cases, however, the problems of multiple meanings must be handled purely on the basis of semantic criteria or on the basis of contexts, both general and specific. Thus if we know the general topic of discourse, e.g. chemistry, theology, or folklore, we will know that terms such as *matter, spirit, heart*, and *person* are likely to have quite different correspondences in other languages, for their multiple meanings are conditioned by the nature of the general discourse. The type of discourse is usually signaled by certain characteristic words in the text—words which are diagnostic of the context. However, the meanings of certain words depend very closely upon immediate context, e.g. *ran . . . down* in the expression *he ran the man down* in contrast with *ran . . . down* in the phrase *he ran the water down* (*the ditch*). But even the expression *he ran the man down* may have three different meanings: (1) he caught up with him (and presumably stopped him) by running after him or going after him (either running himself or in a vehicle), (2) he ran over him with a vehicle, and (3) he spoke against him. Whether one is to take the first, second, or third meaning depends again upon the immediate context, even as *ran . . . down* is differently interpreted depending upon the use of *man* or *water* as object.

As noted in Chapter 5, treating such problems of multiple meanings is extremely difficult when the words or phrases occur in isolation. But such ambiguity is more theoretical than actual, because language tends to be some 50 per cent redundant in meaning as well as in formal symbolism (Gilbert W. King, 1961, p. 60). Thus to a great extent the preceding words give us clues to the understanding of subsequent expressions. The task of the linguist is to determine those particular formal elements in the discourse which are likely to provide the right clues—an area of research on which much has been done, but on which much more must be undertaken before the results are usable on a practical level.

AMBIGUOUS SYNTACTIC SEQUENCES

In the same way that some words have multiple meanings not always easily resolved by context, so certain sequences of words may be interpreted as belonging to more than one structure, e.g. *a son of Pharaoh's daughter* (is one talking about Pharaoh's grandson or granddaughter?). In most instances the syntactic ambiguities in question are resolved if one analyzes the degrees of cohesion between the parts (either in terms of the immediate constituents or the transformational structure) in the light of the context as a whole. But programing a machine to analyze the structure of the source-language text, transfer this into corresponding receptor-language patterns, and then generate the stylistically appropriate form in the receptor language is beyond machine capacity, except for some of the simplest and most straightforward texts.

BASIC LIMITATIONS IN MACHINE TRANSLATING

Despite the enormous storage capacity in modern computers, they are nevertheless incredibly less complicated than the human brain, which has approximately 10^{14} cells. To understand something of what this figure means, let us imagine that a child born at the time of Christ, and living until now, had been given one dollar each minute of his life; he would still not have one billion dollars. But if this number of one billion is then multiplied by 100,000, only then does one approximate the number of cells in the human brain (Edmundson, ed., 1961, p. 352). At present engineers talk in terms of computers with 10^7 bits, but this is very far short of the 10^{14} cells in the brain—only one ten-millionth of the number.

But size is not the only limitation of the computer—it is also stupid. Not that it cannot do certain calculations much faster than man; but it can do only what it is told to do. Of course, computers have been developed primarily for certain arithmetic operations and for logical operations, such as both/and, either/or, and greater-than/less-than. To be a good translator, the computer should also be able to respond "I do not know" and "I do not care, for this is not relevant" (Edmundson, ed., 1961, p. 347).

In addition to problems of size and sophistication, there is also the difficulty of having some appropriate language with which to "speak to" the machine, for the machine is designed principally for filing, ordering, and arithmetical processes. Thus in order to "translate" the structure of language into a form that the machine can handle, there is a need for an intermediate technical language which can be automatically adapted to the special limitations of the machine. In other words, it is convenient to use a kind of special built-in language. For example, some simple linguistic command such as "identify the noun in the following sequence," or "go to the end of the sentence," may require a score or more of detailed computer orders. Several special languages for computers have been developed, e.g. *Comit*, *Fortran*, and *Mimic*, each with its particular system of correspondences between linguistic procedures and machine processes.

There is no doubt that eventually machines will be able to take over some of the humdrum tasks of "low-grade" translating of certain types of material; for example, translating technical documents of a highly specialized nature, in which the multiple meanings of words are at a minimum and literary quality is not required. Even then considerable postediting by a human being will be required for complicated matter. At the present time, however, there is certainly no danger of any competent translator's being forced out of work by this type of automation. Even in that day when engineers build machines to rival the storage capacity of the human brain, such "hardware" will still not pose any substantial threat to the sensitive translator; for memory is not equivalent to empathy, nor is speed a substitute for esthetic feeling.

BIBLIOGRAPHY

The following bibliography has been prepared not only to provide the reader with data on the scores of books and articles cited in the text of *Toward a Science of Translating*, but also to list a wide selection of source materials dealing with many distinct but ultimately related phases of translating. These include articles on linguistic structure, psychology (especially as it may be related to semantics, learning theory, and perception of symbols), anthropology (with special reference to symbolization and value systems), information theory (in the more language-oriented areas), machine translation, theology (dealing with canons of interpretation and special problems of Bible translation), and stylistics and literary criticism (where the subject matter seems particularly applicable to the translator's problems). Quite naturally such a bibliography, which endeavors to cover all these aspects of so many related fields, cannot hope to be in any sense exhaustive. This is particularly true of the non-English sources. Nevertheless, this bibliography is one of the most extensive which has been produced on translating and related fields, and it is hoped that it will be of assistance to the student who wishes to dig more deeply into certain phases of translation which have only been touched on in this volume.

The following is a key to abbreviations:

Key

BT.   The Bible Translator.
IJAL.   The International Journal of American Linguistics.
LT.   The Times, London.
NYT.   The New York Times.
OUP.   Oxford University Press.
PMLA.   Publications Modern Language Association.
PNSMT.   Proceedings National Symposium on Machine Translation, 1961. Edited by H. P. Edmundson. Englewood Cliffs, N. J.: Prentice-Hall, Inc.
PPICL.   Preprints Papers 9th International Congress of Linguists. Cambridge, Mass., 1962.
PW.   Publishers' Weekly.
SR.   Saturday Review, New York.

Bibliography

Aalders, G. C. 1950. Notes on some difficulties of Old Testament translation. BT 1. 9-15.
——. 1953. Some aspects of Bible translating concerning the Old Testament. BT 4.97-102.
——. 1956. Translator or textual critic? BT 7. 15-16.
Aarne, A. and Thompson, S. 1928. The Types of the Folk-Tale. Helsinki: Gripenberg Alexandra.
Abernathy, Robert. 1961. The problem of linguistic equivalence. Proc. 12th Symp. Appl. Mathematics, ed. by Jakobson (q.v.), pp. 95-98.
Adams, A. W. 1954. The Old-Latin Version. BT 5. 101-106.
Adams, Sidney and Powers, Francis F. 1929. The psychology of language. Psych. Bull. 26. 241-260.
Adler, Johannes. 1960. The revision of the reference system in the New Luther Bible. BT 11. 178-181.
Aginsky, B. W. and E. G. 1948. The importance of language universals. Word 4. 168-172.
Aginsky, E. G. 1946. Language and culture. Proc. 8th Am. Scientific Cong., pp. 271-276.
Ahrweiler, Alice. 1952. Réalisme et traduction. Europe 30. 66-70.

Alegria, Fernando. 1954. How good is a translation? Américas 6. 36-38.
Alekseev, M. 1931. Problema xudožestvennogo perevoda. (The problem of artistic translation.) Sbornik Trudov Irkutskogo Gos. Universiteta 18. 149-196.
Allis, Oswald T. 1925. Dr. Moffatt's 'New Translation' of the Old Testament. Princeton Theol. Rev. 23. 267-317.
——. 1928. An 'American' translation of the Old Testament. Princeton Theol. Rev. 26. 109-141.
——. 1951. Review of Ronald Knox, Trials of a Translator (New York: Sheed & Ward, 1949). BT 2. 137-142.
——. 1952. Bible numerics. BT 3. 117-124.
Alphonse, Efrain. 1951. The translator's struggles. BT 2. 106-112.
American Ceramic Society, Research Committee. 1957. Access to Soviet literature on ceramics. Am. Ceramic Soc. Bull. 36. 377f.
American Editorial Board. 1950. Proposed publication of the manuscript evidence for the text of the Greek New Testament. BT 1. 169-171.
Amos, F. R. 1920. Early Theories of Translation. New York: Columbia Univ. Press.
Anderson, Earl. 1950. Lexical problems in the Kipsigis translation. BT 1. 85-90.
Anderson, H. H. and G. L., eds. 1951. An Introduction to Projective Techniques and Other Devices for Understanding the Dynamics of Human Behavior. New York: Prentice-Hall.
Anderton, Basil. 1920. Lure of translation. In his Sketches from a Library Window, pp. 38-70. Cambridge (England): Heffer.
Andreyev, N. D. 1962. Linguistic aspects of translation. PPICL.
Anon. 1820. Translation of the Bible. Quart. Rev. 23. 287-325.
——. 1858. English translations of the Bible. Bibliotheca Sacra 15. 261-288.
——. 1900. Translating the Arabian Nights. Nation 71. 167-168, 185-186.
——. 1924. Note complémentaire. Revue Études Latines 2. 194-195.
——. 1927. Transformation by translation. Living Age 333. 1117-1118.
——. 1935. A translator's Decalogue. J. Educ. (London) 67. 716.
——. 1938. Should the Chinese language be Latinized? Asiatic Rev. 34. 491-493.
——. 1948a. New Catholic text of Genesis issued. NYT, Sept. 3, p. 21.
——. 1948b. Where ignorance is bliss, 'tis folly. Congregational Quart. 25. 337-338.
——. 1949. Translating by machine. NYT, June 1, p. 30.
——. 1951. Further translation questions on Bali. BT 2. 25-30.
——. 1952a. Bible translators conference in Djakarta, Indonesia. BT 3.145-150.
——. 1952b. Biblical terms. BT 3.225-233.
——. 1952c. Discussion of Bible revision in Indonesian. BT 3. 223-225.
——. 1952d. Discussion of Bible translating in the work of the Indonesian churches. BT 3. 158-162.
——. 1952e. Discussion of the problems of the Bible translator in connection with the cultural and religious background of people. BT 3. 170-171.
——. 1952f. Discussion of the translation of Greek Sarks 'flesh.' BT 3. 209-212.
——. 1952g. Discussion of the use of literary or poetic language. BT 3. 219-220.
——. 1952h. Discussion of translating the divine names. BT 3. 196-199.
——. 1952i. General discussion of the Bode translation of the New Testament in Indonesian. BT 3.221-223.
——. 1952j. The Jerusalem Bible. BT 3.50-51.
——. 1952k. New group formed to aid publication of translations. PW 161. 2612-2613.
——. 1952l. New Testament in plain English. LT, July 14, p. 8.
——. 1952m. Practical problems of text and format. BT 3.162-164.
——. 1952n. Translating the divine names. BT 3. 171-196.
——. 1952o. U.S. translation program surveyed by Hodge. PW 161. 1377.
——. 1953a. Language of the Bible. LT, Nov. 19, p. 10.
——. 1953b. New translation of the Bible. LT, Dec. 21, p. 8.
——. 1954a. Electronic translation. J. Franklin Inst. 257. 257-260.
——. 1954b. Electronic translator. Time 63. 83-84.
——. 1954c. Hurdling the language barrier. Chem. & Eng. News 32. 5158f.
——. 1954d. The Welsh Bible. LT, Dec. 9, p. 9.
——. 1955a. La manière de bien traduire d'une langue en autre. Babel 1. 18-19.

——. 1955b. Translations Limited. LT, Oct. 21, p. 5.

——. 1956a. Recommendations of the International Conference of Asian and Middle-East Translators, November, 1956. Babel 2. 166-167.

——. 1956b. II. Technical translation services. Babel 2. 66-68.

——. 1957a. Bishops' move to revise Psalms. LT, Oct. 2, p. 6.

——. 1957b. Computers get smarter, study semantics. Electronics, Aug. 1, pp. 16, 20.

——. 1957c. Four languages interpreted by computer. Elec. Eng., Oct., p. 943.

——. 1957d. Let IBM translate it. Chem. & Eng. News, Sept. 23, p. 116.

——. 1957e. Translation by electronics. NYT, Oct. 28, p. 16.

——. 1957f. Translations by machine. LT, May 13, p. 6.

——. 1958a. Church in South Africa denies Bible racialism. NYT, Feb. 7, p. 5.

——. 1958b. Conférence de traducteurs à Luxembourg. Babel 4. 109-111.

——. 1958c. New South Africa Bible alters Song of Solomon. NYT, Jan. 24, p. 5.

——. 1958d. Première rencontre internationale des traducteurs littéraires à Varsovie. Babel 4. 174.

——. 1958e. Recommendations of the International Conference of Asian and Middle-East Translators, November 1956. Babel 4. 7.

——. 1959a. A new edition of the Greek New Testament. BT 10. 29-35.

——. 1959b. A new edition of the Hebrew Old Testament. BT 10. 110-112.

——. 1959c. Principles of Bible translating in the year 1727. BT 10. 22-27.

——. 1960. The Bible in modern Chinese; A Symposium. BT 11. 100-115.

——. 1961. Questions and answers; Psalms 1-50. BT 12. 80-84.

Antal, L. 1961. Sign, meaning, context. Lingua 10. 211-219.

Appleby, Lee. 1955. Luyia Old Testament translation; I, Unifying the written forms of the language. BT 6. 180-186.

——. 1956a. Luyia Old Testament translation; II, The work of the translation committee. BT 7. 25-30.

——. 1956b. Luyia Old Testament translation; III, Some problems in translation. BT 7. 85-90.

——. 1956c. Luyia Old Testament translation; IV, Translation and people. BT 7. 101-103.

Applegate, Joseph R. 1961. Syntax of the German noun phrase. PNSMT, pp. 280-285.

Arberry, A. J. 1946. Ḥāfiẓ and his English translators. Islamic Culture 20. 111-128, 229-249.

Argyle, A. W. 1953. The elements of New Testament textual criticism. BT 4. 118-125.

——. 1955. The causal use of the relative pronouns in the Greek New Testament. BT 6. 165-169.

——. 1956a. Review of Rudolf Bultmann, Bible Key Words—"Gnosis."* BT 7. 186-192.

——. 1956b. Review of Gottfried Quell and Ethelbert Stauffer, Bible Key Words—"Love."* BT 7. 90-95.

——. 1956c. Review of Karl Ludwig Schmidt, Bible Key Words—"The Church."* BT 7. 138-143.

——. 1958. Review of Karl Heinrich Rengstorf, Bible Key Words—"Apostleship."* BT 9. 44-48.

Armstrong, R. P. 1959. Content analysis in folkloristics. In Pool, ed., Trends in Content Analysis (q.v.), pp. 151-170.

Arndt, W. 1939. Have we the original text of the Holy Scriptures? Concordia Theol. Monthly 10. 105-111.

——. 1946. The RSV of the New Testament. Concordia Theol. Monthly 17. 333-339.

——. and Gingrich, F. Wilbur. 1957. A Greek-English Lexicon of the New Testament. Chicago: Univ. Chicago Press.

* From Gerhard Kittel, Theologisches Wörterbuch zum Neuen Testament, trans. and ed. by J. R. Coates. London: A. & C. Black, 1949.

268   BIBLIOGRAPHY

Arnold, Matthew. 1862. On Translating Homer. (Two essays.) London: Longmans,
    Green.
Arns, Karl. 1921. Über die Kunst der Übersetzung englischer Verse. Zeit. f.
    französischen und englischen Unterricht 20. 12-27.
Arrowsmith, William and Shattuck, Roger, eds. 1961. The Craft and Context of
    Translation. Austin: Univ. of Texas Press.
Arsenian, Seth. 1937. Bilingualism and Mental Development. Contrib. to Educ.
    No. 712. New York: Teachers College, Columbia Univ.
Aschmann, Herman. 1950. A literal translation of 2 Corinthians 1: 1-11 in Totonac.
    BT 1. 171-179.
Auden, W. H. 1953. Translation and tradition. Review of Ezra Pound, Trans-
    lations (New York: New Directions, 1953). Encounter 1. 75-78.
Aulie, Wilbur. 1957a. Figures of speech in the Chol New Testament. BT 8. 109-113.
——— 1957b. High-layered numerals in Chol (Mayan). IJAL 23. 281-283.
Austerlitz, Robert. 1959. Semantic components of pronoun systems: Gilyak.
    Word 15. 102-109.
Austin, H. D. 1932. Multiple meanings and their bearing on the understanding
    of Dante's metaphors. Mod. Philology 30. 129-140.
Austin, J. 1946. Other minds. Proc. Aristotelian Soc., Sup. Vol. 20.
Austin, R. G. 1956. Some English Translations of Virgil. Liverpool: Liverpool
    Univ. Press.
Avis, Walter S. 1957. Suffixorama. J. des Traducteurs 2. 49-52.
Ayoub, Millicent R. 1962. Bi-polarity in Arabic kinship terms. PPICL.
Baba, Bay Nuzhet. 1944. Linguistic reform and historical research in the New
    Turkey. Asiatic Rev. 40. 173-176.
Bach, Emmon. 1962. Subcategories in transformational grammars. PPICL.
Bacon, B. W. 1924. Punctuation, translation, interpretation. J. Religion 4. 243-
    260.
Bagnoli, Ferdinando. 1955. Le Congrès de Rome. Babel 1. 67-68.
Bailey, John W. 1937. William Tyndale and the New Testament. Congregational
    Quart. 14. 104-113.
Baldensperger, F. 1908-1909. Two unpublished letters to Goethe from an English
    translator of Goetz von Berlichengen. Mod. Lang. Rev. 4. 515-517.
Ball, J. 1954. Style in the folktale. Folk-lore 65. 170-172.
Bally, Charles. 1913. Le Langage et la Vie. Geneva: Editions Atar.
Bandini, A. R. 1948. The way of the translator is hard. Catholic World 167. 60-66.
Barclay, William. 1959. Words that intrigue. BT 10. 5-17.
Bar-Hillel, Yehoshua. 1951. The present state of research on mechanical translation.
    Am. Documentation 2. 229-237.
———. 1953a. On recursive definitions in empirical sciences. Proc. 11th Internat.
    Cong. Philosophy 5. 160-165.
———. 1953b. A quasi-arithmetical notation for syntactic description. Language
    29. 47-58.
———. 1953c. Some linguistic problems connected with machine translation.
    Philosophy of Science 20. 217-225.
———. 1954a. Can translation be mechanized? Am. Scientist 42. 248-260.
———. 1954b. Logical syntax and semantics. Language 30. 230-237.
———. 1955a. Can translation be mechanized? J. Symbolic Logic 20. 192-194.
———. 1955b. Can translation be mechanized? Methodos 7. 45-62.
Barker, George C. 1951. Growing up in a bilingual community. Kiva 17. 1-2, 17-32.
Barlow, A. R. 1952. Some problems of translation in Kikuyu. BT 3. 29-33.
Barnes, H. M. 1948. UNESCO sets programme for classics translation. UNESCO
    Courier 1. 1,3.
Barnes, W. E. 1926-1927. Bible translation—official and unofficial. (A study of
    Psalm 4 in English.) J. Theol. Stud. 28. 29-48.
———. 1938a. The New Testament, Authorized and Revised. Theology 36. 337-
    340.
———. 1938b. Thanks due to the Revised Version. Theology 37. 142-145.
Barnett, H. G. 1953. Innovation: The Basis of Cultural Change. New York:
    McGraw-Hill.

Barnhart, C. L. 1962. Problems in editing commercial monolingual dictionaries. In Householder and Saporta, eds., Problems in Lexicography (q.v.), pp. 161-181.

Barnstorff, Hermann. 1940-1941. German literature in translation published in ·Poet Lore, 1891-1939. Mod. Lang. J. 25. 711-715.

Barr, James. 1961. The Semantics of Biblical Language. OUP.

——. 1962. Biblical Words for Time. London: SCM Press.

Barrett, C. K. 1955a. New Testament commentaries; I, Classical commentaries. BT 6. 106-110.

——. 1955b. New Testament commentaries; II, Gospels and Acts. BT 6. 160-165.

——. 1956. New Testament commentaries; III, Epistles and Revelation. BT 7. 9-14.

Barrows, William. 1860. Romanism and a free Bible. Bibliotheca Sacra 17. 323-355.

Bartlett, F. C. 1932. Remembering: A Study in Experimental and Social Psychology. Cambridge Univ. Press.

Bartlett, Phyllis B. 1942. Stylistic devices in Chapman's Iliad. PMLA 57. 661-675.

Barzun, Jacques. 1952. Trial by translations: Plays of Corneille. New Repub. 127. 20-21.

——. 1953. Food for the N.R.F., or My God, what will you have? Partisan Rev. 20. 660-674.

Basilius, H. 1952. Neo-Humboldtian ethnolinguists. Word 6. 95-105.

Basson, A. H. and O'Connor, D. J. 1953. Language and philosophy: Some suggestions for an empirical approach. Methodos 5. 203-220.

Bates, Ernest Stuart. 1936. Modern Translation. OUP.

Bateson, Gregory. 1958. Naven. 2d ed. Stanford, Calif.: Stanford Univ. Press.

Batteux, Charles. 1760. Principles of Translation. Edinburgh: Sands, Donaldson, Murray & Cochran.

Battles, F. L. 1963. Englishing the Institutes of John Calvin. Babel 9. 94-98.

Baum, Paull Franklin. 1922. The Principles of English Versification. Cambridge: Harvard Univ. Press.

Baxter, William L. 1929. The Bible's first verse. Evangelical Quart. 1. 87-92.

Bazell, C. E. 1948. On some definitions in structural linguistics. Garp Filolojileri Dergisi, pp. 279-287. Istanbul University Press.

——. 1949a. On the neutralisation of syntactic oppositions. Travaux du cercle linguistique de Copenhague 5. 77-86.

——. 1949b. On the problem of the morpheme. Archivum Linguisticum 1. 1-15.

——. 1953. Linguistic Form. Istanbul University Press.

——. 1954. The sememe. Litera 1. 17-31.

Beals, Ralph L. 1957. Native terms and anthropological methods. Am. Anthropologist 59. 716-717.

——. 1961. Community typologies in Latin America. Anthropol. Linguistics 3. 8-16.

Beardsley, Wilfred A. and Grace H. 1937-1938. Evaluating popular translations—a duty of the foreign language teacher. Mod. Lang. J. 22. 454-456.

Beck, H. 1960. Problems of orthography and word division in East African vernacular Bantu languages. BT 11. 153-161.

Bedikian, A. A. 1957. Some remarks on the Bible in modern Armenian. BT 8. 75-79.

Beegle, Dewey M. 1957. The meaning of the Qumran Scrolls for translators of the Bible. BT 8. 1-8.

——. 1960. God's Word into English. New York: Harper. (See also review: Bratcher, 1961b.)

Beekman, John. 1952. The value of using translation helpers. BT 3. 24-25.

Beerbohm, Max. 1903. Translation of plays. Sat. Rev. (London) 96. 75-76.

Belasco, Simon. 1961. The role of transformation grammar and tagmemics in the analysis of an Old French text. Lingua 10. 375-391.

Bell, B. C. 1908. The ARV: Its translation of 'en. Union Seminary Mag. 19. 208-212.

Bello, Francis. 1953. The Information Theory. Fortune, Dec., pp. 136-142, 149-158.

Belloc, Hilaire. 1924. On translation. London Mercury 10. 150-156.

——. 1929. A Conversation with an Angel. New York: Harper.

——. 1931a. On Translation. OUP.

——. 1931b. On translation. Bookman 74. 32-39, 179-185. (Reprinted BT 10. 83-100. 1959.)

Belska-Fiserova, Libuše. 1958. Théories tchèques de la traduction. Babel 4. 120-122.

Belskaja, I. K. 1957. Machine translation of languages. Research 10. 383-389.

Benjamin, A. Cornelius. 1936. The Logical Structure of Science. London: Kegan Paul, Trench, Trubner & Co.

Benson, A. C. 1924. Verse translation. Cornhill 57. 586-598.

Bentley, Arthur F. 1932. Linguistic Analysis of Mathematics. Bloomington, Ind.: Principia Press.

Berelson, Bernard. 1952. Content Analysis in Communication Research. Glencoe, Ill.: Free Press.

Berry, R. N. 1960. An extension of Foley's "expression of certainty." Amer. J. of Psychology 73. 639-640.

Bestor, A. E., Jr. 1948. The evolution of the Socialist vocabulary. J. Hist. Ideas 9. 259-302.

Bett, Henry. 1940. John Wesley's translations of German hymns. London Quart. & Holborn Rev. 165. 288-294.

Bieber, Konrad F. 1954-1955. The translator—friend or foe? French Rev. 28. 493-497.

Binder, James. 1947. More's Utopia in English: A note on translation. Mod. Lang. Notes 62. 370-376.

Bishop, Eric F. F. 1951a. A patriotic mistranslation in the Arabic of the London Polyglot. BT 2. 31.

——. 1951b. Some notes on the version of St. Mark in the spoken language of Palestine. BT 2. 124-128.

——. 1953. Pronominal courtesy in the New Testament. BT 4. 32-34.

——. 1954. Interpretations of 'hope' in Arabic. BT 5. 4-9.

——. 1956a. Akouein akouetô. BT 7. 38-40.

——. 1956b. 'The Authorised Teacher of the Israel of God' John 3: 10. BT 7. 81-83.

Bishop, John Peale. 1943. On translating poets. Poetry 62. 111-115.

Bishop of Nyasaland. 1951. The Reader's Corner. BT 2. 177-179.

Bismarck, Klaus von. 1957. The Christian vocabulary an obstacle to communication? Ecumenical Rev. 10. 1-15.

Black, G. A. 1936. James Thomson: His translations of Heine. Mod. Lang. Rev. 31. 48-54.

Black, Max. 1962. Models and Metaphors: Studies in Language and Philosophy. Ithaca, N. Y.: Cornell Univ. Press.

Blackman, E. C. 1953. A study of the words 'thought,' 'mind' and 'heart.' BT 36-40.

Blaszczyk, Stanislas. 1934. Sur une traduction en Polonais. Revue Littératures Comparées 14. 181-183.

Blickstein, B. D. 1961. The high-speed general-purpose computers in machine translation. PNSMT, pp. 485-490.

Bloch, Bernard and Trager, George L. 1942. Outline of Linguistic Analysis. Baltimore: Linguistic Soc. America.

——. 1953. Linguistic structure and linguistic analysis. In Archibald A. Hill, ed., Rept. 4th Ann. Round Table Meeting on Linguistics and Language Teaching, pp. 40-44. Washington: Georgetown Univ. Mon. Ser. Languages and Linguistics No. 3.

Bloom, Lillian D. 1949. Addison as translator. Stud. Philology 46. 31-53.

Bloomfield, Leonard. 1926. A set of postulates for the science of language. Language 2. 153-164. (Reprinted IJAL 15. 195-204. 1949.)

——. 1927. On recent work in general linguistics. Mod. Philology 25. 211-230.

——. 1930. Linguistics as a science. Stud. Philology 27. 553-557.

——. 1933. Language. New York: Holt.

——. 1935. Linguistic aspects of science. Philosophy of Science 2. 499-517.

——. 1936. Language or ideas? Language 12. 89-95.

——. 1939. Linguistic aspects of science. Internat. Encyc. of Unified Science 1:4.

——. 1942. Outline Guide for the Practical Study of Foreign Languages. Baltimore: Special Publ. Linguistic Soc. America.

——. 1943. Meaning. Monatshefte f. Deutschen Unterricht 35. 101-106.

——. 1944. Secondary and tertiary responses to language. Language 20. 45-55.

Blount, Turner. 1953. Obtaining criticism of a Bible translation. BT 4. 34-36.

Bluhm, Heinz S. 1943. Recent American research on Luther's German Bible. Germanic Rev. 18. 161-171.
——. 1947. The 'Douche' sources of Coverdale's translation of the 23rd Psalm. J. English-German Philology 46. 53-62.
——. 1951. The evolution of Luther's translation of the Twenty-third Psalm. Germanic Rev. 26. 251-258.
——. 1952. Luther's translation and interpretation of the Ave Maria. J. English-Germanic Philology 51. 196-211.
Boas, Franz. 1911-1938. Handbook of American Indian Languages. Parts I-III. (Introduction, Pt. 1, 1911.) Washington: U.S. Bureau Ethnology, Bull. 40.
——. 1940. Race, Language and Culture. New York: Macmillan.
Bodde, D. 1955. On translating Chinese philosophical terms. Far Eastern Quart. 14. 231-234.
Bogenschneider, Hans-J. 1958. Der Wert der Dezimalklassifikation für den Übersetzer. Babel 4. 103-108.
——. 1959. Technischer Übersetzer und technische Bibliothek. Babel 5. 200-206.
Bohannan, Paul. 1953. Concepts of time among the Tiv of Nigeria. Southwestern J. Anthropology 9. 251-262.
——. 1958a. On anthropologists' use of language. Am. Anthropologist 60. 161-162.
——. 1958b. Rejoinder to Taylor. Am. Anthropologist 60. 941-942.
Bolinger, Dwight L. 1948. On defining the morpheme. Word 4. 18-23.
——. 1950. Rime, assonance, and morpheme analysis. Word 6. 117-136.
Bonneau, George S. 1938. Le Problème de la Poésie Japonaise. Paris: Libraire Paul Geuthner.
Booth, Andrew D. 1954. Calculating machines and mechanical translation. Discovery 15. 280-285.
——. 1955. Use of a computing machine as a mechanical dictionary. Nature 176. 565.
——. 1956a. The nature of a translating machine. Engineering 182. 302-304.
——. 1956b. Present objectives of M.T. research in the United Kingdom. Babel 2. 108-110.
——. 1958a. The history and recent progress of machine translation. In Forster, ed., Aspects of Translation (q.v.), pp. 88-104.
——; Brandwood, L.; and Cleave, J. P. 1958b. Mechanical Resolution of Linguistic Problems. New York: Academic Press; London: Butterworth.
——. 1962. Machine translation—a challenge to the linguist. The Incorporated Linguist 1. 34-41.
Booth, K. H. V. 1963. An experiment in mechanical translation. Information Storage and Retrieval 1. 19-28.
Borst, Arno. 1957-1961. Der Turmbau von Babel: Geschichte der Meinungen über Ursprung und Vielfalt der Sprachen und Völker. Stuttgart: A. Hiersemann. (See also reviews: Jumpelt, 1959b; Pap, 1962.)
Bothien, Erwin H. and Bodel, Jacques. 1958. Législation et conventions concernant les traducteurs et interprètes. Babel 4. 177-184.
——. 1959a. Magnetton-Übersetzer—der modernste Berufszweig. Babel 5. 123-126.
——. 1959b. Magnetton-Übersetzer und Übersetzer im Pressedienst. Babel 5. 216-219.
Boulding, K. E. 1956. The Image. Ann Arbor: Univ. Michigan Press.
Bowen, C. R. 1922. A notable Roman Catholic version of the New Testament. (A review.) J. Religion 2. 212-214.
Bower, Robert T. 1952-1953. Translation problems in international surveys. Public Opinion Quart. 14. 595-604.
Bowie, W. Russell. 1946. The New Testament—a new translation. Atlantic, Aug., pp. 122-127.
Bradnock, Wilfred J. 1952. The translator at work. BT 3. 125-127.
——. 1953a. The central problem: Conveying the Gospel. BT 4. 1-4.
——. 1953b. The Christian vocabulary. BT 4. 49-51.
——. 1953c. On the use of the name 'Isa. BT 4. 102-106.
——. 1954. Scripture translation through one hundred and fifty years. BT 5. 50-53.
——. 1956. Questions and answers. BT 7. 163-170.

Bradnock, Wilfred J. (cont.). 1975. Travels of a translations secretary in East Africa. BT 8. 62-67.
——. 1963. Religious translation into non-Western languages within the Protestant tradition. Babel 9. 22-35.
Braem, Helmut M. 1960. Einfluss der Verlegers auf die Qualität der Übersetzungen. Babel 6. 172.
Braine, Martin D.S. 1963. The ontogeny of English phrase structure: the first phase. Language 39. 1-14.
Brandwood, Leonard. 1956a. Previous experiments in mechanical translation. Babel 2. 125-127.
——. 1956b. The translation of a foreign language by machine. Babel 2. 111-118.
——. 1958. Some problems in the mechanical translation of German: 1. Relation clauses. 2. Prepositional phrases. Mech. Translation 5. 60-66.
Brang, P. 1955. Das Problem der Übersetzung in sowjetischer Sicht. Sprachforum 1. 124-134.
Bratcher, Robert G. 1953. A note on Mark XI: 3. BT 4. 52.
——. 1958a. The art of translation. BT 9. 84-89.
——. 1958b. A study of Isaiah 7: 14. BT 9. 97-126.
——. 1959a. 'Having loosed the pangs of death.' BT 10. 18-20.
——. 1959b. Review of Dorothy Heiderstadt, To All Nations (New York: Nelson, 1959). BT 10. 192.
——. 1959c. Review of Alfred Marshall, The Interlinear Greek-English New Testament (London: Bagster, 1958). BT 10. 41-43.
——. 1959d. Review of J. B. Phillips, The New Testament in Modern English (New York: Macmillan, 1958). BT 10. 135-143.
——. 1959e . Review of Hugh J. Schonfield, The Authentic New Testament (New York: Mentor Books, 1958). BT 10. 129-132.
——. 1959f. Review of The Amplified New Testament (Grand Rapids: Zondervan, 1958). BT 10. 132-135.
——. 1959g. Review of J.-J. Von Allmen, ed., A Companion to the Bible (OUP, 1958). BT 10. 41.
——. 1959h. Review of Kenneth S. Wuest, The New Testament, An Expanded Translation (Grand Rapids: Eerdmans, 3 vols., 1956, 1958, 1959). BT 10. 188-191.
——. 1959i. Weights, money, measures and time. BT 10. 165-174.
——. 1960a. Review of Ronald Bridges and Luther A. Weigle, The Bible Word Book (New York: Nelson, 1960). BT 11. 186-187.
——. 1960b. Review of James T. Hudson, The Pauline Epistles, Their Meaning and Message (London: Clarke, 1958). BT 11. 93-95.
——. 1960c. Review of H. T. Marroquín, ed., Versiones Castellanas de la Biblia (Mexico: Casa de Publicaciones 'El Faro,' n.d.). BT 11.93.
——. 1960d. Review of Gustavus S. Paine, The Learned Men (New York: Crowell, 1959). BT 11. 140-141.
——. 1960e. Review of E. H. Robertson, The New Translations of the Bible (London: S.C.M. Press, 1959). BT 11. 139-140.
——. 1961a. Changes in the New Testament of the Revised Standard Version. BT 12. 61-68.
——. 1961b. Review of Dewey M. Beegle, God's Word into English (New York: Harper, 1960). BT 12. 93-96.
——. 1961c. Why do we have so many translations? In his Why So Many Bibles?, pp. 29-42. Philadelphia: Evangelical Foundation, Inc. (To be reissued by American Bible Society.)
Brenes, Dalai, 1959. On language and culture. Mod. Lang. J. 43. 175-177.
Bridges, Ronald and Weigle, Luther A. 1960. The Bible Word Book. New York: Nelson. (See also review: Bratcher, 1960a.)
Briet, Suzanne. 1955. Le normalisateur, le bibliographe et le traducteur. Babel 1. 81-82.
Briggs, Harold E., ed. 1949. Language-Man-Society: Readings in Communication. New York: Rinehart.
Bright, William and Ramanujan, A.K. 1962. Sociolinguistic variation and language change. PPICL.

Broadbent, D. E. 1958. Perception and Communication. New York: Pergamon Press.

Brock-Sulzer, Elisabeth. 1956. André Gide als Übersetzer Shakespeares. Shakespeare-Jahrbuch 92. 207-219.

Brøndal, Viggo. 1949. Les parties du discours. (1919.) Trans. by Pierre Naert. Copenhagen: Munksgaard.

Bronowski, J. 1956. The theory and philosophy of language. Mech. Translation 3. 12-13.

Bross, John S. 1963. Problems of equivalence in some German and English constructions. Mech. Translation 8. 8-16.

Brother Basil, F.S.C. 1951. Mind reading and translating. Mod. Lang. J. 35. 153-154.

Brower, Reuben A. 1947. Seven Agamemnons. J. Hist. Ideas 8. 383-408. (Reprinted in his On Translation [q.v.], pp. 173-195.)

——. 1948. The Theban eagle in English plumage. Class. Philology 43. 25-30.

——. 1953. . . . And of recent translations and editions. Yearbk. Comparative and General Lit. 2. 69-72. Stud. Compar. Lit. No. 7. Chapel Hill: Univ. North Carolina.

——, ed. 1959. On Translation. Cambridge: Harvard Univ. Press. (See also reviews: Cary, 1960a; Jumpelt, 1960b; Swellengrebel, 1960b.)

Brown, A. F. R. 1958. Language translation. J. Assoc. Computing Machinery 5. 1-8.

——. 1961. Flexibility versus speed. PNSMT, pp. 444-450.

Brown, Alec. 1949. The translation of certain uses of the Russian imperfective. Slavonic & East European Rev. 26. 503-514.

Brown, Chas. R. 1886. The revision of Genesis. Bibliotheca Sacra 43. 507-527.

Brown, J. V. 1927. The Book in the Greek. Bibliotheca Sacra 84. 255-271.

Brown, Mildred. 1960. The Lwo Bible. BT 11. 31-42.

Brown, Robert. 1962. Meaning and rules of use. Mind 71 (n.s.). 494-511.

Brown, Roger W. and Lenneberg, Eric H. 1954. A study in language and cognition. J. Abn. & Soc. Psych. 49. 454-462.

——; Black, Abraham H.; and Horowitz, Arnold E. 1955. Phonetic symbolism in natural languages. J. Abn. & Soc. Psych. 50. 388-393.

——. 1956. Language and categories. In Jerome S. Bruner, Jacqueline J. Goodnow, and George A. Austin, A Study of Thinking, pp. 247-312. New York: Wiley.

——. 1957. Linguistic determinism and the part of speech. J. Abn. & Soc. Psych. 55. 1-5.

——. 1958a. Review of Charles E. Osgood, George J. Suci and Percy H. Tannenbaum, The Measurement of Meaning (Urbana: Univ. Illinois Press, 1957). Contemp. Psych. 3. 113-115.

——. 1958b. Words and Things. Glencoe, Ill.: Free Press.

—— and Lenneberg, Eric H. 1958c. Studies in linguistic relativity. In Eleanor E. Maccoby, Theodore M. Newcomb, and Eugene L. Hartley, eds., Readings in Social Psychology. 3d ed. New York: Holt.

Browning, Robert. 1889. Poetical Works. London: Smith, Elder.

Bruce, F. F. 1947. Two new versions of the New Testament. Evangelical Quart. 19. 69-73.

——. 1951. The New Testament in the language of the people. Evangelical Quart. 23. 152-154.

——. 1953. The Old Testament in Greek. BT 4. 129-135, 156-162.

——. 1955. Review of W. Schwarz, Principles and Problems of Biblical Translation; Some Reformation Controversies and Their Background (Cambridge Univ. Press, 1955). Evangelical Quart. 27. 230-231.

——. 1960. Review of Adam Fox, Meet the New Testament (London: S. C. M. Press, n.d.). BT 11. 185-186.

Brueggemann, E. A. 1936. The first three Bibles entering Luther's early life. Concordia Theol. Monthly 7. 118-122.

Bryson, Lyman. 1954. Symbols and Values. New York: Harper.

Buber, Martin, with Franz Rosenzweig. 1930. Die Fünf Bücher der Weisung. Berlin: Lambert Schneider.

Buck, Harry M. 1956. On the translation of John 2:4. BT 7. 149-150.

274 BIBLIOGRAPHY

Bull, William E. 1949. Natural frequency and word counts. Class. J. 44. 469-484.
Bullough, S. 1948. English Catholic New Testaments since Challoner. Scripture 3. 13-19.
Burke, Kenneth. 1945. A Grammar of Motives. New York: Prentice-Hall.
——. 1962. What are the signs of what? A theory of 'entitlement.' Anthropol. Linguistics. 4. 1-23.
Burkitt, F. C. 1921-1922. Is Ecclesiastes a translation? J. Theol. Stud. 23. 22-26.
Burrill, Meredith F. and Bonsack, Edwin, Jr. 1962. Use and preparation of specialized glossaries. In Householder and Saporta, eds., Problems in Lexicography (q.v.), pp. 183-199.
Burrows, M. 1951. The Semitic background of the New Testament. BT 2. 67-73.
Bütow, Hans. 1935. Übersetzen—eine edle und schwere Kunst. Zeit. f. Bücherfreunde 39. 23-29.
Cadbury, Henry J. 1946. Revision after revision. Am. Scholar 15. 298-305.
——. 1951. The vocabulary and grammar of New Testament Greek. BT 2. 153-159.
——. 1954. The danger of overtranslation. BT 5. 137-138.
——. 1956. The grandson of Ben Sira. BT 7. 77-81.
Caemmerer, R. R. 1951. A concordance study of the concept 'Word of God.' Concordia Theol. Monthly 22. 170-185.
Caillé, Pierre-François. 1955. Avant-propos. Babel 1. 3-5.
——. 1957. Géographie économique de la traduction. La Parisienne, April, pp. 439-442.
——. 1958. Les traducteurs littéraires à Varsovie. Babel 4. 195-200.
——. 1959. Drapeaux dans le soleil d'été; ou le Congrès de Bad Godesberg. Babel 5. 149-151.
——. 1960. Cinema et traduction. Babel 6. 103-109.
Callot, E. 1949. Langue et culture. Le français moderne 17. 103-121.
Campbell, Caroline. 1955. Bambara people and language. BT 6. 63-68.
Campbell, George. 1789. The Four Gospels. Vol. 1. London: Strahan & Cadell.
Campbell, J. Y. 1948. The New Testament—RSV. J. Theol. Stud. 49. 118-124.
—— and Richardson, Alan. 1956. A study of the words 'authority,' 'might' and 'miracle.' BT 7. 40-47.
Cannon, W. W. 1927. Jerome and Symmachus; Some points in the Vulgate translation of Koheleth. Zeit. f. die Alttestamentliche Wissenschaft 46. 191-199.
Carnap, Rudolf. 1937. The Logical Syntax of Language. London: Kegan Paul, Trench, Trubner & Co.
——. 1947. Meaning and Necessity. Chicago: Univ. Chicago Press.
——. 1950. Logical Foundations of Probability. Chicago: Univ. Chicago Press.
Carpenter, Edmund. 1957. The new languages. Cross Currents 7. 305-315.
Carr, Elizabeth. 1959. Word compounding in American speech. Speech Monographs 26. 1-20.
Carrington, John F. 1954. Lingala and tribal languages in the Belgian Congo. BT 5. 22-27.
Carroll, John B. 1953. The Study of Language; A Survey of Linguistics and Related Disciplines in America. Cambridge: Harvard Univ. Press.
——, ed. 1956. Language, Thought and Reality: Selected Writings of Benjamin Lee Whorf. (Cambridge: Technology Press, Mass. Inst. Technology.) New York: Wiley.
—— and Casagrande, Joseph B. 1958. The functions of language classifications in behavior. In Eleanor E. Maccoby, Theodore M. Newcomb, and Eugene L. Hartley, eds., Readings in Social Psychology, pp. 18-31. 3d ed. New York: Holt.
——. 1959. An operational model for language behavior. Anthropol. Linguistics 1. 37-54.
——. 1960. Language development in children. Encyclopedia of Educational Research. New York: Macmillan.
Carruth, W. H., trans. 1907. Luther on translation. Open Court 21. 465-471.
Cary, Edmond. 1955a. Le droit d'auteur appliqué au traducteur. Babel 1. 69-71.
——. 1955b. Etienne Dolet. Babel 1. 17-20.
——. 1955c. Review of Georges Mounin, Les belles infidèles (Paris: Cahiers du Sud, 1955). Babel 1. 33.

——. 1956a. Mécanismes et traduction. Babel 2. 102-107.
——. 1956b. La traduction dans le monde moderne. Genève: Georg et Cie. (See also review: Olivier, 1956.)
——. 1957a. L'art de traduire. Babel 3. 89-91.
——. 1957b. Review of Theodore H. Savory, The Art of Translation (London: Jonathan Cape, 1957). Babel 3. 89-91.
——. 1957c. Théories sovietiques de la traduction. Babel 3. 179-189.
——. 1957d. Traduction et poésie. Babel 3. 11-32. (See also review: Meynieux, 1957b.)
——. 1958. M. Sankichi Asabuki nous dit. . . Babel 4. 32-33.
——. 1959a. Introduction à la théorie de la traduction. (Review of Andrei Fedorov, Vvedenije v teoriju perevoda. Rev. ed. Moscow: Bibliothèque du Philologue, 1958.) Babel 5. 19-20.
——, ed. 1959b. Notre enquète. Babel 5. 61-106.
——. 1959c. Qualité. Babel 5. 3-5.
——. 1959d. La rencontre internationale des traducteurs littéraires. Babel 5. 151-153.
——. 1960a. De la traduction considérée comme un des beaux-arts. (Reviews of O. Koundzitch, et al., L'art de la traduction, Moscow: Sov. Pisatel, 1959; Reuben A. Brower, ed., On Translation, Cambridge: Harvard Univ. Press, 1959.) Babel 6. 19-24.
——. 1960b. La traduction totale. Babel 6. 110-115.
——. 1962. Pour une théorie de la traduction. Diogène 40. 96-120.
——. 1963. The Word of God into the languages of men. Babel 9. 87-91.
Casagrande, Joseph B. 1954a. Comanche linguistic acculturation; I. IJAL 20. 140-151.
——. 1954b. Comanche linguistic acculturation; II. IJAL 20. 217-237.
——. 1954c. The ends of translation. IJAL 20. 335-340.
——. 1955. Comanche linguistic acculturation; III. IJAL 21. 8-25.
Casares, Julio. 1956. La traducción (deberse y debido a. . .). Babel 2. 5-7.
Cassian, Bishop. 1954. The revision of the Russian translation of the New Testament. BT 5. 27-35.
Cassirer, Ernst. 1933. La langue et la construction du monde des objets. J. Psych. Normale & Pathol. 30. 18-44.
——. 1944. An Essay on Man: An Introduction to a Philosophy of Human Culture. New Haven: Yale Univ. Press.
——. 1946. Language and Myth. New York: Dover Publications.
——. 1953. The Philosophy of Symbolic Forms. Vol. 1, Language. New Haven: Yale Univ. Press. (See also review: Leopold, 1955.)
Cauer, Paul. 1896. Die Kunst des Übersetzens. Berlin: Weidmann.
Cazelles, H. 1958. The Jerusalem Bible. BT 9. 153-155.
Ceccato, Silvio, ed. 1961. Linguistic Analysis and Programming for Mechanical Translation (Mechanical Translation and Thought). Milan: Feltrinelli Editore; New York: Gordon and Breach.
Chafe, Wallace L. 1962. Phonetics, semantics, and language. Language 38. 335-344.
Chalmers, T. W. 1885. Professor Briggs on the Revised Version of the Old Testament. Bibliotheca Sacra 42. 736-765.
Chamberlain, A. F. 1901. Translation: A study in the transference of folk-thought. J. Am. Folk-Lore 14. 165-171.
——. 1910. Some difficulties in Bible translating. Harper's Mag. 121. 726-731.
Chao, Yuen Ren. 1933. The non-uniqueness of phonemic solutions of phonetic systems. Academia Sinica: Bull. Inst. Hist. & Philology 4. 363-397.
——. 1953. Popular Chinese plant words. Language 29. 379-414.
Chapman, George. 1903. The Works of George Chapman. Vol. 3, Homer's Iliad and Odyssey. London: Chatto & Windus.
Chapman, J. J. 1928. Two Greek Plays. Boston: Houghton Mifflin.
Chapman, John. 1922-1923. St. Jerome and the Vulgate New Testament. J. Theol. Stud. 24. 33-51.
Chase, Stuart. 1954. How language shapes our thoughts. Harper's Mag. 208. 76-82.

Chatman, S. 1957. Linguistics, poetics, and interpretation: The phonemic dimension. Quart. J. Speech 43. 248-256.
Chavarria-Aguilar, O. L. and Penzl, Herbert. 1962. Lexicographical problems in Pashto. In Householder and Saporta, eds., Problems in Lexicography (q.v.), pp. 237-247.
Cheek, John L. 1952-1953. Let the translators speak. Religion in Life 22. 438-448.
Cherry, E. Colin; Halle, Morris; and Jakobson, Roman. 1953. Toward the logical description of languages in their phonemic aspect. Language 29. 34-46.
——. 1956. Roman Jakobson's 'Distinctive Features' as the normal co-ordinates of a language. In Halle et al., For Roman Jakobson (q.v.), pp. 60-64.
——. 1957. On Human Communication. (Cambridge: Technology Press, Mass. Inst. Technology.) New York: Wiley. (See also review: Jumpelt, 1957b.)
Chomsky, Noam. 1955a. Logical syntax and semantics: Their linguistic relevance. Language 31. 36-45.
——. 1955b. Semantic considerations in grammar. Mon. Ser. 8, Languages & Linguistics. Washington: Georgetown Univ. Press.
——. 1956a. The Logical Structure of Linguistic Theory. (Mimeographed.) Cambridge: Harvard Univ.
——; Halle, Morris; and Lukoff, Fred. 1956b. On accent and juncture in English. In Halle et al., For Roman Jakobson (q.v.), pp. 65-80.
——. 1957. Syntax and semantics. In his Syntactic Structures, pp. 92-105. 's-Gravenhage: Mouton. (See also review: Lees, 1957.)
——. 1959. Review of B. F. Skinner, Verbal Behavior (New York: Appleton-Century-Crofts, 1957). Language 35. 26-57.
——. 1961a. On the notion 'rule of grammar.' Proc. 12th Symp. Appl. Mathematics, ed. by Jakobson (q.v.), pp. 6-24.
——. 1961b. Some methodological remarks on generative grammar. Word 17. 219-239.
——. 1962. The logical basis of linguistic theory. PPICL.
Chowdhury, D. A. 1953. Should we use the terms ''Isa' and 'Beta'? BT 4. 26-27.
Christensen, Niels Egmont. 1961. On the Nature of Meanings: A Philosophical Analysis. Copenhagen: Munksgaard.
Church, J. 1961. Language and the Discovery of Reality. New York: Random House.
Cicero. 46 B.C. Libellus de optimo genere oratorum IV: 14.
Citroen, I. J. 1955. Training technical translators. Babel 1. 61-64.
——. 1959. The translation of texts dealing with applied science. Babel 5. 30-33.
Clarke, W. K. L. 1945. A note on Basic English. Theology 48. 39-41.
——. 1948. A new translation of the Bible. Theology 51. 303-306.
Cleave, J. P. and Zacharov, B. 1955. Language translation by electronics. Wireless World 61. 433-435.
Climenson, N. D.; Hardwick, N. H.; and Jacobson, S. N. 1961. Automatic syntax analysis in machine indexing and abstracting. Am. Documentation 12. 178-183.
Coates, William Ames. 1962. Meaning in morphemes and compound lexical units. PPICL.
Cocking, J. M. 1949. Mr. Day Lewis and the translation of Valéry. 19th Century 145. 311-318.
Cohen, L. Jonathan. 1962. The Diversity of Meaning. London: Methuen.
Colby, Benjamin N. 1958. Behavioral redundancy. Behavioral Science 3. 317-322.
Coleman, Edward. 1961. Responses to transformations: remembering and understanding. Paper Ann. Meeting Linguistic Soc. America, Chicago.
Collison, Robert. 1962. The continuing barrier: translations as a factor of East-West communication. UNESCO Bulletin for Libraries 16. 296-300.
Collitz, Hermann. 1926. World languages. Language 2. 1-13.
Combet, G. 1956. Sur la nomenclature des techniques. Le Linguiste (Brussels) 4. 11-14; 5. 7-11.
Conant, Francis P. 1961. Jarawa kin systems of reference and address: A componential system. Anthropol. Linguistics 3. 19-33.
Conington, John. 1861. The English translators of Virgil. Quart. Rev. 110. 73-114.

Conklin, Harold C. 1955. Hanunóo color categories. Southwestern J. Anthropology 11. 339-344.
——. 1962. Lexicographical treatment of folk taxonomies. In Householder and Saporta, eds., Problems in Lexicography (q.v.), pp. 119-141.
Connelly, T. 1946. The Haydock Bible. Scripture 1. 81-85.
Cook, C. L. 1955. Languages in the Southern Provinces of the Sudan. BT 6. 122-127.
Cooper, William A. 1928. Translating Goethe's poems. J. English-Germanic Philology 27. 470-485.
Cordasco, Francesco. 1952. Smollett and the translation of the Don Quixote. Mod. Lang. Quart. 13. 23-36.
Cornford, F. M., ed. 1941. The Republic of Plato. OUP.
Cortada, Judith. 1953. The man with three heads. Am. Mercury 77. 129-132.
Covell, Ralph R. 1956a. Questions and answers. BT 7. 162-163.
——. 1956b. Sediq syntax as related to problems of Bible translation. BT 7. 171-185.
Cowan, Florence H. 1947. Linguistic and ethnological aspects of Mazateco kinship. Southwestern J. Anthropology 3. 247-256.
——. 1950. Syntax problems in the Mazateco translation. BT 1. 135-140.
Cowan, Marion M. 1957. Hymn writing—a phase of translation work. BT 8. 20-22.
——. 1960. The translation of questions into Huixteco. BT 11. 123-125.
Cowl, R. P. 1914. The Theory of Poetry in England. London: Macmillan.
Cowley, Abraham. 1656. Preface to "Pindarique Odes." Poems. London: Humphrey Moseley.
Cowper, William. 1791. Preface to Iliad. London. (New York: Putnam, 1850.)
Cox, Mr. & Mrs. Newberry. 1950. Translation problems in Conob. BT 1. 91-96.
Crabtree, A. R. 1946. Translating the Bible into Portuguese. Rev. & Expositor 43. 40-49.
Craig, C. T. 1951. The King James and the American Standard Versions of the New Testament. BT 2. 43-48.
Croce, Benedetto. 1929. Aesthetic—as Science of Expression and General Linguistic. (Trans. by D. Ainslie.) London: Macmillan.
Cromer, E. B. 1913. Translation and paraphrase. Edinburgh Rev. 218. 102-114.
Culshaw, Wesley. 1959. Bible translation in Assam. BT 10. 176-181.
——. 1962. Bible translation in Hindi, Urdu and Hindustani. BT 13. 65-71.
Curme, George O. 1911. Is the Gothic Bible Gothic? J. English-Germanic Philology 10. 151-190, 335-377.
Current Research and Development in Scientific Documentation. Washington: National Science Foundation. Quarterly from 1957.
Curry, Haskell B. 1961. Some logical aspects of grammatical structure. Proc. 12th Symp. Appl. Mathematics, ed. by Jakobson (q.v.), pp. 56-68.
Daggett, Mabel C. 1926-1927. Translation by the A-B-C Method. Mod. Lang. J. 11. 513-516.
Daiches, David. 1955. Translating the Bible. Encounter 5. 82-86.
Dammann, Ernst. 1954. The translation of Biblical and Christian personal names into Swahili. BT 5. 80-84.
Davis, Marjorie. 1952. Translating nouns into the Cuicateco language. BT 3. 34-38.
——. 1954. Cuicateco to English. IJAL 20. 302-312.
Davis, Watson. 1945. Translated books for and from Latin America. PW 147. 1550-1551.
Davis, W. H. 1921. The place of the Greek tenses in the province of New Testament interpretation. Rev. & Expositor 18. 375-386.
Deak, Etienne. 1960. Y a-t-il une langue américaine? Babel 6. 68-71.
Deans, W. A. 1953. Congo-Swahili, a lingua franca of Central Africa. BT 4. 77-82.
de Groot, A. W. 1948. Structural linguistics and word classes. Lingua 1. 427-500.
——. 1957. Phonetics in its relations to aesthetics. In Manual of Phonetics, ed. by L. Kaiser, pp. 385-400. Amsterdam: North-Holland.
——. 1962. The description of a poem. PPICL.
——. 1964. (In press.) An Introduction to Structural Linguistics. (Chapter on Poetics.)
De Juan, Marcela. 1955. Dignificación del Arte de Traducir. Babel 1. 10-12.

de Laguna, G. A. 1927. Speech, Its Function and Development. New Haven: Yale Univ. Press.
Delavenay, Émile. 1959. La Machine à traduire. Collection, Que sais-je? Vol. 834. Paris: Presses Universitaires de France.
——. 1960a. An Introduction to Machine Translation. New York: Praeger.
——. 1960b. Machine translation of languages: Research and organizational problems. Impact (UNESCO) 10. 26-44.
—— and Delavenay, K. 1960c. Bibliography of Mechanical Translation (Janua Linguarum No. 11). 's-Gravenhage: Mouton.
——. 1962. Machines à traduire, mécanismes et contenu de la pensée. Revue Philosophique de la France et de l'Etranger 2. 219-238.
Dempster, W. 1955. Santali New Testament revision. BT 6. 69-72.
Denham, John. 1709. To Sir Richard Fanshawe upon his translation of 'Il Pastor Fido.' In his Poems and Translations, with 'The Sophy,' a Tragedy. London: Jacob Tonson.
Denio, F. B. 1920. Bible authors and the imagination. Bibliotheca Sacra 77. 83-101.
Dent, Edward J. 1921. Song translations. Nation 29. 482-484.
Dentan, R. C. 1956. One man's translation. NYT, April 29, Sec. 7, p. 10.
Deny, Jean. 1956. À propos des traductions en Turc Osmanli des textes religieux chrétiens. Die Welt des Islams 4. 30-39.
de Savignac, J. 1958. Observations on the version of the Bible called 'The Jerusalem Bible.' BT 9. 158-161.
De Vries, Louis. 1956. Making a technical dictionary. Babel 2. 159-162.
d'Haucourt, Geneviève. 1958. Interpretation and the interpreter. Rev. General Semantics 15. 96-102.
Diamond, Stanley. 1960. Anaguta cosmography: the linguistic and behavioral implications. Anthropol. Linguistics 2. 31-38.
Dickinson, G. Lowes. 1929. On translation. Nation (London) 46. 282-283.
Diderichsen, P. 1957. The importance of distribution versus other criteria in linguistic analysis. Proc. 8th Internat. Cong. Linguists, Oslo. 156-182.
Dijk, J. 1955. A new apparatus of references for the Bible in The Netherlands. BT 6. 169-173.
Dillon, Wentworth, Earl of Roscommon. 1684. An Essay on Translated Verse. (Reprinted in J. E. Spingarn, ed., Critical Essays of the Seventeenth Century. OUP, 1908.)
Dinjeart, J. 1958. La demande de traductions s'accroît... Babel 4. 154-157.
Doble, Marion L. 1950. Transliteration in Kapauku. BT 1. 133-135.
——. 1956. A milestone in New Guinea. BT 7. 83-85.
Dodd, C. H. 1960. The translation of the Bible: Some questions of principle. BT 11. 4-9.
——. 1962. Some problems of New Testament translation. BT 13. 145-157.
Doke, C. M. 1954. The concept of hope among the Bantu. BT 5. 9-19.
——. 1956. The points of the compass in Bantu languages. BT 7. 104-113.
——. 1958. Some difficulties in Bible translation into a Bantu language. BT 9. 57-62.
Dolet, Etienne. 1540. La manière de bien traduire d'une langue en autre. (See Cary, 1955b.)
Dollard, J. and Miller, N. E. 1950. Personality and Psychotherapy; An Analysis in Terms of Learning, Thinking, and Culture. New York: McGraw-Hill.
Donald, Trevor. 1963. The semantic field of "folly" in Proverbs, Job, Psalms, and Ecclesiastes. Vetus Testamentum 13. 285-292.
Doob, Leonard W. 1961. Communication in Africa: A Search for Boundaries. New Haven: Yale Univ. Press.
Dosker, H. E. 1912. The Dutch 'Staten-Bybel' of 1637. Princeton Theol. Rev. 10. 86-109.
Dovring, Karin. 1959. Road of Propaganda: The Semantics of Biased Communication. New York: Philosophical Library.
Draper, John W. 1921. The theory of translation in the 18th century. Neophilologus 6. 241-254.

Drinker, Henry S. 1950. On translating vocal texts. Musical Quart. 36. 225-240.
Dryden, John. 1680. Preface to Ovid's Epistles. London: Jacob Tonson.
Dubois, Jean. 1960. Les notions d'unité sémantique complexe et de neutralization dans le lexique. Cahiers de Lexicologie 2. 62-66.
——— and Guilbert, Louis. 1961. La notion de degré dans le système morphologique du français moderne. J. Psych. Normale & Pathol. 58. 57-64.
Duikjer, H. C. J. 1962. Spreeksituatie en taalstructuur. Gawein 10. 191-203.
Dunham, B. 1957. The formalization of scientific languages. Pt. 1: The work of Woodger and Hull. IBM J. Research & Development 1. 341-347.
Dunlop, D. M. 1960. The work of translation at Toledo. Babel 6. 55-59.
Eakin, F. 1924. New translations of the New Testament. J. Religion 4. 133-146.
Eastman, Max. 1936. Pushkin and his English translators. New Repub. 89. 187-188.
Edgerton, Faye. 1962. Some translation problems in Navajo. BT 13. 25-33.
Edmundson, H. P. 1959. Linguistic analysis in machine-translation research. In Modern Trends in Documentation, pp. 31-37. (Proc. Symp. held at Univ. Southern Calif., April, 1958.) Pergamon Press.
———, ed. 1961. Proc. Nat. Symp. on Machine Translation. (Referred to as PNSMT in this bibliography.) Englewood Cliffs, N. J.: Prentice-Hall.
Edwards, C. E. 1938. Inspired translations. Evangelical Quart. 10. 87-91.
Edwards, H. E. 1928. The tongues at Pentecost: A suggestion. Theology 16. 248-252.
Edwards, Oliver. 1957a. Constance Garnett. LT, June 6, p. 13.
———. 1957b. Cynara. LT, July 11, p. 13.
Ege, Niels. 1949. Le signe linguistique est arbitraire. Travaux du cercle linguistique de Copenhague. 5. 11-29.
Eisenstadt, S. N. 1949. The perception of time and space in a situation of culture-contact. J. Royal Anthropol. Inst. 79. 63-68.
Elbert, Samuel H. 1957. Possessives in Polynesia. BT 8. 23-27.
Eliot, T. S. 1920. Euripides and Professor Murray. In his The Sacred Wood. London: Methuen.
———. 1949. Correspondence: New translation of the Bible. Theology 52. 336-338.
Elkin, A. P. 1941. Native languages and the field worker in Australia. Am. Anthropologist 43. 89-94.
Ellegård, Alvar. 1960. Estimating vocabulary size. Word 16. 219-244.
Emden, Cecil S. 1954. St. Mark's use of the imperfect tense. BT 5. 121-125.
Emeneau, Murray B. 1941. Language and social forms: A study of Toda kinship terms and dual descent. In Spier, Hallowell, and Newman, eds., Language, Culture, and Personality (q.v.), pp. 158-179.
———. 1950. Language and non-linguistic patterns. Language 26. 199-209.
Emmet, Dorothy M. 1943. Communication. Theology 46. 53-58.
English, T. R. 1915. The language of the New Testament. Union Seminary Mag. 26. 209-219.
Enslin, M. S. 1946. Review of the RSV New Testament. Congregational Quart. 23. 271-273.
Entwhistle, William J. 1953. Aspects of Language. London: Faber & Faber.
Erasmus, C. J. 1952. Changing folk beliefs and the relativity of empirical knowledge. Southwestern J. Anthropology 8. 411-428.
Ercilla y Zúñiga, Alonso de. 1945. 'La Araucana,' The Epic of Chile. Trans. into English verse by Walter Owen. Buenos Aires: Walter Owen.
Ervin, Susan and Bower, R. T. 1952-1953. Translation problems in international surveys. Public Opinion Quart. 16. 595-604.
——— and Osgood, Charles E. 1954. Second language learning and bilingualism. In Osgood and Sebeok, eds., Psycholinguistics (q.v.), pp. 139-146.
———. 1956. Translation procedures. In John B. Carroll and Susan Ervin, eds., Field Manual: Southwest Project in Comparative Psycholinguistics. Unpublished MS. Cambridge: Harvard Univ.
———. 1961. Semantic shift in bilingualism. Am. J. Psych. 74. 233-241.
Estrich, Robert M. and Sperber, Hans. 1952. Three Keys to Language. New York: Rinehart.
Evans, Helen M. 1954. Experiences in translating the New Testament in Kui. BT 5. 40-46.

Evans, R. J. Monda. 1957. Antiokh Kantemir and his German translators. Slavonic & East European Rev. 36. 150-158.
Everts, W. W. 1925. Paul's contribution to the vocabulary of the New Testament. Rev. & Expositor 22. 193-201.
Ewell, J. L. 1887. Wyclif's Bible honored by the revision. Bibliotheca Sacra 44. 36-45.
Fang, Achilles. 1953. Some reflections on the difficulty of translation. In Wright, ed., Studies in Chinese Thought (q.v.), pp. 263-285. (Reprinted in Reuben A. Brower, ed., On Translation [q.v.], pp. 111-133.)
Fano, Robert M. 1961. Transmission of Information. New York: Wiley.
Fast, P. W. 1952. Problems of basic vocabulary in a culturally restricted area. BT 3. 79-80.
Faulk, Ramon D. 1961. A general-purpose language translation program for the IBM 650 computer. PNSMT, pp. 409-421.
Fearing, Franklin. 1954. An examination of the conceptions of Benjamin Whorf in the light of theories of perception and cognition. In Hoijer, Language in Culture (q.v.), pp. 47-81.
Fergin, A. F. 1953. A critical review of the RSV of the New Testament. Concordia Theol. Monthly 24. 208-213.
Ferguson, Charles A. 1962. Basic grammatical categories of Bengali. PPICL.
Fife, Austin E. 1943. A classroom exercise in poetic translation. Mod. Lang. J. 27. 186-189.
Finney, Robert V. 1940-1941. A case for translation. Mod. Lang. J. 25. 883-886.
Firth, John Rupert. 1935. The technique of semantics. Transactions Philolog. Soc., pp. 36-72.
——. 1937. The Tongues of Men. London: Watts.
——. 1951a. General linguistics and descriptive grammar. Transactions Philolog. Soc., pp. 69-87.
——. 1951b. Modes of meaning. In Essays and Studies, Vol. 4, pp. 118-149. London: English Association.
——. 1956. Linguistic analysis and translation. In Halle et al., For Roman Jakobson (q.v.), pp. 133-139.
——. 1957a. Ethnographic analysis and language with reference to Malinowski's views. In Raymond Firth, ed., Man and Culture: An Evaluation of the Work of Bronislaw Malinowski, pp. 93-118. London: Routledge & Paul.
——. 1957b. Papers in Linguistics. OUP.
Fischbach, Henry. 1953. Suggestions for translating German, French, and Italian chemical literature. J. Chem. Ed. 30. 388-393.
——. 1958. Translating German, French and Italian chemical literature. J. des Traducteurs 3. 78-86.
Fischel, W. J. 1952. The Bible in Persian translation. Harvard Theol. Rev. 45. 3-45.
Fishman, Joshua A. 1960. A systematization of the Whorfian Hypothesis. Behavioral Science 5. 323-339.
Fitts, Dudley. 1959. The poetic nuance. In Brower, ed., On Translation (q.v.), pp. 32-47.
Fitzgerald, Edward. 1859. Works. New York: Houghton Mifflin.
——. 1878. Some New Letters of Edward Fitzgerald. London. (Am. ed., Letters. New York: Putnam, 1924.)
——. 1889. Letters and Literary Remains. Vol. I. London: Macmillan. (Vol. II, 1903.)
Fitzmaurice-Kelly, James. c. 1910. Translation. In Encyclopaedia Britannica, 11th ed.
Flavell, John H. 1961a. Meaning and meaning similarity: I. A theoretical reassessment. J. Gen. Psych. 64. 307-319.
——. 1961b. Meaning and meaning similarity: II. The semantic differential and co-occurrence as predictors of judged similarity in meaning. J. Gen. Psych. 64. 321-335.
—— and Johnson, B. Ann. 1961c. Meaning and meaning similarity: III. Latency and number of similarities as predictors of judged similarity in meaning. J. Gen. Psych. 64. 337-348.

Flourney, Parke P. 1925. Doctor Moffatt's new translation of the Bible. Bibliotheca Sacra 82. 462-471.
——. 1926. The Old Testament—a new translation by James Moffatt. Bibliotheca Sacra 83. 229-232.
Foerster, W. 1951. Neuere Übersetzungen des Neuen Testamentes. Deutsches Pfarrerblatt 51. 410-414.
Foley, J. P. 1959. The expression of certainty. Am. J. Psych. 72. 614-615.
Fónagy, Iván. 1961. Communication in poetry. Word 17. 194-218.
Ford, William H. 1957. Some reflections on the revision of the New Testament in Lokele. BT 8. 203-206.
Forster, Leonard, ed. 1958. Aspects of Translation: Studies in Communication 2. (See also his Introduction, pp. 1-28.) London: Secker & Warburg.
Foust, William D. 1961. Automatic English inflection. PNSMT, pp. 229-233.
Fox, David G. 1959. How intelligible is a literal translation? BT 10. 174-176.
Fox-Strangways, A. H. 1921. Song-translation. Music & Letters 2. 211-224.
Frake, Charles O. 1961. The diagnosis of disease among the Subanen of Mindanao. Am. Anthropologist 63. 113-132.
Frayn, Joan M. 1951. Early English versions of the Scriptures. Congregational Quart. 29. 153-158.
Frei, Henri. 1948. Note sur l'analyse des syntagmes. Word 4. 65-70.
——. 1956. Caractérisation, indication, spécification. In Halle et al., For Roman Jakobson (q.v.), pp. 161-168.
Frere, J. H. 1820. Review of Mitchell's Aristophanes. Quart. Rev. 46. 474-505.
Frerk, Charles W. 1958. . . . Another important milestone. Babel 4. 139-150.
——. 1959. What linguists—and others—ought to know. Review of Alexander Lane et al., Die Fremdsprachenberufe (Munich: Hueber). Babel 5. 182.
——. 1960. The organization of translation services for international congresses. Babel 6. 60-67.
Freudenthal, Hans W. L. 1942. The problem of translating. Mod. Lang. J. 26. 62-65.
Fries, Charles Carpenter. 1940. American English Grammar. New York: Appleton-Century.
——. 1945. Teaching and Learning English as a Foreign Language. Ann Arbor: Univ. Michigan Press.
——. 1952. The Structure of English; An Introduction to the Construction of English Sentences. New York: Harcourt, Brace.
——. 1954. Meaning and linguistic analysis. Language 30. 57-68.
Fromm, Erich. 1951. The Forgotten Language. New York: Grove Press.
Frost, William. 1955. Dryden and the Art of Translation. New Haven: Yale Univ. Press.
Fuerst, Norbert. 1942. Rilke's translation of the Sonnets of Elizabeth Barrett Browning, of Louise Labé, and of Michelangelo. Stud. in Philology 39. 130-142.
Fulke, William. 1843. A Defense of the Sincere and True Translation of the Holy Scripture into the English Tongue, against the Cavils of Gregory Martin. Cambridge Univ. Press. (Reprint of original 1583 ed.)
Fuller, R. H. 1944. The Word of God. Theology 47. 267-271.
Funke, Erich. 1956. Translingua Script: A code of interlinguistic communication. Mod. Lang. J. 40. 22-24.
Furfey, Paul H. 1944. The semantic and grammatical principles in linguistic analysis. Stud. in Linguistics 2. 56-66.
Furley, D. J. 1958. Translation from Greek philosophy. In Forster, ed., Aspects of Translation (q.v.), pp. 52-64.
Furness, N. A. 1956. Georg Büchner's translations of Victor Hugo. Mod. Lang. Rev. 51. 49-54.
Furst, Norbert. 1942. Rilke's translations of English, French, and Italian sonnets. Stud. in Philology 39. 130-142.
Gabris, Karel. 1960. The translation of the Bible into Slovak. BT 11. 145-152.
Galantière, Lewis. 1951. On translators and translating. Am. Scholar 20. 435-445.
Gammon, E. R. 1962. A statistical study of English syntax. PPICL.
Gard, D. H. 1955. The concept of Job's character according to the Greek translator of the Hebrew text. J. Biblical Lit. 72. 182-186.

Gardiner, F. 1881. The New Testament revision. Bibliotheca Sacra 38. 553-578.
Gardner, A. L. 1950. Technical translating dictionaries. J. Documentation 6. 25-31.
Garvin, Paul L. 1954. Delimitation of syntactic units. Language 30. 345-348.
——, ed. and trans. 1955. A Prague School Reader on Esthetics, Literary Structure and Style. Washington: Washington Linguistic Club.
——. 1956. Some linguistic problems in machine translation. In Halle et al., For Roman Jakobson (q.v.), pp. 180-186.
——. 1957. Machine translation. In Proc. 8th Internat. Cong. Linguists, Oslo.
——. 1958. A descriptive technique for the treatment of meaning. Language 34. 1-32.
——. 1961a. Model to procedure. PNSMT, pp. 367-370.
——. 1961b. Syntactic retrieval. PNSMT, pp. 286-292.
——. 1962a. Computer participation in linguistic research. Language 38. 385-389.
——. 1962b. The impact of language data processing on linguistic analysis. PPICL.
——. 1962c. Research in semantic structure. Presented 37th Ann. Meeting Linguistic Soc. America, New York.
——. 1963. An appraisal of linguistics in Czechoslovakia. In Current Trends in Soviet and East European Linguistics, ed. by Thomas A. Sebeok. The Hague: Mouton.
Gathercole, Patricia M. 1954. Laurent de Premierfait: The translator of Boccaccio's De Casibus Virorum Illustrium. French Rev. 27. 245-252.
——. 1956. Two Old French translations of Boccaccio's De Casibus Virorum Illustrium. Mod. Lang. Quart. 17. 304-309.
Gehman, H. S. 1930. The Armenian version of the Book of Daniel and its affinities. Zeit. f. die Alttestamentliche Wissenschaft 48. 82-99.
——. 1949. The theological approach of the Greek translator of Job 1-15. J. Biblical Lit. 68. 231-240.
——. 1950. Exegetical methods employed by the Greek translators of 1 Samuel. J. Am. Oriental Stud. 70. 292-296.
Gelb, Ignace J. 1952. A Study of Writing; The Foundations of Grammatology. Chicago: Univ. Chicago Press.
Gen, Lewis. 1955. Legge's translation of Mencius. Eastern World 9. 36-37.
George, F. H. 1959. Automation, Cybernetics and Society. New York: Philosophical Library.
Gerr, Stanley. 1942. Language and science. Philosophy of Science 9. 146-161.
Gess, Ernst. 1957. Conclusion of the revision of the Luther New Testament. BT 8.155-160.
Gilman, E. W. 1859. Early editions of the Authorized Version of the Bible. Bibliotheca Sacra 16. 56-81.
Gingrich, F. Wilbur. 1958. The most interesting words in the world. BT 9. 161-163.
——. 1959. Leads from a lexicon. BT 10. 35-36.
Gipper, Helmut. 1956a. Die Kluft zwischen muttersprachlichem und physikalischem Weltbild. Physikalische Blatter 97ff., 284-287.
——. 1956b. Muttersprachliches und wissenschaftliches Weltbild. Sprachforum 2. 1-10.
——, ed. 1962. Sprache, Schlüssel zur Welt (Shetter). Language 38. 318-324.
Giuliano, Vincent. 1961. The logic of automatic formula synthesis. PNSMT, pp. 462-471.
Glanzer, Murray. 1962. Toward a psychology of language structure. J. Speech & Hearing Research 5. 303-314.
Gleason, Henry Allan, Jr. 1955. Workbook in Descriptive Linguistics. New York: Holt.
——. 1961. An Introduction to Descriptive Linguistics. (2d ed., rev.) New York: Holt, Rinehart and Winston.
——. 1962. The relation of lexicon and grammar. In Householder and Saporta, eds., Problems in Lexicography (q.v.), pp. 85-102.
Glémet, R. 1958. Conference interpreting. In Forster, ed., Aspects of Translation (q.v.), pp. 105-122.
Glenn, Edmund S. 1954. Semantic difficulties in international communication. ETC.: A Review of General Semantics 11. 163-180.

———. 1955. Languages and Patterns of Thought. (Mimeographed.) Washington: Georgetown Univ.

———. 1958. Interpretation and intercultural communication. ETC.: A Review of General Semantics 15. 87-95.

Glinz, Hans. 1962. Worttheorie auf strukturalistischer und inhaltsbezogener Grundlage. PPICL.

Gode, Aiexander. 1955. Interlingua in chemical writing. J. Chem. Educ. 32. 132-136.

Goethe, J. W. V. 1827. Letter to Carlyle, 20 July. Goethe-Briefe. Berlin: D. Eisner, 1902-1905.

Goldstein, Kurt. 1948. Language and Language Disturbances. New York: Grune & Stratton.

Goodenough, Ward H. 1951. Property, Kin, and Community on Truk. New Haven: Yale Univ. Press.

———. 1956. Componential analysis and the study of meaning. Language 32. 195-216.

Goodman, Nelson. 1961. About. Mind 70 (n.s.). 1-24.

Goodman, Ralph M. 1960. The Degrees of Grammaticalness. Unpublished material amplifying paper presented at Linguistic Soc. America meeting, Austin, Texas.

Goodspeed, Edgar J., ed. 1935. 'The Translators to the Reader' in Preface to the King James Version 1611. Chicago: Univ. Chicago Press.

———. 1945. Problems of New Testament Translation. Chicago: Univ. Chicago Press.

———. 1948. New light on the New Testament. Rev. & Expositor 45. 155-168.

———. 1952. Problems of New Testament translation. BT 3. 68-71.

Gordis, R. 1938. Some effects of primitive thought on language. Am. J. Semitic Languages & Lit. 55.270-284.

Gordon, Cyrus H. 1955. Language as a means to an end. Antiquity 29. 147-149.

Göring, Fritz. 1958. Review of Paulo Ronai, Escola de Tradutores. (2d ed.; Rio de Janeiro: Livraria São José, 1956.) Babel 4. 212.

Gougenheim, Georges. 1960. Structure grammaticale et traduction automatique. La Traduction Automatique 1. 3-10.

Gould, R. 1956. Multiple Correspondence in Automatic Translation. Progress Rept. No. AF-44, Design and operation of digital calculating machinery. Cambridge: Harvard Computation Laboratory.

Graff, W. L. 1932. Language and Languages: An Introduction to Linguistics. New York: Appleton.

Grainger, Jas. M. 1907. Studies in the syntax of the King James Version. Stud. in Philology 2. 5-60.

Grainger, W., et al. 1959. The Institute of Linguists. Babel 5. 225-228.

Gramberg, K. P. C. A. 1960. 'Leprosy' and the Bible. BT 11. 10-23.

de Grand'combe, Félix. 1949. Reflexions sur la traduction. French Stud. 3. 345-350.

———. 1957. Les diverses erreurs de traduction. J. des Traducteurs 2. 162-169.

Grant, Frederick C. 1938. Why change the Bible? Religion in Life 7. 510-524.

———. 1950. Notes on translating the New Testament. BT 1. 145-149.

———. 1951. The Greek text of the New Testament. BT 2. 117-121.

———. 1961. Translating the Bible. Greenwich, Conn.: Seabury Press.

Gray, G. B. 1910-1911. The Greek version of Isaiah: Is it the work of a single translator? J. Theol. Stud. 12. 286-293.

Gray, Louis H. 1939. Foundations of Language. New York: Macmillan. (See also review: Zellig S. Harris, 1940.)

Gray, M. M. 1934. The prose of Wyclif's Bible. London Quart. & Holborn Rev. 159. 354-362.

Grayston, Kenneth. 1953. A study of the word 'sin.' BT 4. 138-140, 149-152.

———. 1958. Review of G. D. Kilpatrick, ed., A New Edition of the Nestle Greek New Testament. BT 9. 185-189.

Green, Julian. 1942. Translation and the 'Fields of Scripture.' Am. Scholar 11. 110-121.

Greenberg, Joseph H. 1948. Linguistics and ethnology. Southwestern J. Anthropology 4. 140-147.

Greenberg, Joseph H. (cont.). 1954a. Concerning inferences from linguistic to non-linguistic data. In Hoijer, ed., Language in Culture (q.v.), pp. 3-19.
——. 1954b. Language in culture. Am. Anthropologist, Vol. 56, Memoir 79.
——; Osgood, C. E.; and Saporta, S. 1954c. Language change. In Osgood and Sebeok, eds., Psycholinguistics (q.v.).
——. 1957a. Essays in Linguistics. Chicago: Univ. Chicago Press.
——. 1957b. The nature and uses of linguistic typologies. IJAL 23. 68-77.
——. 1962. Some universals of word order. PPICL.
Greenlee, J. Harold. 1950a. The genitive case in the New Testament. BT 1. 68-70.
——. 1950b. The Greek definite article. BT 1. 162-165.
——. 1950c. Kurios 'Lord.' BT 1. 106-108.
——. 1951a. *Psuchê* in the New Testament. BT 2. 73-75.
——. 1951b. Word suffixes in the Greek New Testament. BT 2. 159-161.
——. 1952a. The preposition *Eis* in the New Testament. BT 3. 12-14.
——. 1952b. Verbs in the New Testament. BT 3. 71-75.
——. 1954. New Testament participles. BT 5. 98-101.
——. 1955a. *Hina* clauses and related expressions. BT 6. 12-16.
——. 1955b. 'My Father.' BT 6. 119-121.
Gregg, J. R. 1954. The Language of Taxonomy: An Application of Symbolic Logic to the Study of Classificatory Systems. New York: Columbia Univ. Press.
Gregory, Horace. 1944. On the translation of the classics into English poetry. Poetry 64. 30-35.
Grether, Herbert. 1957. The revision of the Thai Bible. BT 8. 9-19.
Griffin, Stuart. 1958. Snail pace language reform. Eastern World 12. 24-25.
Griffiths, J. Gwyn. 1953. 'Within you' (Luke XVII. 21). BT 4. 7-8.
Grimes, Joseph E. 1955. Style in Huichol structure. Language 31. 31-35.
——. 1957a. An Indian's interpretation of St. Luke in simple Spanish. BT 8. 131-135.
——. 1957b. Translation procedure in Huichol. BT 8. 175-179.
——. 1961. Workshop in translation theory. BT 12. 56-60.
——. 1962a. Measures of linguistic divergence. PPICL.
—— and Barbara F. 1962b. Semantic distinctions in Huichol (Ato-Aztecan) kinship. Am. Anthropologist 64. 104-114.
——. 1963. Translating incommensurables. Babel 9. 91-93.
Grosheide, F. W. 1950. The new Dutch translation of the Bible. BT 1. 6-9.
——. 1955. The translation of quotations from the Old Testament in the New. BT 6. 16-20.
Gross, Feliks. 1951. Language and value changes among the Arapaho. IJAL 17. 10-17.
Grossouw, W. 1961. A new Catholic version in Dutch. BT 12. 14-20.
Groves, C. P. 1955. Social anthropology in missionary service. BT 6. 136-140.
Grubb, G. G. 1943. Myles Coverdale: poet and song writer. Rev. & Expositor 40. 338-353.
Gruber, L. F. 1923. Luther's New Testament—a quadricentennial study. Bibliotheca Sacra 80. 97-114.
Gudschinsky, Sarah C. 1957. Handbook of Literacy. Glendale, Calif.: Summer Inst. Linguistics.
——. 1959a. Discourse analysis of a Mazatec text. IJAL 25. 139-146.
——. 1959b. Mazatec kernel constructions and transformations. IJAL 25. 81-89.
Guérard, Albert. 1947. Ten levels of language. Am. Scholar 16. 148-158.
Guillebaud, Rosemary. 1950. Problems of related dialects; A study from experience in the Ruanda and Rundi languages. BT 1. 15-21.
Guillemir, A. 1924. Sur quelques difficultés de la traduction. Revue Études Latines 2. 182-188.
Guiraud, P. 1955. La semantique. Paris: Presses universitaires de France.
Gummere, E. B. 1886. The translations of Beowulf, and the relations of ancient and modern English verse. Am. J. Philology 7. 46-78.
Gumperz, John J. 1961. Speech variation and the study of Indian civilization. Am. Anthropologist 63. 976-988.

——. 1962. Hindi-Punjabi code switching in Delhi: a study in sociolinguistics. PPICL.
Guthrie, Malcolm. 1954. The Bible and current theories about language. In Proc. Victoria Inst., pp. 50-60. Croydon, Surrey: Victoria Inst.
Haas, Mary R. 1944. Men's and women's speech in Koasati. Language 20. 142-149.
——. 1948. Classificatory verbs in Muskogee. IJAL 14. 244-246.
——. 1951. Interlingual word taboo. Am. Anthropologist 53. 338-344.
——. 1962. What belongs in the bilingual dictionary? In Householder and Saporta, eds., Problems in Lexicography (q.v.), pp. 45-50.
Haas, Rudolf. 1958. Übersetzungsprobleme im Feld deutsch-englischer Literaturbegegnung. Die Neueren Sprachen 7. 366-378.
Haas, William. 1962. Semantic value. PPICL.
Hackett, Marion S. 1950. Three major problems in Taungthu translation. BT 1. 150-153.
Haering, Theodor. 1947-1948. Das Problem der naturwissenschaftlichen und geisteswissenschaftlichen Begriffsbildung und die Erkennbarkeit der Gegenstände. Zeit. f. Philosophische Forschung 2. 537-579.
Haggard, J. V. and McLean, M. D. 1941. Handbook for Translators of Spanish Historical Documents. Oklahoma City: Semco Color Press.
Hall, Edward T. and Trager, George L. 1953. The Analysis of Culture. Washington: U.S. Dept. State, Foreign Service Inst.
——. 1959. The Silent Language. Garden City, N.Y.: Doubleday.
Hall, I. H. 1885. The American Arabic Bible. J. Am. Oriental Soc. 11. 276-286.
Hall, John F. 1952. Mossi proverbs and their use in translating and illustrating Gospel messages. BT 3.27-29.
Hall, Robert A., Jr. 1950. Leave Your Language Alone! Ithaca, N.Y.: Linguistica.
Halle, Morris. 1961. On the role of simplicity in linguistic description. Proc. 12th Symp. Appl. Mathematics, ed. by Jakobson (q.v.), pp. 89-94.
Halliday, M. A. K. 1956. The linguistic basis of a mechanical thesaurus. Mech. Translation 3. 81-88.
——. 1957. Some aspects of systematic description and comparison in grammatical analysis. Oxford: Stud. in Linguistic Analysis, pp. 54-67.
——. 1962. The linguistic study of literary texts. PPICL.
Hallowell, A. I. 1955. Culture and Experience. Philadelphia: Univ. Pennsylvania Press.
Hamilton, Edith. 1937. Introduction: On Translating. In Three Greek Plays. New York: Norton.
Hamp, Eric P. 1958. A Glossary of American Technical Linguistic Usage, 1925-1950. Utrecht: Spectrum. (See also review: Joos, 1958.)
Hanks, L. M., Jr. 1954. A psychological exploration in the Blackfoot language. IJAL 20. 195-205.
Hare, R. M. 1952. The Language of Morals. OUP.
Harkin, Duncan. 1957. The history of word counts. Babel 3. 113-118.
Harper, Kenneth. 1961. Soviet research in machine translation. PNSMT, pp. 2-12.
Harrah, David. 1960. The adequacy of language. Inquiry 3. 73-88.
Harries, Lyndon. 1954. Two important Swahili translations. BT 5. 78-80.
Harris, Rendel. 1958. The English New Testament from Revised Version to Moffatt. BT 9. 70-73.
Harris, Zellig S. 1940. Review of Louis H. Gray, Foundations of Language (New York: Macmillan, 1939). Language 16. 216-231.
——. 1941. Linguistic structure of Hebrew. J. Am. Oriental Soc. 61. 143-167.
——. 1942. Morpheme alternants in linguistic analysis. Language 18. 169-180.
——. 1944. Simultaneous components in phonology. Language 20. 181-205.
——. 1945. Discontinuous morphemes. Language 21. 121-127.
——. 1946. From morpheme to utterance. Language 22. 161-183.
——. 1947. Structural restatements: I and II. IJAL 13. 47-58, 175-186.
——. 1951. Methods in Structural Linguistics. Chicago: Univ. Chicago Press. (See also reviews: Householder, 1952; McQuown, 1952.)
——. 1952. Discourse analysis. Language 28. 1-30, 474-494.
——. 1954a. Distributional structure. Word 10. 146-162.

Harris, Zellig S. (cont.). 1954b. Transfer grammar. IJAL 20. 259-270.
——. 1957. Co-occurrence and transformation in linguistic structure. Language 33. 283-340.
——. 1959. The transformational model of language structure. Anthropol. Linguistics 1.27-29.
Harrison, Frederic. 1921. The art of translation. Forum 65. 653-674.
Hart, Helen Long. 1957. Hierarchical structuring of Amuzgo grammar. IJAL 23. 141-164.
Haskell, Juliana. 1908. Bayard Taylor's Translation of Goethe's Faust. New York: Columbia Univ. Press.
Hattori, Shirô. 1956. The analysis of meaning. In Halle et al., For Roman Jakobson (q.v.), pp. 207-212.
Haugen, Einar. 1950a. The analysis of linguistic borrowing. Language 26.210-231.
——. 1950b. Problems of bilingualism. Lingua 2. 271-290.
——. 1951. Directions in modern linguistics. Language 27. 211-222.
——. 1953. The Norwegian Language in America; A Study in Bilingual Behavior. Philadelphia: Univ. Pennsylvania Press.
——. 1956. Bilingualism in the Americas: A Bibliography and Research Guide. Publ. No. 26, American Dialect Society. University, Ala.: Univ. Alabama Press.
——. 1957. The semantics of Icelandic orientation. Word 13. 447-459.
Hawkes, David. 1955. Translating from the Chinese. Encounter 5. 83ff.
Hayakawa, S. I., ed. 1954. Language, Meaning and Maturity. New York: Harper.
Hays, David G. 1961a. Grouping and dependency theories. PNSMT, pp. 258-266.
——. 1961b. Linguistic research at the Rand Corporation. PNSMT, pp. 13-25.
Headlam, Walter. 1907. A Book of Greek Verse. Cambridge Univ. Press.
Hebb, D. O. 1949. The Organization of Behavior. New York: Wiley.
Heberden, M. V. 1956. Teaching the machine grammar. Babel 2. 119-124.
Hebert, A. G. and Snaith, N. H. 1952. A study of the words 'curse' and 'righteousness.' BT 3. 111-116.
Heck, Philipp. 1931. Übersetzungsprobleme im frühen Mittelalter. Tübingen: J. C. B. Mohr (P. Siebeck).
Henderson, R. F. 1955. Problems of Bible translation. BT 6. 127-136.
Hendry, George S. 1949. New translation of the Bible. Theology 52. 203-208, 387-388.
Hennig, John. 1947. John Stuart Blackie's translation of Goethe's *Jahrmarktfest zu Plundersweilern.* Mod. Lang. Quart. 8. 91-100.
Henry, Jules. 1940. A method for learning to talk primitive languages. Am. Anthropologist 42.635-641.
——. 1941. Rorschach technique in primitive cultures. Am. J. Orthopsychiatry 11. 230-234.
Herdan, G. 1956. Language as Choice and Chance. Groningen: P. Noordhoff.
Herzberger, Hans G. 1961. The joints of English. Proc. 12th Symp. Appl. Mathematics, ed. by Jakobson (q.v.), pp. 99-103.
Herzog, George. 1941. Culture change and language: Shifts in the Pima vocabulary. In Spier, Hallowell, and Newman, eds., Language, Culture and Personality (q.v.), pp. 66-74.
Hewitt, Arthur W. 1948-1949. Job and Psalms in the Vulgate. Religion in Life 18. 66-78.
Hewitt, Gordon. 1956. Modern translations of the Bible. World Dominion 34. 191-196.
Hickerson, Harold; Turner, Glen D.; and Hickerson, Nancy P. 1952. Testing procedures for estimating transfer of information among Iroquois dialects and languages. IJAL 18. 1-8.
Hieble, Jacob. 1958. Should operas, lyric songs, and plays be presented in a foreign language? Mod. Lang. J. 42. 235-237.
Higgins, A. J. B. 1945. 'Lead us not into temptation': Some Latin variants. J. Theol. Stud. 46.179-183.
Higham, T. F. 1938. Introduction II. Oxford Book of Greek Verse in Translation. OUP.

Highet, Gilbert. 1949. The Classical Tradition. OUP.
Hill, Archibald A. 1941. Incorporation as a type of language structure. In Humanistic Studies in Honor of John Calvin Metcalf, pp. 65-79. Univ. Virginia Stud., Vol. 1.
——. 1958a. Introduction to Linguistic Structures; From Sound to Sentence in English. New York: Harcourt, Brace.
——. 1958b. A program for the definition of literature. Stud. in English 37. 46-52.
——. 1962. A postulate for linguistics in the sixties. Language 38. 345-351.
Hills, Margaret T. 1952. The progress of Bible translation in Japan. BT 3. 75-79.
——. 1953. Bible translators' conferences. BT 4. 115-117.
Hincha, Georg. 1961. Endocentric vs. exocentric constructions. Lingua 10. 267-275.
Hinkle, L. E. 1951. A translation service as an incentive to language study. Mod. Lang. J. 35. 147-152.
Hintikka, K. Jaakko J. 1959. Aristotle and the ambiguity of ambiguity. Inquiry 2. 137-151.
Hiorth, Finngeir. 1955. Arrangement of meanings in lexicography. Lingua 4. 413-424.
——. 1956. On the relation between field research and lexicography. Studia Linguistica 10. 57-66.
——. 1957. On the foundations of lexicography. Studia Linguistica 11. 8-29.
——. 1959. Origin and control of meaning hypotheses. Lingua 8.294-305.
Hiz, Henry. 1961. Congrammaticality, batteries of transformations and grammatical categories. Proc. 12th Symp. Appl. Mathematics, ed. by Jakobson (q.v.), pp. 43-50.
Hjelmslev, Louis. 1947. Structural analysis of language. Studia Linguistica 1. 69-78.
——. 1953. Prolegomena to a Theory of Language. (Trans. by F. J. Whitfield from Omkring sprogteoriens grundlaeggelse, 1943.) Indiana Univ. Publ. in Anthropology and Linguistics. Memoir 7, IJAL.
——. 1958. Dans quelle mesure les significations des mots peuvent-elles être considérées comme formant une structure? Proc. Internat. Cong. Linguists, Oslo.
Höcker, K. H. 1960. Sollen Amerikanismen unübersetzt bleiben? Probleme der Begriffsbestimmungen am Reaktor. Lebende Sprachen 5. 97-99.
Hockett, Charles F. 1947a. Problems of morphemic analysis. Language 23. 321-343.
——. 1947b. Review of Eugene A. Nida, Morphology (1st ed., Ann Arbor: Univ. Michigan Press, 1946). Language 23. 273-285.
——. 1948. Biophysics, linguistics and the unity of science. Am. Scientist 36. 558-572.
——. 1950a. Language 'and' culture: A protest. Am. Anthropologist 52. 113.
——. 1950b. Which approach in linguistics is 'scientific'? Stud. in Linguistics 8.53-57.
——. 1952. A formal statement of morphemic analysis. Stud. in Linguistics 10. 27-39.
——. 1953. Review of Claude L. Shannon and Warren Weaver, The Mathematical Theory of Communication (Urbana: Univ. Illinois Press, 1949). Language 29. 69-93.
——. 1954a. Chinese versus English: An exploration of the Whorfian theses. In Hoijer, ed., Language in Culture (q.v.), pp. 106-123.
——. 1954b. Translation via I.C. IJAL 20. 213-215.
——. 1954c. Two models of grammatical description. Word 10. 210-234.
——. 1955. A Manual of Phonology. Indiana Univ. Publ. in Anthropology and Linguistics. Memoir 11, IJAL.
——. 1956. Idiom formation. In Halle, et al., For Roman Jakobson (q.v.), pp. 222-229.
——. 1958. A Course in Modern Linguistics. New York: Macmillan.
——. 1961a. Grammar for the hearer. Proc. 12th Symp. Appl. Mathematics, ed. by Jakobson (q.v.), pp. 220-236.
——. 1961b. Linguistic elements and their relations. Language 37. 29-53.
Hockett, Marion S. 1950. Three major problems in Taungthu translation. BT 1. 150-153.
Hoekstra, Harvey T. 1952. Theological implications in translation. BT 3. 17-20.

Hoenigswald, Henry M. 1962. Lexicography and grammar. In Householder and
Saporta, eds., Problems in Lexicography (q.v.), pp. 103-110.
Hoijer, Harry, et al. 1946. Linguistic Structures of Native America. Viking Fund
Publ. in Anthropology, No. 6. New York: Viking Fund.
——. 1948. Linguistic and cultural change. Language 24. 335-345.
——. 1951. Cultural implications of some Navaho linguistic categories. Language
27. 111-120.
——. 1953. The relation of language to culture. In A. L. Kroeber, et al., Anthropology Today, pp. 554-573. Chicago: Univ. Chicago Press.
——, ed. 1954a. Language in Culture. Memoir 79, Am. Anthropologist. Chicago:
Univ. Chicago Press.
——. 1954b. The Sapir-Whorf hypothesis. In his Language in Culture, pp. 92-105.
Hollander, John. 1959. Versions, interpretations, and performances. In Brower,
ed., On Translation (q.v.), pp. 205-231.
Holmstrom, J. E. 1954. The language problem of science. Research 7. 190-
195.
——. 1955. How translators can contribute to improving scientific terminology.
Babel 1. 73-79.
——. 1956. How translators can help in improving scientific terminology. Babel
2. 28.
——. 1958. ASLIB conference on scientific and technical translation. Babel
4.114-115.
——. 1960. Review of D. Yu. Panov, Automatic Translation (trans. from the
Russian by R. Kisch; ed. by A. J. Mitchell; London: Pergamon Press, 1960).
Babel 6. 132-133.
Holter, Åge. 1960. The New Testament translated for the Norwegian youth.
BT 11. 126-132.
Hooper, J. S. M. 1953. Translation of Biblical terms: An illustration. BT 4. 126-129.
——. 1954. The New Testament translation of *elpis* in languages of India. BT
5. 2-4.
Hopgood, Cecil R. 1954. Hope: A brief study from the standpoint of a translator
into Tonga. BT 5. 19-22.
Horrwitz, E. P. 1935. An All-India alphabet. Asiatic Rev. 31. 376-378.
Horton, A. E. 1951. The translation of 'holy.' BT 2. 122-124.
Hoskier, H. C. 1911. The 'Authorized' Version of 1611. Bibliotheca Sacra 68.693-704.
Householder, Fred W. 1952. Review of Zellig S. Harris, Methods in Structural
Linguistics (Chicago: Univ. Chicago Press, 1951). IJAL 18. 260-268.
——. 1961. On linguistic terms. In Psycholinguistics: A Book of Readings, ed.
by Sol Saporta. New York: Holt, Rinehart & Winston. (Condensed version
in Word 15. 231-239.)
—— and Saporta, Sol, eds. 1962. Problems in Lexicography. Publ. 21, Indiana
Univ. Research Center in Anthropology, Folklore, and Linguistics. IJAL 28: 2.
Hovland, C.; Lumsdaine, A.; and Sheffield, F. 1949. Experiments on Mass Com-
munication. Princeton: Princeton Univ. Press.
Howard, H. G. 1952. Questions arising in connection with the 1950 edition of the
Marathi New Testament. BT 3. 25-27.
Howard, Wilbert F. 1950. Some thoughts on a new translation of the Bible. London
Quart. & Holborn Rev. 175. 103-112.
Howerton, Paul W. 1962. Technical translations: Their initiation, production and
use. Special Libraries 53. 21-25.
Hudson, Hoyt H. 1941. Current English translations of *The Praise of Folly*. Philol-
ogy Quart. 20. 250-265.
Hudspith, J. Edwin. 1958. Thailand translators' conference. BT 9.183-185.
Hudspith, Mrs. T. E. 1952. Notes on the translation of the New Testament in
Bolivian Quechua. BT 3. 66-68.
Huebsch, B. W. 1942. Cross-fertilization in letters. Am. Scholar 11. 304-314.
Hughes, Helen S. 1919. Notes on 18th century fictional translation. Mod. Philology
17. 225-231.
Hull, Clark L. 1943. Principles of Behavior. New York: Appleton-Century-Crofts.
Hulst, A. R. 1963. Bible translating into Dutch. Babel 9. 79-82.

Humboldt, Alexander von. 1845. Betrachtungen über die Verschiedenartigkeit des Maturgenusses. Kosmos. Works, Vol. I. Stuttgart.

Humboldt, Wilhelm. 1836. Über die Verschiedenheit des menschlichen Sprachbaues und ihren Einfluss auf die geistige Entwickelung des Menschengeschlechts. Berlin: Dummler.

Humphries, Rolfe. 1959. Latin and English verse—some practical considerations. In Brower, ed., On Translation (q.v.), pp. 57-66.

Hunt, R. J. 1953. The wild Chaco tribes. BT 4. 112-114, 146-149.

Hurteau, Philippe. 1961. Relations exterieurs et traduction. J. des Traducteurs 6. 47-51.

Hurvitz, L. 1963. The problem of translating Buddhist canonical texts into Chinese. Babel 9. 48-52.

Hutson, H. H. and Willoughby, H. R. 1939. The ignored Taverner Bible of 1539. Congregational Quart. 16. 161-176.

Hutton, W. R. 1951. Magazines for the translator. BT 2. 180-182.

——. 1953a. Textual emendation in the Old Testament. BT 4. 13-14.

——. 1953b. Who are we? BT 4.86-90.

——. 1958. Considerations for the translation of Greek en. BT 9. 163-170.

Huxley, Aldous. 1940. Words and Their Meanings. Los Angeles: Ward Ritchie Press.

Hymes, Dell H. 1961a. Linguistic aspects of cross-cultural personality study. In Studying Personality Cross-culturally, ed. by B. Kaplan. Evanston, Ill.: Row, Peterson.

——. 1961b. On typology of cognitive styles in language (with examples from Chinookan). Anthropol. Linguistics 3. 22-54.

Iannucci, James E. 1959. Explanatory matter in bilingual dictionaries. Babel 5. 195-199.

——. 1962. Meaning discrimination in bilingual dictionaries. In Householder and Saporta, eds., Problems in Lexicography (q.v.), pp. 201-216.

Iglauer, Edith. 1947. Housekeeping for the family of nations. Harper's Mag. 194. 295-306.

Iglesias, Mr. and Mrs. Claudio. 1951. Notes on the Cuna translation of Mark. BT 2.85-88.

Im, Young Bin. 1951. The Korean translation of the Bible and the Korean language. BT 2.91-93.

Information Processing. 1960. UNESCO. Proc. Internat. Conf. on Information Processing. London: Butterworth.

International Congress of Linguists. 1958. Proc. Internat. Cong. Linguists, 8, pp. 502-539. Oslo: University Press.

Irvin, Leon P. 1942. Courses in foreign literature in translation. Mod. Lang. J. 26. 533-538.

Irwin, William A. 1954. Textual criticism and Old Testament translation. BT 5. 54-58.

Isenberg, Arnold. 1953. Some problems of interpretation. In Wright, ed., Studies in Chinese Thought (q.v.), pp. 232-246.

Ishikawa, K. I. 1955. Difficulties in translating Japanese into English and vice versa. Pacific Spectator 9. 95-99.

Ives, H. E. 1917. The units and nomenclature of radiation and illumination. Astrophysics J. 45. 39-49.

Ives, Samuel A. 1957. Henry Ainsworth: A founding father of Congregationalism and pioneer translator of the Bible. Trans. Wisconsin Acad. 46. 189-199.

Jackson, Robert Sumner. 1961. The 'inspired' style of the English Bible. J. Bible & Religion 29. 4-15.

Jacobsen, Eric. 1958. Translation, A Traditional Craft. Copenhagen: Gyldendal.

Jakobson, Roman. 1930. O překladu veršu (translation of verses). Plan 2. 9-11.

——. 1936. Beitrag zur allgemeinen Kasuslehre. Travaux de Cercle Linguistique de Prague 6. 240-288.

——. 1944. Franz Boas' approach to language. IJAL 10. 188-195.

——; Fant, C. G. M.; and Halle, Morris. 1952. Preliminaries to Speech Analysis: The Distinctive Features and Their Correlates. Cambridge: Mass. Inst. Technology, Acoustics Laboratory.

Jakobson, Roman (cont.). and Halle, Morris. 1956. Fundamentals of Language. The Hague: Mouton.
——. 1959a. Boas' view of grammatical meaning. Am. Anthropologist 61. 139-145.
——. 1959b. On linguistic aspects of translation. In Brower, ed., On Translation (q.v.), pp. 232-239.
——. 1960. Linguistics and poetics. In Sebeok, ed., Style in Language (q.v.), pp. 350-377.
——. 1961a. Linguistics and communications theory. Proc. 12th Symp. Appl. Mathematics, ed. by Jakobson (q.v.), pp. 245-252.
——, ed. 1961b. Proc. 12th Symp. Appl. Mathematics: On Structure of Language and Its Mathematical Aspects. Providence, R.I.: American Mathematical Society. vi + 279.
——. 1964. (In press.) Efforts toward a means-ends model of language in interwar continental linguistics. In Trends in European and American Linguistics.
Jakobvits, Leon A. and Lambert, Wallace E. 1961. Semantic satiation among bilinguals. J. Exper. Psych. 62. 576-582.
James, E. L. 1948. Soviets as guardians of all civil liberties. . .nice problem in semantics. NYT, May 30, Sec. IV, p. 3.
Jaspers, Karl and Bultmann, Rudolf. 1958. Myth and Christianity; An Inquiry into the Possibility of Religion without Myth. New York: Noonday Press.
Jenkins, James J.; Russell, Wallace A.; and Suci, George J. 1958. An atlas of semantic profiles for 360 words. Am. J. Psych. 71. 688-699.
——; ——; and ——. 1959. A table of distances for the semantic atlas. Am. J. Psych. 72. 623-625.
——. 1960. Degree of polarization and scores on the principal factors for concepts in the semantic atlas study. Am. J. Psych. 73. 274-279.
Jentsch, Gerhart. 1956-1957. Standard Formulierungen in internationalen Verträgen. Lebende Sprachen 1. 86-87, 119-120, 175-176; 2. 76-78.
Jespersen, Otto. 1922. Language: Its Nature, Development, and Origin. London: Allen & Unwin; New York: Holt.
——. 1924. The Philosophy of Grammar. New York: Holt.
——. 1937. Analytic Syntax. Copenhagen: Munksgaard.
Johnson, Jean B. 1943. A clear case of linguistic acculturation. Am. Anthropologist 45. 427-434.
Johnson, Samuel. 1890. Lives of the Poets. London: Bell. (First published 1779-1781.)
Jones, L. Bevan. 1953. On the use of the name 'Isa. BT 4. 83-86.
Joos, Martin. 1948. Acoustic Phonetics. Language Mon. No. 23. Baltimore: Waverly Press.
——. 1950. Description of language design. J. Acoustical Soc. America 22. 701-708.
——. 1953. Towards a First Theorem in Semantics. (A paper delivered before the Linguistic Society of America, Dec. 29.)
——, ed. 1957. Readings in Linguistics; the Development of Descriptive Linguistics in America since 1925. Washington: Am. Council Learned Societies.
——. 1958a. Review of Eric P. Hamp, A Glossary of American Technical Linguistic Usage, 1925-1950 (Utrecht: Spectrum, 1957). Language 34. 279-288.
——. 1958b. Semology: A linguistic theory of meaning. Stud. in Linguistics 13. 53-70.
Josselson, Harry H. 1961. Research in machine translation. PNSMT, pp. 160-172.
Jowett, Benjamin. 1891. Preface to The Dialogues of Plato. (2d ed.) OUP.
Joy, Charles R. 1956. Thoughts on translating Albert Schweitzer. Babel 2. 54-56.
Jumpelt, R. W. 1954-1955. Mehrsprachige Spezialwörterbücher Moderne Herstellungsmethoden nach Vorschlägen der UNESCO. Nachrichten für Dokumentation. 1954, pp. 111-114, 179-183; 1955, pp. 25-28, 49-52.
——. 1955a. FIT and terminology for science and engineering. Babel 1. 72.
——. 1955b. Towards a FIT-policy in scientific and technical translating. Babel 1. 21-25.
——. 1956. Contribution by translators to the improvement of scientific and technical terminology. (Summary of Rome Congress Meetings.) Babel 2. 81-82.
——. 1957a. Language and logic. Review of Benjamin Lee Whorf, Language, Thought and Reality; Selected Writings. John B. Carroll, ed. (Cambridge:

Technology Press, Mass. Inst. Technology, 1956; New York: Wiley, 1956). Babel 3. 41-42.
——. 1957b. Review of E. Colin Cherry, On Human Communication (Cambridge: Technology Press, Mass. Inst. Technology, 1957; New York: Wiley, 1957). Babel 3. 153-154.
——. 1958. Fachsprachen—Fachworte, als Problem der Übersetzung und Dokumentation. Sprachforum 3. 1-13.
——. 1959a. Quality in scientific and technical translation. Babel 5. 107-109.
——. 1959b. Review of Arno Borst, Turmbau zu Babel (Stuttgart: A. Hiersemann, 1958). Babel 5. 23.
——. 1959c. Symposium on scientific and technical translation. Babel 5. 154-160.
——. 1960a. Review of Stephen Ullmann, The Principles of Semantics; A Linguistic Approach to Meaning (2d ed., Glasgow: Jackson, 1959; Oxford: Basil Blackwell, 1959). Babel 6. 184.
——. 1960b. Trois études de On Translation. Babel 6. 24-26.
——. 1961. Die Übersetzung naturwissenschaftlicher und technischer Literatur. Berlin-Schöneberg: Langenscheidt KG. (See also review: Oettinger, 1963.)
Kaardal, J. I. 1952. Producing the printed word. BT 3. 51-53.
Kahane, Henry and Renée. 1962. Problems in modern Greek lexicography. In Householder and Saporta, eds., Problems in Lexicography (q.v.), pp. 249-262.
Kalé, H. 1956a. I. Language learning for scientists. Babel 2. 63-65.
——. 1956b. II. Technical translating services. Babel 2. 66-68.
Kamman, William F. 1942. The problem of a universal language. Mod. Lang. J. 26. 177-182.
Kantor, J. R. 1952. An Objective Psychology of Grammar. Bloomington, Ind.: Principia Press.
Kaplan, Abraham. 1946. Definition and specification of meaning. J. Philosophy 43. 281-288.
Karlgren, H. 1962. Computation of information measures. PPICL.
Katt, Arthur F. 1955. Does the RSV mutilate the New Testament text? Concordia Theol. Monthly 26. 561-568.
Katz, Jerrold J. 1962a. Review of Semantic Analysis, by Paul Ziff (Ithaca, N.Y.: Cornell Univ. Press, 1960). Language 38. 52-69.
—— and Fodor, Jerry. 1962b. What's wrong with the philosophy of language? Inquiry 5. 3. Oslo: Oslo Univ. Press.
—— and ——. 1963. The structure of a semantic theory. Language 39. 170-210.
Katz, Peter. 1960. Mark 10: 11 once again. BT 11. 152.
Kecskemeti, Paul. 1952. Meaning, Communication and Value. Chicago: Univ. Chicago Press.
Keene, Donald. 1953. On appearing in Japanese translation. Twentieth Century 154. 225-228.
Keinath, H. O. A. 1934. Melanchthon and Luther's translation of the New Testament. Concordia Theol. Monthly 5. 842-846.
Kellogg, Dimitri A. 1961. Modern trends in character recognition machines. PNSMT, pp. 511-514.
Kelly, Hugh and Ziehe, Ted. 1961a. Glossary lookup made easy. PNSMT, pp. 325-334.
——. 1961b. Mimic: A translation for English coding. PNSMT, pp. 451-461.
Kelly, Jane A. and Levy, Leon H. 1961. The discriminability of concepts differentiated by means of the semantic differential. Educ. & Psych. Measurement 21. 53-58.
Kendig, M., ed. 1943. Papers from the Second American Congress on General Semantics. Chicago: Inst. General Semantics.
Kenner, Hugh. 1953. Introduction to The Translations of Ezra Pound. London: Faber & Faber.
——. 1954. Hellas without Helicon. Poetry 84. 112-118.
——. 1955. Problems in faithfulness and fashion. Poetry 85. 225-231.
Keppler, Kurt. 1957. Irreführende Fremdwörter. Lebende Sprachen 2. 134-135.
Key, Wilson Bryan Jr. 1959. Cloze procedure: A technique for evaluating the quality of language translation. J. Communication 9. 14-18.

Kijne, J. J. 1953. How the new Dutch translation of the New Testament was criticized. BT 4. 74-77.

Kilduff, Edward Jones. 1941. Words and Human Nature. New York: Harper.

Kilpatrick, G. D. 1956. Some notes on Marcan usage. BT 7. 2-9, 51-56.

——. 1958. The transmission of the New Testament and its reliability. BT 9. 127-136.

——. 1960. Some notes on Johannine usage. BT 11. 173-177.

King, Donald B. 1952. The Greek translation of Augustus' *Res Gestae*. Transactions Wisconsin Acad. 41. 219-228.

King, Gilbert. 1961. Functions required of a translation system. PNSMT, pp. 53-62.

Kirk, Paul L. 1957. Review of W. Schwarz, Principles and Problems of Biblical Translation: Some Reformation Controversies and Their Background (Cambridge Univ. Press, 1955). BT 8. 40-44.

Kitagawa, J. M. 1963. Buddhist translation in Japan. Babel 9. 53-59.

Klijn, A. F. J. 1957. The value of the versions for the textual criticism of the New Testament. BT 8. 127-130.

Klima, Edward S. 1961. Structure at the lexical level and its implications for transfer grammar. In Papers and Discussions, First International Conference on Machine Translation and Applied Language Analysis. London: H. M. Stationery Office.

Kluckhohn, Clyde. 1941. Patterning as exemplified in Navajo culture. In Spier, Hallowell, and Newman, eds., Language, Culture and Personality (q.v.), pp. 109-130.

——. 1945. The personal document in anthropological science. In Louis Gottschalk, Clyde Kluckhohn, and Robert C. Angell, The Use of Personal Documents in History, Anthropology, and Sociology. New York: Social Science Research Council, Bull. 53.

—— and Murray, Henry A., eds. 1948. Personality in Nature, Society and Culture. New York: Knopf.

——. 1949. Mirror for Man. New York: McGraw-Hill.

——. 1956. Toward a comparison of value-emphases in different cultures. In Leonard D. White, ed., The State of the Social Sciences, pp. 116-132. Chicago: Univ. Chicago Press.

——. 1957. General semantics and 'primitive' languages. Gen. Semantics Bull. Nos. 20 & 21.

——. 1961. Notes on some anthropological aspects of communication. Am. Anthropologist 63. 895-912.

Kluckhohn, Florence R. 1960. A method for eliciting value orientations. Anthropol. Linguistics 2. 1-23.

—— and Strodtbeck, Fred C. 1961. Variations in Value Orientations. Evanston, Ill.: Row, Peterson.

Knight, Douglas. 1951. Pope and the Heroic Tradition. New Haven: Yale Univ. Press.

——. 1959. Translation: The Augustan Mode. In Brower, ed., On Translation (q.v.), pp. 196-204.

Knowles, Jas. D. 1837. Principles of translation. Christian Rev. 2. 596.

Knox, Ronald. 1949. Trials of a Translator. New York: Sheed & Ward. (English title: On Englishing the Bible. London: Burns & Oates, 1949.) (See also reviews: Allis, 1951; Malden, 1950.)

——. 1957. On English Translation. OUP.

Koffka, K. 1935. Principles of Gestalt Psychology. New York: Harcourt, Brace.

Köhler, Wolfgang. 1947. Gestalt Psychology. New York: New American Library.

Kolke, Parke R. 1936-1937. On the translation of verse. Mod. Lang. J. 21. 103-108.

Kooiman, Willem Jan. 1961. Luther and the Bible. (Trans. by John Schmidt.) Philadelphia: Muhlenberg Press.

Korzybski, Alfred. 1948. Science and Sanity: An Introduction to Non-Aristotelian Systems and General Semantics. Lakeville, Conn.: International Non-Aristotelian Library Publishing Co. (Publ. 1933 by Science Press Printing Co., Lancaster, Pa.)

Koschmeider, Erwin. 1955. Das Problem der Übersetzung. In Corolla Linguistica

(Festschrift für Ferdinand Sommer zum 80 Geburtstage), pp. 120-128. Wiesbaden.

Kotarbinska, Janina. 1960. On ostensive definitions. Philosophy of Science 27. 1-22.

Koutsoudas, Andreas. 1957. Mechanical translation and Zipf's Law. Language 33. 545-552.

——. 1959a. Defining linear context to resolve lexical ambiguity. Language and Speech 2. 211-215.

—— and Humecky, A. 1959b. Linguistics and machine translation. Word 15. 489-491.

Kovacs, F. 1962. Sign, meaning, society. PPICL.

Kraemer, Hendrick. 1956. The Communication of the Christian Faith. Philadelphia: Westminster Press.

Kramers, R. P. 1956. Some thoughts on revision of the Bible in Chinese. BT 7. 152-162.

Krasner, Leonard. 1958. Studies of the conditioning of verbal behavior. Psych. Bull. 55.148-170.

Krause, E. George. 1953. Textual-critical methods of RSV Revision Committee. Concordia Theol. Monthly 24. 809-830.

Kretzmann, P. E. 1934. The story of the German Bible. Concordia Theol. Monthly 5. 265-296, 344-368, 425-445.

Kroeber, A. L. 1909. Classificatory systems of relationship. J. Royal Anthropol. Inst. 39. 77-84.

——. 1941. Some relations of linguistics and ethnology. Language 17. 287-291.

—— and Kluckhohn, Clyde. 1952. Culture, a critical review of concepts and definitions. Cambridge: Papers Peabody Mus. Am. Archeology & Ethnology 37. 101-136.

Kronasser, Heinz. 1952. Handbuch der Semasiologie—kurze Einführung in die Geschichte, Problematik und Terminologie der Bedeutungslehre. Heidelberg: Carl Winter.

Ku, Tun-Jou. 1957. Notes on the Chinese version of the Bible. BT 8. 160-165.

Kuhn-Foelix, August. 1961. Zur Kunst der literarischen Übersetzung. Lebende Sprachen 6. 84-85.

Kurath, Hans. 1962. Interrelation between regional and social dialects. PPICL.

Lado, Robert. 1957. Linguistics across Cultures; Applied Linguistics for Language Teachers. Ann Arbor: Univ. Michigan Press.

Lamb, Sydney M. 1961a. The digital computer as an aid in linguistics. Language 37. 382-412.

——. 1961b. MT research at the University of California. PNSMT, pp. 140-154.

——. 1961c. Segmentation. PNSMT, pp. 335-342.

Lambek, Joachim. 1961. On the calculus of syntactic types. Proc. 12th Symp. Appl. Mathematics, ed. by Jakobson (q.v.), pp. 166-178.

Lambert, W. E.; Havelka, J.; and Crosby, C. 1958. The influence of language-acquisition contexts on bilingualism. J. Abn. & Soc. Psych. 56. 239-244.

——; ——; and Gardner, R. C. 1959. Linguistic manifestations of bilingualism. Am. J. Psych. 72. 77-82.

—— and Jakobvits, Leon A. 1960. Verbal satiation and change in the intensity of meaning. J. Exper. Psych. 60. 376-383.

Lancashire, D. 1958. Chinese language reform. BT 9. 26-36.

Lane, Alexander. 1959. Urkundenübersetzungen im internationalen Verkehr. Babel 5. 213-215.

Lane, George S. 1933. Some semantic borrowings in Wulfila. Philology Quart. 12. 321-326.

Lang, D. B. 1953. The revision of the Chokwe New Testament. BT 4. 135-138.

Lang, Friedrich. 1958. À la recherche des principes de terminologie et de lexicographie. Babel 4. 112-113.

Langdon, W. M. 1913. Some merits of the American Standard Bible. Bibliotheca Sacra 70.486-497.

Langer, Suzanne K. 1951. Philosophy in a New Key. New York: New American Library.

——. 1953a. Feeling and Form. New York: Scribner.

Langer, Suzanne K. (cont.). 1953b. An Introduction to Symbolic Logic. New York: Dover Publications.
L'Anglais, Paul. 1960. Le doublage, art difficile. J. des Traducteurs 5. 109-113.
Lanier, Sidney. 1900. The English Novel. New York: Scribner.
Larbaud, Valery. 1946. Sous l'invocation de Saint Jerome. Paris: Gallimard.
———. 1957. Divertissement philologique. Babel 3. 3-10.
Larwill, Paul H. 1934. La théorie de la traduction au début de la Renaissance. Munich: Wolf.
Lashley, K. S. 1951. The problem of serial order in behavior. In Cerebral Mechanisms in Behavior, ed. by L. A. Jeffress, pp. 112-136. New York: Wiley.
Lasse, F. G. 1956. The new edition of the Ddu Alur Bible. BT 7. 22-25.
Lasswell, H. D.; Lerner, D.; and Pool, I. de Sola. 1952. The Comparative Study of Symbols. Hoover Inst. Stud., Ser. C. Symbols, No. 1. Stanford, Calif.: Stanford Univ. Press.
Latomus, Jacob. 1518. De trium linguarium. Basel: Froben.
Lattimore, Richmond. 1959. Practical notes on translating Greek poetry. In Brower, ed., On Translation (q.v.), pp. 48-56.
Lauer, Edward H. 1915. Luther's translation of the Psalms in 1523-1524. J. English-Germanic Philology 14. 1-34.
Lauriault, James. 1951a. Lexical problems in Shipibo Mark. BT 2. 56-66.
———. 1951b. A semi-literal translation of Mark 1 in Shipibo. BT 2. 32-37.
———. 1957. Some problems in translating paragraphs idiomatically. BT 8. 166-169.
———. 1958. On handling meanings in the vernacular. BT 9. 145-150.
Law, Howard W. 1960. Problems of ambiguities in Isthmus Aztec translation. BT 11. 87-90.
Leal, Otis M. 1951. Problems in Zapotec translation. BT 2. 164-166.
Lebrun, Yvan. 1962. 'Can' and 'may': a problem of multiple meaning. PPICL.
Lednicki, Waclaw. 1952. Some notes on the translation of poetry. Am. Slavonic & East European Rev. 11. 304-311.
Lee, Dorothy D. 1940. A primitive system of values. Philosophy of Science 7. 355-378.
———. 1943. The linguistic aspects of Wintu acculturation. Am. Anthropologist 45. 435-440.
Lee, Irving J. 1941. Language Habits in Human Affairs. New York: Harper.
———, ed. 1949. The Language of Wisdom and Folly. New York: Harper.
Leenhardt, Maurice. 1951a. Notes on translating the New Testament into New Caledonian. Pt. 1. BT 2. 97-105.
———. 1951b. Notes on translating the New Testament into New Caledonian. Pt. 2. BT 2. 145-152.
Lees, Robert B. 1957. Review of Noam Chomsky, Syntactic Structures ('s-Gravenhage: Mouton, 1957). Language 33. 375-408.
———. 1959. Automata and the generation of sentences. Anthropol. Linguistics 1. 1-4.
———. 1960. The Grammar of English Nominalizations. Bloomington, Ind.: Research Center in Anthropology, Folklore and Linguistics.
——— and Klima, E. S. 1963. Rules for English pronominalization. Language 39. 17-29.
Lees, William. 1958. Pioneers, what first objective? BT 9. 73-75.
Leidecker, K. F. 1947. How to write a technical dictionary. Library J. 72. 1096ff.
Leishman, J. B. 1956. Translating Horace. Oxford: Bruno Cassirer.
Lengyel, Peter. 1956. The UNESCO pilot project in social science terminology. Babel 2. 24-27.
Lenneberg, Eric H. 1953. Cognition in ethnolinguistics. Language 29. 463-471.
——— and Roberts, John M. 1956. The Language of Experience: A Study in Methodology. Indiana Univ. Publ. in Anthropology and Linguistics. Memoir 13, IJAL.
Leonard, Sterling A. 1929. The Doctrine of Correctness in English Usage, 1700-1800. Madison: Univ. Wisconsin.
Leontiev, A. N. and Leontiev, A. A. 1959. The social and the individual in language. Language and Speech 2. 193-204.
Leopold, Werner F. 1954. A child's learning of two languages. Rept. 5th Ann. Round Table Meeting on Linguistics and Language Teaching, pp. 19-30.

Washington: Georgetown Univ. Mon. Ser. on Languages & Linguistics No. 7.
———. 1955. Review of Ernst Cassirer, The Philosophy of Symbolic Forms; Vol. I, Language. Trans. by Ralph Manheim (New Haven: Yale Univ. Press, 1953). Language 31. 73-84.
———. 1956. Roman Jakobson and the study of child language. In Halle et al., For Roman Jakobson (q.v.), pp. 285-288.
Lerbak, Anna E. 1954. Translating the Psalms to Uruund. BT 5. 84-87.
Lermas, Jordi. 1958. Gaps in world translations. UNESCO Features 283. 10-11.
Lerner, Daniel, ed. 1959. The Human Meaning of the Social Sciences. New York: Meridian Books.
Levi, Edward Hirsch. 1949. An Introduction to Legal Reasoning. Chicago: Univ. Chicago Press.
Lévi-Strauss, Claude. 1951. Language and the analysis of social laws. Am. Anthropologist 53. 155-163.
———; Jakobson, Roman; Voegelin, Carl F.; and Sebeok, Thomas A. 1953. Results of the Conference of Anthropologists and Linguists. Indiana Univ. Publ. in Anthropology and Linguistics. Memoir 8, IJAL.
Levin, Samuel R. 1962. Poetry and grammaticalness. PPICL.
Levý, Jiří. 1955. Překladatelský proces-jeho objektivní podmínky a psychologie. Slovo a Slovesnost 16. 65-86.
Lévy-Bruhl, Lucien. 1949. Les Carnets de Lucien Lévy-Bruhl. (Preface by Maurice Leenhardt.) Paris: Presses Universitaires de France.
Lewis, Clive Staples. 1950. The Literary Impact of the Authorised Version. London: University of London.
Lewis, Elaine T. 1960. Hymn translating. BT 11. 49-68.
Lewis, James. 1947. The New English New Testament. London Quart. & Holborn Rev. 172. 50-51.
Lewis, Juan O. Diaz. 1956. The duties of translators under the 'Compulsory Licence' system of the Universal Copyright Convention. Babel 2. 19-23.
Limaye, Shridhar Dattatraya. 1955. Scientific translation in India—some basic aspects. Babel 1. 13-16.
Linsky, L., ed. 1952. Philosophy of Language. Urbana: Univ. Illinois Press.
Loane, George G. 1937. Chapman's Homer. Cornhill 156. 637-644.
Locke, William N. and Booth, A. Donald, eds. 1955a. Machine Translation of Languages. (Cambridge: Technology Press, Mass. Inst. Technology.) New York: Wiley.
———. 1955b. Speech typewriters and translating machines. PMLA 70. 23-32.
Lockyer, Thomas F. 1925. John Wesley's Revised Version of the New Testament. London Quart. Rev. 143.55-62.
Loehlin, C. H. 1953. The Gurmukhi Punjabi Old Testament. BT 4. 66-70.
Loewenson, Leo. 1956. E. G. von Berge, translator of Milton and Russian interpreter. Slavonic & East European Rev. 34. 281-291.
Lofthouse, W. F. 1955. 'I' and 'we' in the Pauline Letters. BT 6. 72-80.
Long, D. B. 1953. The revision of the Chokwe New Testament. BT 4. 135-138.
———. 1954. Further comments on the Chokwe translation. BT 5.87-96.
Longacre, Robert E. 1953. A tone orthography for Trique. BT 4. 8-13.
———. 1956a. Review of Wilbur M. Urban, Language and Reality (New York: Macmillan, 1939). Language 32. 298-308.
———. 1956b. Review of Benjamin Lee Whorf, Four Articles on Metalinguistics (Washington: U.S. Dept. State, Foreign Service Inst., 1949). Language 32.298-308.
———. 1958. Items in context—their bearing on translation theory. Language 34. 482-491.
Lord, Roger. 1957. Evolution du vocabulaire de la Pharmacie. J. des Traducteurs 2. 10-12.
Lorge, Irving. 1949. The Semantic Count of the 570 Commonest English Words. New York: Columbia Univ., Teachers College Bureau of Publications.
Lotz, John. 1947. The semantic analysis of the nominal bases in Hungarian. Travaux du Cercle Linguistique de Copenhague 5. 185-197.
———. 1950. Speech and language. J. Acoustical Soc. America 22. 712-717.

Lotz, John (cont.). 1954. The structure of human speech. Trans. N.Y. Acad. Sciences, Ser. II. 16. 373-384.
——. 1956. Linguistics: symbols make man. In Frontiers of Knowledge, ed. by Lynn White, Jr., pp. 207-231. New York: Harper.
Lounsbury, Floyd G. 1955. The varieties of meaning. Mon. Ser. No. 8, pp. 158-164. Washington: Georgetown Univ., Inst. Language & Linguistics.
——. 1956. A semantic analysis of the Pawnee kinship usage. Language 32. 158-194.
——. 1960. Similarity and contiguity relations in language and culture. Georgetown Univ. Mon. on Language & Linguistics 12. 123-128.
Lowe-Porter, H. T. 1955. Translating Thomas Mann. Symposium 9. 260-272.
Lowie, Robert H. 1940. Native languages as ethnographic tools. Am. Anthropologist 42. 81-89.
Luce, G. H. 1950. Three major problems in Taungthu translation. BT 1. 153-154.
Luehrs, F. U.; Kent, A.; Perry, J. W.; and Berry, M. M. 1955. Machine literature searching. Am. Documentation 6. 33-39.
Lukjanow, Ariadne W. 1961a. Report on some principles of the unified transfer system. PNSMT, pp. 88-120.
——. 1961b. Semantic classification. PNSMT, pp. 394-397.
Lund, N. W. 1943. The significance of chiasmus for interpretation. Congregational Quart. 20. 105-123.
Luria, A. R. and Vinogradova, O. S. 1959. An objective investigation of the dynamics of semantic systems. British J. Psych. 50. 89-105.
Luther, Martin. 1530. Ein Sendbrief von Dolmetschen. Werke.
——. 1936. On the study and use of the ancient languages. (From Luther on Education, trans. by F. V. N. Painter.) Concordia Theol. Monthly 7. 23-27.
Luzzatto, Guido Lodovico. 1957. Opinions sur la traduction. Babel 3. 63-72.
Lyons, John. 1963. Review of Paul Ziff, Semantic Analysis (Ithaca: Cornell Univ. Press, 1960). IJAL 29. 82-87.
Lyttelton, E. 1935. Paraphrasing the New Testament in church. Theology 31. 167f.
MacFarlane, J. W. 1953. Modes of translation. Durham Univ. J. 45. 77-93.
Machwé, Prabhakar. 1958. The problem of translation: Hindi and other Indian languages. Babel 4. 23-31.
Mack, E. 1925. Dr. Moffatt's new translation of the Old Testament. Union Seminary Mag. 36. 135-137.
Maclay, Howard. 1958. An experimental study of language and non-linguistic behavior. Southwestern J. Anthropology 14. 220-229.
—— and Ware, Edward E. 1961. Cross-cultural use of the semantic differential. Behavioral Science 6. 185-190.
Maclure, A. Seton. 1959. Translating the Lugbara Bible. BT 10. 124-127.
Maclure, Hugh L. 1957. Some notes on the New Testament in Temne. BT 8. 85-89.
Macnicol, J. D. A. 1952. Word and deed in the New Testament. Scottish J. Theology 5.237-248.
MacPhail, R. M. 1961. The Santali Union version of the New Testament. BT 12. 36-39.
Macurdy, Grace H. 1919. The diaphragm and the Greek ideal, or the treachery of translations. Class. Philology 14. 389-393.
Magnus, Laurie. 1931. Hours in undress: translation. Cornhill 71. 244-254.
Magnusson, Rudolf. 1954. Studies in the Theory of the Parts of Speech. (Lund Stud. in English, No. 24.) Lund: C. W. K. Gleerup; Copenhagen: Ejnar Munksgaard. (See also review: Whitfield, 1955.)
Mahr, A. C. 1961. Semantic evaluation. Anthropol. Linguistics 3. 1-46.
Malblanc, Alfred. 1961. Stylistique comparée du Français et de l'Allemand. Paris: Didier.
Malden, R. H. 1950. Review of Ronald A. Knox, On Englishing the Bible (London: Burns & Oates, 1949). J. Theol. Stud. 1. 85-88.
Malinowski, Bronislaw. 1922. Argonauts of the Western Pacific. London: Routledge.
——. 1923. The problem of meaning in primitive languages. In his Magic, Science and Religion, pp. 228-276. Boston: Beacon Press.

——. 1935. Coral Gardens and Their Magic. (Vol. 2, The Language of Magic and Gardening.) New York: American Book Co.
——. 1945. The Dynamics of Culture Change. New Haven: Yale Univ. Press.
Malkiel, Yakov. 1962. A typological classification of dictionaries on the basis of distinctive features. In Householder and Saporta, eds., Problems in Lexicography (q.v.), pp. 3-24.
Malone, Kemp. 1940. On defining *mahogany*. Language 16. 308-318.
——. 1962. Structural linguistics and bilingual dictionaries. In Householder and Saporta, eds., Problems in Lexicography (q.v.), pp. 111-118.
Manchester, Paul T. 1951. Verse translation as an interpretive art. Hispania 34. 68-73.
Mandelbaum, David G., ed. 1949. Selected Writings of Edward Sapir. Berkeley: Univ. California Press.
Mandelbrot, Benoit. 1950. An informational theory of the structure of language based upon the statistical matching of messages and coding. In W. Jackson, ed., Proc. Symp. on Information Theory. London: Royal Society.
——. 1961. On the theory of word frequencies and on related Markovian models of discourse. Proc. 12th Symp. Appl. Mathematics, ed. by Jakobson (q.v.), pp. 190-219.
Mandler, G. and Kessen, W. 1959. The Language of Psychology. New York: Wiley.
Manning, B. 1920. Review of Margaret Deanesley, The Lollard Bible and Other Medieval Biblical Versions (Cambridge Univ. Press, 1920). Theology 1. 246-247.
Manning, Clarence A. 1934. A Russian translation of *Paradise Lost*. Slavonic & East European Rev. 13.173-176.
Manrique, Julio Colón and Gómez, Julio Colón. 1954. Arte de Traducir el Inglés. Mexico: Julio Colón Manrique.
Mantey, J. R. 1951a. Inadequately translated words in the New Testament. Rev. & Expositor 48. 169-175.
——. 1951b. New Testament words inadequately translated in English. BT 2. 161-163.
Marchand, Joseph W. 1961. German syntax patterns. PNSMT, pp. 234-244.
Markel, Norman N. and Hamp, Eric P. 1960-1961. Connotative meanings of certain phoneme sequences. Stud. in Linguistics 15. 47-61.
Marouzeau, J. 1924. La traduction et l'ordre des mots (phrase latine et phrase française). Revue Études Latines 2. 189-194.
Marshall, Alfred. 1952. The genitive of quality in the New Testament. BT 3. 14-16.
——. 1953. *Ou* and *Mee* in questions. BT 4. 41-42.
——. 1959. This question of 'synonyms.' BT 10. 121-123.
Marthinson, A. W. 1954. The revision of the Mongolian New Testament. BT 5. 74-78.
——. 1957. Bible translations in Belgian Congo, Ruanda-Urundi, and Angola. BT 8. 191-202.
Martin, Samuel E. 1962. Selection and presentation of ready equivalents in a translation dictionary. In Householder and Saporta, eds., Problems in Lexicography (q.v.), pp. 153-159.
Martinet, André. 1949. Review of Kenneth L. Pike, Phonemics, A Technique for Reducing Languages to Writing (Ann Arbor: Univ. Michigan Press, 1947). Word 5. 282-286.
——. 1952a. Function, structure and sound change. Word 8. 1-32.
——. 1952b. Review of Interlingua-English (Internat. Auxiliary Lang. Assoc.; New York: Storm, 1951). Word 8. 163-167.
——. 1960. Elements of a functional syntax. Word 16. 1-10.
——. 1962. Structural variation in language. PPICL.
Mates, Benson. 1959. Synonymity. In his Meaning and Interpretation, pp. 201-229. Berkeley: Univ. California Press.
Mathews, Jackson. 1954. Campbell's Baudelaire. Sewanee Rev. 62. 663-671.
——. 1959. Third thoughts on translating poetry. In Brower, ed., On Translation (q.v.), pp. 67-77.
Mathieu, George J. 1949. Words before peace; translators and interpreters. UN World 3. 58-59.

Mathiot, Madeleine. 1962. Noun classes and folk taxonomy in Papago. Am. Anthropologist 64. 340-350.
Matteson, Esther. 1951. Translation procedure in Piro. BT 2. 38-42.
Matthew, A. F. 1956. The revision of the Amharic New Testament. BT 7. 72-76.
Matthews, G. H. and Rogovin, Syrell. 1958. German sentence recognition. Mech. Translation 5. 114-120.
——. 1961a. Analysis by synthesis of sentences of natural languages. In Papers and Discussions, First International Conference on Machine Translation and Applied Language Analysis. London: H. M. Stationery Office.
——. 1961b. The use of grammars within the mechanical translation routine. PNSMT, pp. 245-248.
Matthiessen, Francis Otto. 1931. Translation: An Elizabethan Art. Cambridge: Harvard Univ. Press.
May, J. Lewis. 1927. Concerning translation. Edinburgh Rev. 245. 108-118.
Mayers, Marvin and Marilyn. 1955. The place of dialect study in translation. BT 6. 186-191.
Maymi, Protasio. 1956. General concepts on laws in translation. Mod. Lang. J. 40. 13-21.
McCasland, S. V. 1949. Some New Testament metonyms for God. J. Biblical Lit. 68. 99-113.
McFarlane, John. 1953. Modes of translation. Durham Univ. J. 14. 77-93.
McGarry, William J. 1941. The revision of the New Testament. Thought 16. 405-408.
McGee, C. Douglas. 1960. A word for dictionaries. Mind 69 (n.s.). 14-30.
McHardy, W. D. 1956. A translation of an ancient version. BT 7. 66-72.
McIlwaine, W. A. 1954. Translation of the future tense into colloquial Japanese. BT 5. 112-117.
McIntosh, Angus. 1961. Patterns and ranges. Language 37. 325-337.
McKaughan, Howard. 1959. Semantic components of pronoun systems: Maranao. Word 15.101-102.
McKim, Randolph H. 1913. A critical examination of 'The Bible of 1911.' Bibliotheca Sacra 70. 123-144.
McKinsey, J. C. C. 1952. Introduction to the Theory of Games. New York: McGraw-Hill.
McManus, George. 1952. Jiggs and I. Collier's, Jan. 19, pp. 9-11, 66-67.
McQuown, Norman A. 1952. Review of Zellig S. Harris, Methods in Structural Linguistics (Chicago: Univ. Chicago Press, 1951). Language 28. 495-504.
——. 1954. Analysis of the cultural content of language materials. In Hoijer, ed., Language in Culture (q.v.), pp. 20-31.
—— and Hymes, D. H. 1960. Discussion of the Symposium on Translation between Language and Culture. Anthropol. Linguistics 2. 79-84.
Mead, George H. 1934. Mind, Self and Society. Chicago: Univ. Chicago Press.
Mead, Margaret. 1939. Native languages as field work tools. Am. Anthropologist 41. 189-205.
Meecham, H. G. 1953. Old words with new meanings—A New Testament study. BT 4. 4-7, 71-74.
Meek, T. J. 1938. Lapses of Old Testament translators. J. Am. Oriental Soc. 58. 122-129.
——. 1953-1954. The RSV of the Old Testament: An appraisal. Religion in Life 23. 70-82.
——. 1962. Old Testament translation principles. J. Biblical Lit. 81. 143-154.
Meisnest, F. W. 1914. Wieland's translation of Shakespeare. Mod. Lang. Rev. 9. 12-40.
Mencken, H. L. 1935-1936. The American Language. Yale Rev. 25. 538-552.
——. 1944. Designations for colored folk. Am. Speech 19. 161-174.
Mennie, Duncan M. 1935. A note on Goethe as a translator of English prose, 1820-1832. Mod. Lang. Rev. 30. 61-64.
Meredith, G. P. 1955. Language, meaning and mind. Nature 178. 673-674.
——. 1956. Semantics in relation to psychology. Archivum Linguisticum 8. 1-12.
Mersel, Jules. 1961. Research in machine translation at Ramo-Wooldridge. PNSMT, pp. 26-38.

Messing, G. M. 1951. Structuralism and literary tradition. Language 27. 1-12.
Metlen, Michael. 1933. What a Greek interlinear of the Gothic Bible text can teach us. J. English-Germanic Philology 32. 530-548.
——. 1937. St. Jerome's comments on the Psalter. J. English-Germanic Philology 36. 515-542.
Meyer, Richard Moritz. 1910. Altgermanische Religionsgeschichte. Leipzig: Quelle & Meyer.
Meyer-Eppler, W. 1959. Grundlagen und Anwendungen der Informations-theorie. (Kommunikation und Kybernetik in Einzeldarstellungen, Bd. 1.) Berlin: Springer.
Meyers, Russell. 1948. 'Reality' and 'Unreality.' ETC.: A Review of General Semantics 6. 27-38.
Meyerstein, Rud S. 1955. Meaning determinations: objectives and procedures. Lang. Learning 6. 42-50.
Meynieux, André. 1955. Pouchkine traduit, Pouchkine trahi. . . . Babel 1. 45-50.
——. 1957a. Sur l'article d'Edmond Cary 'Traduction et poésie.' Babel 3. 125-140.
——. 1957b. Les traducteurs en Russie avant Pouchkine. Babel 3. 73-79.
Michaeli, Frank. 1957. A new revision of the Segond New Testament. BT 8. 80-85.
——. 1958. The Bible of 'La Pleiade' by Ed. Dhorme. BT 9. 152-153.
Michaels, J. Ramsey. 1957. Some notable readings of Papyrus Bodmer II. BT 8. 150-154.
Michelet, Mme. C. 1958. La formation du traducteur. Babel 4. 166-168.
Micklesen, Lew R. 1956. Form classes: Structural linguistics and mechanical translation. In Halle et al., For Roman Jakobson (q.v.), pp. 344-352.
——. 1961. An experiment in the automatic selection or rejection of technical terms. PNSMT, pp. 398-408.
Middelkoop, P. 1952a. Problems of the Bible translator in connection with the cultural and religious background of the people. BT 3. 165-169.
——. 1952b. The translation of 'flesh' in Timorese. BT 3. 208-209.
——. 1953. The translator and the cultural and religious background of the people. BT 4. 183-187.
——. 1956. About the translation of the word nachash into Timorese. BT 7. 130-138.
Miles, F. G. 1956. The decay of English. Babel 2. 8-10.
Milewski, Tadeusz. 1951. The conception of the word in the languages of North American natives. Lingua Posnaniensis 3. 248-268.
Miller, George A. 1950. Language engineering. J. Acoustical Soc. America 22. 720-725.
——. 1951. Language and Communication. New York: McGraw-Hill.
—— and Selfridge, Jennifer A. 1953. Verbal context and the recall of meaningful material. Am. J. Psych. 63. 176-185.
—— and Beebe-Center, J. G. 1957. Some psychological methods for evaluating the quality of translations. Babel 3. 223.
——. 1958. Free recall of redundant strings of letters. J. Exp. Psych. 56. 484-491.
——; Galanter, Eugene; and Pribram, Karl H. 1960. Plans and the Structure of Behavior. New York: Holt, Rinehart & Winston.
Miller, L. M. 1915. Why did St. Paul write Greek? Bibliotheca Sacra 72. 23-33.
Milligan, E. E. 1957. Some principles and techniques of translation. Mod. Lang. J. 41. 66-71.
Mills, Theodore M. 1953. Power relations in three person groups. Am. Sociolog. Rev. 18. 351-357.
Milner, R. H. 1963. The English Bible 1611-1961: Some literary considerations. Babel 9. 70-79.
Mitton, C. Leslie. 1954. Modern translations of the Bible. London Quart. & Holborn Rev. 179. 113-119.
Moeller, Henry R. 1958a. Review of Gerhard Lisowsky and Leonhard Rost, Konkordanz zum hebräischen alten Testament (Stuttgart: Privileg. Württembergische Bibelanstalt, 1958). BT 9. 189-191.
——. 1958b. Review of G. Ernest Wright, Biblical Archaeology (Philadelphia: Westminster Press, 1957). BT 9. 141-144.

Moeller, Henry R. (cont.). 1958c. Review of Ernst Würthstein, The Text of the Old
    Testament: An Introduction to Kittel-Kahle's Biblia Hebraica, trans. by Peter
    R. Ackroyd (Oxford: Blackwell, 1957). BT 9. 92-96.
——. 1959. Reviews of Harold M. and Alma L. Moldenke, Plants of the Bible
    (Waltham, Mass.: Chronica Botanica, 1952) and Winifred Walker, All the
    Plants of the Bible (New York: Harper, 1957). BT 10. 43-47.
——. 1960. Reviews of A. C. Bouquet, Everyday Life in New Testament Times
    (New York: Scribner, 1955) and E. W. Heaton, Everyday Life in Old Testa-
    ment Times (New York: Scribner, 1956). BT 11. 43-47.
——. 1961. Review of A. R. Hulst, ed., Old Testament Translation Problems
    (Leiden: Brill, 1960). BT 12. 87-93.
——. 1962. Biblical research and Old Testament translation. BT 13. 16-22.
Moles, Abraham A. 1962. On the hierarchy of sign sets in semiotics and the problem
    of integration in perception. PPICL.
Moody, Dale. 1953. God's Only Son: The translation of John 3: 16 in the RSV.
    J. Biblical Lit. 72. 213-219. (Abridged in BT 10. 145-147. 1959.)
Moon, Parry, 1942. The names of physical concepts. Am. J. Physics 10. 134-140.
—— and Spencer, Domina E. 1946. Internationality in the names of scientific
    concepts. Am. J. Physics 14. 285-293, 431-438.
—— and ——. 1947. Internationality in the names of scientific concepts. Am. J.
    Physics 15. 84-92.
—— and ——. 1948. Modern terminology for physics. Am. J. Physics 16. 100-104.
Moore, Olin H. 1959. Some translations of Les Misérables. Mod. Lang. Notes
    74. 240-246.
Moreau, Jules Laurence. 1961. Language and Religious Language. Philadelphia:
    Westminster Press.
Morgan, B. Q. 1917. In defense of translation. Mod. Lang. J. 1. 235-242.
——. 1928-1929. The art of translation. Mod. Lang. J. 13. 80-85.
——. 1956a. On translating feminine rhymes. In his On Romanticism and the
    Art of Translation. Princeton: Princeton Univ. Press.
——. 1956b. What is translation for? Symposium 10. 322-328.
Morgan, Charles. 1948. The death of words. English 7. 56-59.
Moritzen, J. 1921. Is the translator without a literary conscience? Bookman
    53. 133-135.
Morrice, R. J. 1938. Notes on the translation of agapê. Theology 36. 304.
Morris, Charles W. 1938. Foundations of the theory of signs. International En-
    cyclopedia of Unified Science 1. 63-75. Chicago: Univ. Chicago Press.
——. 1946. Signs, Language and Behavior. New York: Prentice-Hall.
——. 1956. Varieties of Human Value. Chicago: Univ. Chicago Press.
Morris, R. P. 1944-1945. The RSV of the New Testament—a first impression.
    Religion in Life 15. 174-181.
Morris, T. E. 1942. A study in tone. Congregational Quart. 20. 58-61.
Morrison, W. M. 1913. Translation of the Bible into the Baluba language of Central
    Africa. Union Seminary Mag. 24. 414-422.
Moss, C. Scott. 1960. Current and projected status of semantic differential research.
    Psych. Record 10. 47-54.
Moule, C. F. D. 1951. 'Fulness' and 'fill' in the New Testament. Scottish J. Theology
    4. 79-86.
Moulton, H. K. 1957. Translation and revision in India. BT 8. 169-175.
——. 1958. An Indian word list. BT 9. 22-25.
——. 1959. Review of A. Van Deusen, Illustrated Dictionary of Bible Manners
    and Customs (London: Marshall, Morgan & Scott, 1958). BT 10. 191.
——. 1961. Biblical words in Indian languages; Report of conference held at
    Jabalpur, Oct. 3-9, 1960. BT 12. 69-71.
Mounin, Georges. 1955. Les belles infidèles. Paris: Cahiers du Sud. (See also review:
    Cary, 1955d.)
——. 1958. Pseudo-langues, interlangues et métalangues. Babel 4. 91-102.
——. 1959a. Linguistique structurale. Critique (Revue Générale des Publications
    Françaises et Étrangères, Paris). 143. 355-367.
——. 1959b. Les Systèmes de communication non-linguistiques et leur place dans

la vie du XXe siècle. Bull. de la Société de Linguistique de Paris 54. 176-200.
——. 1960. Un système de traduction mot à mot pour le dépouillement des publications russes. Babel 6. 126-127.
Mozley, J. F. 1935. Tyndale's knowledge of Hebrew. J. Theol. Stud. 36. 392-396.
Mueller, J. T. 1935. The first complete printed English Bible. Concordia Theol. Monthly 6. 721-731.
Muir, Edwin and Willa. 1959. Translating from the German. In Brower, ed., On Translation (q.v.), pp. 93-96.
Muir, Lawrence. 1935. The influence of the Rolle and Wycliffe Psalters upon the Psalter of the Authorized Version. Mod. Lang. Rev. 30. 302-310.
Muliyil, F. 1957. Christian missions and the versions of the Bible. BT 8. 34-36.
Munsterberg, Margaret. 1926. The gift of tongues. J. English-Germanic Philology 25. 393-406.
Murray, A. H. Jowett. 1953. A review of Lü Chenchung's revised draft of new translation of the New Testament in Chinese. BT 4. 165-167.
Murray, Gilbert. 1913. Euripides and His Age. New York: Holt.
——. 1923. On translating Greek. Living Age 318. 420-423.
Myers, Estella. 1950. Illustrative literal translation from Karré. BT 1. 122-123.
Myron, Herbert B. 1944. Translation made tolerable. Mod. Lang. J. 28. 404-408.
Nabokov, Vladimir. 1941. The art of translation. New Repub. 105. 160-162.
——. 1955. Problems of translation: 'Onegin' in English. Partisan Rev. 22. 496-512.
——. 1959. The servile path. In Brower, ed., On Translation (q.v.), pp. 97-110.
Nadel, S. F. 1937. Experiments on culture psychology. Africa 10. 421-435.
Nader, Laura. 1962. A note on attitudes and the use of language. Anthropol. Linguistics. 4. 24-29.
Naess, Arne. 1953. Interpretation and Preciseness: A Contribution to the Theory of Communication. Oslo: Dybwad.
Narasimhan, Raji. 1958. India's language problem. Eastern World 12. 16-18.
National Physical Laboratory, Teddington. 1961. Papers and Discussions, First International Conference on Machine Translation and Applied Language Analysis. London: H. M. Stationery Office.
Needham, Joseph. 1958a. The translation of old Chinese scientific and technical texts. Babel 4. 8-22.
——. 1958b. The translation of old Chinese scientific and technical texts. In Forster, ed., Aspects of Translation (q.v.), pp. 65-87.
Neiswender, Rosemary. 1962. Russian transliteration—sound and sense. Special Libraries 53. 37-41.
Nelson, Quentin D. 1952. Linguistic problems in Ngbandi. BT 3. 39-45.
——. 1957. Ngbandi terminology in translating Christian ideas. BT 8. 145-149.
Nemiah, Royal C. 1923. Shall we read literature in translation? Educational Rev. 64. 135-141.
Nestle, Erwin. 1951. How to use a Greek New Testament. BT 2. 49-55.
Newald, Richard. 1936. Von deutscher Übersetzungskunst. Zeit. f. Geistesgeschichte, pp. 190-206.
Newberry, William. 1955. Trials of translators. Chem. & Eng. News 33. 2846.
Newman, Francis W. 1861. Homeric Translation in Theory and Practice. London: Williams & Norgate.
——. 1875. Essay on poetical translation. Fraser's Mag. 12. 88-96.
Newman, Stanley S. 1941. Behavior problems in linguistic structure: A case study. In Spier, Hallowell, and Newman, eds., Language, Culture and Personality (q.v.), pp. 94-106.
——. 1954. Semantic problems in grammatical systems and lexemes: A search for method. In Hoijer, ed., Language in Culture (q.v.), pp. 82-91.
——. 1955. Vocabulary levels: Zuñi sacred and slang usage. Southwestern J. Anthropology 11. 345-354.
Newmark, Peter. 1957. Standards of translation. J. Educ. (London) 89. 248-250.
Nida, Eugene A. 1945. Linguistics and ethnology in translation problems. Word 1. 194-208.
——. 1946. Morphology: The Descriptive Analysis of Words. Ann Arbor: Univ. Michigan Press. (See also reviews: Hockett, 1947b; Trager, 1951b.)

Nida, Eugene A. (cont.). 1947a. Bible Translating: An Analysis of Principles and Procedures. New York: American Bible Society.
——. 1947b. Field techniques in descriptive linguistics. IJAL 13. 138-146.
——. 1947c. Linguistic Interludes. (2d ed.) Glendale, Calif.: Summer Inst. Linguistics.
——. 1948a. The analysis of grammatical constituents. Language 24. 168-177.
——. 1948b. The identification of morphemes. Language 24. 414-441.
——. 1949. Morphology, the Descriptive Analysis of Words. (2d ed.) Ann Arbor: Univ. Michigan Press.
——. 1950a. Learning a Foreign Language. New York: Friendship Press.
——. 1950b. Translation or paraphrase. BT 1. 97-109.
—— and Romero, C. Moisés. 1950c. The pronominal series in Maya (Yucatec). IJAL 16. 193-197.
——. 1951. A system for the description of semantic elements. Word 7. 1-14.
——. 1952a. God's Word in Man's Language. New York: Harper.
——. 1952b. A new methodology in Biblical exegesis. BT 3. 97-111.
——. 1953. What is phonemics? BT 4. 152-156.
——. 1954a. Customs and Cultures. New York: Harper.
——. 1954b. Practical limitations to a phonemic alphabet. BT 5. 35-39, 58-62.
——. 1958. Analysis of meaning and dictionary making. IJAL 24. 279-292.
——. 1959. Principles of translation as exemplified by Bible translating. In Brower, ed., On Translation (q.v.), pp. 11-31. (Reprinted BT 10. 148-164.)
——. 1960a. Message and Mission. New York: Harper.
——. 1960b. Some problems of semantic structure and translational equivalence. In William Cameron Townsend en el XXV Aniversario del I.L.V., pp. 313-325.
——. 1960c. A Synopsis of English Syntax. Norman, Okla.: Summer Inst. Linguistics.
——. 1962. Diglot scriptures. BT 13. 1-16.
——. 1963a. Bible translating and the science of linguistics. Babel 9. 99-104.
——. 1963b. Linguistic and semantic structure. In Study in Languages and Linguistics in Honor of Charles C. Fries. Ann Arbor: English Language Institute, Univ. of Michigan.
North, Eric McCoy. 1938. The Book of a Thousand Tongues. New York: Harper.
Northcott, Cecil. 1956-1957. Putting the Bible into modern speech. Religion in Life 26. 122-128.
O'Brien, Justin. 1959. From French to English. In Brower, ed., On Translation (q.v.), pp. 78-92.
O'Dette, Ralph E. 1957. Russian translation. Science 125. 579-585.
Oettinger, Anthony G. 1959. Automatic (transference, translation, remittance, shunting). In Brower, ed., On Translation (q.v.), pp. 240-267.
——. 1960. Automatic Language Translation: Lexical and Technical Aspects, With Particular Reference to Russian. Cambridge: Harvard Univ. Press.
——. 1961a. Automatic syntactic analysis and the pushdown store. Proc. 12th Symp. Appl. Mathematics, ed. by Jakobson (q.v.), pp. 104-129.
——. 1961b. A new theory of translation and its application. PNSMT, pp. 363-366.
—— and Sherry, Murray E. 1961c. Current research on automatic translation at Harvard University and predictive syntactic analysis. PNSMT, pp. 173-182.
——. 1963. Review of Rudolf Jumpelt, Die Übersetzung naturwissenschaftlicher und technischer Literatur (Berlin-Schöneberg: Langenscheidt KG, 1961). Language 39.350-352.
Ogden, C. K. and Richards, I. A. 1952. The Meaning of Meaning: A Study of the Influence of Language upon Thought and of the Science of Symbolism. (10th ed.) New York: Harcourt, Brace.
Öhman, Suzanne, 1953. Theories of the 'linguistic field.' Word 9. 123-134.
Oke, C. Clare. 1960. A suggestion with regard to Romans 8: 23. BT 11. 91-92. (Abridged by J. Harold Greenlee from an article in Interpretation, Oct. 1957, pp. 455-460.)
Oliver, N. 1927. The inadequacy of the Authorized Version. Congregational Quart. 5. 430-435.
Oliver, Robert T. 1934. The Bible and style. Sewanee Rev. 42. 350-355.

Olivier, Daria. 1956. L'éminente dignité des traducteurs. Review of Edmond Cary, La traduction dans le monde moderne (Genève: Georg et Cie., 1956). Babel 2. 175-179.

Olmsted, D. L. 1950. Ethnolinguistics so far. Stud. in Linguistics, Occ. Papers No. 2. Norman, Okla.: Summer Inst. Linguistics.

——. 1954. Towards a cultural theory of lexical innovation: a research design. Rept. 5th Ann. Round Table Meeting on Linguistics and Language Teaching, ed. by H. J. Mueller. Washington: Georgetown Univ. Press.

Olson, Harry F.; Belar, Herbert; and deSobrino, Ricardo. 1962. Demonstration of a speech processing system consisting of a speech analyzer, translator, typer, and synthesizer. J. Acoustical Soc. of America 34. 1535-1538.

O'Neill, Eugene, Jr. 1950. On translating Homer. New Repub. 123.18.

Onvlee, L. 1952a. The present position of Bible translating in the work of the Indonesian churches. BT 3. 151-158.

——. 1952b. The translation of Greek Sarks 'flesh.' BT 3. 204-206.

Opler, Morris Edward. 1946. An application of the theory of themes in culture. Wash. Acad. Sciences J. 36. 137-166.

Orage, Alfred Richard. 1922. When shall we translate? In his Readers and Writers, pp. 48-49. New York: Knopf.

Ornstein, Jacob. 1955. Mechanical translation. Science 122. 745-748.

Orr, C. W. 1941. The problem of translation. Music & Letters 22. 318-332.

Ortega y Gasset, José. 1937. Miseria y esplendor de la traducción. La Nación (Buenos Aires) May-June. (Reprinted Obras Completas, Vol. 5, pp. 427-448. Madrid: Revista de Occidente, 1946-1947.)

——. 1957. Man and People. New York: Norton.

Osgood, Charles E. 1952. The nature and measurement of meaning. Psych. Bull. 49. 197-237.

—— and Sebeok, Thomas A., eds. 1954. Psycholinguistics: A Survey of Theory and Research Problems. IJAL, Memoir 10.

—— and Tannenbaum, P. H. 1955. The principle of congruity in the prediction of attitude change. Psych. Rev. 62. 42-55.

——. 1956. Aptitude and Comprehension Correlates of 'Cloze' Readability Scores. Paper read before the APA, Chicago.

——; Suci, George J.; Tannenbaum, Percy H. 1957. The Measurement of Meaning. Urbana: Univ. Illinois Press. (See also reviews: Roger W. Brown, 1958a; Uriel Weinreich, 1958.)

——. 1960a. The cross-cultural generality of visual-verbal synesthetic tendencies. Behavioral Science 5. 146-169.

——. 1960b. Some effects of motivation on style of encoding. In Sebeok, ed., Style in Language (q.v.), pp. 293-306.

Osgood, Howard. 1887. Is the RV of the Old Testament better than the Authorized? Bibliotheca Sacra 44.71-90.

Osipoff, A. 1956a. Publication of the Russian Bible (Part I). BT 7.56-65.

——. 1956b. More about the Russian Bible. BT 7.98-101.

Oswald, V. A. and Fletcher, S. L. 1951. Proposals for the mechanical resolution of German syntax patterns. Mod. Lang. Forum 36.1-24.

Otto, Ernst. 1954. Stand und Aufgabe der Allgemeinen Sprachwissenschaft. Berlin: Walter de Gruyter.

Paige, D. D., ed. 1950. The Letters of Ezra Pound. New York: Harcourt, Brace.

Paine, Gustavus S. 1959. The Learned Men. New York: Crowell. (See also review: Bratcher, 1960d.)

Pákozdy, Ladislaus M. 1952. The new revision of the Hungarian Bible. BT 3.1-7.

——. 1956. 'I shall be that which I shall be.' BT 7.146-149.

Palfrey, Thomas R. 1932-1933. Literary translation. Mod. Lang. J. 17.410-418.

Palmer, L. R. 1936. An Introduction to Modern Linguistics. London: Macmillan.

Paneth, Eva. 1957. Friedrich van Gentz—a patron of translators? Babel 3.87-88.

Panov, D. Yu. 1956. Concerning the problem of machine translation of languages. Babel 3.109. (Summarized from original publication by USSR Acad. Sciences.)

——. 1960a. Automatic Translation. New York: Pergamon Press. (See also review: Holmstrom, 1960.)

Panov, D. Yu. (cont.). 1960b. La traduction méchanique et l'humanité. Impact (UNESCO) 10.17-25.
Pap, Leo. 1962. Review of Arno Borst, Der Turmbau von Babel (Stuttgart: A. Hiersemann, 1957-59). Language 38.400-404.
Parker-Rhodes, A. F. 1956. The behaviour of language. Science Progress 44.115-118.
Paschal, G. W. 1947. The RSV of the New Testament (a review). Rev. & Expositor 44.171-185, 331-342.
Pasternak, Boris. 1958. Translating Shakespeare. (Trans. by Manya Harari.) Twentieth Century 164. 213-228.
Patterson, Austin M. 1955. Trials of translators. Chem. & Eng. News 33. 1462.
Pattison, Everett W. 1860. Translation. Univ. Quart. 2. 124-135.
Paul, Benjamin D. 1953. Interview techniques and field relationships. In A. L. Kroeber, ed., Anthropology Today, pp. 430-451. Chicago: Univ. Chicago Press.
Pearse, Mark Guy. 1926. William Tyndale and the English New Testament. London Quart. & Holborn Rev. 145. 177-185.
Peggram, Reed E. 1940. The first French and English translations of Sir Thomas More's Utopia. Mod. Lang. Rev. 35. 330-340.
Perrochon, Henri. 1925. H. F. Amiel traducteur de Schiller. Revue Litteratures Comparées 5. 677-681.
Perry, A. M. 1949. Translating the Greek article. J. Biblical Lit. 68. 329-334.
Perston, W. 1963. Borrowing from Sanskrit into Kannada. Babel 9. 68-70.
Petersen, Julius. 1926. Die Wesenbestimmung der Deutschen Romantik. Leipzig: Quelle & Meyer.
—— and Trunz, Erich. 1933. Lyrische Weltdichtung in deutschen Übertragungen. Berlin: Junker & Dünnhaupt.
Peyser, Herbert F. 1922. Some observations on song text and libretto translation. Musical Quart. 8. 353-371.
Phair, Frances Noble. 1951. Why a simplified Gospel of Mark? BT 2. 128-130.
Phillimore, J. S. 1918. Some Remarks on Translating and Translators. London: English Association.
Phillips, Herbert P. 1959. Problems of translation and meaning in field work. Human Organization 18. 184-192.
Phillips, J. B. 1953. Some personal reflections on New Testament translation. BT 4. 53-59.
Piaget, Jean. 1926. The Language and Thought of the Child. Trans. by Marjorie Gabain. New York: Harcourt, Brace. (Meridian Books, New York, 1955.)
Pickthall, Marmaduke. 1931. Arabs and non-Arabs and the question of translating the Qur'an. Islamic Culture 5. 422-433.
Pierce, Charles. 1934. Collected Papers. Cambridge: Harvard Univ. Press.
Pierce, Ellis E. 1954. The translation of Biblical poetry. BT 5. 62-73.
Pike, Kenneth Lee. 1943. Taxemes and immediate constituents. Language 19. 65-82.
——. 1945. The Intonation of American English. Ann Arbor: Univ. Michigan Press.
——. 1947. Grammatical prerequisites to phonemic analysis. Word 3. 155-172.
——. 1948. Tone Languages. Ann Arbor: Univ. Michigan Press.
——. 1949. A problem in morphology-syntax division. Acta Linguistica 5. 125-138.
——. 1954. Language in relation to a unified theory of the structure of human behavior. Pt. I. Glendale, Calif.: Summer Inst. Linguistics.
——. 1955a. Language in relation to a unified theory of the structure of human behavior. Pt. II. Glendale, Calif.: Summer Inst. Linguistics.
——. 1955b. Meaning and hypostasis. Mon. No. 8, Georgetown Univ. Inst. Language and Linguistics, pp. 134-141. Washington: Georgetown Univ.
——. 1957a. Grammemic theory. General Linguistics 2. 35-41.
——. 1957b. A training device for translation theory and practice. Bibliotheca Sacra 114. 347-362.
——. 1958a. Interpenetration of phonology, morphology and syntax. Proc. 8th Internat. Cong. Linguists, pp. 363-374. Oslo: Oslo Univ. Press.
——. 1958b. On tagmemes née graphemes. IJAL 24. 273-278.
——. 1959. Our own tongue wherein we were born. BT 10. 70-82.
——. 1962. Dimensions of grammatical constructions. Language 38. 221-245.

Pillsbury, W. B. and Meader, C. L. 1928. The Psychology of Language. New York: D. Appleton.
Pires, A. S. 1952. At best an echo (soul-searching of a translator). Américas 4. 13-15, 43-44.
Pittman, Richard S. 1948. Nuclear structures in linguistics. Language 24. 287-292. (Reprinted in Martin Joos, ed., Readings in Linguistics [q.v.], pp. 275-278.)
Pius XII, Pope. 1956. Le traducteur—médiateur entre des cultures. Babel 2. 51-53.
Pocar, Ervino. 1956. Il compenso ai traduttori. Babel 2. 15-16.
——. 1960a. Publishers and translators. Babel 6. 166-172.
——. 1960b. Über die Möglichkeit der dichterischen Übersetzung. Babel 6. 72-76.
Podborny, Josef Georg. 1959. Zu einer international einheitlichen Umschreibung der kyrillischen Buchstaben. Babel 5. 207-212.
Poggioli, Renato. 1959. The added artificer. In Brower, ed., On Translation (q.v.), pp. 137-147.
Politzer, R. L. 1956. A brief classification of the limits of translatability. Mod. Lang. J. 40. 319-322.
Pollock, Thomas Clark. 1942. A Theory of Meaning Analyzed. General Semantics Mon. No. III. Chicago: Inst. General Semantics.
Pool, Ithiel de Sola. 1954. Symbols, meanings and social science. In Lyman Bryson, ed., Symbols and Values. New York: Harper.
——, ed. 1959. Trends in Content Analysis. Urbana: Univ. Illinois Press.
Pooley, Robert C. 1946. Teaching English Usage. New York: Appleton-Century.
Pope, Alexander. 1715. Preface to his translation of Homer's Iliad. (London: Donaldson, 1769; New York: D. Appleton, 1901.)
Portier, L. 1926. À propos des traductions de Giacomo Zanella. Revue Litteratures Comparées 5. 455-470.
Pos, Hendrick J. 1936. The philosophical significance of comparative semantics. In R. Klibansky and H. J. Paton, eds., Philosophy and History: Essays Presented to Ernst Cassirer, pp. 265-276. OUP.
Posin, Jack. 1955. Problems of literary translation from Russian into English. ATSEEL J. 13. 9-15.
Postal, Paul M. 1962. Mohawk prefix generation. PPICL.
Postgate, J. P. 1922. Translation and Translations. London: Bell.
Postman, Leo. 1951. Towards a general theory of cognition. In John H. Lohrer and Muzafer Sherif, eds., Social Psychology at the Crossroads, pp. 242-272. New York: Harper.
Potter, Simeon. 1957. Modern Linguistics. London: André Deutsch.
Pound, Ezra. 1929. Guido's relations. Dial 86. 559-568.
——. 1954. Literary Essays of Ezra Pound. (Ed. and introduced by T. S. Eliot.) London: Faber & Faber.
Preus, Herman A. 1955. The written, spoken, and signed word. Concordia Theol. Monthly 26. 641-656.
Priacel, Stefan. 1957. Review of J. F. Rozan, La prise de notes en interprétation consécutive (Genève: Librairie de l'Université, Georg et Cie., 1957). Babel 3. 37-40.
Price, Carl F. 1944-1945. Translating hymns for other tongues. Religion in Life 14. 40-51.
Price, P. Frank. 1946. The 1946 version of the New Testament—from a reader's point of view. Union Seminary Mag. 57. 202-218.
Procházka, Vladimir. 1942. Notes on translating technique. Slovoa slovesnost, Journal of the Linguistic Circle of Prague 8. 1-20. (Reprinted in Paul L. Garvin, ed. and trans., A Prague School Reader on Esthetics, Literary Structure and Style, pp. 108-130. Washington: Washington Linguistic Club, 1955.)
Pronko, N. H. 1946. Language and psycholinguistics: A review. Psych. Bull. 43. 189-239.
Propp, V. 1958. Morphology of the Folktale. Bloomington, Ind.: Indiana Univ. Research Center in Anthropology, Folklore and Linguistics, Publ. 10.
Prothro, E. Terry and Keehn, J. D. 1957. Stereotypes and semantic space. J. Soc. Psych. 45. 197-209.

Purdie, Edna. 1949. Some problems of translation in the 18th century in Germany. English Stud. 30. 191-205.
Putnam, Hilary. 1960. Minds and machines. In Dimensions of Mind, ed. by Sidney Hook. New York: New York Univ. Press.
——. 1961. Some issues in the theory of grammar. Proc. 12th Symp. Appl. Mathematics, ed. by Jakobson (q.v.), pp. 25-42.
Putnam, Samuel. 1949. Translating isn't all beer and skittles. Books Abroad 23. 235-236.
Quadri, Bruno. 1952. Aufgaben und Methoden der onomasiologischen Forschung. Reihe Romanica Helvetica. Vol. 37. Berne: A. Franke.
Quillian, Ross. 1962. A revised design for an understanding machine. Mech. Translation 7. 17-29.
Quine, Willard V. 1953. The problem of meaning in linguistics. In his From a Logical Point of View, pp. 47-64. Cambridge: Harvard Univ. Press.
——. 1959. Meaning and translation. In Brower, ed., On Translation (q.v.), pp. 148-172.
——. 1960. Word and Object. (Cambridge: Technology Press, Mass. Inst. Technology.) New York: Wiley.
——. 1961. Logic as a source of syntactical insights. Proc. 12th Symp. Appl. Mathematics, ed. by Jakobson (q.v.), pp. 1-5.
Rabin, C. 1958. The linguistics of translation. In Forster, ed., Aspects of Translation (q.v.), pp. 123-145.
Radin, Paul. 1925. Maya, Nahuatl, and Tarascan kinship terms. Am. Anthropologist 27. 100-102.
——. 1927. Primitive Man as Philosopher. New York: D. Appleton.
Radnitzky, G. A. 1961. Some remarks on the Whorfian hypothesis. Behavioral Science 6. 153-157.
Rahbar, D. 1963. Aspects of the Qur'an translation. Babel 9. 60-68.
Rainey, William H. 1950. New Guinea language problems. BT 1. 78-85.
Raper, F. J. 1961. Bible translation in the Lushai Hills. BT 12. 32-35.
Ray, Punya Sloka. 1961. The value of a language. Lingua 10. 220-233.
——. 1962. The standardization of writing. PPICL.
Read, Allen Walker. 1934. An obscenity symbol. Am. Speech 9. 264-278.
——. 1935. Lexical Evidence from Folk Epigraphy in Western North America. Paris: Lecram-Servant. (Privately printed.)
——. 1943. The lexicographer and general semantics, with a plan for 'A Semantic Guide to Current English.' Papers 2d Am. Cong. General Semantics, pp. 33-41. Chicago: Inst. General Semantics.
——. 1948. An account of the word 'semantics.' Word 4. 78-97.
——. 1949a. English words with constituent elements having independent semantic value. In T. A. Kirby and H. B. Woolf, eds., Philologia: The Malone Anniversary Studies, pp. 306-312. Baltimore: Johns Hopkins Press.
——. 1949b. Linguistic revision as a requisite for the increasing of rigor in scientific method. Paper given at 3d Am. Cong. General Semantics, pp. 1-14. Denver.
——. 1950. The adjective 'American' in England. Am. Speech 25. 280-289.
——. 1955. The term 'meaning' in linguistics. ETC.: A Review of General Semantics 13. 37-45.
——. 1962a. The labeling of national and regional variation in popular dictionaries. In Householder and Saporta, eds., Problems in Lexicography (q.v.), pp. 217-227.
——. 1962b. The splitting and coalescing of widespread languages. PPICL.
Readett, A. G. 1958. The organisation and work of the National Coal Board translation section. Babel 4. 160-165.
Recínos, Adrián. 1950. Popol Vuh: The Sacred Book of the Ancient Quiché Maya. Norman: Univ. Oklahoma Press.
Reichard, Gladys A. 1945. Linguistic diversity among the Navaho Indians. IJAL 11. 156-168.
——. 1950. Language and cultural pattern. Am. Anthropologist 52. 194-204.
Reichardt, Günther. 1957. Sowjetische Literatur nur Wissenschaft und Technik. Bad Godesberg: Deutsche Forschungsgemeinschaft; Wiesbaden: Franz Steiner.

Reichenbach, Hans. 1947. Elements of Symbolic Logic. New York: Macmillan.
Reichling, Anton. 1948. What is general linguistics? Lingua 1. 8-24.
———. 1956. Feature analysis and linguistic interpretation. In Halle et al., For Roman Jakobson (q.v.), pp. 418-422.
———. 1961. Principles and methods of syntax: cryptanalytical formalism. Lingua 10. 1-18.
——— and Uhlenbeck, E. M. 1962. Fundamentals of syntax. PPICL.
Reichstein, Ruth. 1960. Étude des variations sociale et géographiques des faits linguistiques. Word 16. 59-99.
Reifler, Erwin. 1954. Mechanical determination of the constituents of German substantive compounds. Mech. Translation 2. 3-14.
———. 1961a. Current research at the University of Washington. PNSMT, pp. 155-159.
———. 1961b. The solution of MT linguistic problems through lexicography. PNSMT, pp. 312-316.
Reitwiesner, G. W. and Weik, M. H. 1955. Survey of the Field of Mechanical Translation of Languages. Rept. PB 151147. Washington: U.S. Dept. of Commerce, Office of Tech. Services.
Rescher, N. 1956. Translation as a tool for philosophical analysis. J. Philosophy 53. 219-224.
Reyburn, William D. 1958a. Certain Cameroun translations: Analysis and plan. BT 9.171-182.
———. 1958b. Literacy in a primitive society. BT 9. 76-81.
———. 1959. The role of the heart in the translation of Acts in some northern Bantu languages. BT 10. 1-4.
Reynolds, W. D. 1911. How we translated the Bible into Korean. Union Seminary Mag. 22. 292-303.
Rhodes, Ida. 1961. The National Bureau of Standards' method of syntactic integration. PNSMT, pp. 39-44.
Richards, I. A. 1932. Mencius on the Mind; Experiments in Multiple Definition. London: Kegan Paul, Trench, Trubner & Co.
———. 1936. The Philosophy of Rhetoric. OUP.
———. 1938. Interpretation in Teaching. New York: Harcourt, Brace.
———. 1953. Toward a theory of translating. In Arthur F. Wright, ed., Studies in Chinese Thought (q.v.), pp. 247-262.
———. 1960. Poetic process and literary analysis. In Sebeok, ed., Style in Language (q.v.), pp. 9-23.
Rieu, E. V. 1953. Translation. In Cassell's Encyclopedia of Literature (London), Vol. 1, pp. 554-559.
——— and Phillips, J. B. 1954. Translating the Gospels. Concordia Theol. Monthly 25. 754-765.
——— and ———. 1955. Translating the Gospels. BT 6. 150-159.
Riffaterre, Michael. 1962. The stylistic function. PPICL.
Rischel, Jørgen. 1962. Stress, juncture, and syllabification in phonemic description. PPICL.
Robertson, A. T. 1925. Why the Revised Version? Union Seminary Mag. 36. 133-135.
———. 1935. The New Testament, translated from the Greek text of Westcott and Hort. Rev. & Expositor 32. 22-37, 121-137.
Robertson, E. H. 1959. The New Translations of the Bible. London: SCM Press. (See also review: Bratcher, 1960e.)
Robins, R. H. 1952. Noun and verb in universal grammar. Language 28. 289-298.
Robinson, T. H. 1936. Some principles of Hebrew metrics. Zeit. f. die Alttestamentliche Wissenschaft 54. 28-43.
———. 1951a. A new translation of the English Bible. BT 2. 167-168.
———. 1951b. Special features of Old Testament translation. BT 2. 113-117.
Roble, L. C. 1958. The revision of the Cebuano New Testament. BT 9. 82-84.
Roditi, Edward. 1942. The poetics of translation. Poetry 60. 32-38.
Ronai, Paulo. 1958. The trials of a technical translator. Babel 4. 210-212.
Rondel, Auguste. 1928. Les traductions françaises de Shakespeare. Études Françaises 15. 3-47.

Ronga, Giulio. 1956. Les droits des traducteurs sur le plan international. Babel
    2. 73-76.
Roolvink, R. 1954. An old Malay criticism of an even older translation of the Bible.
    BT 5. 117-120.
Roscommon, Earl of. See Dillon, Wentworth.
Rosenberg, Justus. 1956. Constant factors in translation. In his On Romanticism
    and the Art of Translation, pp. 171-195. Princeton: Princeton Univ. Press.
Rosetti, A. 1962. Sur la categorie du neutre. PPICL.
Rosin, H. 1952. Questionnaire concerning the divine names. BT 3. 199-204.
Ross, Alan S. C. 1944. The fundamental definition of the theory of language. Acta
    Linguistica 4. 101-106.
Rossetti, Dante Gabriel. 1874. Preface (1861) to *Dante and His Circle*. London:
    Ellis & White.
Rothbauer, Anton M. 1957. Zum Problem des literarischen Übersetzens. Babel
    3. 224.
Roulet, E. M. 1956. Translation work in Fulfulde (Fulani). BT 7. 30-33.
——. 1957. The linguistic situation in French West African Territories. BT
    8. 37-40.
Rowe, Thomas L. 1960. The English dubbing text. Babel 6. 116-120.
Rudnyckyj, J. B. 1962. Typological classification of 'immigrant' languages and
    dialects. PPICL.
Rudskoger, A. 1952. Fair, foul, nice and proper: a contribution to the study of
    polysemy. Gothenburg Stud. English No. 1. Stockholm: Almquist & Wiksell.
Rupp, Gordon. 1957. Review of W. Schwarz, Principles and Problems of Biblical
    Translation (Cambridge Univ. Press, 1955). J. Theol. Stud. 8. 203-205.
Rush, F. A. 1952. Standards of translation and the status of translators. Internat.
    PEN Bull. Selected Books, III, 3. 68-70.
Russell, Bertrand. 1940. An Inquiry into Meaning and Truth. New York: Norton.
Ryle, G. 1953. Ordinary language. Philosoph. Rev. 62. 167-186.
——. 1961. Use, usage and meaning. Aristotelian Soc., Sup. Vol. 35.
Sahinbas, Irfan. 1959. Translation from world literature in Turkey. Babel 5. 10-
    14.
Saleska, E. J. 1953. Our English Bible. Concordia Theol. Monthly 24. 13-25.
Salzmann, Zdenek. 1951. Contrastive field experience with language and values
    of the Arapaho. IJAL 17. 98-101.
——. 1954. The problem of lexical acculturation. IJAL 20. 137-139.
——. 1960. Cultures, languages, and translations. Anthropol. Linguistics 2. 43-
    47.
Samarin, William John. 1951. A caution on Greek connectives. BT 2. 131-132.
Samba, Joseph. 1952. The tribal or trade language. BT 3. 49-50.
Sanford, F. H. 1942. Speech and personality. Psych. Bull. 39. 811-845.
Sapir, Edward. 1912. Language and environment. Am. Anthropologist 14. 226-242.
——. 1927. Language as a form of human behavior. English J. 16. 421-433.
——. 1929a. Male and female forms of speech in Yana. Donum Natalicium Schrij-
    nen 79-85.
——. 1929b. The status of linguistics as a science. Language 5. 207-214.
——. 1930. Totality. Language Mon. No. 6. Baltimore: Waverly Press.
——. 1931a. Communication. Encyclopaedia of the Social Sciences 4. 78-81.
    New York: Macmillan.
——. 1931b. Conceptual categories in primitive languages. Science 74. 578.
—— and Swadesh, Morris. 1932. The Expression of the Ending-Point Relation in
    English, French and German. Language Mon. No. 10. Baltimore: Waverly
    Press.
——. 1933. Language. Encyclopaedia of the Social Sciences 9. 155-169. New
    York: Macmillan.
——. 1939. Language: An Introduction to the Study of Speech. New York:
    Harcourt, Brace.
——. 1944. Grading, a study in semantics. Philosophy of Science 11. 93-116.
——. 1949. Selected Writings of Edward Sapir in Language, Culture, and Per-
    sonality. David G. Mandelbaum, ed. Berkeley and Los Angeles: Univ. Cali-

fornia Press. (Includes papers listed above: 1912, 1929a, 1929b, 1931a, and 1944.)

Saporta, Sol. 1960. The application of linguistics to the study of poetic language. In Sebeok, ed., Style in Language (q.v.), pp. 82-93.

Sarndal, O. 1955. Translation of certain Biblical key-words into Zulu. BT 6. 173-178.

Saumjan, S. K. 1962. Concerning the logical basis of linguistic theory. PPICL.

Saussure, Ferdinand de. 1959. Course in General Linguistics. Trans. by Wade Basking from: Cours de linguistique génerale (Paris: Payot, 1916). New York: Philosophical Library.

Savory, Theodore H. 1953. The Language of Science. London: André Deutsch.

——. 1957. The Art of Translation. London: Jonathan Cape. (See also review: Cary, 1957b.)

Sayce, R. A. 1942. Saint-Amant's *Moyse Sauvé* and French Bible translations. Mod. Lang. Rev. 37.147-155.

Schach, Paul. 1952. Types of loan translations in Pennsylvania German. Mod. Lang. Quart. 13. 268-276.

Schachter, Paul. 1962. Kernel and non-kernel in transformational grammar. PPICL.

Schaefer, Edward H. 1954. Non-translation and functional translation—two Sinological maladies. Far Eastern Quart. 13. 251-260.

Schaeffer, Chas. F. 1868. The exegetical punctuation of the New Testament. Bibliotheca Sacra 25. 593-644.

——. 1869. The English version of the New Testament and the marginal readings. Bibliotheca Sacra 26. 486-540.

Schaff, Adam. 1962. Introduction to Semantics (trans. from Polish by Olgierd Wojtasiewicz). Warsaw: Państwowe Wydawnctwo Naukowe; Oxford: Pergamon Press.

Scherer, Edmond. 1886. De la traduction en vers. In his Études sur la littérature contemporaine. Paris: Ancienne Maison Michel Lévy Frères.

Schick, George V. 1953. The Holy Bible, RSV. Concordia Theol. Monthly 24. 1-12.

Schlauch, Margaret. 1942. The Gift of Language. New York: Dover Publications.

——. 1946. Early behaviorist psychology and contemporary linguistics. Word 2. 25-36.

Schlegel, Dom G. D. 1947. The Vulgate Bible. Scripture 2. 61-67.

Schmidt, Wilhelm. 1939. The Culture Historical Method of Ethnology: The Scientific Approach to the Racial Question. (Trans. by S. A. Sieber.) New York: Fortuny's.

Scholz, Karl William Henry. 1918. The Art of Translation. Philadelphia: Americana Germanica Press.

Schorp, A. 1959. Quelques critères de qualité dans les traductions techniques. Babel 5. 110-118.

Schwartz, Theodore and Mead, Margaret. 1961. Micro- and macro-cultural models for cultural evolution. Anthropol. Linguistics 3. 1-7.

Schwarz, W. 1944. Translation into German in the fifteenth century. Mod. Lang. Rev. 39. 368-373.

——. 1945. Theory of translation in 16th century Germany. Mod. Lang. Rev. 40. 289-299.

——. 1955. Principles and Problems of Biblical Translation: Some Reformation Controversies and Their Background. Cambridge Univ. Press. (See also reviews: Bruce, 1955; Kirk, 1957; Rupp, 1957.)

——. 1963. The history of principles of Bible translation in the Western World. Babel 9. 5-22.

Sebeok, Thomas A. 1946. Finnish and Hungarian case systems: Their form and function. Acta Instituti Hungarici Universitatis Holmiensis.

——. 1953. The structure and content of Cheremiss charms. Pt. I. Anthropos 48. 369-388.

—— and Ingemann, F. J. 1956. Studies in Cheremiss: The Supernatural. New York: Wenner-Gren Foundation.

—— and Zeps, V. J. 1958. An analysis of structured content, with application of electronic computer research in psycholinguistics. Lang. & Speech 1. 181-193.

(Abstracted in Thomas A. Sebeok, ed., Style in Language [q.v.], p. 236.)

Sebeok, Thomas A. (cont.). 1959. Approaches to the analysis of folk song texts. Ural-Altaische Jahrbücher 31. 392-399.

——, ed. 1960a. Style in Language. (Cambridge: Technology Press, Mass. Inst. Technology.) New York: Wiley.

—— and Zeps, V. J. 1960b. An analysis of structured content, with application of electronic computer research in psycholinguistics. (Abstract.) In Sebeok, ed., Style in Language (q.v.), p. 236.

Seeber, E. D. and Remak, H.H.H. 1946. The first French translation of *The Deserted Village*. Mod. Lang. Rev. 41. 62-67.

Seely, Francis M. 1957. Some problems in translating the Scriptures into Thai. BT 8. 49-61.

——. 1959. Note on G'RH with especial reference to Proverbs 13: 8. BT 10. 20-21.

Seidensticker, Edward. 1958. On trying to translate Japanese. Encounter 11. 12-20.

Seitz, Rudolph O. 1962. 'Japlish,' the Japanese brand of English. Special Libraries 53. 30-34.

Sellers, O. R. 1946. Limits in Old Testament interpretation. J. Near Eastern Stud. 5. 83-91.

Sevenster, Jan N. 1947. The theological importance of translation. Congregational Quart. 24. 137-145.

Shannon, Claude L. and Weaver, Warren. 1949. The Mathematical Theory of Communication. Urbana: Univ. Illinois Press. (See also review: Hockett, 1953.)

Sharman, J. C. 1957. Some general observations on the translator's art. BT 8. 28-31.

Sheffield, Alfred Dwight. 1912. Grammar and Thinking, A Study of the Working Conceptions in Syntax. New York: Knickerbocker Press.

Sheppard, G. W. 1955. The problem of translating 'God' into Chinese. BT 6. 23-30.

Sheridan, Peter. 1955. Research in language translation on the IBM Type 701. Tech. Newsletter, No. 9, Appl. Science Div., IBM, pp. 5-24.

Sherry, Murray E. 1961. Automatic affix interpretation and reliability. PNSMT, pp. 317-324.

Shields, David L. 1951. What should we translate? Wilson Library Bull. 25. 657f.

Short, Charles. 1881. The new revision of King James' Revision of the New Testament. Am. J. Philology 2. 149-180.

Shouby, E. 1951. The influence of the Arabic language on the psychology of the Arabs. Middle East J. 5. 284-302.

Showerman, Grant. 1916. The way of the translator. Unpopular Rev. 5. 84-100.

Shuey, R. L. 1953. Bits, language efficiency, and Information Theory. General Electronic Rev., Sept., pp. 15-19.

Siertsema, B. 1961. Language learning and language analysis. Lingua 10. 128-148.

Silveira, Brenno. 1954. A Arte de Traduzir. São Paulo: Edições Melhoramentos.

Sime, A. H. M. 1936. William Tyndale. Congregational Quart. 14. 442-448.

Simmons, E. J. 1938. English translations of *Eugene Onegin*. Slavonic & East European Rev. 17. 198-208.

Simpson, G. G. 1961. Principles of Animal Taxonomy. (Jessup Lectures, Columbia University, 1960.) New York: Columbia Univ. Press.

Singh, Kushwant. 1956. Translating the Sikh Scriptures. Eastern World 10. 40-41.

Siro, Paavo. 1962. On the fundamentals of sentence structure. PPICL.

Sjoberg, Andrée F. 1962. Writing, speech, and society: some changing interrelationships. PPICL.

Skilton, J. H. 1943. The basic text for the latest revision of the Roman Catholic New Testament in English. Westminster Theol. J. 6. 1-18.

——. 1944. A translation of a translation. Westminster Theol. J. 7. 23-39.

——. 1945. A revision of a revision. Westminster Theol. J. 8. 61-82.

——. 1947. A Roman Catholic Testament. Westminster Theol. J. 9. 198-219.

Skinner, B. F. 1938. The Behavior of Organisms. New York: Appleton-Century.

——. 1953. Science and Human Behavior. New York: Macmillan.

——. 1957. Verbal Behavior. New York: Appleton-Century-Crofts. (See also review: Chomsky, 1959.)

Sledd, James. 1959. A Short Introduction to English Grammar. Chicago: Scott, Foresman.

Slocum, Marianna C. 1958. Christianization of vocabulary in the translation of the Tzeltal New Testament. BT 9. 49-56.

Slotki, I. W. 1931. Typographic arrangement of ancient Hebrew poetry. Zeit. f. die Alttestamentliche Wissenschaft 49. 211-222.

Smalley, William A. 1953. A programme for missionary language learning. BT 4. 106-112.

——. 1957a. Finding out how close related dialects are. Part I: Language, dialect, and communication. BT 8.68-74.

——. 1957b. Finding out how close related dialects are. Part II: Conducting a dialect survey. BT 8. 114-126.

——. 1958. Dialect and orthography in Kipende. BT 9. 63-69.

——. 1959a. How shall I write this language? BT 10. 49-69.

——. 1959b. Orthography Conference for French West Africa. BT 10. 181-187.

Smeaton, B. Hunter. 1957. Translation, its nature, problems, and limitations. J. des Traducteurs 2. 85-89.

——. 1958. Translation, structure and lexicography. J. des Traducteurs 3. 122-130.

Smith, Edwin W. 1945. A school for translators. Internat. Rev. Missions 34. 243-252.

Smith, Henry Lee, Jr. 1952. An outline of metalinguistic analysis. Rept. 3d Ann. Round Table Meeting on Linguistics and Language Teaching, pp. 59-66. Washington: Georgetown Univ. Press.

Smith, J. M. Powis. 1925. Some difficulties of a translator. J. Religion 5. 163-171.

Smith, Madorah E. 1939. Some light on the problem of bilingualism as found from a study of the progress in mastery of English among preschool children of non-American ancestry in Hawaii. Gen. Psych. Mon. 21. 121-284.

Smith, Miles. 1611. The Translators to the Reader. Preface to Authorized Version of the Holy Bible (King James Version).

Smoke, W. and Dubinsky, E. 1961. A program for the machine translation of languages. Mech. Translation 6. 2-10.

Souter, Alexander. 1920. Hints on Translation from Latin into English. London: Society for Promoting Christian Knowledge.

Spaeth, Sigmund. 1915. Translating to music. Musical Quart. 1. 291-298.

Spearing, Evelyn M. 1920. Alexander Nevile's translation of Seneca's 'Oedipus.' Mod. Lang. Rev. 15. 359-363.

Spencer, Harold. 1951. Humpty Dumpty—the problem of theological language. Internat. Rev. Missions 40. 185-189.

——. 1953. Musalmani Vernacular Gospels used in India (Part I). BT 4. 162-165.

Spicer, Edward H. 1943. Linguistic aspects of Yaqui acculturation. Am. Anthropologist 45. 410-426.

Spier, Leslie; Hallowell, A. Irving; and Newman, Stanley S., eds. 1941. Language, Culture and Personality: Essays in Memory of Edward Sapir. Menasha, Wis.: Sapir Memorial Publ. Fund.

Spinka, M. 1933. Slavic translations of the Scriptures. J. Religion 13. 415-432.

Spiro, Melford E. 1954. Human nature in its psychological dimensions. Am. Anthropologist 56. 19-30.

Spitzer, Leo. 1948. Essays in Historical Semantics. New York: S. F. Vanni.

Spitzer, M. 1958. Hebrew translation in Israel. Babel 4. 62-65.

Stafford, T. P. 1938. The language of the Bible. Rev. & Expositor 35. 298-303.

Stamm, W. A. 1956. Revision of the Twi Bible in the Gold Coast. BT 7. 34-38.

Stankiewicz, Edward. 1960a. Expressive language. (Abstract.) In Sebeok, ed., Style in Language (q.v.), pp. 96-97.

——. 1960b. Linguistics and the study of poetic language. In Sebeok, ed., Style in Language (q.v.), pp. 69-81.

Stevenson, Charles L. 1948. Meaning: Descriptive and emotive. Philosoph. Rev. 57. 127-144.

Stewart, J. S. 1953. Review of the Gospel of St. Mark, A New Translation in Simple English. Scottish J. Theology 6. 99 f.

Storr, Francis. 1909. The art of translation. Educational Rev. 38. 359-379.

Stroll, Avrum. 1961. Meaning, referring and the problem of universals. Inquiry 4. 107-127.

Studley, Marian H. 1925. Milton and his paraphrases of the Psalms. Philology Quart. 4. 364-372.

Sturtevant, E. H. 1947. An Introduction to Linguistic Science. New Haven: Yale Univ. Press.

Suci, George J. 1960. A comparison of semantic structures in American Southwest culture groups. J. Abn. & Soc. Psych. 61. 25-30.

Surzur, Roland. 1957. Existe-t-il une stylistique publicitaire? J. des Traducteurs 2. 39-48, 111-117.

Swadesh, Morris. 1934. The phonemic principle. Language 10. 117-129. (Reprinted in Joos, ed., Readings in Linguistics [q.v.], pp. 32-37.)

——. 1960. On the unit of translation. Anthropol. Linguistics 2. 39-42.

Swanson, Don R. 1961. The nature of multiple meaning. PNSMT, pp. 386-393.

Swellengrebel, J. L. 1950a. Bible translation and politeness in Bali. BT 1. 124-130.

——. 1950b. A literal translation of Mark 1 in Balinese. BT 1. 75-78.

——. 1951. Further translation questions on Bali. BT 2. 25-30.

——. 1953a. Questions and answers on Balinese Luke. BT 4. 59-66.

——. 1953b. The renderings of some Biblical terms in languages of the Indonesian Archipelago. (Part I.) BT 4. 168-182.

——. 1954. The Bible in Bahasa Indonesia. BT 5. 130-136.

——. 1955a. The renderings of some Biblical terms in languages of the Indonesian Archipelago. (Part II.) BT 6. 32-46.

——. 1955b. The translation of the divine names in the Bahasa Indonesia. BT 6. 110-119.

——. 1960a. 'Leprosy' and the Bible; The translation of 'Tsara'ath' and 'Lepra.' BT 11. 69-80.

——. 1960b. Review of Reuben A. Brower, ed., On Translation (Cambridge: Harvard Univ. Press, 1959). BT 11. 187-190.

——. 1961. Review of John D. W. Watts, Lists of Words Occurring Frequently in the Hebrew Bible (Leiden: Brill, 1959). BT 12. 46.

Sywulka, Edward F. 1952. Notes on the translation of the Mam New Testament. BT 3.54-61.

Szaley, Loránd. Untersuchungen zur semantischen Struktur der Zeitwörter. Zeitschrift f. experimentelle une angew. Psychologie 9. 140-163.

Takahashi, Masashi. 1959. The colloquial Japanese Bible of 1955. BT 10. 101-106.

Tancock, L. W. 1958. Some problems of style in translation from French. In Forster, ed., Aspects of Translation (q.v.), pp. 29-51.

Taube, Mortimer. 1961. Computers and Common Sense. New York: Columbia Univ. Press.

Tax, Sol. 1950. Animistic and rational thought. Papers Kroeber Anthropol. Soc. 2. 1-5.

Taylor, Douglas. 1958. On anthropologists' use of linguistics. Am. Anthropologist 60. 940-941.

Taylor, Douglas Rae; Keller, Hans E.; and Fay, Percival B. 1963. Remarks on the lexicon of Dominican French Creole. Romance Philology 16. 402-415.

Taylor, Vincent. 1955. The syntax of New Testament Greek. BT 6. 20-23.

Taylor, W. C. 1938. The first Catholic version of the Greek New Testament in Portuguese. Rev. & Expositor 35. 54-61.

Taylor, W. L. 1953. 'Cloze procedure': A new tool for measuring readability. Journalism Quart. 30. 415-433.

——. 1954. Application of Cloze and Entropy Measures to the Study of Contextual Restraints in Samples of Continuous Prose. Ph. D. thesis. Urbana: Univ. of Illinois. Dissertation Abstracts 15. 464-465.

——. 1956. Recent developments in the use of 'cloze procedure.' Journalism Quart. 33. 42-48, 99.

Teele, Roy E. 1949. Through a Glass Darkly. Ann Arbor: Univ. Michigan Press.

Teile, R. E. 1957. Translations of Noh plays. Comparative Literature 9. 345-368.

Tesniere, Lucien. 1959. Eléments de syntaxe structurale. Paris: Klinksieck.

Thackeray, H. St. John. 1903a. The Greek translators of Ezekiel. J. Theol. Stud. 4. 398-411.
——. 1903b. The Greek translators of Jeremiah; The relation of the Greek Jeremiah to the Book of Baruch. J. Theol. Stud. 4. 245-266.
——. 1903c. The Greek translators of the Prophetical Books. J. Theol. Stud. 4. 578-585.
——. 1908. Renderings of the infinitive absolute in the LXX. J. Theol. Stud. 9. 597-601.
——. 1917. The Letter of Aristeas. London: Society for Promoting Christian Knowledge.
Thieme, Karl. 1955. Die geschichtlichen Haupt-Typen des Dolmetschens. Babel 1. 55-60.
——; Herman, A.; and Gläser, E. 1956a. Beiträge zur Geschichte des Dolmetschens. Bd. 1, Schriften des Auslands- und Dolmetscher-instituts der Johannes-Gutenberg-Universität Mainz in Germersheim. München: Isar.
——. 1956b. Das Problem der sachverständigen öffentlichen Kritik an Buchübersetzungen. Lebende Sprachen 1.27-28.
——. 1963. Martin Buber and Franz Rosenzweig's translation of the Old Testament. Babel 9. 82-86.
Thierfelder, Franz. 1955. Darf der Übersetzer den Text des Originals verändern? Babel 1.51-54.
Thistle, Mel. 1957. Communication Barriers in Our World of Technology. Paper delivered before National Council of Teachers of English, Minneapolis, Nov. 29.
Thomas, David. 1955. Three analyses of the Ilocano pronoun system. Word 11. 204-208.
——. 1957. An Introduction to Mansaka Lexicography. 6 pp., typescript. Nasuli, Philippines: Summer Inst. Linguistics.
Thompson, John A. 1955. The origin and nature of the chief printed Arabic Bibles. BT 6. 2-12, 51-55, 98-106, 146-150.
Thompson, Stith. 1946. The Folktale. New York: Dryden Press.
Thompson, William E. 1950. Gender, pronominal reference, and possession in Guajiro. BT 1. 165-169.
Thornton, Thomas P. 1954. Luther and the translation of Liber Generationis (Matt. 1: 1). Neophilologus 38. 254-259.
Thrall, Margaret E. 1962. Greek Particles in the New Testament: Linguistic and Exegetical Studies. In Bruce M. Metzger, ed., New Testament Tools and Studies, Vol. III. Leiden: E. J. Brill.
Thursfield, Hugh. 1936. Translation. Cornhill 153. 482-486.
Tibawi, A. L. 1962. Is the Qur'an translatable? Muslim World 52. 4-16.
Tietze, Andreas. 1962. Problems of Turkish lexicography. In Householder and Saporta, eds., Problems in Lexicography (q.v.), pp. 263-272.
Tillich, Paul. 1957. The Dynamics of Faith. New York: Harper.
Tin, Pham Xuan. 1952. Translating the Word of God. BT 3. 20-23.
——. 1957. Time spent in translating the Jorai New Testament. BT 8. 74.
Tolman, H. C. 1901. The Art of Translating. Boston: Sanborn.
Torrance, T. F. 1950. A study in New Testament communication. Scottish J. Theology 3. 298-313.
Tosh, Wayne. 1962. Content recognition and the production of synonymous expressions. PPICL.
Towner, L. B. 1935. Versions of the Psalter. Theology 31. 32.
Toynbee, Paget. 1913. Dante's remarks on translation in the 'Convivio.' Mod. Lang. Rev. 8. 101-102.
Trager, George L. 1949. The Field of Linguistics. Stud. in Linguistics: Occ. Papers, 1. Norman, Okla.: Battenburg Press.
—— and Smith, Henry Lee, Jr. 1951a. An Outline of English Structure. Stud. in Linguistics, Occ. Papers, 3. Norman, Okla.: Battenburg Press.
——. 1951b. Review of Eugene A. Nida, Morphology, the Descriptive Analysis of Words (2d ed.; Ann Arbor: Univ. Michigan Press, 1949). IJAL 17. 126-131.
——. 1960. Taos III: paralanguage. Anthropol. Linguistics 2. 24-30.
——. 1961. The typology of paralanguage. Anthropol. Linguistics 3. 17-21.

Trever, John C. 1951. Scrolls from a Dead Sea cave. BT 2. 75-79.
Triandis, Harry C. and Osgood, Charles E. 1958. A comparative factorial analysis of semantic structure in monolingual Greek and American college students. J. Abn. & Soc. Psych. 57. 187-196.
——. 1960. Some determinants of interpersonal communication. Human Relations 13. 279-287.
Trier, Jost. 1931. Der deutsche Wortschatz im Sinnbezirk des Verstandes: die Geschichte eines sprachlichen Feldes. Heidelberg, C. Winter.
——. 1934. Das sprachliche Feld. Eine Auseinandersetzung. Neue Jahrbücher für Wissenschaft u. Jugendbildung 10. 428-449.
Tritton, A. S. 1933. The Bible text of Theodore Abu Kurra. J. Theol. Stud. 34. 52-54.
Trubetskoy, Nikolai Sergieevich. 1939. Principes de Phonologie. Paris: Klinksieck. (Trans. by J. Cantineau from Grundzüge der Phonologie. Prague: Cercle Linguistique.)
Tsien, Tsuen-Hsuin. 1954. Western impact on China through translation. Far Eastern Quart. 13. 305-327.
Turbayne, Colin Murray. 1962. The Myth of Metaphor. New Haven: Yale Univ. Press.
Turner, C. H. 1910-1911. Curiosities of Latin interpretation of the Greek New Testament. J. Theol. Stud. 12. 273-275.
Turner, C. W. 1950. Revision of the Spanish Bible. BT 1. 155-158.
Turner, Nigel. 1956a. The Greek translators of Ezekiel. J. Theol. Stud. 7. 12-24.
——. 1956b. The translation of *Moichatai ep' Autēn* in Mark 10: 11. BT 7. 151-152.
——. 1959. The preposition *en* in the New Testament. BT 10. 113-120.
Tustin, Arnold. 1952. Feedback. Scientific American 187. 48-55.
Twaddell, W. Freeman. 1935. On defining the phoneme. Language Monograph No. 16. Baltimore: Waverly Press. (Reprinted in Joos, ed., Readings in Linguistics [q.v.], pp. 55-79.)
——. 1949. Meanings, habits and rules. Lang. Learning 2. 4-11.
Twentyman, John H. 1951. Proposed revision of the Bible in Spanish. BT 2. 88-90.
Twyman, L. and E. 1953. Suki Translation. BT 4. 91-95.
Tyler, A. W. 1873. Paul's panegyric of love—a new critical text, translation and digest. Bibliotheca Sacra 30. 128-143.
Tytler, Alexander Fraser (Lord Woodhouselee). 1790. Essay on the Principles of Translation. London: Dent.
Ullman, Stephen. 1953. Descriptive semantics and linguistic typology. Word 9. 225-240.
——. 1959. The Principles of Semantics; A Linguistic Approach to Meaning. (2d ed. rev.) Glasgow: Jackson; Oxford: Blackwell. (See also review: Jumpelt, 1960a.)
——. 1962. Semantics, an Introduction to the Science of Meaning. New York: Barnes & Noble.
Underhill, Ruth. 1938. Singing for Power. Berkeley: Univ. California Press.
UNESCO. 1957. Report on Scientific and Technical Translation. Paris: UNESCO.
Unwin, Stanley. 1946. On translations. PW 149. 151-153.
Urban, Wilbur M. 1939. (2d printing, 1951.) Language and Reality: The Philosophy of Language and the Principles of Symbolism. New York: Macmillan. (See also review: Longacre, 1956a.)
van der Veen, H. 1950. Difficulties of translating the Bible into the South-Toradja language. BT 1. 21-25.
——. 1952a. On translating the Greek word 'Sarks' in the South Toradja language. BT 3. 207-208.
——. 1952b. The use of literary or poetic language in poetic parts of the Bible. BT 3.212-218.
——. 1961. Experience with Bible reading-books. BT 12. 1-13.
Van Doren, Mark. 1950. Uses of translation. Nation 170. 474.
Vanhoye, Albert. 1963. La Structure Littéraire de L'Epître aux Hebreux (Studia Neutestamentica). Paris-Bruges: Desclee de Brouwer.
Vellacott, Philip. 1954. Four Plays of Euripides. (Introduction.) London: Penguin.
Vendryes, J. 1925. Language. London: Kegan Paul, Trench, Trubner & Co.

Verhaar, John W. M. 1962. Speech, language and inner form. (Some linguistic remarks on thought.) PPICL.

Verkuyl, Gerrit. 1951. The Berkeley version of the New Testament. BT 2. 80-85.

Vickery, B. C. 1956. The language barrier in science. Linguists' Rev. (London) Jan., pp. 5-8; May, pp. 10-12.

Vielhauer, Adolf. 1956. A glimpse into the workshop of a Bible translator. BT 7. 122-130.

Vigotsky, L. S. 1939. Thought and speech. Psychiatry 2. 29-52.

Vinay, Jean-Paul, ed. 1952. Traductions—mélanges offerts en mémoire de Georges Panneton. Montréal: Institut de Traduction.

——. 1956. Rubrique de langage. I. Néologismes et Création lexicologique. II. Vision comparative et vision absolue. III. Les déictiques. J. des Traducteurs 1. 27-30, 59-63, 91-95.

——. 1957. Peut-on enseigner la traduction? ou Naissance de la Stylistique comparée. J. des Traducteurs 2. 141-148.

Virtue, Leila M. and Bakalanoff, N. W. 1952. The technique of translation. Mod. Lang. J. 36.396-401.

Voegelin, C. F. and E. W. 1935. Shawnee name groups. Am. Anthropologist 37. 617-635.

—— and Harris, Zellig S. 1945. Linguistics in ethnology. Southwestern J. Anthropology 1.455-465.

—— and ——. 1947. The scope of linguistics. Am. Anthropologist 49. 588-600.

——. 1948. Distinctive features and meaning equivalence. Language 24. 132-135.

——. 1949. Linguistics without meaning and culture without words. Word 5. 36-45.

—— and Harris, Zellig S. 1951. Methods for determining intelligibility among dialects of natural languages. Proc. Am. Philosoph. Soc. 95. 322-329.

——. 1952a. Linguistically marked distinctions in meaning. In Selected Papers, 29th Internat. Cong. Americanists. Sol Tax, ed. Chicago: Univ. Chicago Press.

—— and Harris, Zellig S. 1952b. Training in anthropological linguistics. Am. Anthropologist 54. 322-327.

——. 1954a. A modern method for field work treatment of previously collected texts. J. Am. Folklore 67. 15-20.

——. 1954b. Multiple state translation. IJAL 20. 271-280.

——; Yegerlehner, John F.; and Robinett, Florence M. 1954c. Shawnee laws: perceptual statements for the language and for the content. In Hoijer, ed., Language in Culture (q.v.), pp. 32-46.

——. 1956. Subsystems within systems in cultural and linguistic typologies. In Halle et al., For Roman Jakobson (q.v.), pp. 592-599.

—— and Voegelin, Florence M. 1957a. Hopi Domains, A Lexical Approach to the Problem of Selection. IJAL Memoir No. 14.

——. 1957b. Meaning correlations and selections in morphology-syntax paradigms. Academia Sinica: Bull. Inst. History and Philology 29. 91-111.

——. 1959. Model-directed structuralization. Anthropol. Linguistics 1. 9-25.

——. 1960a. Casual and noncasual utterances within unified structure. In Sebeok, ed., Style in Language (q.v.), pp. 57-68.

—— and Voegelin, Florence M. 1960b. Selection in Hopi ethics, linguistics, and translation. Anthropol. Linguistics 2. 48-78.

——. 1961a. Typology of density ranges II: Contrastive and non-contrastive syntax. IJAL 27.287-297.

—— and Voegelin, Florence M. 1961b. Typological classification of systems with included, excluded and self-sufficient alphabets. Anthropol. Linguistics 3. 55-96.

Vogel, George A. W. 1935. A comparison of the King James and the Douay Version. Concordia Theol. Monthly 6. 18-24.

Vogt, Hans. 1954. Contact of languages. Word 10.365-374.

von den Steinen, H. 1956. Neugriechische Lyrik in deutscher Übertragung. Babel 2. 57-62.

Vonnegut, Kurt, Jr. 1955. Der Arme Dolmetscher. Atlantic 196. 86-88.

Voorhoeve, J. 1957. Missionary linguistics in Surinam. BT 8. 179-190.

——. 1961. Spelling difficulties in Sranan. BT 12. 21-31.

Voronin, V. A. 1961. An independent system of analysis of a Chinese text for mechanical translation to Russian (in Russian). Mashinnyj Perevod 2. (Abstracted in La Traduction Automatique 3.17. 1962.)

Wach, Joachim. 1926-1929. Das verstehen; grundzüge einer geschichte der hermeneutischen theorie im 19 jahrhundert. Tübingen: Mohr.

Waismann, F. 1945. Verifiability. Proc. Aristotelian Soc., Sup. Vol. 29.

Waley, Arthur. 1941. Translations from the Chinese. (1st ed., 1919.) New York: Knopf.

Walker, William H. 1960. Translation and teaching; one without the other is not enough! BT 11. 42-43.

Wall, Robert E. 1961. System design of a computer for Russian-English translation. PNSMT, pp. 491-510.

Wallace, Anthony F. C. and Atkins, John. 1960. The meaning of kinship terms. Am. Anthropologist 62. 58-60.

——. 1961. The psychic unity of human groups. In Bert Kaplan, ed., Studying Personality Cross-Culturally, pp. 129-164. Evanston, Ill.: Row, Peterson.

Wallington, D. H. 1961. 'Leprosy' and the Bible; conclusion. BT 12. 75-79.

Wang, S. L. 1926. A demonstration of the language difficulty involved in comparing racial groups by means of verbal intelligence tests. J. Applied Psychology 10. 102-106.

Ward, Dennis. 1957. On translating *slovo o polku Igoreve.* Slavonic & East European Rev. 36. 502-512.

Ward, R. A. 1955. Salute to translators. BT 6. 80-94.

Warfel, Harry R. 1952. 1460 U.S. books translated in 1950. PW 161. 1450-1452.

Warren, E. B. 1934. The pastor and his Greek New Testament. Rev. & Expositor 31. 208-210.

Warren, T. H. 1895. The art of translation. Quart. Rev. 182. 324-353.

Wartensleben, G. von. 1910. Beiträge zur Psychologie des Übersetzens. Zeit. f. Psychologie 57.89-115.

Waterhouse, Viola. 1963. Independent and dependent sentences. IJAL 29. 45-54.

Waterman, G. Henry. 1952. What is Koiné Greek? BT 3. 127-131.

——. 1957. Report on the Formosa Translators' Conference. BT 8. 32-34.

——. 1960a. Problems of syntax in the translation of the Scriptures in Philippine dialects. BT 11. 162-172.

——. 1960b. The translation of theological terms in some of the major dialects of the Philippines. BT 11. 24-31.

Weber, Hans. 1954. Das Tempus System des deutschen und des französischen. Berne: A. Francke. (No. 45 in Romanica Helvetica.)

Weigle, Luther A. 1945-1946. The making of the RSV Version of the New Testament. Religion in Life 15. 163-173.

——, ed. 1946. An Introduction to the Revised Standard Version of the New Testament. New York: International Council of Religious Education.

——. 1952. The English of the RSV New Testament. BT 3. 8-11.

Weinberg, Harry L. 1959. Levels of Knowing and Existence: Studies in General Semantics. New York: Harper.

Weinreich, Uriel. 1953. Languages in Contact. New York: Linguistic Circle of New York.

——. 1958. Review of Charles E. Osgood, George J. Suci, and Percy H. Tannenbaum, The Measurement of Meaning (Urbana: Univ. of Illinois Press, 1957). Word 14. 346-366.

——. 1962. Lexicographic definition in descriptive semantics. In Householder and Saporta, eds., Problems in Lexicography (q.v.), pp. 25-43.

Weisgerber, Leo. 1927. Die Bedeutungslehre—ein Irrweg der Sprachwissenschaft? Germ.-Romanische Monatsschrift 15. 161-183.

——. 1928. Vorschläge zur Methode und Terminologie der Wortforschung. Indogermanische Forschungen 305-325.

——. 1951. Das Gesetz der Sprache (als Grundlage des Sprachstudiums). Heidelberg: Quelle & Meyer.

——. 1953-1954. Vom Weltbild der deutschen Sprache. I. Die inhaltbezogene grammatik; II. Die Sprachliche Erschliessung der Welt. Dusseldorf.

——. 1955a. Der Begriff der Wörter. Corolla Linguistica (Festschrift für Ferdinand Sommer zum 80 Geburtstage), pp. 248-254. Wiesbaden.
——. 1955b. Das Dolmetschen und die sprachliche Verwandlung der Welt. Babel 1. 7-9.
Weiss, A. P. 1925. Linguistics and psychology. Language 1. 52-57.
Welby, V. 1911. Significs and Language. London: Macmillan.
Weld-Blundell, Dom Adrian. 1947. The revision of the Vulgate Bible. Scripture 2. 100-105.
Welford, A. T. 1948. The use of archaic language in religious expression. Brit. J. Psychology 38. 209-217.
Wellard, James H. 1928. The art of translating. Quart. Rev. 250. 128-147.
Wellek, René. 1956. The concept of evolution in literary history. In Halle et al., For Roman Jakobson (q.v.), pp. 653-661.
Wells, Rulon S. 1945. The pitch phoneme of English. Language 21. 27-39.
——. 1947a. De Saussure's system of linguistics. Word 3. 1-31.
——. 1947b. Immediate constituents. Language 23. 81-117.
——. 1949. Automatic alternation. Language 25. 99-116.
——. 1954. Meaning and use. Word 10.235-250.
——. 1957. Is a structural treatment of meaning possible? Proc. 8th Internat. Cong. Linguists, pp. 654-666.
——. 1960. Nominal and verbal style. In Sebeok, ed., Style in Language (q.v.), pp. 213-220.
——. 1961. A measure of subjective information. Proc. 12th Symp. Appl. Mathematics, ed. by Jakobson (q.v.), pp. 237-244.
Wentz, Abdel Ross. 1953. Luther and his methods of translating. BT 4. 27-32.
Werbow, Stanley N. 1961. Report on the Texas project. PNSMT, pp. 121-125.
Werner, C. F. 1955. Die Fachausdrücke und 'lateinischen' Namen in der Biologie. Sprachforum 1. 259-264.
Werner, Heinz. 1948. Comparative Psychology of Mental Development. Chicago: Follett.
West, Constance B. 1932. La théorie de la traduction au XVIIIe siècle. Revue Littérature Comparée 12. 330-355.
Westburg, Sigurd F. 1956. Some experiences in the translation of Genesis and Exodus into Lingala. BT 7. 117-122.
Whatmough, Joshua. 1957. Language; A Modern Synthesis. Mentor Books 209. New York: New American Library.
White, Leslie A. 1949. The Science of Culture. New York: Farrar, Straus.
White, Peter T. 1955. The interpreter: Linguist plus diplomat. NYT Mag., Nov. 6, pp. 10-11, 32-33.
Whitehall, H. 1956. From linguistics to criticism. Kenyon Rev. 18. 411-421.
——. 1957. From linguistics to poetry. In Northrop Frye, ed., Sound and Poetry, pp. 134-146. New York: Columbia Univ. Press.
Whitehorn, John. 1956. Some language problems of Formosa. BT 7. 17-21.
Whiteley, W. H. 1961. Further problems in the study of Swahili sentences. Lingua 10. 148-174.
Whitfield, Francis J. 1955. Review of Rudolf Magnusson, Studies in the Theory of Parts of Speech (Lund: Gleerup; Copenhagen: Munksgaard, 1954). Language 31. 245-247.
——. 1956. Linguistic usage and glossematic analysis. In Halle et al., For Roman Jakobson (q.v.), pp. 670-676.
Whitley, W. T. 1911. The character and history of the 1611 version. Rev. & Expositor 8. 483-510.
Whitney, H. M. 1902-1911. The latest translation of the Bible. Bibliotheca Sacra: 59. 217-237, 451-475, 653-681. 60. 109-120, 342-357. 61.248-271. 62.71-89, 245-263. 64.464-488. 66. 467-497. 68.405-415.
Whorf, Benjamin Lee. 1945. Grammatical categories. Language 21. 1-11.
——. 1950. An American Indian model of the universe. IJAL 16. 67-72.
——. 1956. Language, Thought and Reality; Selected Writings. John B. Carroll, ed. (Cambridge: Technology Press, Mass. Inst. Technology.) New York: Wiley. (See also review: Jumpelt, 1957a.)

Wickens, G. M. 1953. The transliteration of Arabic: An approach in the light of current problems of printing and publication. J. Near Eastern Stud. 12. 253-256.

Widmer, Walter. 1959. Fug und Unfug des Übersetzens. Cologne: Kiepenheuer & Witsch.

Wiener, Norbert. 1948. Cybernetics, or Control and Communication in the Animal and the Machine. New York: Wiley.

———. 1954. The Human Use of Human Beings; Cybernetics and Society. New York: Houghton Mifflin.

Wikgren, Allen (with E. C. Colwell & Ralph Marcus). 1947. Hellenistic Greek Texts. Chicago: Univ. Chicago Press.

———. 1950. The use of marginal notes in the English Bible. Congregational Quart. 27. 143-153.

Willans, H. C. 1953. Translators' conference in Burma. BT 4. 21-25.

———. 1954. Centenary of the Sgaw Karen Bible. BT 5. 126-130.

Williams, C. B. 1915. Grammatical glimpses at some Scriptures. Rev. & Expositor 12. 234-245.

Williams, Charles Kingsley. 1952. The New Testament: A new translation in plain English. BT 3. 61-66.

Williams, Edwin B. 1960. Analysis of the problem of meaning discrimination in Spanish and English bilingual lexicography. Babel 6. 121-125.

Williams, S. W. 1878. The controversy among the Protestant missionaries on the proper translation of the words God and Spirit into Chinese. Bibliotheca Sacra 35. 732-778.

Williams, Thyllis. 1961. From text to topics in mechanized search systems. PNSMT, pp. 358-362.

Willoughby, L. A. 1921. English translations and adaptations of Schiller's *Robbers*. Mod. Lang. Rev. 16. 297-315.

Wils, J. 1963. Aspects of sacral language. Babel 9. 36-48.

Wilson, A. J. 1909. Emphasis in the New Testament. J. Theol. Stud. 10. 255-266.

Wilson, R. McL. 1960. Light on sayings of Jesus; interpreting the 'Gospel of Thomas.' BT 11. 132-135.

Wilson, W. 1948. The annotations to the Psalms. Theology 51. 45-59.

Winburne, John N. 1962. Sentence sequence in discourse. PPICL.

Winny, James, ed. 1960. Elizabethan Prose Translation. Cambridge Univ. Press.

Winston, Richard. 1950. The craft of translation. Am. Scholar 19. 179-186.

Winter, Ralph D. 1961a. Review of Earl W. Stevick, Helping People Learn English. (New York: Abingdon Press, 1957). BT 12. 44-46.

———. 1961b. Translation and transduction. BT 12. 39.

Winter, Werner. 1962. Styles as dialects. PPICL.

Winton, Alwyn. (With Joint Committee.) 1961. Preface and Introduction to the New English Bible: New Testament. Oxford and Cambridge Univ. Presses.

Wirl, Julius. 1956. Erwagungen zum Problem des Übersetzens. Vienna: Festschrift Leo Hibler-Lebmannsport. Anglo-Americana, pp. 173-184.

———. 1958. Grundsätzliches zum Problematik des Dolmetschens und des Übersetzens. Stuttgart: Wilhelm Braumüller.

Withers, A. M. 1948. On translations. Hispania 31. 315.

Wittgenstein, L. 1953. Philosophical Investigations. New York: Macmillan; Oxford: Blackwell.

Wolff, Kurt H., trans. and ed. 1950. The Sociology of Georg Simmel. Glencoe Ill.: Free Press.

Wonderly, William L. 1952a. Information-correspondence and the translation of Ephesians into Zoque. (Pt. 1.) BT 3. 138-142.

———. 1952b. Semantic components in Kechua person morphemes. Language 28. 366-376.

———. 1953. Information-correspondence and the translation of Ephesians into Zoque. (Pt. 2.) BT 4. 14-21.

———. 1956. What about italics? BT 7. 114-116.

———. 1959. The Scriptures: Translation and distribution. BT 10. 27-29.

——. 1961. Some factors of meaningfulness in reading matter for inexperienced readers. In William Cameron Townsend en el XXV Aniversario del I.L.V., pp. 387-397.

Woodhouselee, Lord. See Tytler, A. F.

Woodward, Julia. 1950. Translation problems in Ecuadorean Quechua. BT 1. 140-144.

Workman, H. B. 1921. The first English Bible. London Quart. Rev. 135. 187-199.

Worth, Dean S. 1958. Transform analysis of Russian instrumental constructions. Word 14. 247-290.

——. 1959. Linear contexts, linguistics and machine translation. Word 15. 183-191.

——. 1962. Suprasyntactics. PPICL.

Wright, Arthur F. 1953a. The Chinese language and foreign ideas. In his Studies in Chinese Thought (q.v.), pp. 286-303.

——, ed. 1953b. Studies in Chinese Thought. (Am. Anthropol. Assoc., Vol. 55, Memoir 75.) Chicago: Univ. Chicago Press.

Wright, H. G. 1936. The first English translation of the 'Decameron.' Mod. Lang. Rev. 31. 500-512.

Wüster, E. 1957. Das Worten der Welt—schaubildlich und terminologisch dargestellt. Sprachforum 3. 183-204.

——. 1959. Die Struktur der sprachlichen Begriffswelt und ihre Darstellung in Wörterbüchern. Studium Generale 12. 615-627.

Yegerlehner, John. 1954. The first five minutes of Shawnee laws in multiple stage translation. IJAL 20. 281-294.

Yngve, Victor H. 1954. The machine and the man. Mech. Translation 1. 20-22.

——. 1955a. Sentence-for-sentence translation. Mech. Translation 2. 29-37.

——. 1955b. Syntax and the problem of multiple meaning. In Locke and Booth, eds., Machine Translation of Languages (q.v.), pp. 208-226.

——. 1956a. The outlook for mechanical translation. Babel 2. 99-101.

——. 1956b. The technical feasibility of translating languages by machine. Elec. Eng., Nov., pp. 1-5.

——. 1956c. Terminology in the light of research on mechanical translation. Babel 2. 128-132.

——. 1957. Framework for syntactic translation. Mech. Translation 4. 59-65.

——. 1958. A programming language for mechanical translation. Mech. Translation 5. 25-41.

——. 1960. A model and an hypothesis for language structure. Proc. Am. Philosoph. Soc. 104.444-446.

——. 1961a. The Comit System. PNSMT, pp. 439-443.

——. 1961b. The depth hypothesis. Proc. 12th Symp. Appl. Mathematics, ed. by Jakobson (q.v.), pp. 130-138.

——. 1961c. MT at the Massachusetts Institute of Technology. PNSMT, pp. 126-132.

Yokawa, Fumihiko. 1960. Über die Übersetzungen der alemannischen Gedichte J. P. Hebels. Babel 6. 175-176.

You-Kuang, Chou. 1957. Chinese gets a Latin alphabet. UNESCO Courier, July, pp. 18-19.

Young, G. M. 1941. On translation. English 3. 209-211.

Zaitzeff, Boris. 1960. The Book Eternal. BT 11. 97-99.

Zarechnak, Michael. 1959. Three levels of linguistic analysis in machine translation. J. Assoc. Computing Machinery 6. 24-32.

——. 1961a. Nesting within the prepositional structure. PNSMT, pp. 267-279.

—— and Brown, A. F. R. 1961b. Current research at Georgetown University. PNSMT, pp. 63-87.

Zeydel, Edwin H. 1936. Ludwig Tieck as a translator of English. PMLA 51. 221-242.

——. 1940-1941. Can we rely on translations? Mod. Lang. J. 25. 402-404.

——. 1955. Preface, Goethe the Lyrist. Chapel Hill: Univ. North Carolina Press.

Ziff, Paul. 1960. Semantic Analysis. Ithaca, N.Y.: Cornell Univ. Press. (See also review: Katz, 1962a.)

Zipf, George Kingsley. 1935. The Psycho-Biology of Language; An Introduction to Dynamic Philology. Boston: Houghton Mifflin.

——. 1949. Human Behavior and the Principle of Least Effort. Cambridge, Mass.: Addison-Wesley Press.

Zvegincev, V. A. 1962. Meaning as a fact of 'langue' and as a fact of 'parole.' PPICL.

GENERAL INDEX

Abstracts, 63
Achooli, 54
Adaptation, in translating, 158
Additions, 227-231
  categories of the receptor language, 230
  classifiers, 230
  connectives, 230
  doublets, 230
  elliptical expressions, 227
  explicit status, 228
  grammatical restructuring, 228
  implicit status, 228
  obligatory specification, 228
  rhetorical questions, 229
Adjustment
  justification for, 226
  of language usage, 55
  techniques of, 226-239
Adjustments, obligatory, 228
Algonkian languages, 47, 202
Alterations, 233-240
  categories, 234
  clause structure, 235
  semantic problems involving idiomatic phrases, 237
  semantic problems involving single words, 236
  sentence structure, 235
  sounds, 233
  word classes, 234
  word order, 235
Ambiguities, 61, 101
  in sentence structure, 262
American Bible Society, 22, 143
American College Dictionary (1947), 88
American Standard Version of the Bible (1901), 20, 24, 175, 180, 185
Amos, F. R., 14, 16, 17
Amuesha, 228
Anachronisms, 169
Analysis
  chain, 72
  of communication load, 140-142
  componential, 35-36, 82-87
    of individual words, 90
    limitations of, 87
  derivational, 89
  discourse, 243
  hierarchical, 73
  of source and receptor languages, 241
  of types of translations, 184

Anderton, Basil, 151
Anthropology, 6, 35
Anuak, 54, 91, 92, 93, 198
Apocrypha (Ecclesiasticus), 12
Aquila, 12, 23
Arabic, 14, 51, 124, 160, 176, 181
Aramaic, 11, 13
Arberry, A. J., 151
Aristeas, 26
Armenian, 12
Arnold, Matthew, 20, 163, 164
Art of translating, 3
Aspect, 199
Atkins, John, 6, 82, 83, 87
Attributives, restrictive and non-restrictive, 135
Augustine, 26, 27
Austerlitz, Robert, 82
Authority, in translating, 28
Aymara, 195, 207, 208
Aztec, Zacapoastla, 197, 208, 228, 229

Babel, 22
Babylon, 11
Back transformations, 68
Baghdad, 13
Balinese, 202
Bambara, 214
Bantu languages, 112, 203
Bar-Hillel, Yehoshua, 253
Barker, James, 79
Barr, James, 5
Bassa, 215
Batteux, Charles, 18
Bauré, 157
Beerbohm, Max, 163
Behavioral meaning, 36
Behavioral meanings, 41
Behaviorism, 7, 33
Belloc, Hilaire, 159
Bett, Henry, 177
Beza, 28
Bible, versions of; *see also* Apocrypha; New Testament; Old Testament
  American Standard Version (1901), 20, 24, 175, 180, 185
  Bible de Jérusalem (1955), 28
  English Revised Version (1885), 20, 180
  Holy Bible: A New Translation (Moffatt, 1926), 202

Ponapean, 51, 202
Pope, Alexander, 18
Portier, L., 151
Portuguese, 94
Possession, grammatical, 205
Pound, Ezra, 162, 168
Pragmatic meaning, 35, 46
Pragmatics, 36
Predictability, 127
Prepositional phrases, 208
Pribram, Karl H., 7, 33, 122, 146, 254
Price, Carl F., 177
Primitive mentality, 53
Principles of translating, 15, 18-19,
  25, 27-29, 165, 166, 171-175
  statement of, 248
Principles of Translation, The, 19
Procedures
  organizational, 245-251
  technical, 241-245
  in translating, 241-251
Processes in communication, 122
Procházka, Vladimir, 21, 161, 164, 180
Projection rules, 114
Pronominal structure, 86-87
Proper names, transliteration of, 194
Prostaxis, 210
Psychiatry, 8
Psychological distance, 129
Psychological noise, 121-122
Psychological terms, 218
Psychologists, 7
Psychology, 34
  Gestalt, 7
Purdie, Edna, 18
Purposes of communication, 53
Purposes of translating, 157
Purveyors of information, 52

Quechua, 135, 195, 196
  Bolivian, 174, 197, 215, 218
  Ecuadorian, 238
  Huanuco, 208
Quine, Willard V., 7
Quintilian, 12

Rapoport, Anatol, 6, 7
Rare forms, 133, 225
Rawang, 202
Read, Allen Walker, 89, 91
Receivers of information, 52
Recomposition of the structure, 68
Redundancy
  calculations of, 128
  in language, 127
  and noise, 128
  percentage of, 132
  and rare forms of words, 133
  two way, 128
Reference, specification of, 231

Referential meaning, 43
Referential meanings, 70-119
  of series of words, 71-87
  of single words, 88-94
Referents, classes of, 47
Reformation, 15, 16, 27, 28, 29, 46
Reichenbach, Hans, 30, 45, 62
Reina, Casiodoro de, 16, 28
Relationals, 63
Religions; see Episcopalians, Pente-
  costal, Roman Catholicism
Religious communication, 46
Renaissance, 14, 46
Repetitions, 231
Response, 40
Restructuring, grammatical, 228
Review committees, 248
Revised Standard Version of the Bible
  (1946, 1952), 24, 185, 202, 235
Revision
  by a committee, 247
  pressures, 179
Rheims-Douay Bible, 17
Rhetorical questions, 229
Rhyming, 195
Richards, I. A., 10, 38, 41, 45, 122
Rieu, E. V., 25, 157, 159
Roditi, Edward, 151
Role of the translator, 145-155
Roman Catholicism, 2, 28
Rosenzweig, Franz, 23, 194, 195
Rosetta stone, 11
Rossetti, D. G., 156
Rufinus, 13
Rules, projection, 114
Russell, Bertrand, 7
Russia, 253

San Blas, 157
Sapir, Edward, 6, 21, 36, 62
Saporta, Sol, 126, 222
Saussure, Ferdinand de, 6, 21
Savory, Theodore H., 162, 163, 238
Schlegel, A. W., 18
Schwarz, W., 2, 14, 26
Science of translating, 3
Scientific language, 222
Seely, Francis M., 233
Segmentation of meaning, 35
Selection of categories, 197
Semantic classes, 62-64
Semantic context, 37
Semantic domains, 38, 48, 70, 85
Semantic field, 37
Semantic formulae, 227
Semantic laws, 182
Semantic markers, 39, 103, 111
  types of, 109
Semantic meaning, 36
Semantic overloading, 137